Beginning Xcode

Swift 3 Edition

Matthew Knott

Apress®

Beginning Xcode

Matthew Knott
Ammanford, United Kingdom

ISBN-13 (pbk): 978-1-4302-5004-3   ISBN-13 (electronic): 978-1-4302-5005-0
DOI 10.1007/978-1-4302-5005-0

Library of Congress Control Number: 2016957886

Managing Director: Welmoed Spahr
Lead Editor: Aaron Black
Editorial Board: Steve Anglin, Pramila Balen, Louise Corrigan, James DeWolf, Jonathan Gennick, Robert Hutchinson, Celestin Suresh John, Nikhil Karkal, Michelle Lowman, James Markham, Susan McDermott, Matthew Moodie, Jeffrey Pepper, Douglas Pundick, Ben Renow-Clarke, Gwenan Spearing
Coordinating Editor: Jessica Vakili
Copy Editor: Kezia Endsley
Compositor: SPi Global
Indexer: SPi Global

Distributed to the book trade worldwide by Springer Science+Business Media New York, 233 Spring Street, 6th Floor, New York, NY 10013. Phone 1-800-SPRINGER, fax (201) 348-4505, e-mail orders-ny@springer-sbm.com, or visit www.springer.com. Apress Media, LLC is a California LLC and the sole member (owner) is Springer Science + Business Media Finance Inc (SSBM Finance Inc). SSBM Finance Inc is a Delaware corporation.

For information on translations, please e-mail rights@apress.com, or visit www.apress.com.

Apress and friends of ED books may be purchased in bulk for academic, corporate, or promotional use. eBook versions and licenses are also available for most titles. For more information, reference our Special Bulk Sales–eBook Licensing web page at www.apress.com/bulk-sales.

Any source code or other supplementary materials referenced by the author in this text is available to readers at www.apress.com. For detailed information about how to locate your book's source code, go to www.apress.com/source-code/.

Printed on acid-free paper

Dedicated to all those who keep going no matter what obstacles life throws at them.

Contents at a Glance

Contents

About the Author

Matthew Knott has been writing code for as long as he can remember, from marveling at moving pixels on a BBC Micro to writing ridiculous text adventures for his mother on an overheating ZX Spectrum 48k. Knott has been a professional software developer for the past 14 years and now leads a software section in Swansea, Wales. Matthew's work and hobby are basically the same things, but when he's not working, he loves spending time with his wife, Lisa, their two kids, Mikey and Charlotte, and Eva the dog.

Acknowledgments

Writing a book for the Swift programming language proved to be a blessing and a curse. The rapidly evolving ecosystem meant many a weekend producing code updates to stay relevant. For this book, I'd like to acknowledge all the great people who bought the last book and who sent kind messages and stories of how they're learning and developing their own apps.

Thanks to my family for the encouragement to put in another long shift at the keyboard and for keeping the tea flowing.

Introduction

Welcome to *Beginning Xcode,* the book that aims to give you all of the knowledge to start writing applications using what is probably the most powerful integrated development environment (IDE) ever, and it's free.

As with many Apple products, Xcode has simplicity and ease of use in abundance, but don't be fooled; the shiny exterior masks a workhorse of a tool, incredibly powerful with an extensive set of integrated tools for every eventuality. Xcode is the development environment that all other IDEs want to be when they grow up.

Xcode hasn't always been this shining Rock God of awesomeness; it used to be a sorry band of ragtag applications. When I first picked up Xcode 3 in 2007, I remember switching through an array of different applications to create an app, such as the very basic Interface Builder, and finding out how to adapt my knowledge of C into Objective-C. Back then what I really wanted was something that would show me how to get the most out of Xcode and would give me the understanding I needed to get going with the hundreds of app ideas I had in my head.

Fast-forward nine years. Xcode and I have both come a long way. I feel as if I've gone from a kid, bumping my leaky paddleboat aimlessly around a boating lake, to a handsome sea captain at the prow of my vessel, gazing forth as I slice through choppy waves with grace and ease. Well, aside from the handsome part, the analogy is a good one. Xcode 7 is more complete and powerful than ever before; an integrated product that puts the same power in your hands as the developers at Apple who write the apps found in iOS and macOS as well as WatchOS and tvOS to boot.

I've always had a mixed experience of development books in the past and was often sick of building the same old apps again and again. What I've aimed to do in this book is take you through almost every facet of Xcode, helping you to understand the capabilities of each of the key areas as you build a number of cool and exciting projects along the way, and begin to get to grips with the new Swift programing language. By the end of the book, you should be ready to turn the ideas in your head into reality, and I can't wait to see what that looks like.

Prior Assumptions

Before you dive in and start reading this book, it's assumed that you have at least some familiarity with developing for Cocoa Touch and are familiar with the concepts of object-oriented programming. This book is geared toward those developing for iOS; however, it's possible to get a lot out of this book if you're developing macOS applications, because many of the principles presented can be applied to either platform.

It's assumed that you are using a Mac and are preferably running the latest version of macOS. Unlike the Objective-C based equivalent of this title, it's absolutely necessary that you run the latest version of Xcode. There is a common misconception that you need the greatest and latest "souped-up" Mac, but many previous-generation iMacs, MacBooks, Mac Minis, and Mac Pros will work just fine.

It's also assumed that you know how to operate your Mac and how to use macOS. For example, you need to know how to use the Finder, save files, and so forth—all the basics. Finally, a couple of the chapters present scenarios in which an active Internet connection is required, and some features of Xcode perform better when you're connected. Additionally, some later chapters require a physical device and a paid developer account to complete, but for the most part you can use an iOS simulator to run your apps.

It's also worth mentioning that the purpose of this book is not to teach you how to create applications for iOS or teach you how to program in Swift or Objective-C; the purpose of this book is to get you up and running with Xcode so you can apply your current knowledge of Swift and macOS/iOS development and use the latest version of Xcode to its full potential to enable you to work more productively and create fantastic applications.

What's Covered in This Book

Part 1: Getting Acquainted

- *Chapter 1*: This chapter starts you on your journey into the world of Xcode and explains how to get Xcode onto your machine and prepare it for first use. You are shown how to sign up as an Apple developer, and you get a look at the wealth of resources provided by Apple to iOS and macOS developers.

- *Chapter 2*: Here, you start a project and get the ball rolling in terms of becoming familiar with Xcode. You learn the basics of how to create projects and build applications, along with how to get around in Xcode.

- *Chapter 3*: Next, the focus shifts to how to choose from Xcode's different project templates. You also get a guided tour of Xcode's interface along with an introduction to many of the menus, inspectors, and panels you should use to work efficiently.

- *Chapter 4*: This chapter focuses solely on how to design your interfaces using Xcode's built-in interface editor, Interface Builder. It gives you an in-depth look at the libraries and inspectors available.

- *Chapter 5*: Next, you're shown how to access the invaluable help resources that are built right in to Xcode and also how to make the most of its intelligent code-completion feature.

- *Chapter 6*: Building on Chapter 4, you see the Auto Layout system and learn how it works with constraints and size classes to create a single layout for any device.

Part 2: Diving Deeper

- *Chapter 7*: This chapter shows you how to use a key feature for rapid development in Xcode: Storyboards. You see how Storyboards can add a certain degree of logic to how you display and push views in your application.

- *Chapter 8*: This chapter explains how Xcode makes it easy to populate and create table and collection views, with the addition of how to customize their appearance and functionality.

- *Chapter 9*: Here you learn how to add features to your application by adding frameworks and libraries. You also learn how to create a different version of your application in the same project with targets.

- *Chapter 10*: This chapter shows you how to add your own personal touches to Xcode in terms of editing code. In particular, the code editor is the focus of this chapter, and you see how to work more productively and how to customize its appearance and behavior to suit your tastes and requirements.

- *Chapter 11*: This chapter presents the idea of making your application run more efficiently and faster. This is done by looking at the range of different tools and methods included in Xcode. For example, using breakpoints to step through your code systematically. You also learn about the Swift Playground for prototyping and testing your code.

Part 3: Final Preparations and Releasing

- *Chapter 12*: Here you learn how you can protect your code and work effectively as a team by using Git, Xcode's integrated version control software.

- *Chapter 13*: This chapter examines the idea of localization and how to use Xcode to accurately support multiple languages in your app.

- *Chapter 14*: This chapter looks at the Organizer, what it's for, how to navigate around in it, and how to keep your developer assets in good standing order.

- *Chapter 15*: To conclude, you make final touches to your application, build it for release, and then share it either as an IPA file or via the App Store using either Application Loader or the Organizer.

PART I

Getting Acquainted

CHAPTER 1

■ ■ ■

Welcome to Xcode

Apple provides Xcode to developers to help them create applications for Macs, iPhones, and iPads (macOS and iOS). Xcode was used to create many of your favorite iOS and macOS applications. Arguably, without such a powerful, refined, integrated development environment (IDE), the thriving ecosystem that is the App Store would not exist as it does today.

What Is Xcode?

All developers, regardless of the platform for which they're developing, use an array of tools to take an application from an idea to something that is readily available to millions of people. Apple is no exception, and it provides a cultured, powerful, and polished set of development tools. These tools come together in one application called Xcode. Xcode provides everything you need to create, test, deploy, and distribute applications for iOS and macOS. With the release of iOS 10 and Xcode 8, Apple has continued to build on the radical changes introduced in the previous version of both the operating system and in Xcode. One of the most significant developments in the last two years was that Apple, for the first time, introduced its own proprietary language called Swift.

The purpose of this book is to guide you in becoming familiar with Xcode 8, in the hope that you'll become more confident and embrace it as a means to create amazing, innovative new applications for iOS and macOS. As in many other technical books, as you progress through each chapter, you build on your knowledge and will create a variety of iOS applications that challenge the knowledge you gain through the course of the book.

Although Xcode was created primarily for developers working on iOS and macOS applications, it's also great if you work with other languages such as C, Java, and C++, among others. Xcode has a long, interesting history of releases, some having a very good reception and some less so. First released in 2003, Xcode has had six major releases and has seen a couple of major interface overhauls. After more than 10 years of active development, it's safe to say that Xcode is incredibly powerful and a leading professional set of development tools. What's more, Xcode is available to developers at absolutely no cost; all you need is an iTunes account and you're good to go.

What Is Swift?

Before WWDC 2014, Apple's World Wide Developer conference, if you created a project in Xcode, the code that was added behind the scenes was written in a programming language called Objective-C. At WWDC14, Apple unveiled a new and highly streamlined programming language called Swift. This new language greatly reduced the amount of code needed to achieve equivalent outcomes in Objective-C. Swift is far less rigid than Objective-C and is very similar in structure to Python, a move that will no doubt encourage more developers into what is already one of the most accessible development ecosystems in existence today.

Electronic supplementary material The online version of this chapter (doi:10.1007/978-1-4302-5005-0_1) contains supplementary material, which is available to authorized users.

To make Swift even more appealing, Apple also introduced a new piece of software called Swift Playground with Xcode 6. Playground gives you the ability to experiment with snippets of code to see the result without putting them into your application, meaning you have a code sandbox in which to try things such as loops or regular expressions and instantly see the result.

Swift has developed very quickly, yet the early days of Swift were difficult as Apple regularly changed how the language and the compiler worked. Code that was valid in one version of Xcode became invalid in the next—not a great situation for authors looking to write a print book about the language. Thankfully, now in version 3.0 at the time of this writing, Swift has continued to develop but also stabilized a great deal. In 2015, Apple made the Swift programming language and it is now available for Linux as well. Head over to https://swift.org to find out more about the language and to connect with the development community. Going open source has expanded and accelerated the development of Swift, with large organizations such as IBM becoming its biggest contributors.

The purpose of this book is to teach you how to create apps using Swift in Xcode 8—it isn't a definitive Swift language guide. Apple, however, has released a free book that *is* a definitive guide to the Swift programming language and has made it available via iBooks. Search iBooks for Swift programming or visit https://itunes.apple.com/us/book/swift-programming-language/id881256329?mt=11. Although you'll be using Swift version 3, I'll just refer to it as Swift for the course of the book.

Why Choose Xcode?

If you have experience developing for other platforms, then you probably want to know what makes Xcode so great. The main thing is that there's simply no other IDE like it. It's unique in the sense that Apple has created it to be simple, yet at the same time it masks a powerful interior. You have the ability to work with a range of technologies, and you also have a phenomenal developer toolkit at your disposal. Xcode contains everything you could need: an intuitive code editor, advanced debugging, seamless interface-editing features, and the benefit of being constantly updated and maintained by Apple.

In addition, using Xcode is arguably the only practical way to develop applications for iOS and macOS that can truly be called native. Xcode is what Apple itself uses to produce its own innovative software, which is used by millions of people.

Aside from Xcode, it's hard to find a commendable alternative if you want to develop native iOS or macOS applications. Of course, there are third-party services and tools, but when using these, you may often find yourself battling inconsistencies and a lack of compatibility rather than focusing on what's really important: creating great apps (and enjoying doing so). The purpose of Xcode isn't to simply be an IDE: it also helps and guides you on your quest to create something that has the potential to reach a staggeringly large audience. For that reason, Xcode is a fantastic choice.

Getting and Installing Xcode

Before you can download Xcode, there are a couple of things you need to do. You need an iTunes account (or an Apple ID) that allows you to download content from the Mac App Store. Then you're good to go. If you don't have an Apple ID, you can sign up for one at no cost at http://appleid.apple.com. This book is written for Xcode 8, and to run it you also need a Mac that's running the latest version of macOS or at least macOS 10.11.5.

Once you're equipped with an Apple ID and a Mac running macOS 10.11.5+, you can begin downloading Xcode. As with many other Mac apps, you simply download it from the Mac App Store at no additional cost. Open the App Store on your Mac, select Categories from the top bar of the window, and then click the Developer Tools category. Usually, you can find Xcode right away, either at the top of the window or in the sidebar on the right, displaying the top free apps. Alternatively, you can use the Search bar at top right and enter xcode. Xcode's icon is a hammer over an "A" blueprint, as shown in Figure 1-1.

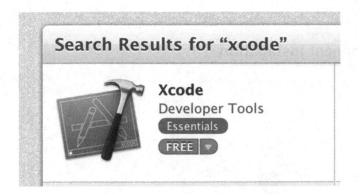

Figure 1-1. *Xcode in App Store search results*

■ **Note** If you don't have access to the latest version of macOS or are running an older version that isn't supported, you can download previous versions of Xcode from the iOS Dev Center, but for this you need to have a registered Apple developer account. This is explained later. However, this book covers the latest version of Xcode (which is 8.0 at the time of this writing).

Select the icon and you're taken to Xcode's App Store page. Here you can view all the features of Xcode along with the latest additions to the current version of Xcode (at the time of this writing, this is 8.0) and preview some screenshots of Xcode. To download Xcode, click the gray Free button and enter your Apple ID e-mail address and password. Your download will commence. Xcode is about 4.4 GB, so you can go and make some coffee while you wait for the download to finish, as shown in Figure 1-2.

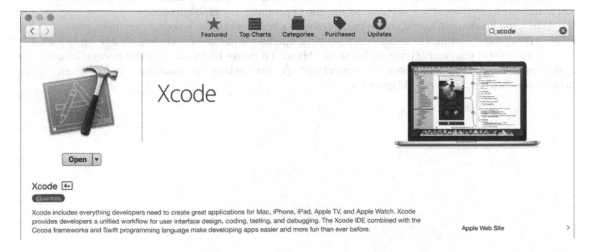

Figure 1-2. *Xcode in the Mac App Store*

With Xcode downloaded, open it from your Applications folder. You're prompted to install some additional packages. Click Install and enter your user password. This installation should take a matter of seconds, as shown in Figure 1-3.

5

Figure 1-3. Installing additional tools required by Xcode

Firing Up Xcode

Once you've successfully downloaded and installed the additional components, you can begin using Xcode. In Chapter 2, you create your first project and become familiar with the basic areas of Xcode; but for now, just make sure everything is in good order so you don't encounter any problems later.

When you first launch Xcode, you're presented with a Welcome splash screen. From there, you can create a new project, connect to an external repository, open documentation, visit Apple's developer portal, and browse a list of your recent projects. For some, this screen causes irritation—you can prevent it from appearing each time you open Xcode by simply checking or unchecking the Show This Window When Xcode Launches box, as shown in Figure 1-4.

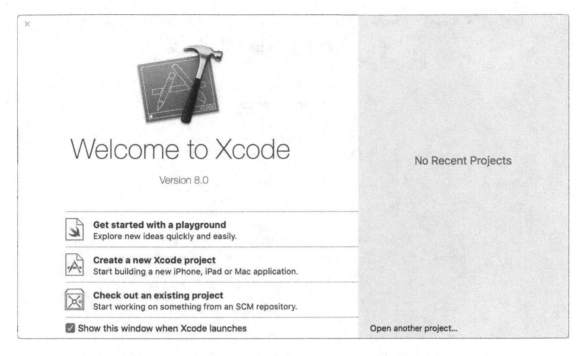

Figure 1-4. *Xcode's Welcome window, which is displayed optionally each time you open Xcode*

To create a new project, click the Create A New Xcode Project button on the Welcome screen or navigate to File ➤ New ➤ Project, where you're presented with a range of templates provided by default by Xcode.

If you have gotten to this point, it's safe to assume that you've successfully installed Xcode and that you're ready to start creating projects. However, let's save this for a deeper explanation in Chapter 2 and for now look at the variety of resources provided to developers by Apple.

Apple's Resources for Developers

At this point, you have Xcode downloaded to your machine, and you've fired it up to make sure it runs. If there's one thing that makes Apple stand out from its competitors, it's the wealth of knowledge, resources, and tools that are made just for developers. There are thousands of documents, thousands of samples to download, and dozens upon dozens of videos you can watch. Currently you have Xcode installed, but that alone isn't going to make you a great developer of iOS and macOS applications. You also need to use the vast library provided by Apple. To gain access to Apple's resources, I urge you to sign up as a registered Apple developer. To do this, all you need is an Apple ID; you can create a new one or use the same ID you use to download content from iTunes or the App Store.

First, head over to `http://developer.apple.com`. This is the central web site for Apple developers. Until recently, Apple had a dedicated area called the iOS Dev Center. This has now been replaced with a one-stop-shop solution in line with the new holistic approach Apple has taken toward its paid-for developer accounts. The key areas for you as a developer looking for support and guidance is the Resources page shown in Figure 1-5 and the Support page.

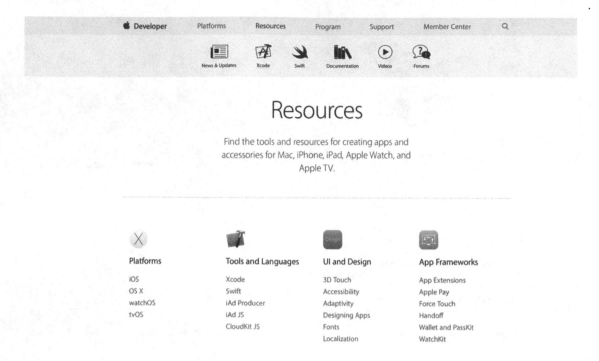

Figure 1-5. *The Apple Developer Resources Page*

You don't need to be subscribed to the Apple Developer Program in order to gain access to these resources, which includes the Developer Library, a wealth of example applications and their source code, release notes, and much more besides. To access the developer libraries for any of the core Apple technologies, go to Resources ➤ iOS/macOS/watchOS/tvOS ➤ Documentation.

The Dev Center

As mentioned previously, Apple really does like to take care of its developers. As a developer, your first port of call is the Developer Library, because it houses most of the resources provided by Apple. If you select the iOS Developer Library link under Documentation and Videos, you're taken to an invaluable section of Apple's developer web site. The Developer Library is a simple and straightforward site: simply use the links on the left to navigate around and to filter the results. You can search for specific keywords or sort the results using one of the column titles, as shown in Figure 1-6.

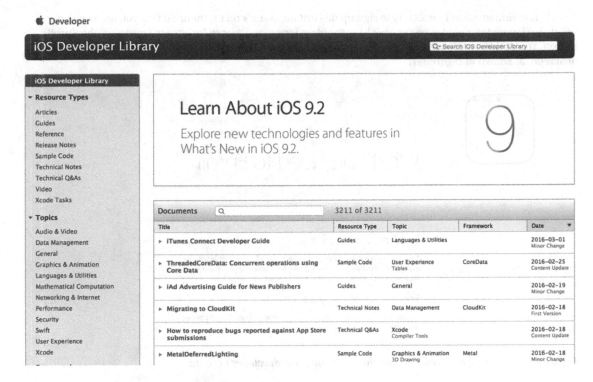

Figure 1-6. *The iOS Developer Library*

In addition to the iOS Developer Library, you also have access to an array of getting-started videos that explain core Swift, Objective-C, and Cocoa Touch concepts. You can also access a direct link to the latest version of Xcode on the Mac App Store and can download previous versions of Xcode if you're not running the latest version of macOS or would like to target older versions of iOS.

Your Developer Account

Currently, your Apple ID gives you access to Xcode and all the resources you need to get started as an Xcode developer, but if you're planning to release applications to the App Store or test your applications on your own device, you're going to need to enroll in the Apple Developer Program. Although this isn't necessary at this point in the book, it's a good idea to sign up as a paid developer, because doing so gives you access to the Apple developer forums, prerelease versions of iOS before they're available to the public, prerelease versions of Xcode, the ability to test your applications on your iOS devices, and, of course, the ability to submit applications to the iOS, macOS, or tvOS App Stores.

The cost of signing up at the time of the writing of this book was $99 per year, but it's required only when you want to publish an application to the App Store or need early access to Xcode or operating system betas. Apple has done a couple of neat things with the developer program in recent years. First, Apple combined all of its developer programs into one, meaning you only need to pay a single fee to develop for all of the available platforms and App Stores. Secondly, they removed the requirement to have a paid up developer account for testing on physical hardware, so you can take your apps on the go with you and show off your progress as you go through the book.

As mentioned, it isn't necessary to sign up this instant, but it's recommended that you do so at some point. To sign up for a paid account, visit `https://developer.apple.com/programs/` and click the Enroll button. You're then guided through the process of signing up; it's straightforward if you follow the steps onscreen, as shown in Figure 1-7.

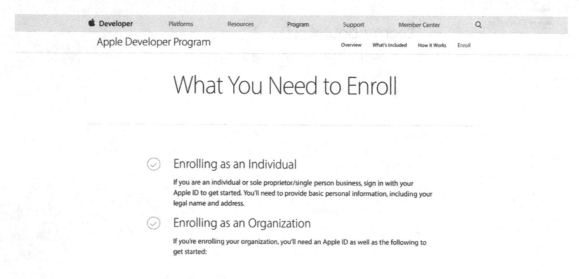

Figure 1-7. *Choosing between an individual or a company developer account*

It's useful to note that when you're prompted to choose between an individual or company account, if you're planning to operate under a name other than your own, you have to register as an official company (this is verified by Apple) and then acquire what's called a Data Universal Numbering System (DUNS) number that uniquely identifies your company; this takes around seven days to process, so plan ahead. If selling applications under your own name suffices, then go for the simpler option of signing up as an individual. Both accounts are essentially equal in terms of the resources you're able to access. This choice mainly determines the name with which you operate under on the App Store.

Don't worry if you're not ready to do this right now—it's covered in detail later in the book when it becomes essential if you're planning to release applications on the App Store (free or paid). Chapter 14 takes you through enrollment and looks at using Provisioning Profiles and the deployment of an app onto an actual iOS device as opposed to the virtual iOS Simulator.

If you've had an Apple Developer account in the past, you may not be able to enroll. Instead, head over to `https://developer.apple.com/program/renew/index.action` and you will be able to renew your membership and regain access to the program.

Source Code

I strongly recommend that one of the first things you do is to go to the Apress web site for this book and download the entire source code. Either search for the book at `www.apress.com` or go directly to `www.apress.com/9781430250043`. When you get to the page for this book, scroll down until you see the section of the web site with four tabs, the third of which is Source Code/Downloads, as shown in Figure 1-8.

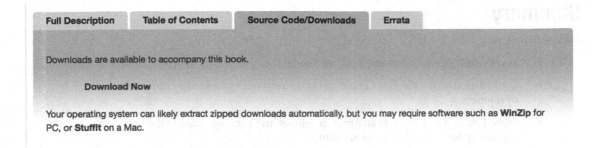

Figure 1-8. *The source code download page for this book*

Additional Resources

In addition to Apple's own resources, an extensive amount of third-party resources are available if you ever have a burning question or get stuck somewhere:

Forums: Forums are a great way to ask questions, learn from other people's questions, and help other people. In particular, Stack Overflow (http://stackoverflow.com/) has been invaluable to the entire developer spectrum for years and has a vibrant, active collection of iOS developers. There are also the Apple developer forums, which are available to those with a paid Apple developer account.

Mailing lists: There's a handy Xcode users mailing list that I recommend you subscribe to and periodically check. Many other developers, including myself, participate in answering questions relating to Xcode. You can subscribe at https://lists.apple.com/mailman/listinfo/xcode-users.

Xcode overview: Apple provides a handy user's guide that's always being updated to accompany the latest release of Xcode, so it's a good idea to refer to it when there's a new update or if you want to follow up on something. It's available at https://developer.apple.com/library/ios/documentation/ToolsLanguages/Conceptual/Xcode_Overview. Similarly, it's handy to glance over the latest release notes when Xcode is updated. These are available at https://developer.apple.com/library/ios/releasenotes/DeveloperTools/RN-Xcode.

Search engines: It's easy to underestimate the power of a simple Google search (and it's apparent many people on online forums don't have access to them). It can save you a lot of time, because someone, somewhere, at some point has undoubtedly had the same question you have—all you need to do is find out where they asked it!

Videos: If you type "Xcode" into iTunes U search, you'll find a couple of good university courses that focus not only on Xcode but also on iOS development in general. Similarly, type "Xcode" into a YouTube search, and you'll be amazed at what you can learn from the short screencasts that have been uploaded.

Contact me: I am happy to field questions via e-mail at matthewknott@me.com or via the Facebook page for this book at https://www.facebook.com/BeginningXcode.

Summary

In this chapter, you:

- Successfully downloaded and installed Xcode
- Looked around the iOS Dev Center and at the resources provided by Apple to aid developers
- Signed up and registered as an Apple developer and became aware of the option of signing up for a paid developer account

Chapter 2 explains how to create your first project and helps you become more familiar with Xcode's interface and basic concepts.

CHAPTER 2

■ ■ ■

Diving Right In

In Chapter 1, you downloaded Xcode, made sure it was correctly configured, signed up for a developer account, and explored the wealth of resources provided by Apple to help you get started with not only Xcode but also some of its fantastic new technologies. This chapter explains how to create a working application using Xcode's visual interface building tool (aptly named Interface Builder) and its built-in code editor and then run the app on your machine.

As mentioned, as you progress through this book, the ultimate goal is not only to get a grip on the latest and greatest version of Xcode but also, by the end of the book, to have walked through building a series of varied applications that give you many of the essential skills needed to go out and start writing your own applications. The application you build in this chapter familiarizes you with Xcode as a development environment before you start looking at sharing data between pieces of your application in Chapter 3. For now, you develop a very simple application that has a custom background color and a label, and you programmatically update the text in the label.

Be forewarned that in this chapter, a lot of the concepts are new and therefore require more explanation to do them justice. As a result, on several occasions you're told that later chapters revisit many of the concepts presented. This is because the main goal of this chapter isn't to turn you into an Xcode pro, but rather to get you started and give you the confidence to believe that Xcode isn't as overwhelming as it may first appear. In Figure 2-1, you get a glimpse of the example application; although it's simple, it will make you at least a little familiar with the workings of Xcode and help you to understand that Xcode can help you produce a working application in next to no time.

© Matthew Knott 2016

M. Knott, *Beginning Xcode*, DOI 10.1007/978-1-4302-5005-0_2

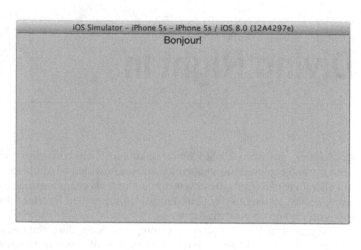

Figure 2-1. *The application you create in this chapter*

Creating Your First Xcode Project

First you need to bring this project into existence. To do this, start by running the Xcode application, and then click Create A New Xcode Project on the Welcome Screen or choose File ➤ New ➤ Project (⌘+Shift+N). You're presented with a new window asking what kind of project you want to create. Apple provides, by default, a variety of different project templates for iOS, macOS, and the newer watchOS and tvOS. These templates are useful for getting started on different types of projects; Chapter 3 covers each of the iOS templates in more detail. Continue as follows:

1. Because you're creating a basic one-view application, it seems appropriate to choose Single View Application, which can be found in the Application category under iOS on the left side of the dialog.

2. Once you've selected the Single View Application project template, click the Next arrow in the bottom-right corner. Figure 2-2 shows the template screen.

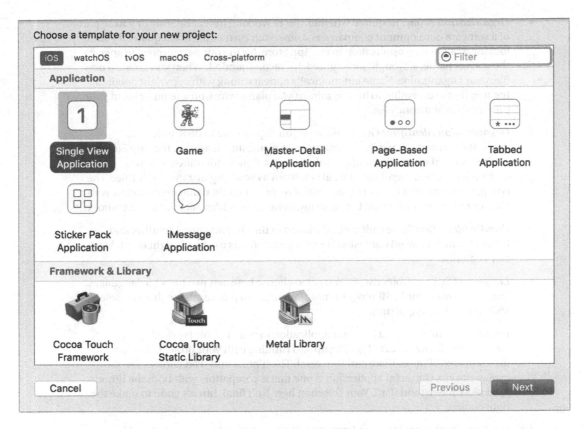

Figure 2-2. *The variety of different templates provided by Apple to help you get started creating your app quickly*

You need to specify a couple of things before you can actually get started. Once you select your project template, a screen identical to that in Figure 2-3 is displayed. Following is a brief overview of each of the values required to proceed—bear in mind that you learn more about the significance of some of the values you enter here as the book progresses:

- **Product Name:** What you would like to call your application. For example, if you wanted to create an application called Chocolate Recipes, you'd specify the Product Name to be something along the line of ChocolateRecipes. Although not required, it's generally good practice to omit any spaces and instead capitalize each new word. The Product Name can be amended during the development of your application, so you're not obliged to stick with what you specify; but regardless, the Product Name is a rather important detail that you're required to specify at this stage.

- **Team:** This is where you select which development team you are working as. The values displayed here are derived from the Apple Developer accounts set up within Xcode. Assuming this is the very first time that you have run Xcode, there's a chance that there is a button titled Add Account. There is no need to do this at this stage and it will be covered later in the book.

- *Organization Name:* Required whether you're working independently or you're part of a software development company. For now, your own name is adequate. If you're looking to submit an application to the App Store, it's in your best interest to specify the correct name; although not required, it's recommended. When you create a new file, your Organization Name automatically appears along with copyright details at the top; that's something to bear in mind if you plan to work on a team or hand your project off to someone else.

- *Organization Identifier:* Only required if you're planning to distribute your application in some capacity. For example, to distribute an app via the App Store, you're required to specify an App ID along with a Bundle Identifier, which is created by Xcode depending on what you input as your Organization Identifier. The company identifier is written in the style of reverse domain name notation; my web site, for example, is mattknott.com, so my Organization Identifier is com.mattknott.

- *Bundle Identifier:* By default, a combination of the Organization Identifier and the Product Name, to avoid confusion (I won't focus on this too much right now). You can't edit this.

- *Language:* Swift or Objective-C. You get to choose between two possible languages. This book covers the Swift programming language, so please ensure that you select Swift for each example project.

- *Devices:* The device you'd like your application to run on. This is possibly the most straightforward part of getting up and running with your project. You have three choices: iPhone, iPad, and Universal. The iPhone and iPad choices are self-explanatory. A Universal application is one that is compatible with both the iPhone (and iPod Touch) and iPad. Your selection here isn't final, but it's good to make the right choice.

- *Use Core Data:* Core Data is a large framework designed by Apple to simplify and unify the methods for storing data in iOS. For example, if you wanted to create a database for storing relational information in your application, you might want to set up an SQLite database. Core Data does all this for you and gives you a simple interface to set up the tables, fields, and relationships.

- *Include Unit Tests:* Unit testing is a long-established method of testing the functions and methods within your application to ensure the results meet expectations. Leave this checked.

- *Include UI Tests:* A new feature for Xcode 7, UI Tests are unit tests for the user interface, and they allow developers and testers to evaluate the application against a set of acceptance criteria. There is no harm in leaving this checked.

3. Now that you vaguely know what these values are for and what they correspond to, you're probably wondering what you should input to create this project. As shown in Figure 2-3, type in HelloWorld as the Product Name; input your own first and last name as your Organization Name; use com.*LASTNAME* as your Organization Identifier (obviously change *LASTNAME* to your actual last name), set the Language value to Swift if it isn't set already, specify iPhone as the Device, and, finally, ensure that Use Core Data isn't selected.

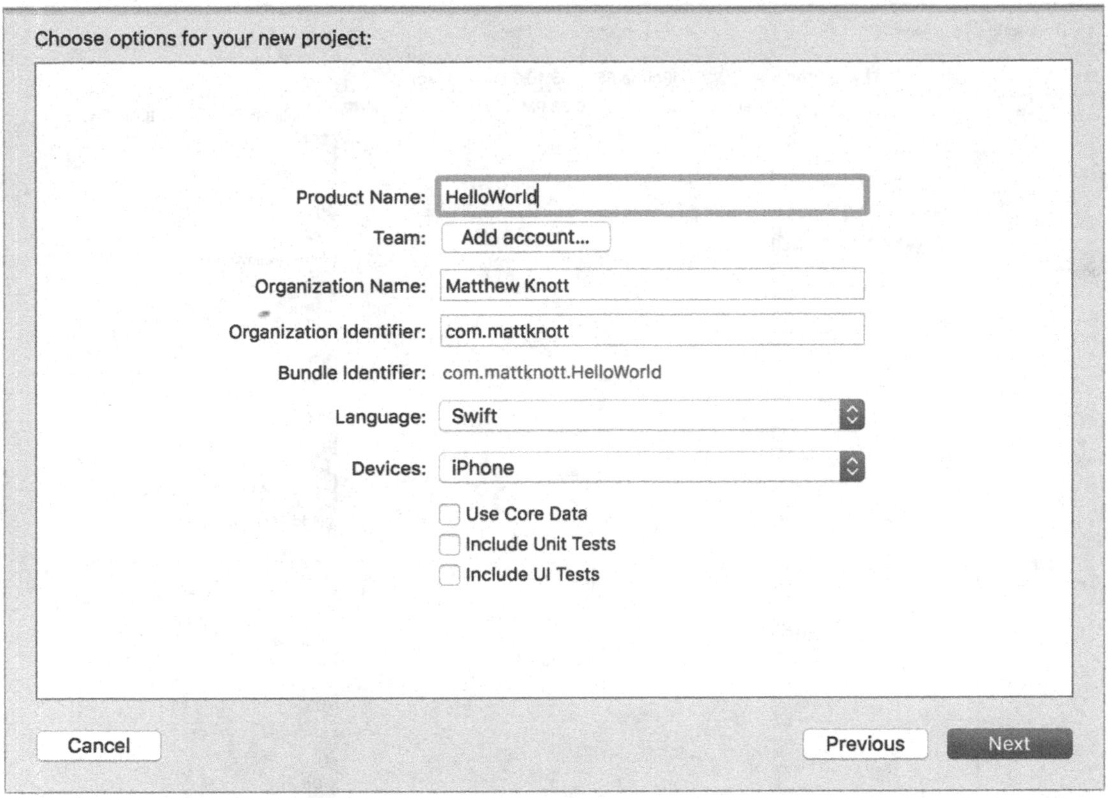

Choose options for your new project:

Product Name:	HelloWorld
Team:	Add account...
Organization Name:	Matthew Knott
Organization Identifier:	com.mattknott
Bundle Identifier:	com.mattknott.HelloWorld
Language:	Swift
Devices:	iPhone

☐ Use Core Data
☐ Include Unit Tests
☐ Include UI Tests

Cancel   Previous   Next

Figure 2-3. Specifying the project's details

4. Once you've made sure all your values are correct, click Next. You're required to save your project to disk.

5. When prompted to, use the familiar macOS dialog to find a location. Make sure the box next to Source Control is unchecked, and then click Create.

■ **Note** Git is a popular system used for version control and source code management. You can integrate a local Git repository with a web site such as GitHub or Bitbucket if you want to back up or share your code online. If none of these things is familiar to you, Chapter 12 explains.

So, you've given Xcode all the relevant details and specified what kind of project you're looking to create. As a result, Xcode conveniently creates a basic, functioning application for you to use as a starting point. The code that Xcode creates for you is just enough to get the application to run; it's a working, if slightly pointless, app that you can run right now if you like.

Choose Product ➤ Run (⌘+R), and you'll find the application builds successfully and the iOS Simulator pops up with the app running, as shown in Figure 2-4. It's nothing spectacular, nor will it reach the top 25 in the App Store anytime soon, but it's a functioning application created by Xcode with very little input from you. Return to Xcode and click the Stop button in the top-left corner or choose Product ➤ Stop (⌘+.).

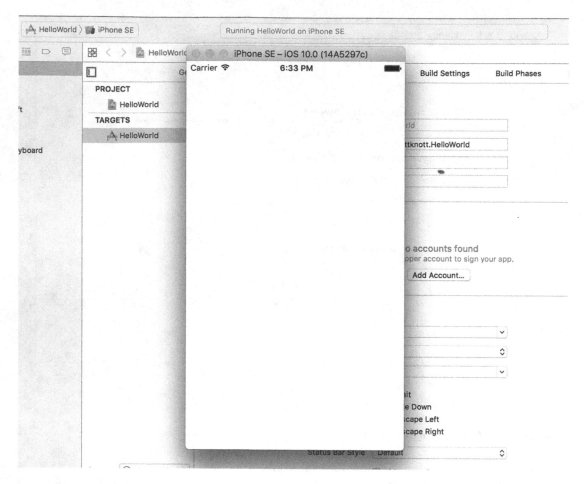

Figure 2-4. The initial application created by Xcode

■ **Tip** With the high resolution of modern iOS devices, unless you have a top-of-the-range Mac and a very high desktop resolution, the simulator may be too large for your computer screen. If this is the case, then with the simulator selected, choose Window ➤ Scale ➤ 50% or use the shortcut key ⌘+3. The Scale menu also gives you the option to go to 100% or 75% scale using ⌘+1 or ⌘+2, respectively, or down as low as 25%, which reflects the increasing resolution of mobile devices relative to macOS devices.

The Project

In order to make the app a little more interesting than a simple white screen, you need to open some files that Xcode created. As with previous versions of Xcode, the way in which it organizes your project's file is somewhat strange. Upon returning to Xcode, if you look to the left of the interface, you should see what appears to be an arrangement of folders and files. These are the files that make up your project (see Figure 2-5). This part of Xcode is called the Project Navigator. If you're unable to find it, choose View ➤ Navigators ➤ Show Project Navigator (⌘+ 1). It's important to note that when you create a folder in the Project Navigator, it doesn't correspond to the structure in which the files are saved in the Finder. The folders and organization of the Project Navigator are purely to help you locate files in Xcode. If you create a folder in the Navigator, the same folder isn't present in your project when you browse in Finder. I revisit this issue when you add a file to your project later in this chapter.

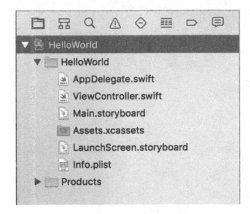

Figure 2-5. *The Project Navigator*

If you've used Xcode with Objective-C in the past, then you've almost certainly noted that when using the Swift language, there are far fewer files in the project. The reason is that in Objective-C, each class file is created with a header (.h) file and an implementation (.m) file. Swift combines all class information into a single file.

With that in mind, select Main.storyboard from the Project Navigator. Xcode opens its built-in graphical user interface (GUI) design tool, usually referred to as Interface Builder. Xcode 4.0 introduced a major overhaul of Apple's developer tools. Interface Builder, which was previously a separate application, was conveniently integrated into Xcode, making it easy to switch between the built-in code editor and interface design tool in a single application, as shown in Figure 2-6. One warning is worth mentioning: the more you learn to do with Xcode, the more you may wish for a larger screen!

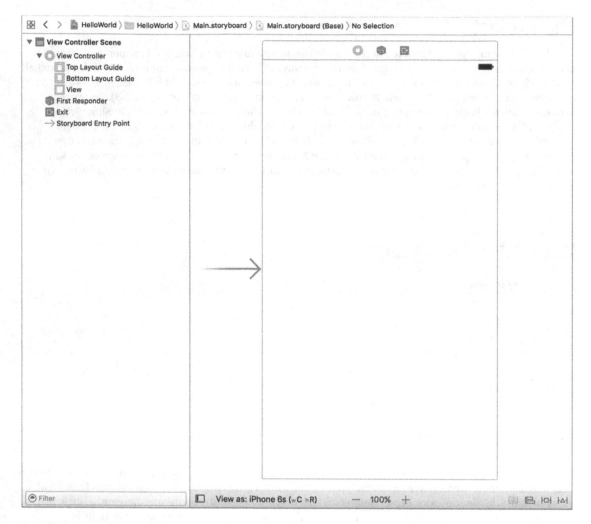

Figure 2-6. *Xcode's built-in graphical interface designer*

Designing the Interface

At this point, the application's interface is a blank canvas in the shape of an iPhone, and although throughout this chapter, the application you create is straightforward, the basic lessons imparted here are the building blocks behind almost any app you could want to build. You will use these techniques time and again as you progress through the book. To begin making this application into something other than a blank page, let's look at the Attributes Inspector. You can find this by selecting the fourth tab in the sidebar on the right side of Xcode's interface; alternatively, you can choose View ➤ Utilities ➤ Show Attributes Inspector (⌘+⌥+4). The Attributes Inspector plays an important role when it comes to layout and fine-tuning interface elements. Now follow these steps:

1. To change the background color of the application, first make sure the view is selected by clicking the white area with an arrow pointing to it, as shown in Figure 2-6.

2. Under the View heading of the Attributes Inspector, select the color-picking option for the Background attribute. Then use macOS's default color picker to choose a background color, as shown in Figure 2-7. In this example, I use the RGB sliders and a background of Red: 181, Green: 218, and Blue: 225, but you're free to choose whichever colors you wish.

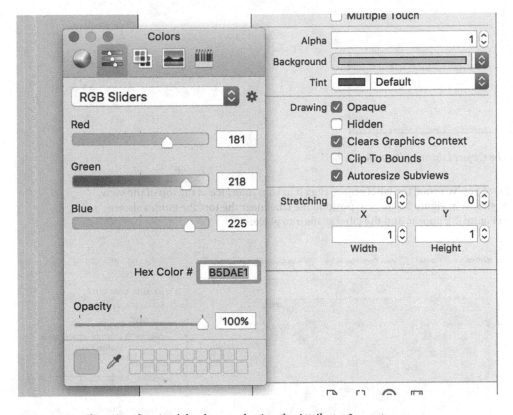

Figure 2-7. *Changing the view's background using the Attributes Inspector*

■ **Tip**   Since Xcode 7, you can now specify a color Hex Code, which is useful if you want your app to match the color scheme of your companion or corporate web site.

---

3. Add a label to your view. To do this, open the Object Library (shown in Figure 2-8) and drag a label object to your view. Generally, the Object Library is right below the Attributes Inspector and is accessible by selecting the third tab; you can also access it via View ➤ Utilities ➤ Show Object Library (^+⌘+⌥+3).

4. With the library open, use the small search bar to search for "label".

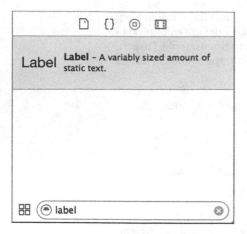

Figure 2-8. *The Object Library, filtered for "label"*

5. Once you've found the label object, drag it to your interface at the top of the view, as shown in Figure 2-9. As you position the label near the top, the guides shown in Figure 2-9 appear, and the label snaps into place.

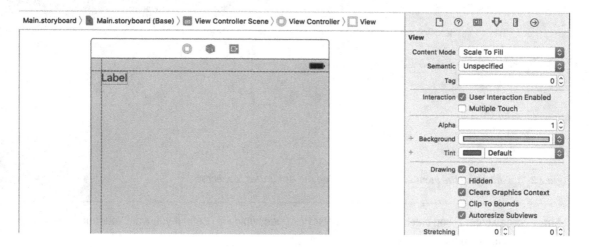

Figure 2-9. *Dragging the label onto the view*

6. Select your new label and use the handles to extend its width so it fills the width of the view. Then double its height to accommodate a larger font size.

7. Set the Alignment attribute in the Attributes Inspector to Center.

8. Click the T symbol in the Font attribute to alter the font. Set Font to Custom, Family to Avenir, and Size to 32, as shown in Figure 2-10.

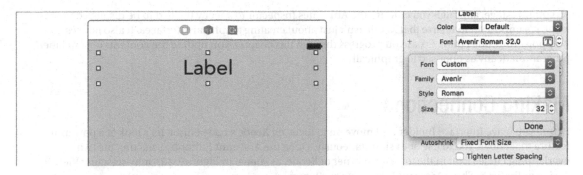

Figure 2-10. *The Attributes Inspector's Font property*

9. Because you have Size Classes enabled for this view, it's essential to set a couple of parameters called ***constraints*** that tell iOS how to position the label in the view as the device and screen orientation changes. I cover this in detail later in the book, but for now, locate the pin icon in the bottom-right corner of the design area and click it. A popup window appears.

10. At the top of the pin popup window, you see a square with a bar on each side followed by a numeric value. Click the top, left, and right bars to highlight them in red and check the Height constraint, as shown in Figure 2-11. Then click the Add 4 Constraints button.

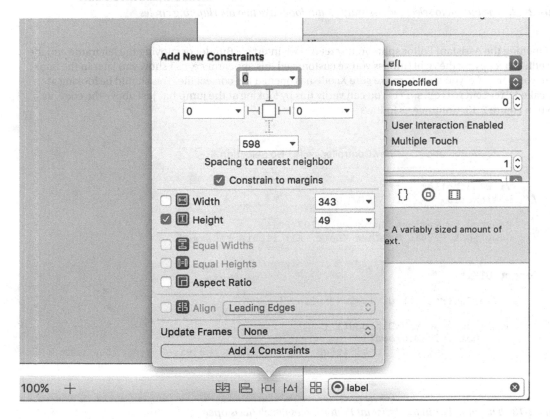

Figure 2-11. *Setting some constraints for the label*

At this stage, although you *can* use the Attributes Inspector to specify the text to be displayed in the label, it's important to realize that Xcode isn't just about creating graphical interfaces. It also houses a very powerful code editor. So, as you progress through this chapter, you update the contents of your label programmatically as opposed to graphically.

Making Connections

Before you leave Interface Builder and move on to focus on Xcode's code editor, let's look at a powerful feature that allows you to use both simultaneously. Open the Assistant Editor by selecting the two overlapping circles icon in the top-right corner of Xcode, as shown in Figure 2-12, or by selecting View ➤ Assistant Editor ➤ Show Assistant Editor (⌘+⌥+Return).

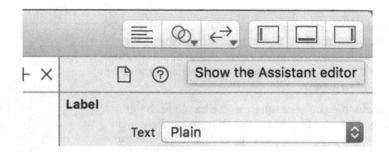

Figure 2-12. *The button to select the Assistant Editor looks like two overlapping circles*

Opening the Assistant Editor splits your screen, with Interface Builder occupying the left frame and the code editor occupying the right (unless you've customized this appearance, as I show you later in the book). Before you continue, you need to make sure Xcode has opened the correct file. You should be looking at a file called ViewController.swift. You can verify this by looking at the jump bar just above the code, as shown in Figure 2-13. Continue as follows:

```
//
//  ViewController.swift
//  HelloWorld
//
//  Created by Matthew Knott on 10/07/2016.
//  Copyright © 2016 Matthew Knott. All rights reserved.
//

import UIKit

class ViewController: UIViewController {

    override func viewDidLoad() {
        super.viewDidLoad()
        // Do any additional setup after loading the view, typically from a
            nib.
    }
```

Automatic ⟩ ViewController.swift ⟩ No Selection

Figure 2-13. *The jump bar in the Assistant Editor shows which file is open*

1. With Interface Builder and the code displayed using the Assistant Editor, click the label you added to your view in Interface Builder to highlight it.

    Now you're going to create a variable called an outlet (IBOutlet) to make the label accessible through your code. In older versions of Xcode, the process of creating an outlet and then wiring it into Interface Builder was quite long-winded, but Apple has simplified this greatly over the past few versions of Xcode by allowing you to drag connections directly from Interface Builder into the code.

2. Holding down the Control key, click the label and drag a connection to the ViewController.swift file. Position the cursor in the class scope, just below the line class ViewController: UIViewController {, as shown in Figure 2-14.

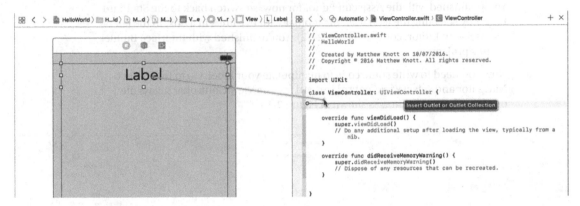

Figure 2-14. *Creating an outlet using the Assistant Editor*

When you release the mouse button, a Connection dialog appears, asking for a number of values (see Figure 2-15). The key option you need to be aware of here is the Name text field. If the object you're connecting to code can be tapped or trigger an event, you can choose one of two options for your connection: Outlet or Action. But in this instance, Xcode intelligently knows that this label isn't interactive and therefore restricts your choices.

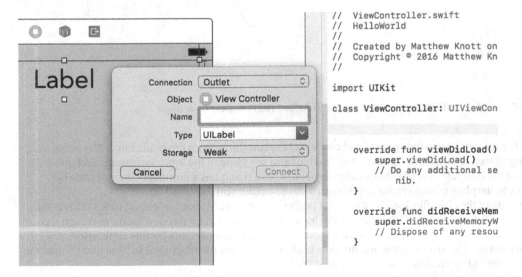

Figure 2-15. *Creating an outlet for your label*

3. The Name text field value determines how you refer to your label in code. For now, type in lblOutput and click Connect.

    If everything's gone according to plan, the first few lines of code should look like this:

    ```
    import UIKit

    class ViewController: UIViewController {
        @IBOutlet weak var lblOutput: UILabel!
    ```

4. You're finished with the Assistant Editor for now, so switch back to the Standard Editor by selecting the icon from the toolbar with five lines in a box, to the left of the Assistant Editor icon (see Figure 2-12). You're finished with Interface Builder for this project.

5. Now you need to write some code to manipulate your label. Go to the Project Navigator and select ViewController.swift. The View Controller's class file opens in the code editor, as shown in Figure 2-16.

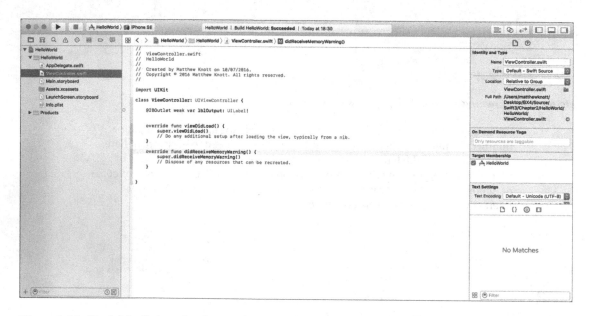

Figure 2-16. *Xcode's built-in code editor with the* ViewController.swift *file open*

This chapter touches on many areas and concepts I explain throughout the book; but at this point, you're going to start using Xcode's powerful code editor and see some of the intuitive features that make Xcode one of the best IDEs ever. With the class file open, notice that it has a number of lines of code by default. This boilerplate code gives the application a starting point you can build on.

In the code of the class file, look for a line that begins with override func viewDidLoad(). This is the start of the viewDidLoad function, a piece of code that is executed each time the view loads, making it a great place to put code that alters the view on-load. To complete the very simple code for this application, you need to tell the View Controller that when the view loads, it should set the label's text to "Bonjour!". Add the highlighted code to the viewDidLoad function, as shown:

```
override func viewDidLoad() {
     super.viewDidLoad()
     // Do any additional setup after loading the view, typically from a nib.

     lblOutput.text = "Bonjour!"
}
```

Here you can see Xcode's powerful code-completion feature in action; it can assist you in writing code much more efficiently. As you type lbl, a popup appears that says UILabel! lblOutput; when this is highlighted, press the Tab or Return key to complete the word lblOutput. Next type .te. Again Xcode's code completion snaps into action and shows a number of options, but the first one in the list is the one you want: String? text. With that item selected, press Return and continue typing the code. You can easily see from this example how Xcode's code completion helps you become a really efficient programmer, as well as how it helps cut down on errors.

To recap, what you've done here is declare a variable that is linked to the UILabel you added to the view in Interface Builder using the Assistant Editor. You then added a single line of code to the viewDidLoad function to set the text of the label programmatically—well done!

Running and Testing Your Application

It's hard to stress enough how important it is to test your application thoroughly before even thinking about submitting it to the App Store. There are many reasons for this. First, the App Store review process is very thorough—if your app isn't up to par, Apple isn't afraid to let you know in the form of a rejection. So testing means you reduce your chances of being rejected by Apple. When you submit your app, if you're rejected, you have to make the amendments and then resubmit your application, all of which is time consuming—time that could otherwise have been used to sell your app. Second, when someone downloads your application, they're parting with their money and expect a certain standard. When they purchase and download an app, it's disappointing to find that it's slow and hard to use. Finally, testing makes you a better developer. Smoothing out the creases in your applications now helps you build good habits, and you carry these on until they become second nature. Testing can save you a lot of time when working on larger, more demanding projects.

Now that your application is ready to be run, the quickest way to check if it will build successfully without crashing is to choose Product ➤ Build (⌘+B). If everything's in order, you should see a small dialog stating that the build has completed successfully. It's time to run your application: choose Product ➤ Run (⌘+R), and Xcode will build and then run the application using the target specified, which is (by default at this stage) the iOS Simulator.

The iOS Simulator is invaluable when you need to test your application quickly or test a feature that you've recently implemented. However, it's important to note that testing your app using the iOS Simulator isn't the same as testing it on an iOS device—that is, an actual iPhone/iPod Touch or an iPad. Applications may not perform the same on a device as they do on iOS Simulator, because the simulator doesn't simulate all software and hardware functionality. To change the type of device you want your application to be tested on via the iOS Simulator, go back to Xcode and click the Stop button in the top-left corner. With the application no longer running, go back to the iOS Simulator and choose Hardware ➤ Device and then select from the list of devices available. Figure 2-17 shows the application running in the iOS Simulator.

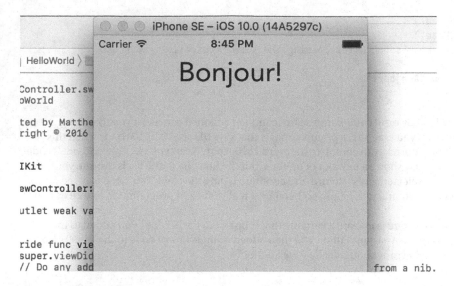

Figure 2-17. *The iOS Simulator running the app using the iPhone 6s as the simulated hardware*

Additionally, in the iOS Simulator you can change the orientation of the device, the scale at which the device displays, and an array of other options covered later in this book. What's recommended now is that you browse through the menus of the iOS Simulator while your app is running and play around with the options to get a little familiar with the different features.

Adding Files

One final point worth mentioning at this early stage is how to add your own files to your project. Applications can be made up of literally hundreds upon hundreds of files, ranging from images to sounds. Let's add some images to the example application: let's change the app's icon without writing any code and then add a background image to the main view.

Before you add an icon file, you need to create one or download the source code for this book from the Apress web site and use the included files. Because this isn't a book on iOS design or even iOS development, I won't digress about how to create perfect iOS app icons. Instead, I'll just state that you need to create a PNG file that, in this instance, I'm calling icon120.png, with dimensions 120 px by 120 px (pixels). Include whatever you like as the graphic, making sure it conforms to these specifications. I created a file with a basic gradient and a speech bubble saying "Hi!" in the middle. To set the application icon, you work with a feature that Apple introduced in Xcode 5, called Asset Catalogs; these are covered in more detail later in the book, but suffice it to say they make the headache of managing retina and standard-resolution images far easier than having a folder with lots of different-sized images. Here are the steps:

1. From the Project Navigator, select Assets.xcassets.

2. You're presented with a single item in the left column of the Asset Catalog called AppIcon. Click this item.

3. Bring the Finder window with the icon file in it over the top of Xcode, and then drag the icon file to the 2x box above the area labeled iPhone App iOS 7-9 60pt, as shown in Figure 2-18.

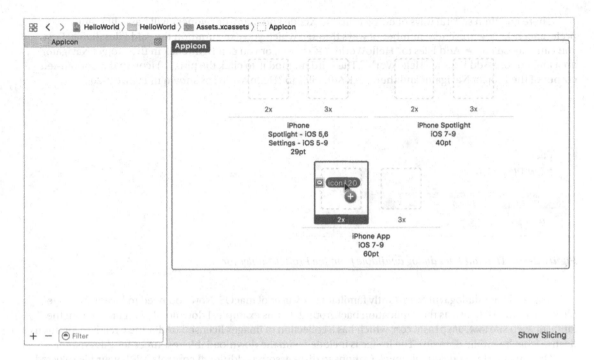

Figure 2-18. *The Images Asset Catalog is where you set the application icon*

For completeness you would add the other required icons in a final version of your application; however, for this quick demo, there is no need to do so. Run the application to see the icon in action. Once the app is running in the Simulator, choose Hardware ➤ Home (⌘+Shift+H). If you've done everything right, you should see something like the image in Figure 2-19.

■ **Note**   As you'll learn as you progress through the book, Apple requires you to create icons in numerous sizes for the App Store, currently including up to 1,024 pixels square. It's good to get into the habit early of adding the resolution to the filename to help you keep track of your assets.

Figure 2-19. *The application's new icon in the iOS Simulator*

With the icon successfully set, let's look at another, more traditional, way of adding files to the project. (You expand your Asset Catalog knowledge later in the book.)

There are often several ways of doing things in Xcode and many developers will have different preferences. Xcode presents a number of ways through which you can summon the Add Files dialog. First, you can choose File ➤ Add Files to "HelloWorld" (⌘+⌥+A), or you can right-click in the Project Navigator area and choose Add Files to "HelloWorld". The third method is to click the plus (+) icon in the bottom-left corner of the Project Navigator and then click Add Files to "HelloWorld", as shown in Figure 2-20.

Figure 2-20. *The Add Files dialog available from the Project Navigator*

The Add Files dialog will be instantly familiar to any user of macOS. Now you need to locate an image file you would like to use as the application background. In this example, I downloaded an image from the fantastic web site `www.unsplash.com`, which has a collection of images licensed under the Creative Commons license (they're public domain). The image is included with the downloadable resources for this chapter.

Once you've located your file, click Options to display some additional controls. With your file selected, ensure Copy Items If Needed is checked, as shown in Figure 2-21, and click Add.

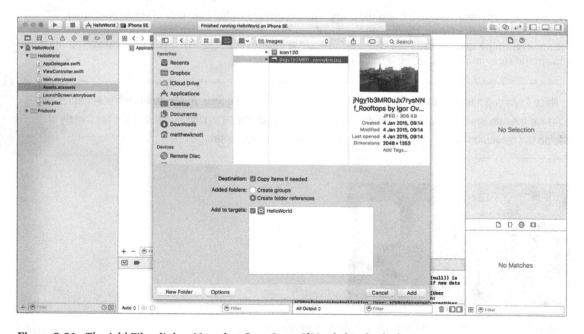

Figure 2-21. *The Add Files dialog. Note that Copy Items If Needed is checked*

At this point you return to Xcode. Look at the Project Navigator, where you see that your file has been added to the project's file structure. When I asked you to add the file, I also asked you to ensure that Copy Items If Needed was checked. The reason is that if you don't check this option, the file appears in the project structure as it does now, but the file itself isn't copied into the project. Hence, if you were to send the project to someone or to archive it, the image would be omitted.

■ **Note** Although adding an image to your project in this fashion is fine, it is no longer the recommended method, which is to use Asset Catalogs. This is because of the variety of resolutions images have to be in order to be considered optimized for the device; Asset Catalogs provide a great way of controlling this.

Organizing Files in Xcode

Before you proceed and make this image appear in your view, let's talk about organizing files. As I mentioned earlier, Xcode gives the illusion of organization: a kind of faux-folder structure that in Xcode is made up of items called Groups.

1. Right-click on the file you just added and click New Group from Selection, as shown in Figure 2-22.

Figure 2-22. *Creating a new group for your file*

2. Name the new group "Backgrounds".

3. If you right-click the HelloWorld project in the Project Navigator and select Show in Finder, you can explore the actual file structure behind your project. Note that there is no sign of a folder called Backgrounds, because Xcode organizes the files while leaving the underlying file structure intact.

You've done the hard work of adding the file to Xcode. Now let's do the fun part—adding the image to the View Controller using the Storyboard. Start by selecting Main.storyboard from the Project Navigator. Now, from the Object Library, select an image view (UIImageView) object and drag it to your View Controller. If you're having trouble finding it in the list, remember that you can filter the list by typing "image" in the search field. Resize the image view so it fills the entire view. Your screen should look something like Figure 2-23.

■ **Tip**   Remember, if you can't see the Object Library, you can access it via View ➤ Utilities ➤ Show Object Library (^+⌘+⌥+3).

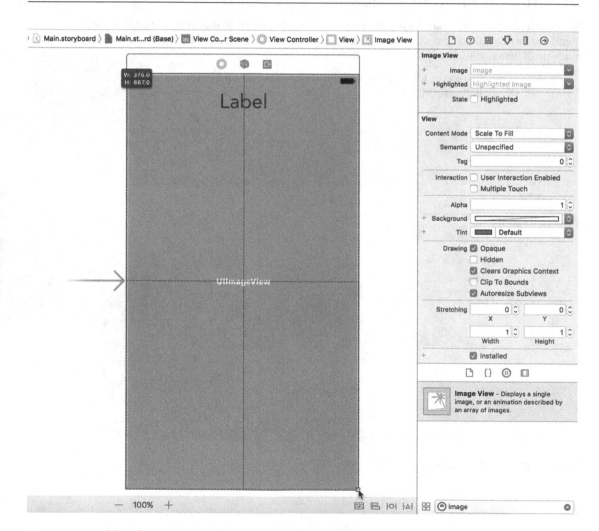

Figure 2-23. *Adding the image view and resizing it to fill the view*

With the image view positioned, it's time to specify which image to use:

1. With the image view selected, go to the Attributes Inspector.

2. From the Image drop-down, select the file you added. If you're using the image from the download, then this is the file starting with jNgy.

3. The image fills the image view, but it may have been distorted in doing so. You want the photo to fill the image view but maintain its aspect ratio. To achieve this, click the Content Mode drop-down list and change it from the default Scale To Fill option to Aspect Fill. Your image still fills the image view, but the ratio is maintained, preserving the original look of the image.

4. You once again need to apply constraints, this time to the image view. Ensuring that the image view is still selected, click the Pin button at the bottom of the design area. This time, all four values should say 0; if they don't, ensure you have not checked Constrain to Margins. If the values still don't say 0, change them manually and then click all four bars, as shown in Figure 2-24. Click the Add 4 Constraints button.

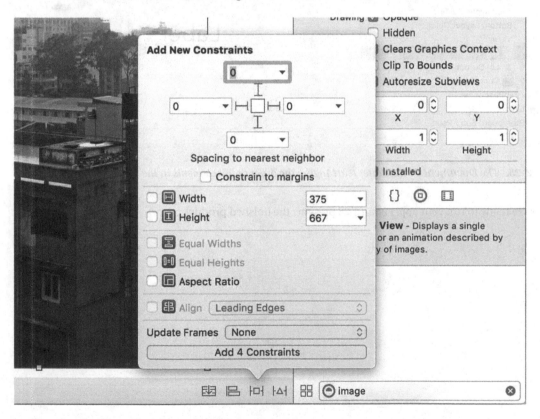

Figure 2-24. *Applying constraints to the image view*

So you're finished, right? Not quite. With the image view filling all the available space, you can't see the label you added at the start of the project! This is because of the way these two items are ordered, or rather how they're layered: the image view is rendered in a layer above the label, obscuring it. To resolve this, let's look at the Document Outline. If you can't see the Document Outline (the column between the design area and the Project Navigator), click the Show Document Outline button in the bottom-left corner of the Storyboard design area, or choose Editor ➤ Show Document Outline.

Expand all the items in the Document Outline. Beneath View, you should have your label which Xcode will name `Lbl Output`, followed by the image view named after the image. Drag the image view carefully to move it above the label, as shown in Figure 2-25. Because of the hierarchy of the objects in the view, the image view is now rendered beneath the label, although you may need to tweak the color of your label to make sure it's visible against the image background.

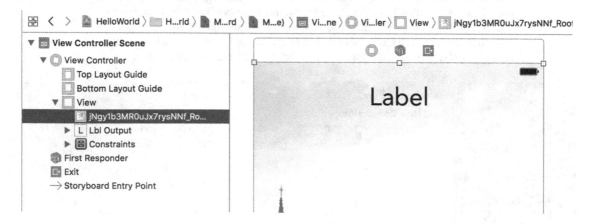

Figure 2-25. *The Document Outline after rearranging the order of the elements in the view*

You're ready to run your app! Figure 2-26 presents the finished product.

Figure 2-26. *The finished app*

Summary

You've learned a lot in this chapter. Specifically, you did the following:

- Set up a new Xcode project and found that Xcode generates a functioning, yet boring, application.

- Designed an interface using Xcode's built-in graphical Interface Builder and used the Attributes Inspector to change some basic properties of the objects you added to your view.

- Used the Assistant Editor to visually create connected outlets quickly and efficiently with drag and drop.

- Looked at Xcode's code editor, updated the contents of a `UILabel` programmatically, and had an introduction to Xcode's code-completion tool.

- Built and run your application in iOS Simulator and looked at some different features of the iOS Simulator.

- Compared and contrasted the basics of the structure of your files in the Project Navigator and the structure of your project in the Finder and added new files to your project, which gave your application an icon without your having to write any code.

- Added an image view (or UIImageView, to use its correct but less-friendly name) to your view controller and set its image in the Attributes Inspector.

- Moved objects in the Document Outline hierarchy.

Essentially, the main purpose of this chapter wasn't to create a groundbreaking application but rather to give you a degree of comfort when it comes to working with the latest version of Xcode. It's easy to become overwhelmed with the sheer number of menus, tools, dialogs, and inspectors; however, as you've seen, creating an app isn't too daunting when you know where to look and what to press.

Chapter 3 introduces you to the different project templates that come with Xcode. You set up a new project and get a guided tour of the array of panels, windows, and menus that come with Xcode, along with learn how to quickly access them.

CHAPTER 3

■ ■ ■

Project Templates and Getting Around

In Chapter 2, you created a very basic application and then tested it on the iOS Simulator. You were also introduced to the basics of the Project Navigator and looked at the Attributes Inspector. In addition, you programmatically updated the contents of a label that had been placed onto the view using Interface Builder and made it show an image file that had been added to the project, and you used an Asset Catalog to set the application's icon. In the first half of this chapter, you take a step back from app creation and look at the array of tabs, inspectors, panels, buttons, and windows that come with Xcode, along with the different project templates that Xcode provides.

In order to be an accomplished app developer, it's important that you train your developer's muscle memory around the key areas of your IDE; there's a good chance you already knew this, which is why you bought this book. By the end of this chapter, you should be a lot more familiar with many of the interface elements of Xcode, should be able to quickly access the most common Xcode features, and should have a great knowledge of the more obscure ones. You should also be able to choose a project template without having to worry about whether you've picked the right one, and you'll have some of the key knowledge required to start creating your own applications.

In this chapter, you create a working multi-view application; then you learn how to pass information from one view to another and display that information in the ShowMe application. Passing information between views is essential for many applications. In this chapter, you simply pass text between views, but in Chapter 8 you discover how to pass a selection from a table view to another view and how to pass certain objects.

Without further ado, let's get started!

Project Templates

As a developer, you have the somewhat daunting task of making many, many decisions throughout the development of your application. With iOS and macOS apps, arguably the first decision you need to make is which project template to choose in Xcode. At this point you're optimistic, excited about the adventure ahead, and eager to get in there and begin writing your application, but not so fast! Choosing the right project template can have a huge impact on the direction your application takes, and that's why this section goes through each of them and explains the cases in which you should choose a project template provided by Xcode. It's worth mentioning here that, because the main focus of this book is iOS development, I don't go into detail about the macOS templates and instead focus more on templates targeted at iOS application development.

To begin, you need to fire up Xcode if you haven't done so already, and either choose Create A New Xcode Project from the Welcome screen or go to File ➤ New ➤ Project (⌘+Shift+N). You're greeted with a screen that presents an array of different project templates to choose from, as illustrated in Figure 3-1.

© Matthew Knott 2016
M. Knott, *Beginning Xcode*, DOI 10.1007/978-1-4302-5005-0_3

Figure 3-1. *Xcode's different project templates*

By default, when you first open Xcode and choose a project template, you can choose only from the ones provided by Apple; however, if you'd like to see what really goes into making an Xcode project and perhaps tinker with one yourself, the default location of Xcode's project template is /Applications/Xcode. app/Contents/Developer/Platforms/iPhoneOS.platform/Developer/Library/Xcode/Templates/Project Templates (this is, of course, assuming that you have Xcode located in your /Applications folder). There, you can open the different project templates provided by Apple and dissect them. However, I recommend that before you do this, you back up that folder just in case you change something that corrupts the template.

■ **Note**   Notice that throughout this book you're given the keyboard shortcut equivalent whenever you need to access a menu item, open a window, or show a navigator or inspector. I strongly encourage you to take advantage of keyboard shortcuts, because using them can drastically improve your workflow and allow you to become a more productive developer—or, at the very least, make you appear to know what you're doing. It can also help make tiresome tasks somewhat bearable. What's more, many of the shortcuts that apply to Xcode can be brought over to other applications: for example, to Finder. You can also visit Xcode's preferences (⌘+,) and modify some of the shortcuts if they're not quite to your liking.

Master-Detail Applications

The Master Detail Application template is a starting point if you're looking to create an application that presents the user with a UITableView and then pushes a detail view when the user taps a row. By default, Xcode creates a project that, if targeting an iPhone, has one table view; the user can add rows by tapping the plus button in the top-right corner of the navigation bar. If you're targeting the iPad, a new row is added to the table view; however, the layouts of both the table and detail view fit much more nicely in the iPad's larger display.

Figure 3-2 shows the default project created when you specify Master Detail View as your project template. It's running universally via the iOS Simulator: iPad on the left and iPhone on the right.

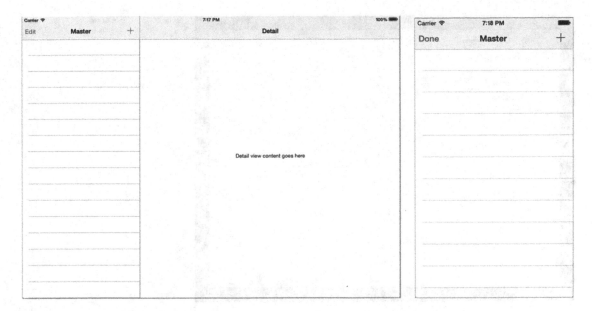

Figure 3-2. *Master Detail View template running on the iPad (left) and iPhone (right)*

Page-Based Applications

Creating an application using the ***page-based*** template gives users the impression that they're swiping through the pages of a book. With a page-based project, Xcode gives you everything you need to create an application that displays information in a book-like format: that is, it reveals information as the user swipes the screen either left or right. By default, you're provided with an object that adheres to the `UIPageViewControllerDelegate` protocol, which specifies the root view controller and initializes the view by loading `PageViewModelController`.

Figure 3-3 shows the default project created by Xcode when you choose to create a page-based application; on the left you can see it running on the iPad, and on the right it's running on the iPhone. If you swipe or click the left- or right-most side of the screen, the content is pulled over as if you're reading a book.

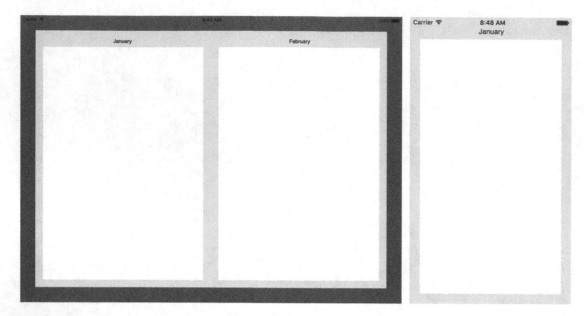

***Figure 3-3.** Page-based template running on an iPad (left) and iPhone (right)*

Single View Applications

This is perhaps the most organic project template provided by Xcode, and it will inevitably be the starting point for many applications. The ***Single View*** project template provides you with a single `UIViewController` that's loaded when the application runs. It's like a completely blank canvas in which the application can take any shape you like. This is especially useful if you're creating a custom iOS application, if you aren't sure of the exact approach you're going to take, or if the alternative templates don't seem appropriate for your project.

Figure 3-4 illustrates what you're given by Xcode when you choose this project template. Surprisingly, it's a blank, white view.

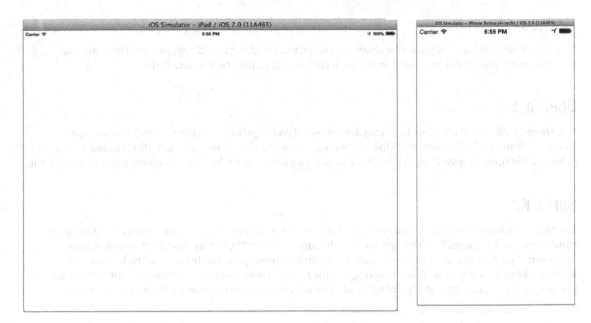

Figure 3-4. *Single View template running on an iPad (left) and iPhone (right)*

Tabbed Applications

Because many applications use tab bars to display different parts, it's no surprise that Apple has created a project template that allows you to quickly implement UIViewControllers in a UITabBarController. By default, you're provided with two view controllers, each of which has its own tabs.

Figure 3-5 shows a tabbed application. As you can see, the application consists of a tab bar with two tabs: the first loads FirstViewController and the second SecondViewController.

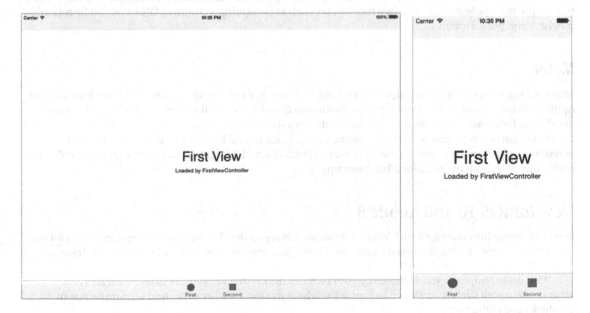

Figure 3-5. *Tabbed template running on an iPad (left) and iPhone (right)*

Games

Xcode provides a single template that allows you to get started with game development. There are four different technologies that you can use and each comes with its own boilerplate code.

OpenGL ES

The *OpenGL ES Game* template is an excellent choice if you're planning to create a game using Apple's OpenGL ES and GLKit frameworks. OpenGL is used across multiple platforms, including consoles, PCs, and other mobile operating systems like Android; hence it's a good choice for cross-platform game development.

Sprite Kit

The Sprite Kit framework was introduced in Xcode 5 with iOS 7. Sprite Kit is Apple's answer to third-party game engines like Cocos2D. It may not have the features of Cocos2D, but its simplicity, coupled with its powerful physics and the animation tools it provides to developers, made it one of the hottest new frameworks in Xcode 5. In addition to giving you the tools to create your own version of your favorite 2D physics game, you can also use Sprite Kit to add complex animations to more traditional applications.

■ **Note**   If you're interested, go to my blog at www.mattknott.com and search for Sprite Kit. I've written a tutorial on adding Sprite Kit particle effects to regular iOS apps.

Scene Kit

Scene Kit is a 3D graphics API that was first introduced with OS X 10.8 and has now made its way into iOS in version 8. Whereas Sprite Kit is a complete game engine, Scene Kit is designed to create and render assets and integrate with other technologies such as Sprite Kit, Core Image, and Core Animation. Scene Kit lets you render and manipulate 3D models in a regular app, such as presenting a strand of DNA that can be rotated, pinched, and pulled around.

Metal

Metal is a huge deal for iOS game developers; there isn't any other way to describe it. In a huge leap forward, Apple has created this new technology as an alternative OpenGL ES and it was introduced in iOS 8. Apple's developers have basically created a bespoke API that can squeeze every ounce of power out of the current A9 chip in the latest iOS hardware. The performance specs being touted by Apple imply that Metal will be able to redraw models on the screen ten times faster than with OpenGL ES. This means better graphics and better performance without the need for a hardware upgrade.

New for iOS 10 and Xcode 8

In iOS 10, Apple introduced a new Messages framework that enables developers to create extensions for the core Messages app. To support this development, Apple provided two templates in the form of iMessage Application and Sticker Pack Application.

With these templates you can develop your own extensions that allow users to share stickers and other content with friends, as shown in Figure 3-6, where you see a sticker collection featuring some of the graphics used in the book.

Figure 3-6. *An example of a sticker book extension for Messages*

Template Selection

Now that I've explained each of the five default project templates provided by Apple, let's start looking at the various panels and panes you see in Xcode. To help with this, you're going to build a simple application with two views or screens, using an innovative system for constructing interfaces and linking views together. Storyboards make the development process much quicker, more visual, and more accessible. I hope that through this example, even though it isn't complex, you can appreciate the real benefits of storyboards ahead of later chapters where they're used more extensively. For this project, called ShowMe, you use the Single View Application template.

Once you've started the process of creating this app, you need to specify which application template you want to use—that is, which one will best suit this application. In this instance, and as I just mentioned, select the Single View Application template. Typically, when choosing a template, you go through a thought process like the following to make sure you start with the right template:

- *How users will navigate around your application*: If you're using a good-old UINavigationController as the crux of the application, chances are you need to choose a single-view application and then implement a UINavigationController manually. However, if users will navigate using the UITabBarController, then your best choice, surprisingly, is a tabbed application.

- *How you'd like your screens to be laid out*: Again, if screens will be pushed via a UINavigationController or displayed as a single UIViewController, a single-view application will suffice. However, if you're creating a book or magazine, the page-based template is your best bet.

- *Whether you're creating a game*: If you're creating a game, Apple provides the Game template, which supports OpenGL ES; Sprite Kit for 2D games; Metal for 3D games; and Scene Kit to render 3D assets. Combined, these give you the tools and features for almost any game project.

As with any other application created using Xcode, you need to start by creating a new project. Let's begin:

1. Create a new Xcode project by going to File ➤ New ➤ Project (⌘+Shift+N) or, alternatively, clicking Create A New Xcode Project from the Welcome screen (⌘+Shift+1).

2. As I've already specified, select Single View Application from the Project Templates dialog and click Next.

3. You're required to provide Xcode with those all-important little details such as Product Name, Organization Name, and so on. Figure 3-7 illustrates the values to put in (remember to enter your own first and last names in the relevant fields, though!). For Product Name, use ShowMe.

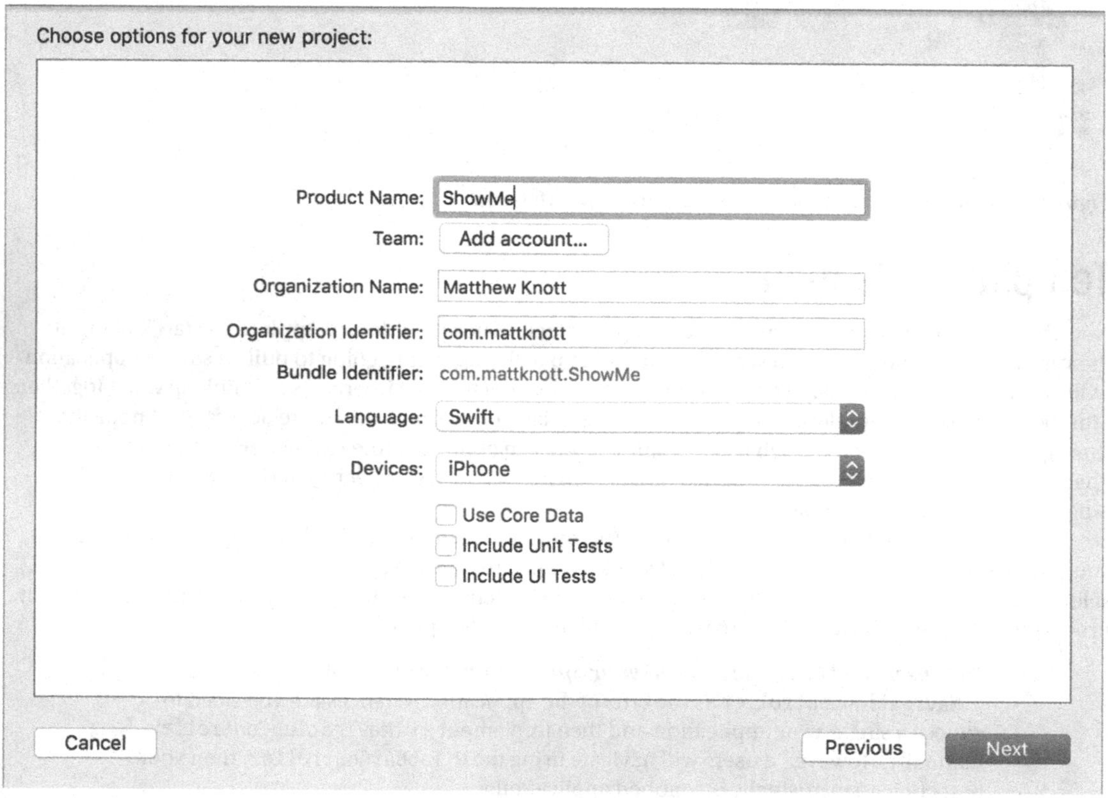

Choose options for your new project:

Product Name:	ShowMe
Team:	Add account...
Organization Name:	Matthew Knott
Organization Identifier:	com.mattknott
Bundle Identifier:	com.mattknott.ShowMe
Language:	Swift
Devices:	iPhone

☐ Use Core Data
☐ Include Unit Tests
☐ Include UI Tests

Cancel   Previous   Next

Figure 3-7. *Inputting the options to create the application*

4. For this project, you can specify your own name (that is, your first and last name) as the Organization Name; for example, in my case this would be Matthew Knott.

5. For Organization Identifier, I used reverse domain notation and entered com.mattknott, but you could just as easily use com.YOURSURNAME.

6. Ensure that Device is set to iPhone and Language is set to Swift, and that you've unchecked Use Core Data, Include Unit Test, and Include UI Tests.

7. To finish, click Next. You're prompted to choose a location for your project. Save it somewhere that's easy for you to find, and ensure that Source Control is unchecked. Click Create. Now you're now ready to explore the many areas of Xcode.

Getting Around

Now that your application is ready and the project is set up, it's be useful to become familiar with the main areas of Xcode's interface: the navigators, toolbar, editor, utilities panel, and debugging area. Essentially, most actions you need to perform are in those main areas of the interface, with the exception of actions contained in the menu bar. This section focuses on each of these areas so that when they come up again later in the book, you know where to look and what purpose they serve. Figure 3-8 shows a breakdown of the main area of Xcode's interface.

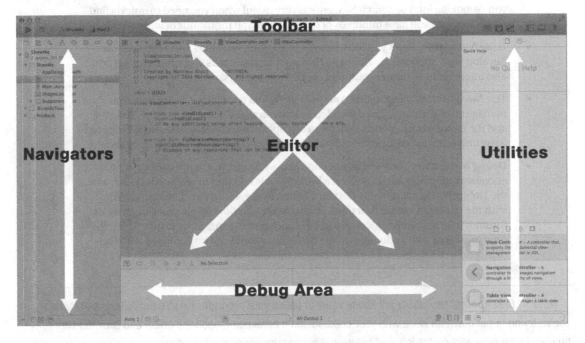

Figure 3-8. *The five main parts of Xcode's interface*

Navigators

Let's first focus on the far-left side of Xcode: the section that houses the navigators. A *navigator* in Xcode is something that allows you to browse various things, such as files, folders, warnings, build errors, memory leaks, breakpoints, and so on. If you look at the top of the navigator panel, you see that you can toggle the view using eight different tabs, as shown in Figure 3-9.

Figure 3-9. Xcode's different navigators, among which you can toggle

- *Project Navigator*: This is perhaps one of the most important features of the entire navigator panel. It allows you to explore the files in your project and displays what frameworks and interface files your project is made of. As previously mentioned, the file structure of the Project Navigator doesn't correspond to that of the Finder; things like folders are there just to make it easier for you to navigate your project in Xcode.

- *Symbol Navigator*: Where you can browse what Xcode considers a *symbol* in your project. A symbol is generally the name of a class or a function. In the bar at the bottom of the Symbol Navigator, you can filter what's displayed and view Cocoa's built-in symbols or symbols defined in your project. The Symbol Navigator is especially useful when you have dozens of Swift class files and you need to quickly browse them to find a specific class declaration or function.

- *Find Navigator*: A very useful means of searching your project to find a certain bit of code. If you select the small magnifying glass in the search area, you can specify search options such as where Xcode should look, and you can more accurately define what you're looking for. The Search Navigator is very useful when you need to quickly find something and you have hundreds of different files and thousands of lines of code.

- *Issue Navigator*: Alerts you to any issues by flagging warnings and errors as you develop your application. The Issue Navigator not only tells you what's wrong but also attempts to accurately pinpoint exactly where the issue lies.

- *Test Navigator*: Where you find your test targets and test classes. From here, you manage all of your tests. They're coded in a way similar to how the Project Navigator and the editor work together: selecting a test opens the relevant code and allows you to write unit tests that ensure that individual classes and functions work as they should.

- *Debug Navigator*: Used when your code pauses. By default, it opens if a pause is encountered. It also appears when a breakpoint is reached in your code. Otherwise, the Debug Navigator remains dormant. When in use, it displays call stacks along with the names of nested functions. If you click a function name, you can navigate through it further. In addition, useful CPU and memory monitors display the real-time impact of your code. The Debug Navigator should not be confused with the debug area of Xcode, which I cover later in this chapter.

■ **Note** *Breakpoints* essentially tell Xcode when to pause your program. They're especially useful when you're trying to pin down an issue with your code. To add a breakpoint, open the editor and click the line number in the gray area on the left, just between the navigator panel and the editor.

- *Breakpoint Navigator*: The hub in which you manage breakpoints. With a project that has dozens of breakpoints, you'll soon become accustomed to using this tab. In the Breakpoint Navigator, you can also create different types of breakpoints: for example, symbolic breakpoints.

- • *Report Navigator*: Like the history option of your Internet browser, except that instead of recording what you open, it records your actions. Specifically, it lists the status of a build (whether it failed, succeeded, or succeeded but has errors). To reveal all the details of something like a build, simply click the log item. Xcode brings up a new dialog in the editor, showing all the necessary details regarding what you clicked.

Now that you know exactly what each of the eight different tabs corresponds to, there must be a quicker way to access them, as opposed to having to click them each time. Well, first and foremost, Xcode has a tendency to spontaneously hide some of its interface elements (usually because you've clicked a button mistakenly). If you ever lose the navigator sidebar, go to View ➤ Navigators ➤ Show Project Navigator to bring up the Project Navigator. To quickly switch between the tabs of the navigator, press ⌘+1 (for the Project Navigator) or ⌘+8 (for the Report Navigator). Again, it's handy to use keyboard shortcuts, because they can dramatically increase your productivity—which, to a developer working through the night to complete a project for a tight deadline, is everything. If you're short on space, you can press ⌘+0 to hide the navigator panel.

Toolbar

Moving on from the navigators section, there is the Toolbar. The Toolbar is present throughout many familiar macOS applications (such as Finder), and it houses many useful buttons and displays important information regarding build results. If you've previously used Xcode 4 or an earlier version, you see a number of changes, most notably the size: the Toolbar has been compressed somewhat from those earlier versions. To tackle the Toolbar, let's examine each of the default buttons, starting on the left and moving to the right. Figure 3-10 shows the default layout of the Toolbar.

Figure 3-10. *The Xcode Toolbar's default layout*

First you see two buttons on the left: Run and Stop. These are rather self-explanatory at this point, but clicking the Run button starts a build of your project and then launches it using whatever target is specified in the active scheme, just to the right. In this instance, the scheme is set to ShowMe and iPhone 6s Plus. Once it's running, you can stop your project by clicking the Stop button. Additionally, if you click and hold your mouse over the Run button, you can choose from Run, Test, Profile, and Analyze. I explain what these do later in this book; briefly, if you select an option from the menu, it takes the place of Run and performs the specified action each time you click it.

Next are the active scheme and device target. This is where you can choose a scheme, which specifies how you'd like to run your project. Select ShowMe, and you're given the option to choose Edit Scheme, New Scheme, or Manage Scheme. A scheme allows you to specify in more detail how you want your application to be run or debugged. If you click the iPhone 6s Plus section, a drop-down menu appears in which you can choose from different platforms on which to test your project.

Next is the Activity Viewer, which tells you what is happening when Xcode is performing an action. For example, if you choose to clean your project, the Activity Viewer displays the progress of the clean, similarly to when you're building an application. What's also nice about the Activity Viewer is that, if you're running the latest versions of Xcode and macOS, it displays the last action performed along with when it was performed. Finally, the Activity Viewer displays small icons near the button that let you quickly see the number of issues or errors found in your project.

On the right of the Activity Viewer are three editor buttons that change how the editor in Xcode looks and behaves. You can choose the Standard, Assistant, or Version editor, respectively. Click to open `Main.storyboard` from the Project Navigator (⌘+1), and then toggle between the three different editors and see what happens. These editors are covered in the next section of this chapter.

Finally, you have three view buttons. These are very useful when you lose one of the main elements of Xcode's interface. The first button toggles the navigators section, the middle button toggles the debug area, and the third button toggles the utilities section.

As with many other macOS applications, if you right-click a gray area of the Toolbar, you can choose to show or hide the toolbar. This will only grant you an extra line of code. It is far more useful to have the toolbar visible than to suppress it.

As with many macOS apps, Xcode has fullscreen support. This is especially useful when you're working with the Assistant Editor, previewing layouts with size classes or storyboards, or designing iPad application interfaces. To toggle fullscreen mode, select the green circle in the top-left corner of Xcode.

Editor

The most important part of any integrated development environment is its code editor. Xcode's editor is exceptional in many ways. It has three different view options—Standard, Assistant, and Version Editor.

If you open `AppDelegate.swift`, you see that the editor is front and center. Simply click where you'd like to begin coding, and then code away. As you type code, Xcode's code-completion feature appears. To choose an option from the code-completion dialog, use the arrow keys on your keyboard to navigate the suggestions (sometimes there are multiple ways to instantiate a class), and press Return or Tab.

Notice that just above the editor window is a small jump bar. You can use this to open files, see function declarations, and more efficiently navigate through your project and your code. I revisit this bar in Chapter 10.

Standard Editor

The Standard Editor displays a single window and focuses on what has been selected from the Project Navigator on the left (see Figure 3-11). This is the editor you will use most frequently simply because you have the most room to work on your code.

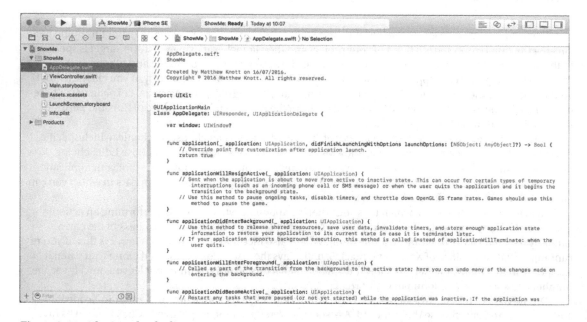

Figure 3-11. *The Standard editor*

Assistant Editor

The Assistant Editor is far more utilitarian, and chances are it will make you want to go out and purchase a larger display. The Assistant Editor displays separate windows and by default contains logical contents depending on which file you're working with. For example, in Figure 3-12, I have the Main.storyboard open on the left; as a result, Xcode opens ViewController.swift on the right automatically. This allows you to work simultaneously on both files without having to worry about switching constantly.

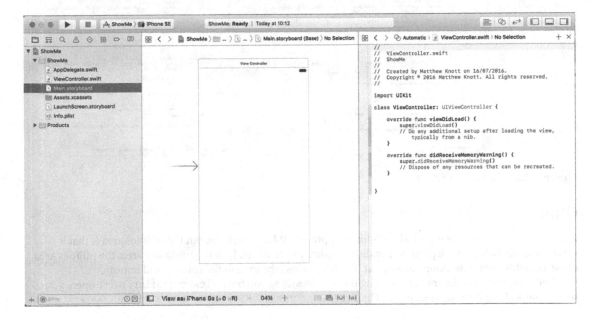

Figure 3-12. *The Assistant Editor*

Notice on the far right, along the jump bar, a small button with a plus symbol on it. If you click this button, Xcode allows you to have multiple editors open—as many as you and your display can handle. In addition, it's important to understand that you aren't restricted to the automated file: you can choose any file in the project to view. This can be useful when you're referencing keys in a strings file for localization of an app, which is something you do toward the end of the book.

Holding down the mouse button on the overlapping circles icon for the Assistant Editor allows you to adjust the positioning of the editor windows.

Version Editor

The Version Editor is used exclusively with projects that use source control. This hasn't been enabled for this project, but later on in the book when you start working with source control you will see the significance of being able to compare your current source to an older version of the file. The Version Editor is shown in Figure 3-13; the most recent version of a file is selected on the left. Xcode opens another version of that file on the right and lets you track and view the changes made to this file. It also presents a timeline mode to view changes over time.

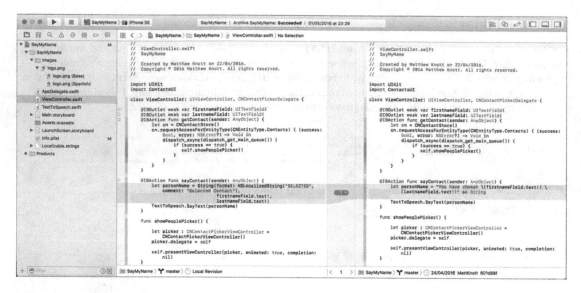

Figure 3-13. *The Version Editor*

Utilities

The utilities area provides essential tools for your project. What's useful about the utilities area is that it varies in terms of what it displays, depending on what you're using. Like the navigator area, the utilities area consists of different tabs along the top, but it also includes tabs toward the middle and bottom.

Let's first focus on the main tabs along the top. Providing you have `ViewController.swift` open, you see two tabs along the top, as shown in Figure 3-14.

Figure 3-14. *The tabs in the utilities area of Xcode with a code file open*

First is the File Inspector. It lets you manage attributes of a file: for example, its name, type path, and location in your project. As with many other inspectors in the utilities area, additional options can be changed if you scroll down. The File Inspector is one of two inspectors that are always present in the utilities area, regardless of which file you're working with.

Second is the Quick Help Inspector. Here you can easily access information about a symbol in Xcode. This is especially useful when you want to know where something has been declared, how it was declared, and its scope and parameters. This tab is always present in the utilities area.

The utilities area really comes to life when you're working with Interface Builder. Interface Builder was introduced in Chapter 2, when you used it in conjunction with the `Main.Storyboard` file. This is the same file you will start with in this chapter.

1. Open `Main.storyboard` from the Project Navigator. You have only a single view in the storyboard, but this will be a multi-view application, so let's add a second view. Just as you did with the label and image views in the previous chapter, you can drag view controllers in from the Object Library. Drag in a view controller from the Object Library and position it to the right of the current view controller, as shown in Figure 3-15.

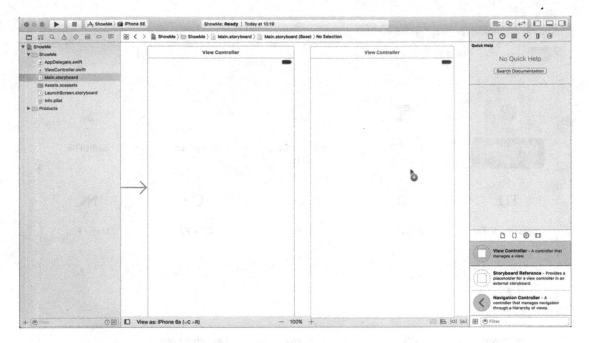

Figure 3-15. *Dragging a view controller from the Object Library to the design area*

2. Once you've released the view controller, use the small bar at the top of the view controller to maneuver it neatly beside the existing view controller, as shown in Figure 3-16.

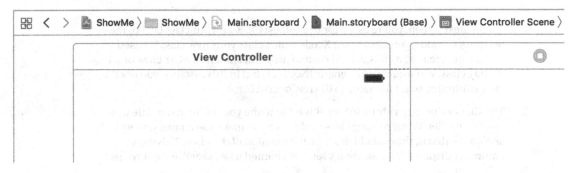

Figure 3-16. *Moving the view controller so that it snaps neatly into place beside the existing view controller*

3. You now have two view controllers on the storyboard. But remember from Chapter 2 that a view controller in a storyboard needs a corresponding view controller code file in order to interact with the visual portion. You need to create a new view controller file called `MessageViewController` that subclasses `UIViewController`. Subclassing is explained in detail later in the book; for now create the file by going to File ➤ New ➤ File... (⌘+N) and selecting Cocoa Touch Class, as shown in Figure 3-17. Click Next.

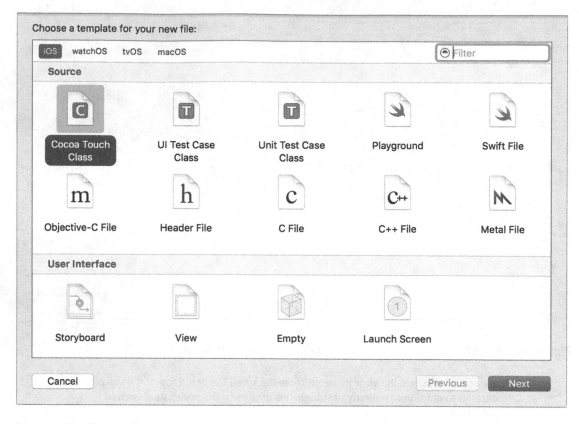

Figure 3-17. *The new file template selection*

4. On the next screen, you're asked for two values: Class and Subclass Of. For the Subclass Of value, you need to tell Xcode which class your new class is based on. If you were creating a class to hold custom properties, such as a Car class or an Animal class, you would use a generic NSObject; but in this instance you need a view controller, so set the value to UIViewController.

5. The Class value is largely up to you; this is the name you use to instantiate this view controller. When naming classes, always try to make the names semantically accurate—that is, they should describe the function of the class. This view controller displays the message it's sent, so I named it MessageViewController.

6. Ensure that Language is Swift. Check that your values match Figure 3-18 and click Next.

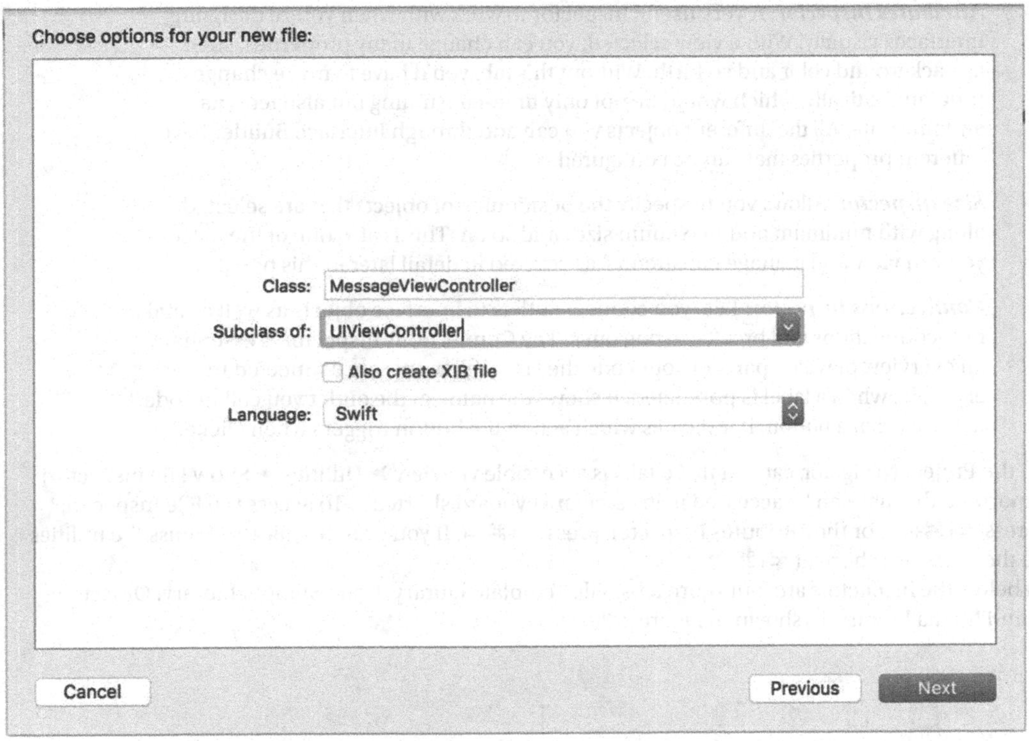

Choose options for your new file:

Class: MessageViewController

Subclass of: UIViewController

☐ Also create XIB file

Language: Swift

Cancel   Previous   Next

Figure 3-18. *Subclassing* `UIViewController`

7. On the next screen, you're prompted for a save location for your new file. Stick with the default settings. Ensure that in the Targets box, ShowMe is selected; then click Create.

You should now have a new file in your Project Navigator called `MessageViewController.swift`, which means you have all the files needed for the project and you're ready to put together the interface for the first view controller.

Reopen `Main.storyboard` from the Project Navigator. Before you add anything to the view, click the left view in the storyboard, and then look back to the utilities area on the right. You should see that the two tabs in Figure 3-14 have become six tabs, as shown in Figure 3-19.

Figure 3-19. *The utilities tabs in Interface Builder*

I've already covered the first two tabs, so let's look at the remaining four:

- ***Identity Inspector***: Here you can change details regarding an object, similar to the File Inspector. You can change and access the class name, accessibility details, runtime attributes, and so on. The Identity Inspector is only active when you have an object selected. With `Main.storyboard` open, select the first view, and the information in the Identity Inspector should become visible. You'll use this tab often when adding views to a storyboard.

- *Attributes Inspector*: A very useful inspector to work with when you're designing interfaces visually. With a view selected, you can change many properties, such as background color and so forth. Without this tab, you'd have to make changes programmatically, which would be not only time-consuming but also tedious and tiresome. All the different objects you can add through Interface Builder have different properties that can be configured.

- *Size Inspector*: Allows you to specify the positioning of objects that are selected, along with minimum and maximum sizes and so on. This is also one of the places you can view and manage constraints, as covered in detail later in this book.

- *Connections Inspector*: Lets you connect outlets to interface objects as well as make new connections and break existing ones. The Connections Inspector is essentially an overview of which parts of your code the visual elements are connected to. For example, when a label is populated, it shows the name of the outlet you call in code; in the case of a button, it indicates which action the button triggers when clicked.

Like the Project Navigator, each of these tabs is accessible via View ➤ Utilities ➤ Show File Inspector; more important, the tabs can be accessed using similar keyboard shortcuts. To access the File Inspector, simply press ⌥+⌘+1. For the Attributes Inspector, press ⌥+⌘+4. If you want to quickly dismiss the utilities area, use the keyboard shortcut ⌥+⌘+0.

Just below the inspectors are four more tabs: File Template Library, Code Snippet Library, Object Library, and Media Library, as shown in Figure 3-20.

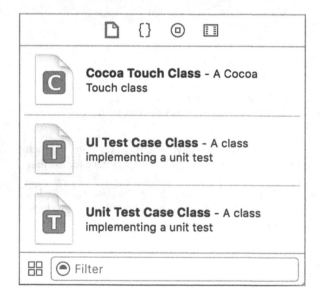

Figure 3-20. *The File Template, Code Snippet, and Object, and Media library tabs*

- The *File Template library* contains templates for common classes, heads, protocols, and so forth. To add one to your project, click and drag it to the Project Navigator.

- The *Code Snippet library* contains short pieces of code that you can use by clicking and dragging them into the editor with a code file open.

- The *Object library* is where you find the standard Cocoa controls for applications. You make extensive use of this library throughout this book. Simply click and drop an item onto a view with Interface Builder open.

- The *Media library* tab contains useful graphics, sounds, and icons you can use in your interfaces, again, by dragging and dropping them onto your interface.

These four tabs are accessible via View ➤ Utilities ➤ Show File Template Library or with the keyboard shortcut ^+⌥+⌘+1. The tabs are always visible, regardless of what file type you're working with; however, they're most useful while working with Interface Builder.

Before adding any objects to your view, you need to add an element called a *navigation controller* to manage the navigation back and forth through the different views. Xcode makes this very easy to do:

1. If you haven't already, select the left-most view in the storyboard by clicking the large white area in the design area. This should be the view with a large arrow pointing to its left side.

2. Go to Editor ➤ Embed In ➤ Navigation Controller, as shown in Figure 3-21. You should see a navigation controller appear to the left of the view. Once it's there, you can pretty much ignore it for the rest of the project, because the focus will be on the two views. Without it, navigating views would be extremely troublesome.

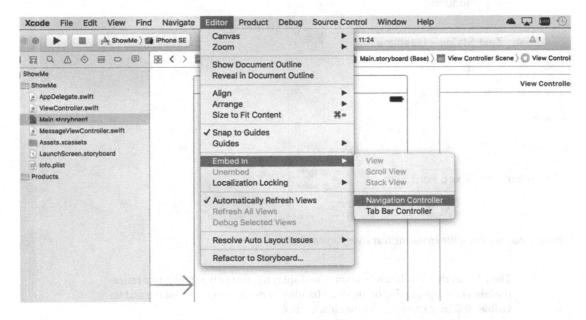

Figure 3-21. Adding a navigation controller to the view controller

3. Position the design area so you can see the first view, which is now attached to the navigation controller.

4. From the Object library, you need to add three items to the view. First, drag a label onto the view and position it toward the top of the view in the center.

5. Click the label once to select it, and then select the Attributes Inspector. Here you can really appreciate the range of minute customizations available to you. The second property in the Attributes Inspector for this label is a text field that says Label. Change this to say "Text to Send". You can also edit labels by double-clicking on the view, but this method helps you see some of the minute adjustments you can make in the Attributes Inspector.

6. Click the T in the Font box and select Headline from the font list, as shown in Figure 3-22.

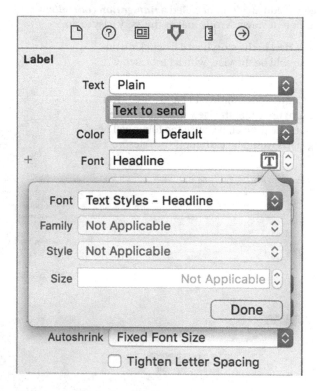

Figure 3-22. *Selecting the Headline text style for your label*

7. The label in the view is now too small to display the text you entered; rearrange the label by dragging one of the small handles in the corners until all the text is visible. You may need to re-center it after this.

8. Now that the label is in place, drag a text field from the Object Library onto the view and position it below the label. As you move the text field, you should get a feel for the vertical positioning as the object snaps into place below the label. Drag out the sides of the text field until a blue line appears on the side of the view; this indicates the view's margin.

9. Drag a button onto the view from the Object Library. Position it a little below the text field. Then double-click the button and change its text to "Show Me". That's it! You've built your interface, and you should have something resembling Figure 3-23.

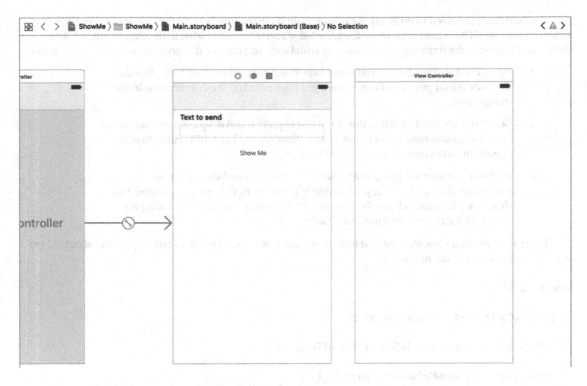

Figure 3-23. *The* Main.storyboard *with all of its elements*

10. You need to add some constraints in order to make sure the elements line up correctly when the application runs. Click a white area of the view, and then click the Resolve Auto Layout Issues button in the bottom-right corner of the design area. Select Add Missing Constraints, and Xcode will do the hard work for you, as shown in Figure 3-24.

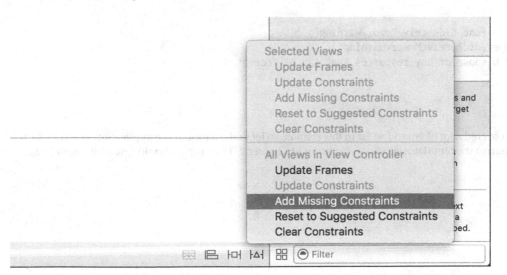

Figure 3-24. *Adding missing constraints to the view to get all elements lined up nicely*

The final thing you need to do is link the objects from Interface Builder into the view controller code as outlets and actions. These next steps reuse the knowledge and skills you started to develop Chapter 2. As a challenge, I'll present the steps for you without any visual aids. You can see if everything matches up at the end.

1. Open the Assistant Editor. You should see ViewController.swift displayed in the code editor portion. If not, ensure you have selected the correct view in the design area.

2. Select the text field. Holding down the Ctrl key, click and drag a connection to the class file, positioning it just below class ViewController: UIViewController. Create an outlet named textToSendField.

3. Perform a similar action on the Show Me button. Control-drag another connection to the class file, positioning it below the outlet you just created; but this time when you release the mouse button, specify that you're creating an action, not an outlet, and name it showMe.

That's it for the first view for now. But before you move on, check that the code in your ViewController.swift file is the same as the following:

```swift
import UIKit

class ViewController: UIViewController {

    @IBOutlet weak var textToSendField: UITextField!

    @IBAction func showMe(sender: AnyObject) {

    }

    override func viewDidLoad() {
        super.viewDidLoad()

        // Do any additional setup after loading the view.
    }

    override func didReceiveMemoryWarning() {
        super.didReceiveMemoryWarning()
        // Dispose of any resources that can be recreated.
    }

}
```

You've covered a lot of ground so far in this chapter, so let's take a look at the application in action. Run the application in the Simulator, as you were shown in Chapter 2. The output should resemble Figure 3-25.

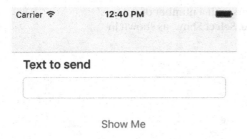

Figure 3-25. *The application running in the Simulator*

At this point, if your app runs successfully and you're staring at the result of your hard work, give yourself a pat on the back. You've built the first part of the application; now it's time to configure the second view controller and bring the two together using a linkage called a *segue*.

Configuring the Second View Controller

Hopefully you're feeling pleased with what you've done so far. You should be—but the application isn't finished. The idea behind this application is to type some text in the text field and have it display on another view controller when you click the Show Me button. Using storyboards to build an application comes into its own when you're working with multiple views. First you need to create a linkage called a *segue* between the Show Me button and what will be the Message view controller; by creating this linkage, you can move between view controllers without writing a single line of code. After you've created the segue, you need to create the second view's interface and, finally, the underlying code to tie it all together.

Now that you know what you're aiming for, let's get started. Again, you'll be tested on how much you remember from creating the previous view controller:

1. Switch back to the Standard Editor by clicking the button to the left of the Assistant Editor on the toolbar.

2. Position the storyboard so that you can see both view controllers.

3. Click the Show Me Button, and then Control-drag a connection from it to the view controller on the right, as shown in Figure 3-26.

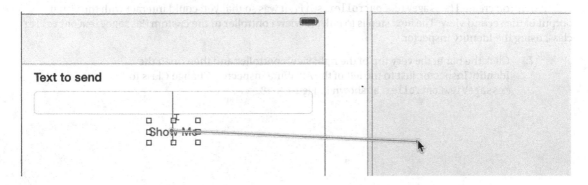

Figure 3-26. *Making a connection from the Show Me button to the second view controller*

4. When you release the mouse button, a dialog appears with a number of options in it; these are the different types of segues available. Select Show, as shown in Figure 3-27.

Figure 3-27. *Selecting the Show segue type*

■ **Note**   You will take a closer look at the different types of segues when you learn about storyboards in Chapter 7.

You've created a relationship between the button and the second view controller. To see what this means, run the application again. Note that when you click the button, the second view slides in nicely and there is a Back button to take you back to the initial view, but it's all a bit simplistic at the moment. Let's finish configuring the second view controller.

5. Stop the Simulator and then align the storyboard so that you can see the second view controller.

6. Drag two labels onto the view, one below the other, and position them near the top of the view under the navigation bar placeholder. Double-click the first label and set its text to "You Said...". Then resize the second label so that it's the width of the view.

When you created MessageViewController.swift, it was so that you could interact with the visual output of the second view. The next step is to link this view controller to the custom MessageViewController class, using the Identity Inspector.

7. Click the bar at the very top of the right view controller and then open the Identity Inspector, just to the left of the Attribute Inspector. Change Class to MessageViewController, as shown in Figure 3-28.

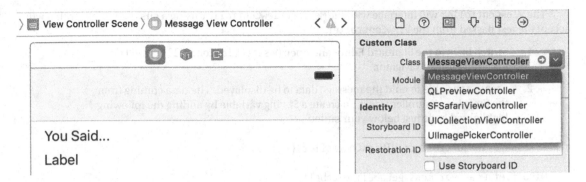

Figure 3-28. *Selecting the* MessageViewController *class for the second view controller*

8. Now that you've created this relationship, turn on the Assistant Editor and, with MessageViewController.swift showing in the code portion, Control-drag a connection from the bottom label to below the line starting class MessageViewController and create an outlet named messageLabel.

9. Click the view and then add the constraints required for a flexible layout by clicking the Resolve Auto Layout Issues button and clicking Add Missing Constraints.

Hopefully, your view should now resemble Figure 3-29.

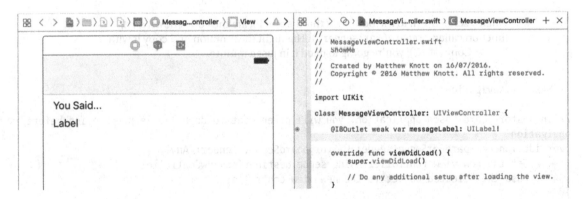

Figure 3-29. *The complete, very simple layout for the second view controller, called MessageViewController*

Before you go any further, let's recap what the objective is for this project. The users should be able to push the Show Me button on the ViewController and have whatever they have written in the text field appear in the MessageViewController. To make this happen, you need to add some code to the MessageViewController class file so it can receive the message from the initial ViewController.

■ **Note** When a new view is loaded on to the screen by a navigation controller replacing another one in an iOS application, this is referred to as **pushing** a view.

The ViewController will interface with the MessageViewController using a custom initializer that will accept the text passed from the ViewController.

1. Switch back to the Standard Editor and open MessageViewController.swift from the Project Navigator.

2. Create a variable to hold the message data to be displayed. The data coming from the first view controller is text, so create a String variable by adding the following highlighted code just below your outlet:

```
class MessageViewController: UIViewController {

    @IBOutlet weak var messageLabel: UILabel!

    var messageData: String?
```

3. Next, you need to take the supplied text and display it on the label. You do this by setting the text property of the messageLabel outlet. Add the highlighted code below to the viewDidLoad method:

```
override func viewDidLoad() {
    super.viewDidLoad()

    // Do any additional setup after loading the view.
    messageLabel.text = messageData
}
```

4. Finally, scroll down to the bottom of this file and locate the code shown next, a function called prepare(for:sender:). Highlight the function and copy it with Edit ➤ Copy (⌘+C); you're going to need it in just a minute.

```
// MARK: - Navigation

// In a storyboard-based application, you will often want to do a little preparation before navigation
override func prepareForSegue(segue: UIStoryboardSegue, sender: Any?) {
    // Get the new view controller using segue.destinationViewController.
    // Pass the selected object to the new view controller.
}
```

Now all that remains is to complete the code to send the data to the MessageViewController.

1. Open ViewController.swift from the Project Navigator.

2. Underneath the didReceiveMemoryWarning function, paste in the code you copied from the other view controller using Edit ➤ Paste (⌘+V) so that the bottom of your code file looks exactly like this:

```
override func didReceiveMemoryWarning() {
    super.didReceiveMemoryWarning()
    // Dispose of any resources that can be recreated.
}
```

```
// MARK: - Navigation
// In a storyboard-based application, you will often want to do a little preparation before
navigation
override func prepare(for segue: UIStoryboardSegue, sender: Any?) {
    // Get the new view controller using segue.destination.
    // Pass the selected object to the new view controller.
}
```

3.   The prepare(for:sender:) method is called just before a segue linking view is executed. Normally, you would name your segue and control the actions based on the segue that has been triggered, but in this instance, you only have one segue, so when this method is called, you know that the destination of the segue is the MessageViewController. You're going to create an instance of MessageViewController based on the segue's destination controller, and then set the messageData string with the text of your text field. Add the following highlighted code into the prepare(for:sender:) method, removing the two comments:

```
override func prepareForSegue(segue: UIStoryboardSegue, sender: AnyObject?) {
    let messageController = segue.destination as! MessageViewController
    messageController.messageData = textToSendField.text
}
```

Xcode automatically understands that you have a MessageViewController class without having to make any specific references or include statements in your code file, and when you type messageController. on the second line of the method, it knows you have a variable called messageData ready and waiting for you to pass it the contents of the text field.

That's it; you should now be able to run the application and find that you can click in the text field, type a message, and click Show Me. This will take you to the MessageViewController and display whatever you typed, as shown in Figure 3-30.

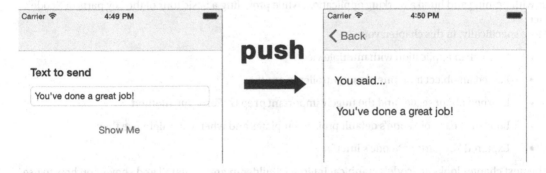

Figure 3-30.   The finished application

Debugging Area

The final focus is the debugging area. In order to see this in action, you need to add some code to the project that captures the text that was entered when the button is clicked, and you use NSLog to add a message to the console. Go to ViewController.swift and go to the showMe action that you've left empty so far. Add the following highlighted code:

```
@IBAction func showMe(sender: AnyObject) {
    NSLog("User Wrote: %@", textToSendField.text!)
}
```

The debug area allows you to pin down any issues with your program. Because the debug area can quickly become very complex and can be used for a variety of different things, I'll only show you the basics for now and revisit it later in the book. Now run your application and try to click the Show Me button without adding any text to the text field. You should see that when you click the button, a message is added to the output console, as shown in Figure 3-31.

Figure 3-31. *The result of the NSLog method call is displayed in the output console*

For now all you need to know is that the debugger included with Xcode is the LLVM-GCC debugger, this means you can debug a variety of code in a variety of languages. This is especially useful as Swift can use frameworks and libraries written in Objective-C.

Summary

This chapter covered two rather contrasting topics: project templates and the basics of Xcode's interface. The purpose of doing so was, first, to give you the confidence to start an Xcode project and choose correctly a project template suitable for your projects and, second, to drop you in at the deep end to understand how to start with nothing and build a working application, while providing a basic tour of the key parts of Xcode's interface.

More specifically, in this chapter, you:

- Created an application with multiple views

- Passed an object from one view controller to another

- Learned about segues and the hugely important prepareForSegue method

- Looked at each of Xcode's default project templates and when you might use them

- Explored key parts of Xcode's interface

The next chapter looks at Xcode's graphical Interface Builder in greater detail and shows you how to use it to build interfaces efficiently.

CHAPTER 4

■ ■ ■

Building Interfaces

A lot was covered in Chapter 3: You looked at each of Xcode's default iOS project templates, examined when exactly you should use them, and then took a tour of the main areas of Xcode's workspace. And if that wasn't enough, you created an application with multiple views that could share information between the views.

The focus of this chapter is to delve deeper into Xcode's graphical interface design tool, Interface Builder. Interface Builder has always been a key part of the Xcode set of development tools. However, with the release of Xcode 4, Interface Builder became part of Xcode itself, as opposed to previous versions in which it was a separate application. As already discussed in previous chapters, what makes Interface Builder an attractive addition to Apple's developer tools is that it removes the need to write code in order to design great interfaces for your applications. It allows you to lay out your views and windows by dragging built-in Cocoa objects from the Object Library and placing them on the screen.

What's even more useful is that by using the Attributes Inspector, you can make many changes that would otherwise require lines upon lines of code. As a developer, this is good news for two reasons. First, you don't have to continuously test, build, and run your application in order to see if what you're designing with code looks good. With Interface Builder, you can see this right away. Second, similar to what's just been mentioned, you can make changes graphically, which saves a lot of time and effort. All this—plus using Interface Builder makes designing views fun!

This chapter explains how to set up an application using the Tabbed Application template. The great thing about using a Tabbed Application is that each of the tabs can act as an app within an app, each one showing a drastically different set of tools and styles. The two initial tabs you set up will showcase some of the interface elements you haven't seen yet, as well as use your device's GPS function. Once you've done this, you set up a third tab that will allow you to demonstrate some of the important interface elements that can't be added using Interface Builder. A goal of this chapter is to show how much you can achieve while using as little code as possible, and it's important to note how little code this example requires compared to how much you would need to write if Interface Builder were not a part of Xcode. The last thing you look at is how you can alter interface elements with code to achieve results that Interface Builder alone can't do but that are important in building beautiful, easy-to-use interfaces. Here is an outline of what each of the tabs will include:

- *Track It*: Here you create a text view that displays detailed telemetry from the GPS receiver, on either a physical device or in the simulator. You also use a switch to turn the GPS on and off.

- *Slide It*: As the name implies, in the second tab you look at how to implement the slider tab, where to build a series of sliders to alter the background color of the entire view, and how to output their values into text fields. You also learn the answer to one of the burning questions all iOS developers ask: "How do I dismiss the keyboard?"

- *Alert*: In the final tab, you see how to use a segmented control to determine what happens when a button is pushed. The choice is between an alert view and an action sheet, two popular elements in many applications.

© Matthew Knott 2016
M. Knott, *Beginning Xcode*, DOI 10.1007/978-1-4302-5005-0_4

Getting Ready

Now that you've had a sneak peek at the aim of this chapter, hopefully you're raring to go. Let's get to it:

1. Open Xcode and create a new project by clicking Create A New Xcode Project on the Welcome screen or choosing File ➤ New ➤ Project (⌘+Shift+N). Select the Tabbed Application template and click Next.

2. Name your project Showcase and ensure that the device is set to iPhone. Configure the other settings as you did in previous applications. Make sure the key settings match those shown in Figure 4-1 and click Next.

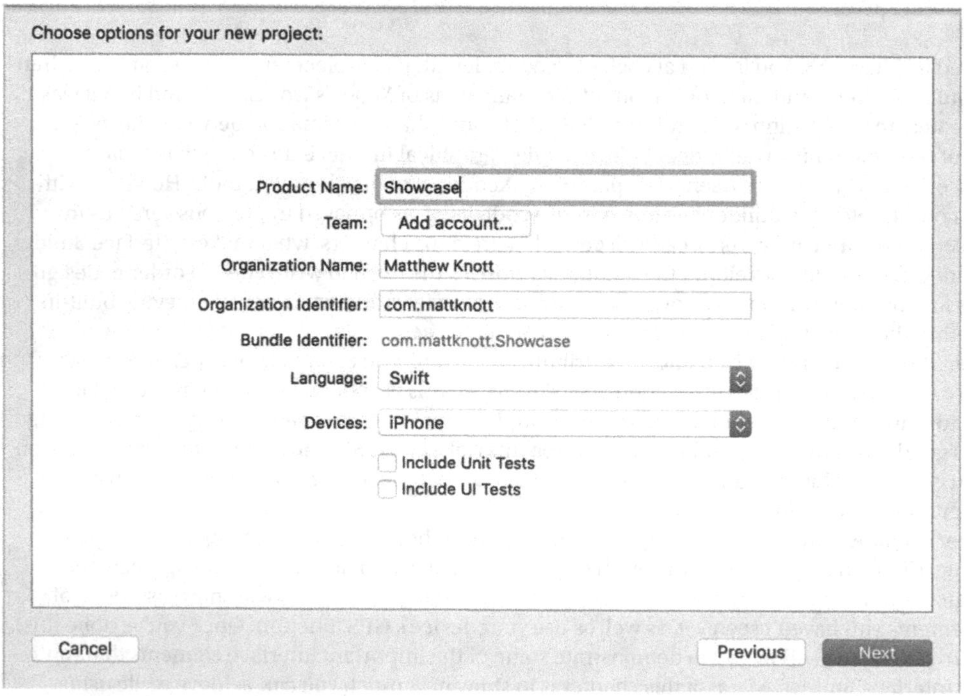

Figure 4-1. *Configuring the Showcase application*

3. You don't want to create a Git repository, so leave the Source Control option unchecked. Ensure that your project is going to be saved where you want it to be and click Create.

You've now created the bare bones of your Showcase tabbed application. To see what Apple's template has given you as a starting point, click Main.Storyboard; you should see a screen resembling that shown in Figure 4-2.

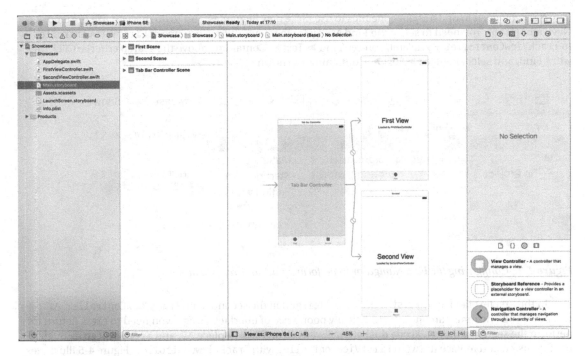

Figure 4-2. *The starting point for the Showcase application*

By default, the template gives you a tab bar controller (UITabBarController) with two view controllers (UIViewController) attached named FirstViewController and SecondViewController. Although these names are perfectly good, tab orders can change as a project develops, so it's always better to use names that are semantically accurate. So, before you add a third tab, let's rename the files to something more appropriate.

With the Project Navigator open (⌘+1), highlight the FirstViewController.swift file and press Return on your keyboard. You should now be able to rename the file. Remove the text and type TrackViewController.swift (remember to add the .swift extension). Repeat this for SecondViewController.swift, but call it SliderViewController.swift. Your Project Navigator should closely resemble what you see in Figure 4-3.

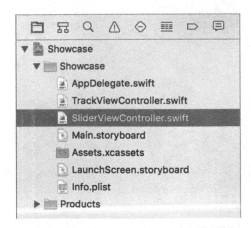

Figure 4-3. *The current project's files as shown in the Project Navigator*

Next you need to update your code files to use these new filenames, and to do this you use the Find Navigator (⌘+3). You need to set up the Find Navigator to rename every instance of FirstViewController to TrackViewController. By default, you see Find ➤ Text ➤ Containing above the search criteria. Click the word Find, and select Replace ➤ Text ➤ Containing, as shown in Figure 4-4.

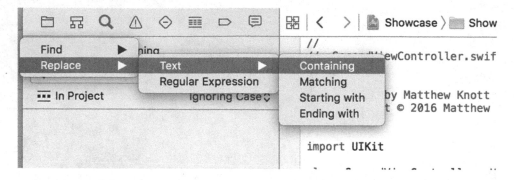

Figure 4-4. *Configuring the Find Navigator to perform a find-and-replace task*

In the first text field, type FirstViewController, and in the second, type TrackViewController. At this point you encounter an uncharacteristically poor piece of interface design: you need to press Return to perform the search, although Xcode doesn't make this clear. Click Replace All, and Xcode will go through all the files listed and replace the word FirstViewController with TrackViewController. Figure 4-5 illustrates the results of this find-and-replace operation in the Find Navigator.

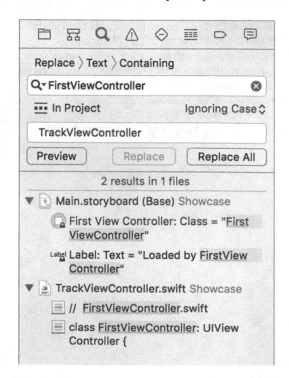

Figure 4-5. *The Find Navigator updating references to old file and class names*

Once the find-and-replace operation has completed, repeat the task, but in the first box enter SecondViewController as the text you're searching for and in the second type SliderViewController as the text you want to replace it with. Press Return and then click Replace All.

You've now updated all references to your renamed view controllers. Next you create a third view controller called ActionViewController:

1. Switch back to the Project Navigator from the Find Navigator so you're ready to start interacting with the project files again.

2. Create a new file (⌘+N). Select Source from the left sidebar under iOS, and then choose Cocoa Touch Class, as you did in Chapter 3. Click Next.

3. Specify ActionViewController as the class name. Type UIViewController in the Subclass Of field, and ensure that Also Create XIB File is *not* checked. Click Next. Create this file in the same location where all your other files are stored and click Create.

Adding Tab Bar Icons to an Asset Catalog

Since they were introduced in Xcode 5, Asset Catalogs have been used to store the icons that appear on tabs in the Tabbed Application template. Although this isn't the way you *have* to store the images, it's certainly best practice, and it makes storing retina and regular versions of the same icon much easier and less cluttered. Chapter 2 briefly explained the Asset Catalogs, but here I go into the topic a little deeper.

For this project, I have created three purpose-built icons that are available in the Chapter 4 source code available from the Apress web site. If you don't want to create your own icons, a fantastic range of free tab-bar icons created by Charlene are available for download at www.iconbeast.com. Once you've downloaded the icons, you're ready to begin working with the Asset Catalog in this project:

1. In Xcode, select Assets.xcassets. You should see the three images shown in Figure 4-6.

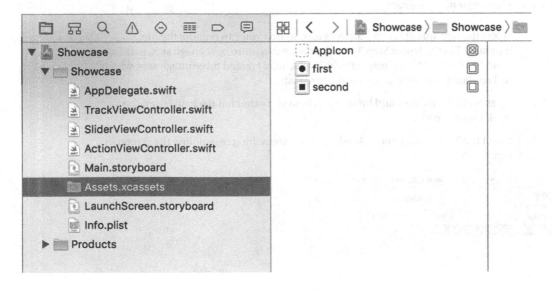

Figure 4-6. The contents of the Assets.xcassets library

2. Select the image named first and delete it by pressing the Backspace key or right-clicking and selecting Remove Selected Items. Repeat this step for the image named second.

3. Click the plus symbol at the bottom of the list of images, and from the menu that appears, select New Image Set, as shown in Figure 4-7. This creates a new image set called image.

Figure 4-7. Creating a new image set

4. Select the new image set and press Return so that you can rename the file; rename it Track. Repeat Step 3 twice to create two more new image sets, naming them Slider and Alert, respectively. You've now created three image sets, which will contain the tab-bar icons for the three tabs.

5. Open a Finder window and browse to where you extracted the icons from the book's source code.

6. Select the Track image set in Xcode. You see something resembling the screen in Figure 4-8.

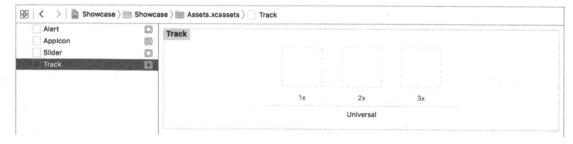

Figure 4-8. The three new image sets

One of the benefits of using Asset Catalogs for storing images is that they make it easy to group identical images that have multiple resolutions, which you need in order to ensure your app displays properly on any compatible device. Within the image set, there are three containers: a 1x container, 2x container, and a 3x container. Traditionally, in the 1x container you would place the standard-resolution image, and in the 2x container the retina, or higher-resolution image. Because of the even higher resolutions of devices such as the iPhone 6 plus and retina iPads, Apple has introduced a 3x container to ensure your icons are crisp and sharp. This image set does not rigidly enforce a specific icon resolution, but as a guideline for tab-bar icons, use 30px × 30px for standard-resolution icons, 60px × 60px for 2x retina icons, and 90px × 90px for 3x retina icons, which is the exact resolutions of the icons you downloaded.

7. In the Finder window, locate the icon named mapicon.png, and drag it into the 1x container. Then drag the mapicon@2x.png file into the 2x container and mapicon@3x.png into the 3x container.

8. Repeat Step 7 for the two remaining image sets, dragging slidericon.png, slidericon@2x.png, and slidericon@3x.png into the containers for the Slider image set, and alerticon.png, alerticon@2x.png, and alerticon@3x.png into the Alert image set. Your Asset Catalog should now resemble that shown in Figure 4-9.

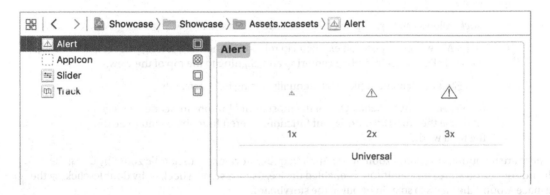

Figure 4-9. *The three image sets with the icons in place*

The benefit to using Asset Catalogs for managing images is that you're left with a much neater project in the Project Navigator. Now you're set up and can begin working on your interfaces using Interface Builder. Let's start by taking a closer look at the different areas of the Interface Builder.

Before You Start

Storyboards are a relatively new feature of Xcode. They allow you to logically lay out how views are connected, pushed, and managed as a user navigates through your application. They can greatly simplify applications, plus they add a degree of logic to how you develop your projects.

Because you work with them a little more in this chapter than the last, it's important to know the basics because they are now a part of Interface Builder. Open Main.storyboard, and let's take a look at the key controls. Conveniently, all the controls for your storyboard are located at the bottom of the storyboard design area and are separated into three groups, as shown in Figure 4-10.

☐ View as: iPhone 6s (wC hR) — 100% +	▦ ⧉ ⊢◻ ⊢◪

Figure 4-10. *The storyboard controls*

Let's look at the groups and their icons:

- *Document Outline toggle*: This first button, located by itself in the bottom-left corner of the design area, hides and displays the document outline, which is covered in more detail in Chapter 7 and throughout the book.

- *Form Factor toggle*: Located in the middle of the design area's icons, this control allows you to alter how view controllers in the storyboard are displayed. This is incredibly useful if you're designing a single interface for multiple form factors, because you can quickly move between orientations and sizes and have that reflected for the entire storyboard.

- *Zoom controls*: Apple finally added a quick zoom control to interface builder in Xcode 8. As expected, this allows you to control the zoom of the design area.

- *Constraint controls*: These are described in greater detail in Chapter 6. For now, these four buttons, which are grouped together, let you control the behavior of the elements in your view when faced with differing resolutions or different screen resolutions:

  - *Stack*: Allows you to group selected elements into a stack view.

  - *Align*: Allows you to position elements in relation to the view, letting you set a range of alignments including centering and aligning to the top of the view.

  - *Pin*: Fixes an element in place by manually setting its constraints.

  - *Resolve Auto Layout Issues*: One of the most useful buttons in Xcode. You can often use the powerful auto-layout functions offered from this menu to do all the hard work for you.

There are no buttons to control zoom level; Apple requires developers to handle zoom by using the pinch and squeeze gestures on a multitouch-enabled device, using a scroll wheel, or by double-clicking the whitespace around the views to snap in or out of the storyboard.

This concludes our brief look at the storyboard design area controls. Chapters 6 and 7 examine all of these functions in more detail, for now let's move on and build the interface.

Building the Interface

Now that you're familiar with the storyboard controls, you can start to get your interface in order. To do that, you first remove the two views that were added by default. With Main.storyboard selected, you have two view controllers, as you saw in Figure 4-2. Just like you did in Chapter 3, you begin by removing the bulk of the boilerplate content so that you can see for yourself exactly how the different elements are created:

1. Above each of the two view controllers is a bar. Click the bar, and three icons appear as shown in Figure 4-11. Press the Backspace key to delete the bar.

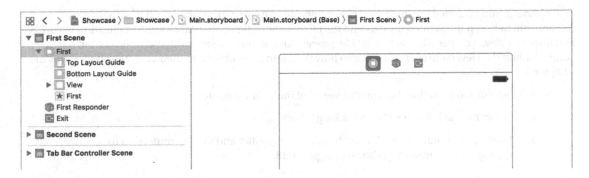

Figure 4-11. *The view controller, outlined in blue after selecting the top bar*

2. Repeat this step for the other view controller so you're left with only a tab bar controller.

3. All your views are going to be based on standard view controllers, so locate the view controller object in the Object Library and drag three of them to the design area. Position them as shown in Figure 4-12.

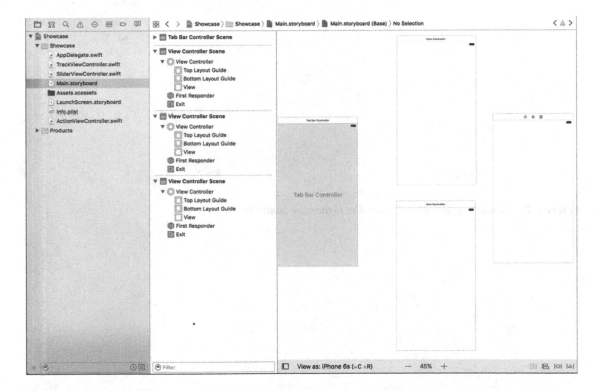

Figure 4-12. `Main.storyboard` *with the three orphaned view controllers. The Utilities pane can be hidden to give extra room.*

Although you've added the three view controllers, they're currently orphans—that is, there is no relationship between the view controllers and the tab bar controller, so in order for the application to run and display a view, you need to create one. The process for creating a relationship between the tab bar controller and the view controllers is similar to how you connected objects to their actions and methods in Chapter 3:

1. Set the zoom level so that you can see all of the view controllers.

2. Select the tab bar controller by clicking it once.

3. Holding the control key (^), click the tab bar controller and drag a connection to the top view controller, as shown in Figure 4-13.

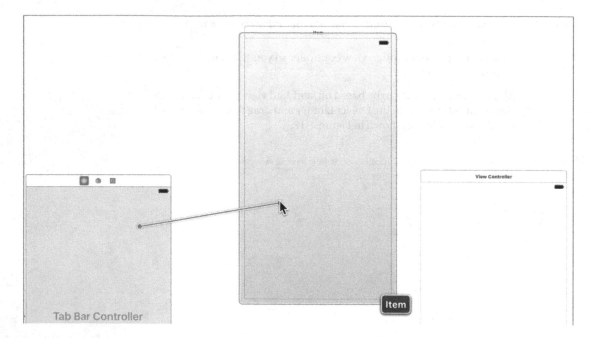

Figure 4-13. *Connecting the tab bar controller to the view controller*

4. When you release the mouse button, a dialog appears, asking you to choose the segue type. Chapter 7 covers segues; for now, select View Controllers under the Relationship Segue heading, as shown in Figure 4-14.

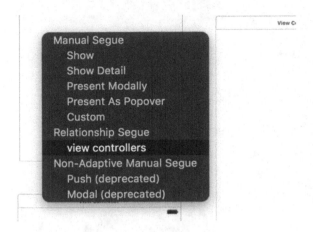

Figure 4-14. *The segue selection dialog*

Now that you've created a relationship between the tab bar controller and the view controller, notice that a few changes have been made in your design area. The tab bar controller has a tab showing on the tab bar, as does the view controller. Also, a line connects the tab bar controller to the top view controller; this is called a segue, and it's a visual representation of the relationship between two elements in a storyboard. Segues can link elements in several different ways, but on this occasion you only choose the View Controllers branch to create a relationship segue.

5. Repeat Step 4 for the remaining two view controllers—first the bottom view controller, then the middle one—until you're left with something resembling the screen shown in Figure 4-15.

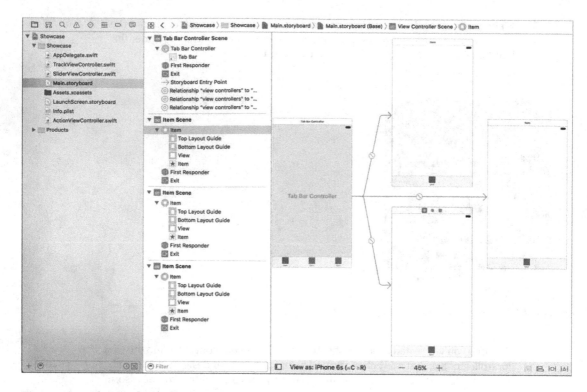

Figure 4-15. *The view controllers are all connected to the tab bar controller*

Setting the Tab Icons

You're nearly ready to focus on the individual views in your application, but before you do, there are a couple more tasks to complete. You need to implement the icons you added to the image Asset Catalog:

1. Zoom back in to the design area.

2. Locate the topmost view controller and select the square icon above the text Item, as shown in Figure 4-16.

Figure 4-16. *Selecting the tab bar icon in the top view controller*

3. Open the Attributes Inspector (⌥+⌘+4). Set the Title attribute to Track It and the Image attribute to Track. Be sure not to set the Selected Image attribute—it needs to stay blank.

4. Select the bottom view controller's tab bar item and set Title to Slide It and Image to Slider.

5. Select the tab bar item from the middle view controller and set Title to Action and Image to Alert.

Using the Asset Catalog and the storyboard, you've successfully named your tabs, set their icons, and created a relationship with the tab bar controller. The tabbed application is really starting to take shape. The visual relationship between the tab bar controller and the view controllers is in place, and if you want to, you can build and run the application in the simulator—it will work fine. However, there is one other relationship you've yet to establish.

The three views on the design area are currently controlled by the default view controller class. But you want to use the purpose-made view controllers that you created earlier in this chapter.

1. Select the top bar above the Track It view controller, as in Figure 4-11, and then open the Identity Inspector (⌥+⌘+3).

2. Click the drop-down list for the Class attribute and select `TrackViewController`, as shown in Figure 4-17.

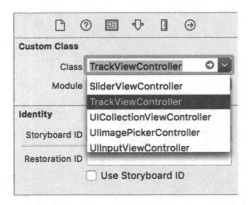

Figure 4-17. *Selecting the custom view controller class*

3. Select the top bar above the bottom view controller, and this time set the class to `SliderViewController`.

4. Repeat Step 3 with the middle view controller and set its class to `ActionViewController`.

5. Build and run the application using the simulator; you should find that at this stage you have three bland but working tabs.

That's it: the preparation work is complete! So far you've renamed the default view controller classes and created an extra one, created entries in the Asset Catalog and populated it with some icons, removed the default view controllers from the storyboard and replaced them with three new ones all before setting the classes, icons, and titles of each tab. You're now ready to learn more about building great interfaces.

Tracking Location with the Track It Tab

For the first tab, you create a view that allows you to display detailed information about the current location, including speed, course, longitude, latitude, and positional accuracy. To do this, you will use the CoreLocation framework.

CoreLocation is used in many applications in the App Store, whether in an obvious way such as in a map-based application or in a more subtle way such as providing localized information wherever you go. The skills you learn here will give you a good grounding in applying CoreLocation in your own applications.

CoreLocation by itself isn't that useful without something to control and display its information. To do this, you add a switch control to turn positional tracking on and off and a text view to display the output information. By the end of this section, you should have created something resembling the screen shown in Figure 4-18.

Figure 4-18. *The Track It tab in action*

UITextViews and UISwitches

To build a simple but effective view, let's use two of the most common and useful controls provided by Apple: UITextView and UISwitch. The UISwitch control (or Switch, as it appears in the Object Library) is found throughout the Settings app on your iPhone or iPad. It has on and off states, and you use it to turn tracking on and off again:

1. Search the Object Library for Switch and drag the object to the view. Position it in the middle, as shown in Figure 4-19. Blue guidelines appear as you approach the middle of the view.

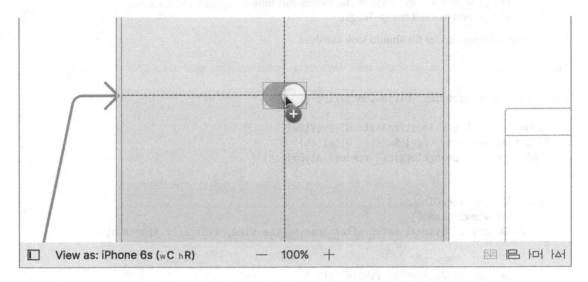

Figure 4-19. *Snapping the switch into place using the guidelines*

2. With the switch selected, open the Attribute Inspector and change the State attribute to Off.

3. Add a UITextView (or Text View, as it appears in the Object Library). A text view can contain a large amount of text; the user can type in it, like a text field, or scroll through it. Search the Object Library for Text View and drag it so it appears just above the switch (refer back to Figure 4-18 for size and positioning reference).

4. With the text view selected, open the Attributes Inspector and remove the placeholder text from the Text attribute. Next, uncheck the Editable behavior.

5. To change the view's background color, select a patch of whitespace on the view and then, in the Attributes Inspector, click the Background drop-down list and select Dark Gray Color from the list of specified colors to the right of the color indicator.

6. As you have in previous chapters, with the view still selected, bring up the Fix Auto Layout Issues menu and click Add Missing Constraints under the All Views in View Controller heading.

You've added the two controls needed for this tab. Next you need to create the actions and outlets within the TrackViewController class file that will allow your code to manipulate them:

1. Switch to the Assistant Editor and ensure that you have the TrackViewController.swift file selected. If you have a different file open, go back to double-check whether you correctly set the view controller's class.

2. Select the text view and control-drag a connection from the text view to the class file, just below the line that says class TrackViewController: UIViewController.

3. Create an outlet named `locationText`. Type this in and click the Connect button.

4. Repeat Step 3 for the switch, this time naming the outlet `toggleSwitch`.

5. Drag another connection from the switch, this time being sure to create an action, and name it `changeToggle`.

The code of your header file should look like this:

```
import UIKit

class TrackViewController: UIViewController {

    @IBOutlet weak var locationText: UITextView!
    @IBOutlet weak var toggleSwitch: UISwitch!
    @IBAction func changeToggle(_ sender: AnyObject) {
    }

    override func viewDidLoad() {
        super.viewDidLoad()
        // Do any additional setup after loading the view, typically from a nib.
    }

    override func didReceiveMemoryWarning() {
        super.didReceiveMemoryWarning()
        // Dispose of any resources that can be recreated.
    }
}
```

You've created all your outlets and actions. But before you can write any code, you need to add the CoreLocation framework to the project so you can interact with the GPS features of your device.

■ **Tip**   If you accidentally create an outlet instead of an action you may have trouble running your application after removing the erroneous line. This is because your control is still looking for that outlet. Select the control and open the Connections Inspector. You can remove the reference to the nonexistent outlet there.

Adding Frameworks to a Project

A framework is a collection of classes and functions that provides additional functionality to your project. In iOS, all the GPS and location-based features are accessed through the CoreLocation framework. Some of the most commonly used frameworks are CoreData, MapKit, and CoreImage.

As of iOS 7 and Xcode 5, Apple gave Objective-C developers an alternative to manually adding frameworks, called *modules*. Modules are a very simple concept: instead of going through Xcode to select a framework, physically add it to a project, and reference it in code with an `#import` statement, you simply reference it with the `@import` statement, and Xcode automatically identifies the framework and adds it into your project.

In Swift, Apple has kept this functionality and made it the default approach. Thus you never again need to add a core Apple framework manually. Chapter 9 explains modules and frameworks in more detail. As I've already mentioned, you need to add CoreLocation, and what have previously been a protracted process of locating and importing the framework is now as simple as writing a single line of code:

1. From the Project Navigator, select the `TrackViewController.swift` file and close the Assistant Editor in favor of the Standard Editor.

2. Drop down a line from `import UIKit` and type `import CoreLocation`. This single line makes the classes, functions, and protocols of the CoreLocation framework available to your application.

3. You need to specify that the view controller can act as a delegate for the `CLLocationManager` class. This means when the location manager is running, it knows this file contains the functions that handle certain events, such as the position of the device changing. Add `, CLLocationManagerDelegate` after `class TrackViewController: UIViewController`. As shown in Figure 4-20, code completion appears to help you complete the protocol name.

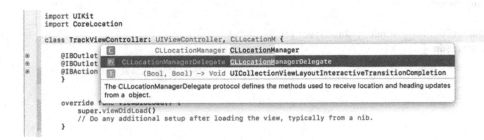

Figure 4-20. *Adding the `CLLocationManagerDelegate` protocol to `TrackViewController`*

The first few lines of your `TrackViewController.swift` file should resemble the following code:

```
import UIKit
import CoreLocation

class TrackViewController: UIViewController, CLLocationManagerDelegate {

    @IBOutlet weak var locationText: UITextView!
    @IBOutlet weak var toggleSwitch: UISwitch!
    @IBAction func changeToggle(sender: AnyObject) {
    }
```

4. You're ready to start setting up your interface into the device's GPS and location tracking technology, which is done via a class called `CLLocationManager`. Before the first `@IBOutlet`, add the following highlighted code to create an instance of the location manager class:

```
var locationManager: CLLocationManager!
@IBOutlet weak var locationText: UITextView!
```

■ **Note**   You have created the instance of the location manager in what is called the *global scope*; this means any of your functions in the `TrackViewController` class can see and use the location manager. This is important because the location manager is the primary interface into the location functions, and you want to be efficient and consistent by having only a single instance of the class declared in your application.

Next, you need to implement the action of the toggle switch being turned on or off. The code you add here does the majority of the work in this tab. A little below the line you just added should be the `changeToggle` action. Let's go through the code step by step before you see the final code block:

1. You need to determine whether the switch was turned on or off when the action is called. You do this with an `if ... else ...` statement. Add the highlighted code into the action:

```
@IBAction func changeToggle(_ sender: AnyObject) {
    if toggleSwitch.isOn {

    }
    else
    {

    }
}
```

The `.on` property of the `UISwitch` class returns a true or a false value, depending on the switch's position. If true or on, the code in the first set of braces is executed; otherwise, if false or off, the code in the second set of parentheses is executed.

■ **Tip**   In Swift, parentheses containing the conditions of an `if` statement are optional.

---

2. All the code you write in this view controller will be ignored if the device's location services are disabled. To account for this, the next block of code will prevent the switch from being turned on if location services are disabled. Add the highlighted code:

```
@IBAction func changeToggle(_ sender: AnyObject) {
    if toggleSwitch.isOn {
        if (CLLocationManager.locationServicesEnabled() == false) {
            self.toggleSwitch.isOn = false
        }
    }
    else
    {

    }
}
```

3. The next step is to check whether the locationManager object has been
    initialized and, if not, to initialize it. There are numerous ways of initializing
    a CLLocationManager object, but in this case you do four things: initialize the
    object, tell it that this view controller is acting as its delegate, tell it to be accurate
    within 10 meters, and tell it to update when it moves more than 10 meters from
    the last recorded position. So, drop down a line after the last statement and add
    the following highlighted code:

```
@IBAction func changeToggle(_ sender: AnyObject) {
    if toggleSwitch.isOn {
        if (CLLocationManager.locationServicesEnabled() == false) {
            self.toggleSwitch.isOn = false
        }

        if locationManager == nil {
            locationManager = CLLocationManager()
            locationManager.delegate = self
            locationManager.distanceFilter = 10.0
            locationManager.desiredAccuracy = kCLLocationAccuracyNearestTenMeters
            locationManager.requestWhenInUseAuthorization()
        }
    }
    else
    {

    }
}
```

4. The last thing you need to do in this half of the if statement is tell the
    locationManager object to start updating the location. You do this by calling
    the startUpdatingLocation function. Once activated, it begins tracking your
    location; then, every time the conditions you initialized it with are met, it fires the
    delegate function didUpdateLocations, which you add later. For now, drop down
    a line and add the following highlighted code:

```
@IBAction func changeToggle(_ sender: AnyObject) {
    if(toggleSwitch.isOn)
    {
        if (CLLocationManager.locationServicesEnabled() == false) {
            self.toggleSwitch.isOn = false
        }

        if locationManager == nil {
            locationManager = CLLocationManager()
            locationManager.delegate = self
            locationManager.distanceFilter = 10.0
            locationManager.desiredAccuracy = kCLLocationAccuracyNearestTenMeters
            locationManager.requestWhenInUseAuthorization()
        }
```

```
        locationManager.startUpdatingLocation()
    }
    else
    {

    }
}
```

5. You now need to write the else outcome, which is triggered when the switch is set to off. All you want to do in this instance is tell the locationManager object to stop tracking by calling the stopUpdatingLocation function. Complete the action by adding the highlighted code between the else braces:

```
@IBAction func changeToggle(_ sender: AnyObject) {
    if(toggleSwitch.isOn)
    {
        if (CLLocationManager.locationServicesEnabled() == false) {
            self.toggleSwitch.isOn = false
        }

        if locationManager == nil {
            locationManager = CLLocationManager()
            locationManager.delegate = self
            locationManager.distanceFilter = 10.0
            locationManager.desiredAccuracy = kCLLocationAccuracyNearestTenMeters
            locationManager.requestWhenInUseAuthorization()
        }

        locationManager.startUpdatingLocation()
    }
    else
    {
        if locationManager != nil {
            locationManager.stopUpdatingLocation()
        }
    }
}
```

Those few lines can be used as boilerplate code any time you want to initialize a CLLocationManager. I mentioned the didUpdateLocations delegate method that the locationManager object looks for every time an update is triggered. It's a very simple implementation that takes the last reported location information and outputs its description value to the text view. To do this, add the following highlighted code after the didReceiveMemoryWarning function:

```
override func didReceiveMemoryWarning() {
    super.didReceiveMemoryWarning()
    // Dispose of any resources that can be recreated.
}
```

```
func locationManager(_ manager: CLLocationManager, didUpdateLocations locations:
[CLLocation]) {
    let location:CLLocation = locations[locations.endIndex-1] as CLLocation
    self.locationText.text = location.description
}
```

You need to implement one final delegate method: the `didFailWithError` function that is called if there is a fault while trying to obtain a location and that writes the error description to the text view. It's not essential for this example, but I'm trying to give you some useful boilerplate code; plus, you should always account for and handle failures such as this. Add the highlighted function below your last delegate function:

```
func locationManager(_ manager: CLLocationManager, didUpdateLocations locations:
[CLLocation]) {
    let location:CLLocation = locations[locations.endIndex-1] as CLLocation
    self.locationText.text = location.description;
}

func locationManager(_ manager: CLLocationManager, didFailWithError error: Error) {
    locationText.text = "failed with error \(error.localizedDescription) "
}
```

That's it—you've finished the code for the Track It tab. But before you run it, you need to do something new: add several entries to the application's `info.plist` file. For a number of frameworks and classes, Apple likes you to add a privacy declaration that explains to the users what you're doing with their location information. Since iOS 8, these are mandatory, and the code won't function without them:

1. In the Project Navigator, select `Info.plist`.

2. Move your mouse cursor over the first line, titled `Information Property List`. A small plus symbol appears, as shown in Figure 4-21. Click it.

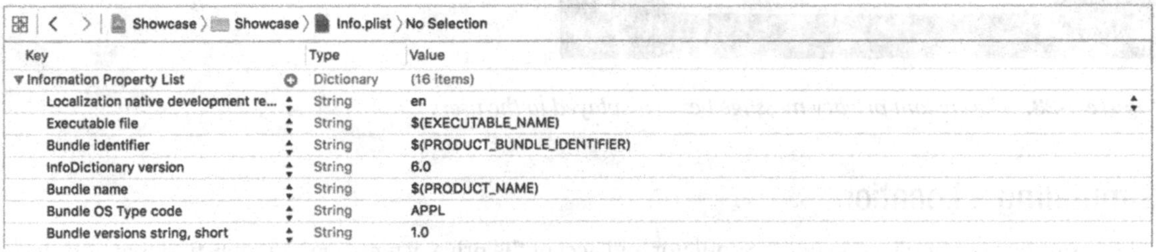

Key		Type	Value
▼ Information Property List	○	Dictionary	(16 items)
Localization native development re...	↕	String	en
Executable file	↕	String	$(EXECUTABLE_NAME)
Bundle identifier	↕	String	$(PRODUCT_BUNDLE_IDENTIFIER)
InfoDictionary version	↕	String	6.0
Bundle name	↕	String	$(PRODUCT_NAME)
Bundle OS Type code	↕	String	APPL
Bundle versions string, short	↕	String	1.0

Figure 4-21. Adding an item to the application's `info.plist` file

3. A new row is inserted. In the list on the left, scroll until you see the item Privacy - Location Usage Description. Select it, double-click the empty Value field, and type `Testing CoreLocation` or whatever message you want to present to the users. Your finished entry should resemble that shown in Figure 4-22.

Key	Type	Value
▼ Information Property List	Dictionary	(17 items)
Privacy - Location Usage Des... ↕ ⊕ ⊖	String	↕ Testing CoreLocation
Localization native development re... ↕	String	en
Executable file ↕	String	$(EXECUTABLE_NAME)
Bundle identifier ↕	String	$(PRODUCT_BUNDLE_IDENTIFIER)
InfoDictionary version ↕	String	6.0
Bundle name ↕	String	$(PRODUCT_NAME)
Bundle OS Type code ↕	String	APPL
Bundle versions string, short ↕ ⊕ ⊖	String	1.0

Figure 4-22. *The privacy statement in the* `info.plist` *file*

4. Repeat Step 2 to create another entry under Information Property List. This time, you need to find the Privacy - Location When In Use Usage Description. Under Value, again enter `Testing CoreLocation`.

This may seem like an unnecessary chore, but without it, not only won't your app work, but it will also be rejected by Apple if you submit it to the App Store.

With the privacy message set, the last thing to do is test it in the simulator. When you flip the switch, you should see the privacy message, as shown in Figure 4-23.

Figure 4-23. *The custom privacy message being displayed to the users*

Simulating a Location

When you run your application in the Simulator and accept the privacy message, you may find that nothing happens. The reason for this is simple: by default, the Simulator doesn't have a location, and therefore it's unable to give you any details about a location, let alone update the location as it's moving.

■ **Note**   If nothing happens, you may not have Location Services enabled. Return to the home screen on your virtual device by going to Hardware ➤ Home, and then open the Settings app. In Privacy, select Location, and then ensure that Location Services is enabled.

Fortunately, Apple has provided some pretty nifty tools for specifying a location. It can also simulate a drive or bike ride, which is the preset you use in this case. In the simulator menu bar, choose Debug ➤ Location ➤ City Bicycle Ride. All of a sudden your text view begins filling as a virtual bike peddles through California, near Apple headquarters in Cupertino. (Chapter 11 explains more about location debugging.)

That does it for this tab! You've created a really neat app that you could deploy to your phone while you take a run to view your location and meters run per second reflected in real time, which is pretty amazing.

Mixing Colors with the Slide It Tab

The second tab uses `UISlider` controls to create a RGB (red green blue) color mixer that alters the background color in real time and outputs the values to a series of text fields. This is another tab with real-world, practical applications. RGB is a color system that defines colors by assigning three values between 0 and 255 to each primary color. Any web developer, graphic designer, or even iOS app programmer will at some point need a tool that gives them the RGB value for a certain color. With this tab, you can play around with different combinations before implementing the one you like.

The interface for this tab is by far the most complex of the three, so let's begin. You create one block of elements for the red color and then repeat the steps two times for the green and blue colors:

1. Add a Label object from the Object Library to the Slide It view. Position it near the top of the view and then double-click it and change the text to Red, as shown in Figure 4-24.

Figure 4-24. *The color label in position*

2. Search for Slider in the Object Library and drag it onto the view. Position it below the label and resize it so it fills about two-thirds of the view's width, as shown in Figure 4-25.

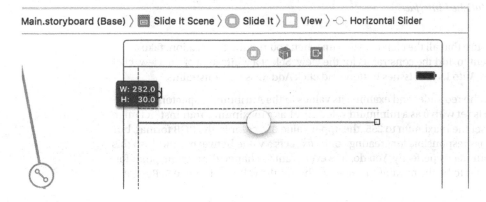

Figure 4-25. *The slider added to the view and made wider*

3. You want to add a text field to display the RGB value. Drag in a text field from the Object Library and position it to the right of the slider, as shown in Figure 4-26.

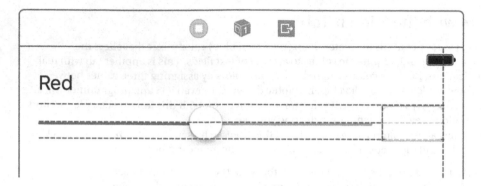

Figure 4-26. *The text field added to the view and positioned to the right of the slider*

4. Repeat Steps 1 through 3, positioning each group of elements one under the other until your view resembles Figure 4-27.

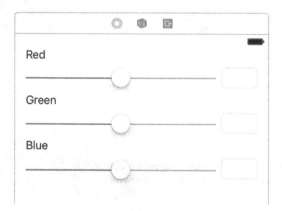

Figure 4-27. *The finished interface*

5. To ensure that all the elements line up when you run the application, take a moment to add the constraints for the view. Select a white area of the view, click the Fix Auto Layout Issues button, and click Add Missing Constraints.

6. Select the red slider and examine its values in the Attributes Inspector. Its value range is set with 0 as a minimum value and 1 as a maximum. Your instinct might be to set the maximum to 255, the upper value of a color in the RGB format, but the class responsible for creating colors expects a value between 0 and 1, so this fits your needs perfectly. You do, however, want to change the starting point for the slider to be the maximum value, so change the value to 1 from 0.5. Repeat this for the green and blue sliders.

This completes the interface, leaving you ready to create your outlets and actions before moving on to the code, which is very simple for this tab. As you did in the previous tab, open the Assistant Editor and ensure that it shows the SliderViewController.swift file:

1.   Create an outlet for each of the UISlider controls, naming them redSlider, greenSlider, and blueSlider, respectively.

2.   Create outlets for each of the UITextFields, naming them redValue, greenValue, and blueValue, respectively.

3.   Create actions for all the UISlider controls, naming them changeRed, changeGreen, and changeBlue, respectively.

4.   For reasons that I go into shortly, make your view controller a text field delegate by adding , UITextFieldDelegate after class SliderViewController: UIViewController.

Before you move on, check that the start of your code looks like this:

```
import UIKit

class SliderViewController: UIViewController, UITextFieldDelegate {

    @IBOutlet weak var redSlider: UISlider!
    @IBOutlet weak var greenSlider: UISlider!
    @IBOutlet weak var blueSlider: UISlider!
    @IBOutlet weak var redValue: UITextField!
    @IBOutlet weak var greenValue: UITextField!
    @IBOutlet weak var blueValue: UITextField!
    @IBAction func changeRed(_ sender: AnyObject) {
    }
    @IBAction func changeGreen(_ sender: AnyObject) {
    }
    @IBAction func changeBlue(_ sender: AnyObject) {
    }
```

That's it for Interface Builder for this tab. This has been one of the most complex interfaces you've encountered so far. Switch back to the Standard Editor and open SliderViewController.swift from the Project Navigator:

1.   As with the previous tab, you need to store the value specified by the sliders by declaring and initializing some global variables that are of CGFloat type. Add the following code after the line class SliderViewController: UIViewController, UITextFieldDelegate {:

```
var redColor:CGFloat = 1.0
var greenColor:CGFloat = 1.0
var blueColor:CGFloat = 1.0
```

2.   Navigate to the viewDidLoad function. Under the line super.viewDidLoad(), you need to set the delegate property of the text fields in order to use the UITextViewDelegate protocol. Add these lines:

```
redValue.delegate = self
```

```
greenValue.delegate = self
blueValue.delegate = self
```

3. You're going to call a function that you haven't written yet, so don't panic when Xcode doesn't help you through code completion and then adds a red exclamation mark next to this line. You call the function by adding `updateColor()` to the `viewDidLoad` function after the last code you wrote. Your completed `viewDidLoad` function should now look like this:

```
override func viewDidLoad() {
    super.viewDidLoad()

    redValue.delegate = self
    greenValue.delegate = self
    blueValue.delegate = self

    updateColor()
}
```

4. You need to write the `updateColor` function, which takes the red, green, and blue values and uses them to set the view's background color. Under the `viewDidLoad` function, add the following code:

```
func updateColor() {
    self.view.backgroundColor =
UIColor(red: redColor, green: greenColor, blue: blueColor, alpha: 1.0)
}
```

In this code, you create a `UIColor` object from the red, green, and blue values. The `alpha` property controls the opacity of the background, with 1.0 being totally opaque and 0.0 being transparent.

Now you need to add the code to the three actions that are linked with their corresponding sliders: `changeRed`, `changeGreen`, and `changeBlue`. All of these actions use practically the same code—only the variable and outlet names change, depending on the color. Let's set the `changeRed` code step by step, after which you complete the remaining two methods yourself:

1. Take the value from the slider and assign it to the `redColor` float. In the action for the red slider, simply write `redColor = CGFloat(redSlider.value)`.

2. You want to update the text field with the correct RGB value. To do that, you need to convert the value from between 0.0 and 1.0 to between 0 and 255, so, you multiply the value of `redColor` by 255. Finally, you ensure that there are no decimal places by using the `String(Format:` function and the `%.0f` placeholder, which in plain English means "put the float value here but limit it to 0 decimal places." The number before f controls the number of decimal places shown in the string. Also, in order to make the format function recognize the float, you need to convert it from a `CGFloat` to a `Float`. The code to achieve this is `redValue.text = String(format: "%.0f",Float(redColor*255.0))`.

3. A change has been made, so you need to call the `updateColor` function to make sure the change is reflected in the color set in the view's background. The code for this is the same as in the `viewDidLoad` function, so type `updateColor()`.

The code for the finished action should look like this:

```
@IBAction func changeRed(sender: AnyObject) {
    redColor = CGFloat(redSlider.value)
    redValue.text = String(format: "%.0f",Float(redColor*255.0))
    updateColor()
}
```

Your challenge is to implement the remaining two actions by yourself. When you're done, check that your code matches mine:

```
@IBAction func changeGreen(sender: AnyObject) {
    greenColor = CGFloat(greenSlider.value)
    greenValue.text = String(format: "%.0f",Float(greenColor*255.0))
    updateColor()
}
@IBAction func changeBlue(sender: AnyObject) {
    blueColor = CGFloat(blueSlider.value)
    blueValue.text = String(format: "%.0f",Float(blueColor*255.0))
    updateColor()
}
```

You need to write one final function to complete this tab: the textFieldShouldReturn method, which the text fields will look for now that they know this view controller is acting as a delegate for those text fields.

The UITextViewDelegate Implementation

Text fields are probably the most common control in an iOS app—they're everywhere. You tap inside them, the keyboard slides in, and you add your text. It's probably second nature to you that tapping the Return key dismisses the keyboard. Hold that thought; go ahead and run your application and select the Slide It tab.

Play around with the sliders and see how the background color changes as you modify the values. You've created something that can be usefully applied in the real world, which, as I mentioned previously, is done by giving the RGB values so they can be selected. Let's test this. Tap in one of the text fields: as expected, the keyboard slides in. Great—now try to go to the Track It tab. Hmm, not so great: the keyboard is blocking the path, so you're effectively stuck and must quit and relaunch the app to have any hope of accessing the other tabs.

You want to make it so that when you press Return, the keyboard dismisses itself. This is why you made your view controller take on the UITextViewDelegate role. By doing this, when you press Return, the text field tries to call the textFieldShouldReturn function; but because you haven't added this function yet, it doesn't do anything. Add the following code beneath your viewDidLoad function:

```
func textFieldShouldReturn(textField: UITextField) -> Bool {
    textField.resignFirstResponder()
    return true
}
```

When you tap the text field, it assumes responsibility for everything that happens thereafter—in other words, it becomes the *first responder*. When this function is called, you're telling it to give up this status with the resignFirstResponder function before returning a Boolean value, which in this case can be true or false (the result is the same). Rerun your application: you should find that you can dismiss the keyboard with the Return key and that you have a fully functional color slider view, as shown in Figure 4-28.

■ **Note**   If you're running this in the simulator, as of Xcode 6 and iOS 8, the keyboard doesn't automatically show—the simulator assumes you want to use your physical keyboard. But on a device, you experience the problem of not being able to dismiss the keyboard, which is why you must always test on a physical device before releasing to the App Store. To summon the keyboard in the simulator, go to Hardware ➤ Keyboard ➤ Toggle Software Keyboard (⌘+K).

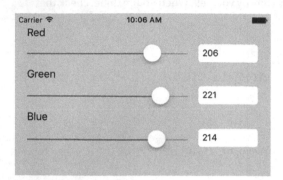

Figure 4-28. *The finished Slide It tab, complete with dismissible keyboard*

Adding "Off the Menu" Controls

You've created two hugely different but incredibly cool tab views so far. For the third tab, you look at another common control you add through Interface Builder: the segmented control. In addition, you look at two important controls that you can't add through Interface Builder: the alert view and the action sheet.

Alert Views and Action Sheets with UIAlertController

Before you begin building your interface, let's clarify what I mean when I talk about alert views and action sheets. Figure 4-29 shows how both are used in the iCloud settings area of the Settings application in iOS 8. You already encountered an alert view, when the Track It tab asked for access to your location.

Figure 4-29. *An example of an action sheet (left) and an alert view (right)*

Action sheets, as their name implies, can be used to present the users with several options for a specific action. For example, when you tap the flag icon while looking at an e-mail, you're asked whether you want to Flag, Mark as Read/Unread, or Move To Junk. If you give the users the option to add account details to your application, you might use an action sheet to ask whether the users want to add an account for your site or a third-party account, such as an OpenID account.

Alert views are coded in a way very similar to action sheets. Alert views are used to draw user attention to an event, such as a timer ending, or to confirm whether users want to activate a feature or delete some data. You'll use them often, and the good news is that they're easy to set up and use.

In iOS 8, Apple introduced a new class called UIAlertController, which combines the older UIAlertView and UIActionSheet classes into a single class. This is a fairly sensible move on Apple's part; the legacy classes were almost identical in syntax.

Building the Action Tab Interface

Now that you have a clearer understanding of what alert views and action sheets do, you're ready to build the third and final tab: the Action tab. Just the middle-right view controller remains to be built. Adjust your storyboard so it's visible in the design area:

1. Search for Segmented Control in the Object Library, as shown in Figure 4-30.
   Drag it onto the view and position it in the center, at the top of the view.

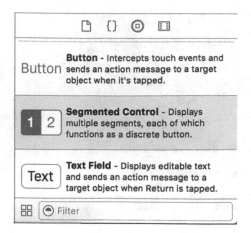

Figure 4-30. *Searching for Segmented Control in the Object Library*

2. Change the values of the segments by selecting the segmented control you added to the view. Open the Attributes Inspector. Change the segment Title attribute from First to Alert and press return.

3. Changing the second segment's title isn't as obvious. Looking at the Attributes Inspector for the segmented control, notice the drop-down list above the Title attribute that you just changed. Click it and select Segment 1- Second.

4. You can now change the Title attribute of the second segment from Second to Action, as shown in Figure 4-31.

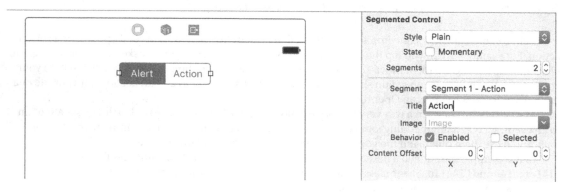

Figure 4-31. *Changing the second segment's Title attribute*

5. Using the square handles on either side of the segmented control, resize it so that you can see all of the text in the second segment. Reposition it so it's centered again.

6. Add a button control to the view to trigger whichever option is selected. Search for Button in the Object Library, and drag it on to the view, positioning it dead center in the middle of the view as you did with the switch in the Track It tab.

7. Using the Attributes Inspector, change the button's Title attribute from Button to Show Me. Again, you need to reposition it to be dead center after changing the text. Your view should resemble Figure 4-32.

Figure 4-32. *The completed interface for the Action tab*

8. Click the view, go to Fix Auto Layout Issues, and click Add Missing Constraints.

9. You're now ready to create the outlets and actions. As usual, switch to the Assistant Editor and ensure that you have `ActionViewController.swift` selected. Control-drag a connection from the segmented control into the header and create an outlet named `actionControl`, as shown in Figure 4-33.

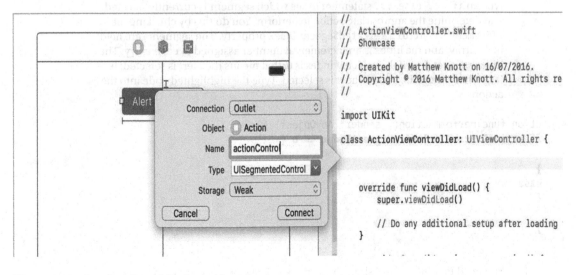

Figure 4-33. *Creating the `actionControl` outlet*

10. Create an outlet for the button called showmeButton, and then create an action for it named performAction.

The first lines of your ActionViewController.swift file should now resemble the following code:

```
import UIKit

class ActionViewController: UIViewController {

    @IBOutlet weak var actionControl: UISegmentedControl!
    @IBOutlet weak var showmeButton: UIButton!
    @IBAction func performAction(_ sender: AnyObject) {
    }

    override func viewDidLoad() {
        super.viewDidLoad()

        // Do any additional setup after loading the view.
    }
```

It's important to check the class documentation when experimenting with different controls and frameworks, because quite often you need to specify that your view controller is acting as a delegate for the classes you're adding. This can be the case with action sheets and alert views if you want to take advantage of any of their delegate methods for handling user responses. Missing a delegate reference can lead to your application failing or your code not being called in some situations. Because you won't be using the delegate methods in this example, there is no need to add them.

You're now ready to begin coding the action in this class file. Switch back to the Standard Editor and open ActionViewController.swift from the Project Navigator. All you need to look at in the file is the stub for the performAction action:

1. Scroll down until you find the performAction action. Inside its braces, you'll type an if ... else ... statement to see which segment is currently selected and determine the appropriate action to perform. You do this by checking the UISegmentedControl's selectedSegmentIndex property. The segments are held in an array, and the index is an incremental number assigned to each entry. The index starts at 0, so if the selected index is 0, that means the alert is selected; if it's 1, that means the action sheet is selected. Type the highlighted code into the action:

```
@IBAction func performAction(_ sender: AnyObject) {
    if actionControl.selectedSegmentIndex == 0 {

    }
    else
    {

    }
}
```

2. You need to initialize and show the alert view. The new UIAlertController takes far more code to initialize than its predecessor, but it's far more flexible. Type the highlighted code; once the action sheet code is written, you can see the completed result:

```
@IBAction func performAction(_ sender: AnyObject) {
    if actionControl.selectedSegmentIndex == 0 {
        let controller : UIAlertController = UIAlertController(title: "This is an alert",
            message: "You've created an alert view",
            preferredStyle: UIAlertControllerStyle.alert)

        let okAction : UIAlertAction = UIAlertAction(title: "Okay",
            style: UIAlertActionStyle.default,
            handler: {
                (alert: UIAlertAction!) in controller.dismiss(animated: true, completion:
                nil)
        })

        controller.addAction(okAction)

        self.present(controller, animated: true, completion: nil)
    }
    else
    {

    }
}
```

3. To code the else eventuality, type this very similar highlighted code inside the second set of parentheses:

```
@IBAction func performAction(_ sender: AnyObject) {
    if actionControl.selectedSegmentIndex == 0 {
        let controller : UIAlertController = UIAlertController(title: "This is an alert",
            message: "You've created an alert view",
            preferredStyle: UIAlertControllerStyle.alert)

        let okAction : UIAlertAction = UIAlertAction(title: "Okay",
            style: UIAlertActionStyle.default,
            handler: {
                (alert: UIAlertAction!) in controller.dismiss(animated: true, completion: nil)
        })

        controller.addAction(okAction)

        self.present(controller, animated: true, completion: nil)
    }
    else
    {
        let controller : UIAlertController = UIAlertController(title: "This is an action
        sheet",
            message: "You've created an action sheet",
            preferredStyle: UIAlertControllerStyle.actionSheet)

        let okAction : UIAlertAction = UIAlertAction(title: "Okay",
```

```
        style: UIAlertActionStyle.default,
        handler: {
            (alert: UIAlertAction!) in controller.dismiss(animated: true, completion:
            nil)
    })

    controller.addAction(okAction)

    self.present(controller, animated: true, completion: nil)
    }
}
```

You've just written code that performs four distinct tasks. First, you define a UIAlertController called controller. Next, you define a UIAlertAction that adds a button to either the alert view or the action sheet to dismiss the controller. Third, you add the action to the controller, associating the two. Finally, you tell the main view to present the UIAlertController. The only difference between these two pieces of code is that UIAlertControllerStyle is alert for an alert view and actionSheet for an action sheet.

That's it—you've configured your view controller to show either an alert view or an action sheet depending on the selected index of a segmented control. Because the focus of this book is Xcode, not iOS app development, I'm only scratching the surface of what you can do with these two controls, but they're extremely easy to build on and are a key addition to any developer's bag of tricks.

You've coded the third and final tab, so go ahead and run the application in the simulator. It should produce results similar to those shown in Figure 4-34. Look at all the great things you've been able to achieve in this chapter, with a relatively small amount of effort and code! Hopefully your confidence with the Xcode IDE, iOS, and the Swift language is beginning to build.

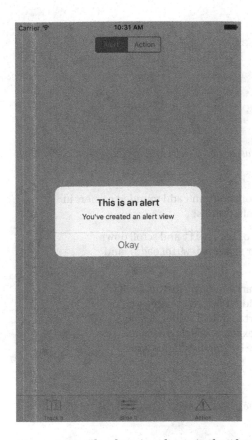

Figure 4-34. The alert view shown in the Alert tab

Changing the Interface with Code

In this chapter, you've taken a good look at how you can adjust the interface elements' attributes using the Attribute Inspector. But just as you can't use Interface Builder to add action sheets and alert views, there are some visual effects that you can only achieve through code. You've already done a lot of hard work in this chapter, and you won't learn any more about Xcode here. So, look at this section as totally optional. However, you'll probably want to use the skills you can develop here to build your own applications for iOS devices, in which case these examples will prove invaluable.

Styling Buttons

With iOS 7, Apple introduced the most radical change in design since the launch of the first iPhone: moving away from *skeuomorphism* to a *flat* design style. The decision was controversial when announced, but many are now warming to the change and have adapted their applications to fit with the new styles.

One area that changed that many want to alter in their applications is the standard button. Figure 4-35 shows the three buttons from the Contact screen in iOS 6 and iOS 7. In iOS 6, buttons *looked* like traditional buttons, whereas in iOS 7 onwards, they're shown in the same style as hyperlinks on a web page.

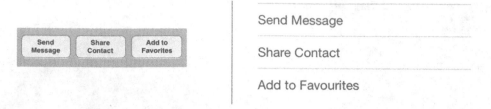

Figure 4-35. *The three buttons from the Contact app's detail view for iOS 6 (left) and updated for iOS 7 (right)*

Although you can change the background color of the button, you can't add rounded corners in Interface Builder, so you need to delve into code to make these alterations:

1. From the Project Navigator, open `ActionViewController.swift` and scroll down to the `viewDidLoad` function. Drop down a line after `super.viewDidLoad()`, and you're ready to add some custom code.

2. You're going to change the background color to a dark blue. You do this similarly to how you changed the background color in the Slide It tab, by creating a color using RGB values. But this time, you need to convert real RGB values, which range from 0 to 255, to fit in with what the method expects, which is a value between 0.0 and 1.0. To do this, you divide the value by 255.0. Add this line of code:

```
showmeButton.backgroundColor =
        UIColor(red: 9/255.0, green: 95/255.0, blue: 134/255.0, alpha: 1.0)
```

3. The button will be hard to read with blue text on a blue background, so the next task is to change the text color to white. You could do this in Interface Builder, but then you wouldn't be able to read the button's text when looking at the storyboard. Type the following code on the next line:

```
showmeButton.setTitleColor(UIColor.white, forState: UIControlState.normal)
```

4. You can easily apply a curved corner to the button by specifying a float value greater that 0.0 to the button's `cornerRadius` property. You do this using the following code:

```
showmeButton.layer.cornerRadius = 4.0
```

```
Your viewDidLoad function should now look like this:override func viewDidLoad() {
    super.viewDidLoad()
    showmeButton.backgroundColor =
        UIColor(red: 9/255.0, green: 95/255.0, blue: 134/255.0, alpha: 1.0)
    showmeButton.setTitleColor(UIColor.white, for: UIControlState.normal)
    showmeButton.layer.cornerRadius = 4.0
}
```

Run the application in the simulator: you see the difference immediately in your button on the Action tab. The problem is that the button isn't set at a suitable size to make the most of your effects.

1. Open Main.Storyboard from the Project Navigator, make the button on the Action view much bigger, and then reposition it to the center.

2. Click the Resolve Auto Layout Issues button and choose Reset to Suggested Constraints.

3. Now run the application again: your button should look great and resemble that shown in Figure 4-36.

Figure 4-36. *The customized button*

That's it for this chapter. As a final challenge, try to apply curved corners to the text view in the Track It tab using the code you used to curve the button. If you get stuck, the answer can be found at the end of the summary for this chapter.

Summary

This has been a long chapter, but you've made it through and should be really proud of what you've achieved. The objective of the chapter was to learn more about creating interfaces in Xcode, and you did that with a mix of Interface Builder and writing custom code. The application you created was called Showcase, mostly because it gives you a cool app that you can load on your phone so you can show your friends and colleagues the kind of amazing things you're now able to develop!

Specifically, in this chapter, you did the following:

• Created an application from the Tabbed Application template

• Renamed the default view controllers and created your own from scratch

- Removed the default views from the storyboard and created three of your own

- Tied your new view controllers to their respective classes

- Created image sets in the images Asset Catalog and populated them

- Linked views to a tab bar controller in a storyboard

- Learned about frameworks and accessed the device's GPS function

- Learned about the `UITextView`, `UISegmentedControl`, `UISwitch`, and `UISlider` controls

- Programmatically created an alert view and an action sheet using `UIAlertController`

- Learned how to modify the visual appearance of controls using code

When you go through that list, you can see how many new skills you've learned in this chapter. Before moving on, though, I promised the solution to rounding the corners of the text view in the Track It tab. If you did it right, you should have added the following line to the `viewDidLoad` function in `TrackViewController.swift`:

```
locationText.layer.cornerRadius = 5.0
```

Very well done if you got that right.

Now on to Chapter 5, where you begin to look at the help provided by Apple through Xcode, along with how Xcode's intelligent code-completion feature makes coding much quicker and more efficient.

CHAPTER 5

■ ■ ■

Getting Help and Code Completion

In Chapter 4, you accomplished quite a lot. You should be starting to feel more confident with the tools and features available in Xcode, and hopefully you're seeing how it can help you build your own applications.

This chapter focuses on the wealth of help that Xcode offers while you create the next big macOS and iOS apps. You see how Xcode makes writing code quick and easy with its intelligent code-completion feature. Looking at code completion will also help you grasp the basics of working with Xcode's code editor. The main focus of Chapter 4 was Interface Builder with a dash of storyboarding. You went from having a default tab bar application to an application that had three very different tabs. This chapter explains how to create the project shown in Figure 5-1, which demonstrates how to interact with some of the built-in applications: Mail, Messaging, and Safari.

Figure 5-1. The InTouch application

Getting Help

Xcode provides help in a variety of ways, not only on how to use Xcode but also on how to program using Swift, Objective-C and how to use Apple's frameworks. This section explains how Xcode helps you find a solution when you're stuck, whether you're using the code editor, the property list editor, or the Interface Builder, or you've simply encountered a problem while coding.

© Matthew Knott 2016
M. Knott, *Beginning Xcode*, DOI 10.1007/978-1-4302-5005-0_5

Creating the Project

Okay, you know what the aim of the chapter is, let's start building the project.

1. Open Xcode and create a new project by clicking Create A New Xcode Project on the Welcome screen or going to File ➤ New ➤ Project (⌘+Shift+N). Select the Single View Application template and click Next.

2. Name your project InTouch and ensure that Language is set to Swift and the Devices option is set to Universal. Configure the other settings as you did in the previous applications. Make sure the key settings match those shown in Figure 5-2. Click Next.

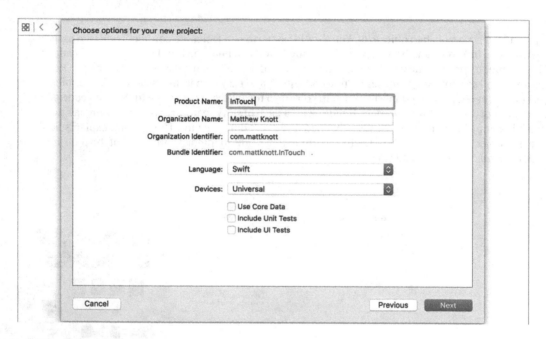

Figure 5-2. *The initial settings for the InTouch application*

3. You don't want to create a Git repository, so leave Source Control unchecked. Make sure your project will be saved where you want it to be. Click Create.

That's the foundation of the project setup. You'll be amazed how much you can achieve beyond this with very little code and effort. Before you proceed, it's important to understand that you don't have to go to your favorite search engine if you're stuck. Xcode has one of the best support systems of any IDE out there, if not *the* best.

Downloading Additional Documentation

Large parts of this chapter are dependent on you having the relevant documentation installed on your computer. Xcode does not give you all of this by default, so it's well worth checking that you have everything you need installed; otherwise, you miss out on some excellent application programming interface (API) and system documentation.

To check the state of your documentation, start by selecting Xcode ➤ Preferences from the menu bar (⌘+,). Click the Components tab, and you're presented with two tabs, as shown in Figure 5-3. You can download legacy simulators from the Simulators tab, and additional documentation sets from the Documentation tab. It's optional for this chapter, but if you want to bolster your documentation, you should download Xcode 7.3 Documentation and iOS 9.3 Documentation. Click the down-pointing arrow next to the file size, and the documentation begins downloading.

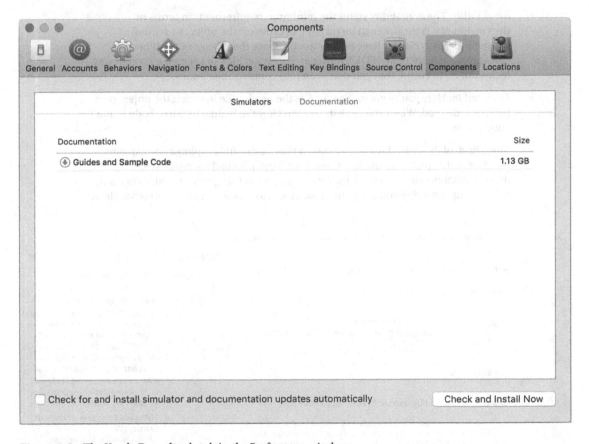

Figure 5-3. *The Xcode Downloads tab in the Preferences window*

Quick Help

To begin, let's focus on Quick Help. Quick Help provides a concise definition of symbols, interface objects, and build settings. The beauty of using Quick Help is that it resides in the Utilities area of Xcode and doesn't take away your focus when you're working on a project. To access the Quick Help Inspector, go to View ➤ Utilities ➤ Show Quick Help Inspector (⌥+⌘+2). To see Quick Help in action, open AppDelegate.swift and highlight UIResponder. Quick Help instantly updates to give you useful information. Figure 5-4 shows Quick Help in action.

You can see from Figure 5-4 that a range of information appears—exactly what is displayed varies with what class or object you select. However, following are the main entries of a Quick Help entity:

- *Declaration:* The declaration gives you an overview of the class's definition, including its base class and any adopted protocols, to help you understand the class's capabilities.

- *Description:* This is rather self-explanatory, but the main point is that the description of a symbol, an object, or a setting covers how it should be used and also gives an overview of event handling.

- *Availability:* The availability states the minimum requirements in terms of the version of iOS the user can be running in order for the object or symbol to function. Many classes have been available since the release of the iPhone software development kit (SDK); however, it's a good idea to keep an eye on newer technologies to ensure that you don't run into compatibility issues.

- *Declared In:* Here you're given the name of the header file in which the object or symbol is defined. When you click it, you can view the header's source code in the code editor.

- *More:* Each of the main classes has a class reference that fully explores and explains the class and its protocols and functions. Also, if you installed the relevant iOS documentation, guides are available for certain classes that give you straightforward help for implementing and using the class, as well as how it can work with other classes.

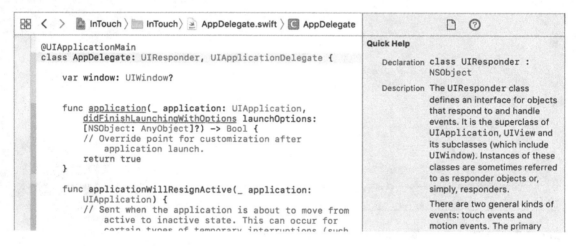

Figure 5-4. *Quick Help showing information about the* UIResponder *class*

If you come across a symbol, an object, or a setting that doesn't have a Quick Help entry, you can search Xcode's documentation for whatever you've selected. For instance, in AppDelegate.swift, if you highlight func, you see that there isn't a Quick Help entry. With @func still highlighted, click Search Documentation, as shown in Figure 5-5, and the Documentation Viewer window appears.

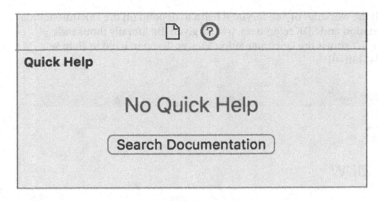

Figure 5-5. *Quick Help's Search Documentation button, which you can click when no entry exists for the highlighted entity*

Another way to access Quick Help is to press the Option key (⌥p and select a class in the code editor. Figure 5-6 illustrates the dialog displayed when the UIWindow class is selected in AppDelegate.swift. This is only accessible from the code editor, but it's very useful if you need to quickly look up a class definition. You're provided with a description of the class, the version of iOS in which it was introduced, where it's declared, and a link to additional documentation (any text that's blue is a link that opens an external file, either source code in the code editor or a class reference in the Documentation Viewer).

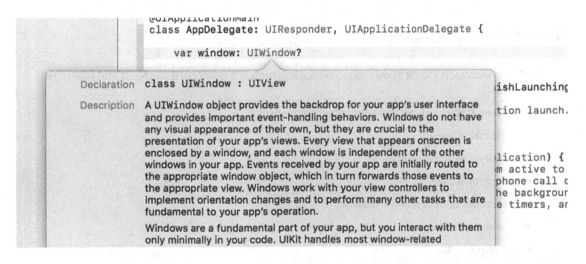

Figure 5-6. *A more compact version of Quick Help, displaying information regarding the UIWindow class*

Documentation Viewer

Before I focus on the Documentation Viewer in detail, I want to talk about how this facet of Xcode has changed from previous versions. Documentation Viewer was introduced in Xcode 5, having previously been a part of the Organizer tool, which is examined in Chapter 14.

As you become more familiar with the workings of Xcode, you'll learn to depend on the Documentation Viewer for its quick access to documentation and SDK references, which, given the literally thousands of APIs, are remarkably detailed. Figure 5-7 shows the Documentation Viewer. To open it, go to Help ➤ Documentation and API Reference (⌘+Shift+0).

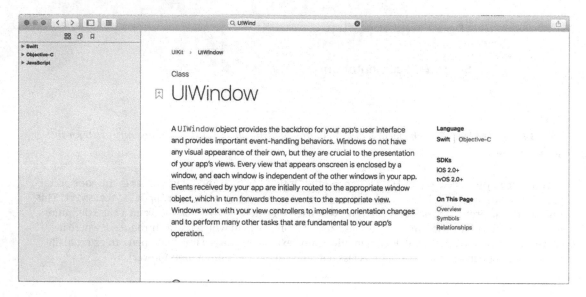

Figure 5-7. *The Documentation Viewer*

The Documentation Viewer allows you to search and browse a variety of documents and resources, including these:

- Class, framework, protocol, and object references
- Technical guides
- Getting started documents
- Technical Q&A
- Change logs and revision histories
- Technical videos
- Sample code

Notice that in addition to the document being viewed, the Documentation Viewer has three key areas: the Toolbar, the Navigator, and the Table of Contents. I cover all three of these in detail in the following sections.

___

■ **Note**   What's really useful about the documentation sets in Xcode is the fact that they're completely accessible offline. This means if you're working where there isn't an Internet connection, you still have access to this wealth of documentation and references.

___

Toolbar

The Toolbar contains all of Documentation Viewer's navigation and sharing features. They're as follows, moving left to right across the bar:

- *Backward/forward navigation:* The Documentation Viewer works very much like a web browser in that the content is HTML based. You can bookmark pages of interest; you can navigate backward and forward through the history of your research. This can be invaluable as you dip in and out of API references, trying to find how to correctly instantiate a new class or get a better understanding of the class properties. Holding down the mouse on either control allows you to select a page from your history.

- *Sidebar controls:* Immediately after the backward and forward navigation arrows are two buttons. The first controls the visibility of the Navigator, and the second controls the visibility of the Table of Contents.

- *Search:* The sheer amount of documentation provided by Apple can overwhelm even the most seasoned iOS developers, and it would be absurd for Apple to assume developers can find the correct documentation for the nitty-gritty details of underlying Swift and Objective-C technologies, classes, and functions. That's why the Documentation Organizer has a very useful search functionality that allows you to search for a particular term.

- To demonstrate, search for a broad term: for example, *gesture*. This can relate to a variety of different things, but luckily Xcode helps you find just what you're looking for. Figure 5-8 illustrates the results that are displayed when searching for *gesture*.

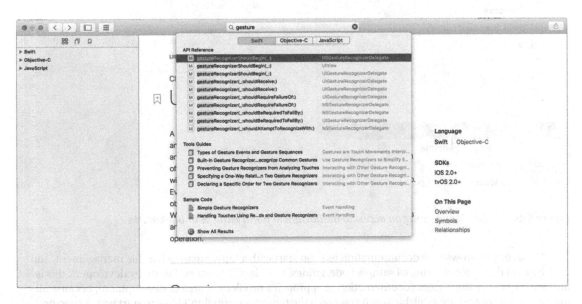

Figure 5-8. *The top results displayed when searching for gesture*

- Notice that as you type, only a few results are displayed. Click Show All Results to see the full set of results spread across a number of sections. In this case, API Reference, SDK Guides, Tool Guides, and Sample Code are shown.

- *Share:* A familiar icon to most people, and almost identical in function to its equivalent in Safari, the Share button presents a list of ways to share or export the current document: Open In Safari, Add Bookmark, Email Link, Message, and, if available, the option to open a PDF copy of the document. Because documentation in the Documentation Viewer is often spread over numerous pages, it can be difficult to search in the scope of the entire document. This is where opening the PDF copy can be useful, and most classes and APIs support this. Another new feature is the ability to open sample code in the Swift Playground, which you learn about in detail in Chapter 11.

The Navigator Sidebar

The Navigator provides you with three methods of accessing help and documentation. First, you can browse the entire library of API documentation installed on the machine; you can focus on just guides and sample code, or you can place bookmarks in various pieces of documentation. Access to each feature is controlled by three icons at the top of the Navigator, as shown in Figure 5-9.

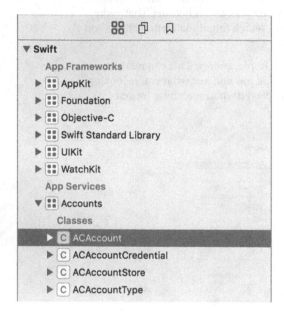

Figure 5-9. The Navigator gives you access to the document library and your bookmarks

The ability to browse the documentation lets you start with a topic area, such as file management, and then expand that topic, viewing all sample code, guides, and class references. For many developers, this is the best way to use the system documentation to approach a problem or area of development, because all the relevant resources are available when you reach the topic area; you don't have to start with a specific class or framework.

Being able to bookmark articles, guides, references, and sample code is another heavily used feature of the Documentation Viewer. This makes it easy to refer to a piece of documentation at a later date. It's inevitable that at some point you're going to stumble on something that may not be useful right away but that you may want to refer to later—so a bookmark is just what you need!

Adding a Bookmark

To bookmark a piece of documentation you have three choices. You've already seen the Add Bookmark option from the Share icon on the Toolbar. Alternatively, you can simply click the bookmark icon found throughout the documentation such as next to the page title, or you can right-click the documentation while you're viewing it and select Add Bookmark, as shown in Figure 5-10.

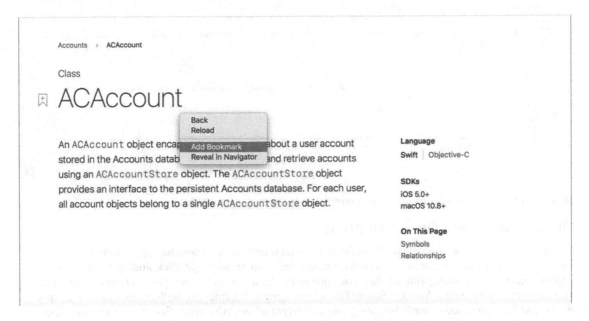

Figure 5-10. Two of the three ways to bookmark documentation

Viewing Your Bookmarks

Once you've bookmarked documentation, when you want to access it again, ensure that the Navigator is active using the relevant Toolbar icon and then select the bookmarks icon. You see a list of everything you've bookmarked. Simply click the documentation item in the Navigator, and it opens. To delete a bookmark, select the item from the sidebar and then press Backspace, or right-click the item and select Delete.

Unfortunately, your bookmarks aren't synced anywhere, so you have to be on your device to access them. It's sometimes useful to use Apple's online documentation library if you want to access your bookmarks on other devices, such as your iPhone or iPad.

The Table of Contents Sidebar

The Table of Contents sits to the left of the document you're viewing. As you would expect, it provides a hierarchical overview, allowing you to quickly navigate a large document and see any associated source code or example projects (see Figure 5-11).

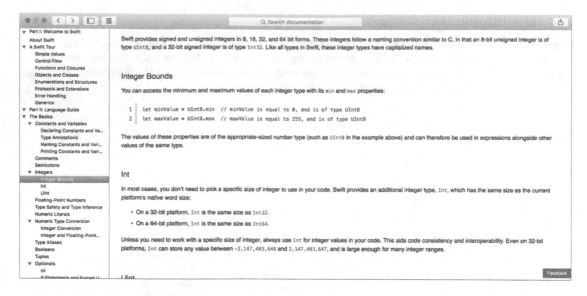

Figure 5-11. *The Table of Contents lets you navigate large documents quickly*

Quickly Accessing Documentation

Xcode makes it easy to access help while you're working on your project without having to open the Documentation Viewer each time you want to look something up. Simply right-click, and, depending on what part of Xcode you're working with, a help menu appears in which you can access relevant help for that area. You can access these menus from the Source Editor (see Figure 5-12), Interface Builder (see Figure 5-13), and the Project Navigator (see Figure 5-14), along with a variety of others. When you choose the contextual help menu, the Documentation Viewer is displayed and shows the relevant guide or reference. This is useful when you want to look something up quickly or want to know how to perform a task in the part of Xcode you're using.

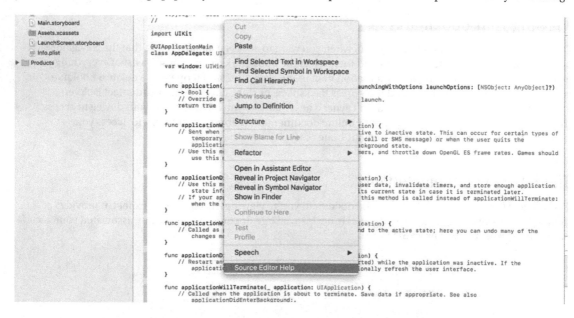

Figure 5-12. *The Source Editor's help menu*

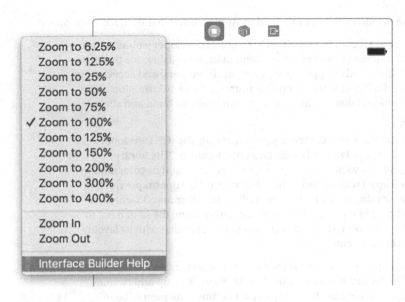

Figure 5-13. *The Interface Builder's help menu*

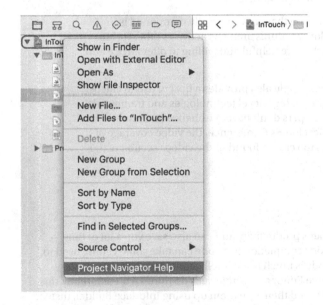

Figure 5-14. *The Project Navigator's help menu*

Apple's Web Site

As mentioned previously in this chapter and also at the beginning of this book, Apple's developer web site also provides an excellent library of information. In fact, when you download a documentation set, you're in fact downloading an offline version of Apple's reference library—the Documentation Viewer is essentially a glorified web browser.

Here is a list of useful online resources that are provided by Apple, aimed mainly at iOS developers:

- `http://developer.apple.com`: The main home of Apple's developer web site. Here you can access the developer centers and all documentation available; see the latest and greatest news in the world of Apple, specifically for developers; and access many other parts of Apple's developer world, such as resource centers, information about copyright, and much more. I discuss these later when it's time to build and share your application.

- `https://developer.apple.com/library/ios/navigation`: The iOS Developer Library is what's used to populate the Documentation Organizer. The library includes technical guides, a wealth of references, sample code, and documentation. Apple really sets itself apart with the overwhelming amount of support provided to developers. If you're working with a certain technology in iOS or macOS, chances are there's a detailed guide for it. You can search the library using the search bar to the left. It's easy to become overwhelmed, but once you get familiar with its layout, finding what you need will become easy.

- `https://developer.apple.com/library/ios/navigation/#section=Resource%20 Types&topic=Sample%20Code`: It's always useful to see something up and running, and seeing a working example can also save you a lot of time. The sample code provided by Apple allows you to test a particular technology yourself, dissect the code, and even use the code in your own applications.

- `https://devforums.apple.com`: Something that I haven't really mentioned is Apple's Developer Forums. The Developer Forums aren't as active as other forums available online, but the users are much more helpful and willing to offer advice and solutions.

- `https://developer.apple.com/videos`: Apple also provides a host of useful videos. Topics range from low-level technologies to high-level technologies and frameworks provided by Apple. Because many developers don't have the chance to attend WWDC, Apple's annual World Wide Developers Conference, the video coverage of the conference can also be useful. This too can be found in the videos section of the developer web site.

Code Completion

Code completion can greatly increase any developer's productivity and can also save you a lot of time—that is, if you know how to use it correctly. Using code completion in Xcode can take some getting used to, depending on your prior experience; however, Xcode is much more intelligent than some other IDEs.

To get a taste of code completion and the Source Editor as a whole, let's do things a bit differently this time. Specifically, you'll code your actions manually and then wire them up using Interface Builder, instead of using Interface Builder to create the action stubs and linkages as you did in previous chapters:

1. Open `ViewController.swift` and, under the line `import UIKit`, begin typing the following (remembering that it's case sensitive):

```
import MessageUI
```

2. As you type the code, Xcode continually suggests the code you are attempting to write so that you can write it quicker.

■ **Note** You have imported the MessageUI framework because it gives you access to
MFMailComposeViewController, among other classes, so try out some of the skills you learned earlier in this
chapter. Go ahead and search for it in Documentation Viewer; you'll find a wealth of information, including
confirmation of its parent framework.

3. You need to tell the view controller to act as a delegate
   for MFMessageComposeViewControllerDelegate and
   MFMailComposeViewControllerDelegate. To do this, immediately next to class
   ViewController: UIViewController, type the following, using the code-
   completion dialog to insert the correct code, as shown in Figure 5-15:

MFMessageComposeViewControllerDelegate, MFMailComposeViewControllerDelegate

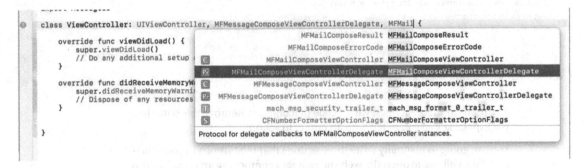

Figure 5-15. *The code-completion dialog appears as you add the delegate protocols*

■ **Note** You can use the up and down arrows to change the selection in the code-completion dialog. Then, with
the correct item highlighted, press Enter: your cursor focuses on the end of the line, and the code is entered.

4. When you add the MFMessageComposeViewControllerDelegate protocol, you
   receive an immediate error; it's important to note that you haven't done anything
   wrong. The issue is that this protocol has a single delegate function that must be
   implemented in the class adopting the protocol. This means if you want to add that
   protocol onto this view controller, the next thing to do is add the delegate function.
   Before you do that, ensure that the start of your view controller looks like this:

```
import UIKit
import MessageUI

class ViewController: UIViewController, MFMessageComposeViewControllerDelegate,
MFMailComposeViewControllerDelegate {

    override func viewDidLoad() {
        super.viewDidLoad()
        // Do any additional setup after loading the view, typically from a nib.
    }
```

5. To remove the error, you can use Xcode's powerful code completion to quickly add the missing delegate method. After the `viewDidLoad` function, drop down a couple of lines and start typing `messageComposeViewController`. As you do, code completion kicks in and presents you with the delegate function, as shown in Figure 5-16. Press the Tab key to create the method.

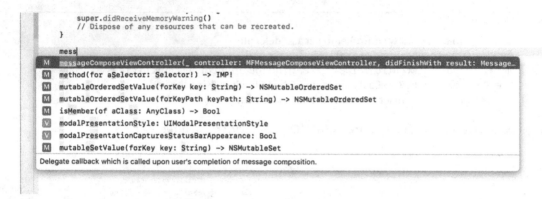

Figure 5-16. *Using code completion to create the missing delegate function*

6. The method was generated with a code placeholder. Remove this with the Backspace key so you're left with an empty function.

7. You are going to manually write three actions that the buttons in your app's interface will use to open the web site or begin composing an e-mail or text message. Begin typing the following highlighted code just before the `override func viewDidLoad()` line:

```
import UIKit
import MessageUI

class ViewController: UIViewController, MFMessageComposeViewControllerDelegate,
MFMailComposeViewControllerDelegate {

    @IBAction func sendEmail(_ sender: AnyObject) {

    }
    @IBAction func sendText(_ sender: AnyObject) {

    }
    @IBAction func openWebsite(_ sender: AnyObject) {

    }
```

Now that you've created the stubs for each action, let's go through the actions and focus on what the code will do before writing it.

Opening Web Sites in Safari

Many applications that you download from the App Store use web views in the native application to load visual information from the Web or from locally stored assets. This is generally frowned on by Apple, which prefers you to write everything natively. In the InTouch app, your goal is to direct users to your company web site, and you do this by forcing Safari to open and display a specified web address. There are some good reasons for using Safari in this instance: first, it's overkill to implement a web view for something that will require a lot of work to create a completely functional implementation with back and forward controls; and, second, if the users open the home page in Safari, they will be able to bookmark it, sync the tab with other iOS devices, and share it on social media.

Locate the openWebsite action stub you just created. Between the braces, begin to type the highlighted code, but feel free to replace http://apress.com with your own URL:

```
@IBAction func openWebsite(sender: AnyObject) {
    UIApplication.shared().open(URL(string: "http://apress.com")!, options: [:],
completionHandler: nil)
}
```

In this code, notice that you aren't creating any variables: you access the UIApplication class and use what are called *type methods* in Swift. Although this book isn't a guide to the Swift language as such, it's important to understand some of the basic concepts of the language. If you have experience with other C-based languages, you may be familiar with static methods; a type method is the same thing. In essence, a type method is a function that you can access without instantiating the parent class—that is, without assigning it to a variable. Type methods are great when you want to quickly access a function without setting a bunch of parameters.

■ **Note**   Each time you add a bracket, notice that for a brief moment a little yellow box appears around its counterpart (that is, the one you're closing). This is to make sure you don't add too many or too few brackets; this also applies to braces.

Sending an E-Mail with MFMailComposeViewController

Next, let's write the code that will allow the users to send an e-mail from your application. What's significant is that you don't need to create an interface for this; you simply use MFMailComposeViewController and preset the values. This is a great approach because unless Apple changes the class, your application will always use the iOS Mail application's compose view, instantly making it familiar to users, more future-proof, and requiring less work than writing your own view.

To implement the view controller, you also have to write another delegate function to handle what happens after the e-mail has been sent. First write the action by adding the following highlighted code:

```
@IBAction func sendEmail(sender: AnyObject) {
    if MFMailComposeViewController.canSendMail()
    {
        let mailVC = MFMailComposeViewController()

        mailVC.setSubject("Beginning Xcode")
        mailVC.setToRecipients(["xcode@mattknott.com"])
        mailVC.setMessageBody("<p>I am really enjoying the book!</p>", isHTML: false)
        mailVC.mailComposeDelegate = self;
```

```
        self.present(mailVC, animated: true, completion: nil)
    }
    else
    {
        print("This device is currently unable to send email")
    }
}
```

Feel free to change xcode@mattknott.com to your own e-mail address, and also feel free to change the subject and presumptuous contents of the e-mail message to whatever you'd like the users to see before they begin to compose their e-mail messages to you.

Next you need to create a new function mailComposeController: didFinishWithResult. This is a delegate function that is called when the users want to dismiss the mail-compose view controller. In this instance, you account for each of the possible outcomes of trying to send an e-mail before you let the users dismiss the compose view, which they can do after they've sent their message or if they decide to cancel it. Add the following function before the other delegate function, messageComposeViewController: didFinishWith:

```
func mailComposeController(_ didFinishWithcontroller: MFMailComposeViewController,
    didFinishWith result: MFMailComposeResult, error: NSError?) {

    switch result {

    case MFMailComposeResult.sent:
        print("Result: Email Sent!")

    case MFMailComposeResult.cancelled:
        print("Result: Email Cancelled.")

    case MFMailComposeResult.failed:
        print("Result: Error, Unable to Send Email.")

    case MFMailComposeResult.saved:
        print("Result: Mail Saved as Draft.")
    }

    self.dismiss(animated: true, completion: nil)
}
```

You've written all the code needed to send an e-mail. Next you will look at text messaging and how the process is similar to sending an e-mail.

Sending a Text Message

Short Message Service (SMS) messaging is still one of the most popular forms of communication in the world today, and just like e-mail, Apple makes it easy to send a text message from your application. The code is very similar to the previous two methods, but there is one big distinction: you have to test this on a physical device, because the Simulator can't simulate SMS.

With that in mind, in the sendText action, type the following highlighted code:

```
@IBAction func sendText(sender: AnyObject) {
    if MFMessageComposeViewController.canSendText()
```

```
{
    let smsVC : MFMessageComposeViewController = MFMessageComposeViewController()
    smsVC.messageComposeDelegate = self
    smsVC.recipients = ["1234500000"]
    smsVC.body = "I am interested in your products, please call me back."
    self.present(smsVC, animated: true, completion: nil)
}
else
{
    print("This device is currently unable to send text messages")
}
}
```

Just as with the e-mail implementation, you now need to complete the code for the delegate function that is called when the process of sending the text message is completed. Once again, you compare the result of the attempt to send a text message against several possible results and print text to the console based on the outcome. Add the highlighted code to the messageComposeViewController: didFinishWithResult: function:

```
func messageComposeViewController(_ controller: MFMessageComposeViewController,
didFinishWith result: MessageComposeResult) {

    switch result {

    case MessageComposeResult.sent:
        print("Result: Text Message Sent!")

    case MessageComposeResult.cancelled:
        print("Result: Text Message Cancelled.")

    case MessageComposeResult.failed:
        print("Result: Error, Unable to Send Text Message.")
    }

    self.dismiss(animated:true, completion: nil)
}
```

Building the Interface

You've written all the code your application needs to perform three essential communication tasks. Now you need to build and connect your interface to harness the code you've just written:

1. Open Main.storyboard from the Project Navigator.

2. Drag a label and three buttons onto the view. Position the label at the top of the view and the three buttons beneath it, one on top of the other.

3. Resize the label so it fills the full width of the view, and then open the Attributes Inspector (⌥+⌘+4). Set the Text attribute to say Ways to get in touch. Center the text and then in the Font attribute, click the T icon to customize the font. Set Font to Custom, Family to Helvetica Neue, Style to Thin, and Size to 23, as shown in Figure 5-17. You may need to increase the height of the label.

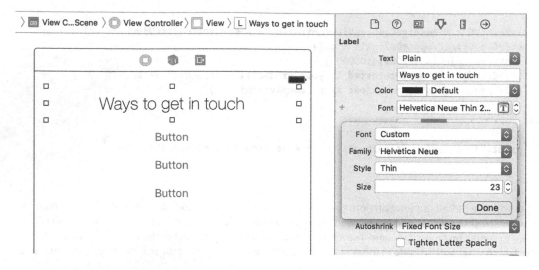

Figure 5-17. *Setting the custom font properties*

4. In order, double-click each of the buttons and name them Email, Text Message, and Website, respectively, before centering them.

5. Use the Resolve Auto Layout Issues button and select Add Missing Constraints under the All Views in View Controller heading to pin the elements in place.

Your finished interface should look something like Figure 5-18.

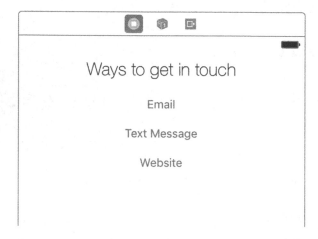

Figure 5-18. *The finished interface*

Making Connections

The code is written and the interface is assembled, but there is no linkage between the two. To address this, you need to connect the actions you've created to the buttons using the Connections Inspector (the sixth and final inspector):

1. Be sure you still have `MainStoryboard.storyboard` open. If it isn't, open it from the Project Navigator.

2. Open the Connections Inspector (⌥+⌘+6) with the view controller selected from the document outline, as shown in Figure 5-19. Note that you can select the view controller by clicking the bar at the top in the design area.

Figure 5-19. *Main.storyboard with the view controller selected and the Connections Inspector open*

3. Under the Received Actions heading in the Connections Inspector, you see the three actions with a hollow circle next to each one. From the `sendEmail` method's circle, click and drag a connection to the button, as shown in Figure 5-20.

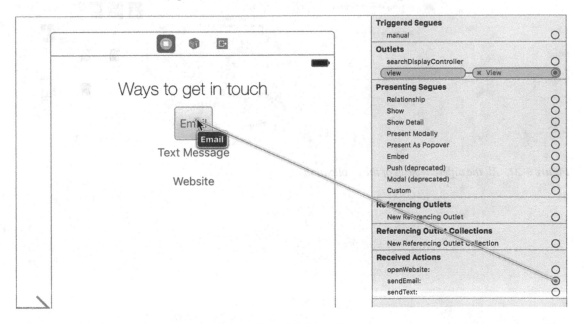

Figure 5-20. *Connecting an action to a button from the Connections Inspector*

4. A menu appears when you release the connection, presenting you with a list of trigger events. The action is called when the correct type of event occurs. Select Touch Up Inside from the bottom part of the list.

■ **Note** When a button in an iOS application is tapped, the Touch Up Inside event is triggered. By linking the action to this event, you can be sure the code will be executed when the user taps your button.

---

5. Repeat these steps, linking the two remaining actions to their respective buttons, and making sure to select the Touch Up Inside event from the list.

You've now learned one of several ways to link buttons to preexisting actions! Well done—you're well on your way to becoming an Xcode master.

Running the Application

Run the application on your device or on the iOS Simulator. When you tap the Website button, InTouch is placed in the background and Safari opens. Similarly, if you click the Email or Text Message button, a view is pushed in which the users can send an e-mail or SMS. Figure 5-21 illustrates, in order on the main view, the Email compose screen, the Text Message compose screen, and Safari with the web site.

Figure 5-21. *All the different views of the application*

■ **Note** You can't send an e-mail from the iOS Simulator, and you can't even see the SMS dialog in it; so in order to fully test this feature, you need to run InTouch on an actual iOS device that has an e-mail account configured. You commence testing on a physical device in Chapter 14; if you haven't skipped ahead to find out how to test on a physical device, this will be a great project to come back to. For now, though, take my word for it and assume that it works.

Summary

This chapter explored quite a few different topics, and you added some interesting communication features to your application. Here is what you achieved:

- Looked at the Documentation Viewer
- Saw how Xcode makes it easy to access help from wherever you're working in Xcode
- Learned about Quick Help
- Explored Apple's online documentation
- Became more familiar with the Source Editor
- Used code completion to speed up how you code
- Connected actions using the Connections Inspector
- Added a framework to your project

The next chapter looks at constraints. If you've been testing on a physical device or have tried rotating the Simulator, you've probably noticed that things can get a little messed up. I explain in detail how to quickly fix this in Interface Builder, and I also provide your first look at programmatically adding objects to the view controller while using programmatically generated constraints to keep them aligned.

CHAPTER 6

■ ■ ■

Constraints

Chapter 5 detailed the many ways Xcode gives you access to help, documentation, and guidance. You created a handy communications application along the way that could compose a text message or an e-mail, or even open a web site in another browser. You also looked at an alternative to the Assistant Editor for making connections between Interface Builder controls and your outlets and actions.

This chapter introduces you to a feature of Xcode that is still relatively new and has been over the last few versions of Xcode: the Auto Layout system. Auto Layout (or Autolayout, as Apple sometimes refers to it) had its last significant revision in Xcode 6 with the addition of size classes to allow for more adaptable storyboards, the subject of the next chapter. In this chapter, you use Auto Layout to build an example application that adapts to changing resolutions and screen orientations the way you want it to. What's great is that the techniques you learn here are largely applicable to both iOS and macOS development.

Understanding Auto Layout

In Xcode, Auto Layout provides you with a comprehensive set of tools to automatically lay out your controls in a view and constrain how those controls react to each other when the resolution changes or when the iOS device is rotated, also known as changing the orientation. In the past there was a lot of stigma around Auto Layout because of its shortcomings: it was inaccurate and offered poor flexibility. A couple of years ago in Xcode 5, Apple completely overhauled Auto Layout, creating something totally new that gave developers very fine control over the behavior of the elements in a view.

Although many of the tools and principles remain, Apple has added an extra layer of configuration with the introduction of *size classes*. This mechanism means a single storyboard can work on both iPhone and iPad, which in the past were separate storyboards. The catalysts for this were the iPhone 6 and 6 Plus, which bridged the gap between phone and tablet. The so-called *phablet* blurred the lines, and Xcode 6 changed to embrace this, making life easier for developers by allowing them to use a single storyboard if they want to.

This chapter takes you through the principles of Auto Layout before focusing specifically on how size classes affect these principles. I'll present four ways to add constraints to your controls:

- Manually, using the Control+click-and-drag method you're familiar with for creating connections

- Using the Add Missing Constraints function to automatically add constraints

- Using Reset To Suggested Constraints to update constraints when you move constrained controls

- Using the Pin menu to set constraints with numeric precision

As a context for demonstrating the power of Auto Layout, you create a login dialog similar to those in many password-protected services. Let's begin!

© Matthew Knott 2016
M. Knott, *Beginning Xcode*, DOI 10.1007/978-1-4302-5005-0_6

Building an Authentication View

The authentication view you create in this chapter will be a familiar sight to users of Twitter, Facebook, or any of the countless other web service–based apps in the App Store. You build the project in this chapter in a way that teaches you how to lay out the elements of a view with Auto Layout and constraints; at the same time, you learn some of the finer points of configuring text fields that will be crucial when you develop your own applications.

Figure 6-1 shows LoginApp, the project you create in this chapter. Here you can see constraints in action. When the device rotates, the text field resizes and adapts to the new orientation. I also explain in depth the text field's attributes; you can see in the finished application that you set placeholder text on the e-mail address, but a number of hidden refinements contribute to a rich user experience.

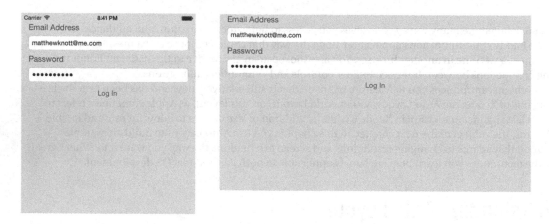

Figure 6-1. *The login page for the app resizes automatically when rotated*

You've done this several times already, so you should be pretty familiar with creating new projects by now. But to give you a heads-up, it's always important to read the setup steps, because in the next chapter you try something new:

1. Open Xcode and create a new project by going to File ➤ New ➤ New Project (⌘+Shift+N) or, alternatively, choosing Create A New Xcode Project from the Welcome screen (⌘+Shift+1).

2. Select Single View Application and click Next.

3. Name the project LoginApp, ensure that Devices is set to Universal, and leave the other options at their defaults, as shown in Figure 6-2. Click Next.

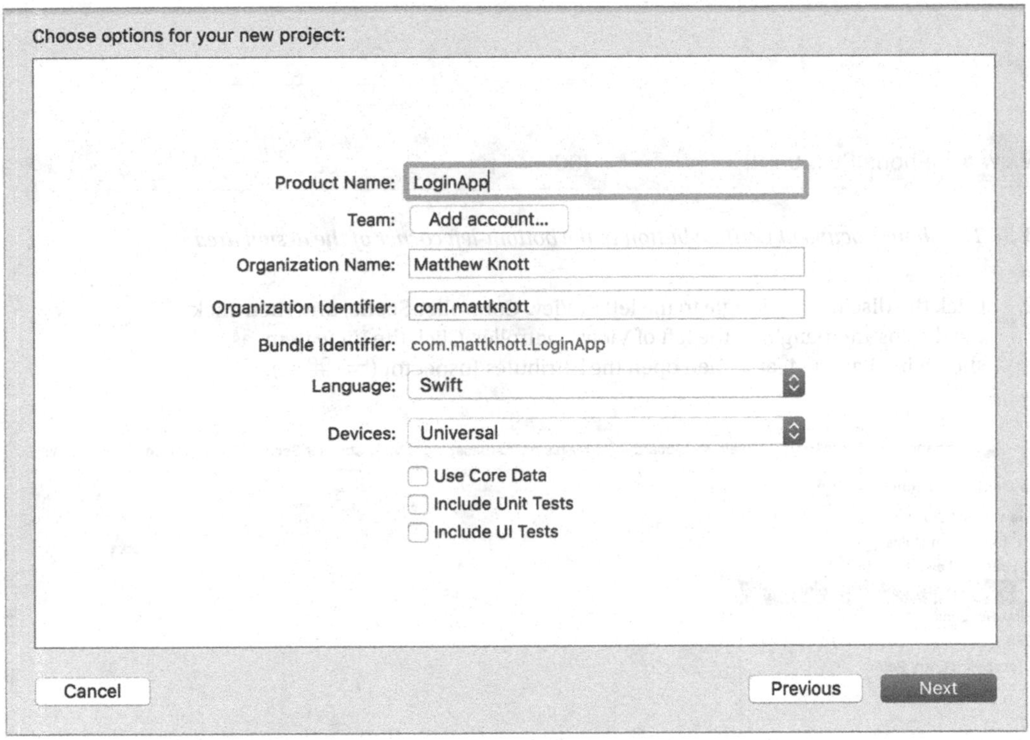

Choose options for your new project:

Product Name: LoginApp

Team: Add account...

Organization Name: Matthew Knott

Organization Identifier: com.mattknott

Bundle Identifier: com.mattknott.LoginApp

Language: Swift

Devices: Universal

☐ Use Core Data
☐ Include Unit Tests
☐ Include UI Tests

Cancel   Previous   Next

Figure 6-2. Setting up the project

4. Do not create a Git repository for this project. Select a location to save the project and click Create.

That's it! You're ready to start building your application. But before you begin building up your view, note that everything you do in this chapter relating to Auto Layout and setting constraints is done purely from Interface Builder—you don't write a single line of code. However, at the end of the chapter you look at using a little code just to add the finishing touches to your form. With that in mind, open Main.storyboard and get to work on the interface.

Design Considerations

If you haven't already, I hope that after reading this book you start writing your own applications using Xcode, whether for fun, to solve a problem you encounter, or maybe because of a gap you've spotted in the market. When you're a beginner, you'll make design decisions that, when you run the application, make you realize you've made an error of judgment about how you've arranged the layout.

The good thing is that most of the time there's a simple solution, and the whole thing becomes a valuable learning experience. Login dialogs are a potential banana skin when you're starting out: when you design a beautiful layout on a static view, it's easy to forget about the keyboard that in many cases slides up and covers the fields, making them inaccessible. To address this problem, make sure you position the text fields and labels in a way that ensures that the keyboard will not obscure them in any of the iOS screen formats. Follow these steps:

1. After you open Main.storyboard, open the Document Outline, if it isn't already visible, by clicking the button in the bottom-left corner of the design area that has a box with a solid line down the left inside it, as shown in Figure 6-3.

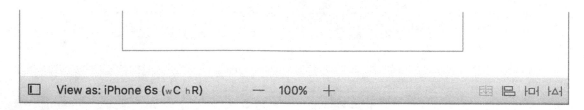

Figure 6-3. The Show Document Outline button in the bottom-left corner of the design area

2. Click the disclosure triangle to the left of View Controller Scene, and then click the disclosure triangle to the left of View Controller. Click the View item, as shown in Figure 6-4, and then open the Attributes Inspector (⌥+⌘+4).

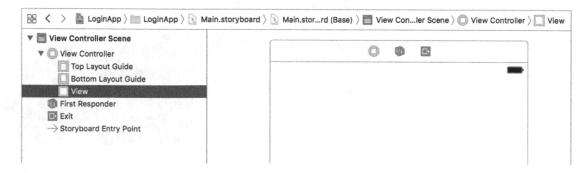

Figure 6-4. Selecting the view from the Document Outline

■ **Note**   The Document Outline bar can be extremely useful when you're working with a large number of controls in a view. You can alter the hierarchy of the elements to make one appear above or below another, or you can add controls to a scroll view instead of the main view. It's also useful for creating connections between view controllers that are physically far apart in the design area, to save zooming out many times.

---

3. To make this view more appealing, change the background color. I selected a pale green color for my view, but you can select whichever color you like. Click the Background drop-down list, and either select a preset color or click Other if you want to choose from the pallet or specify an RGB color. I used Red 206, Green 228, and Blue 188: You can use the same colors by using the color sliders from the color picker and setting RGB sliders from the drop-down menu, as shown in Figure 6-5.

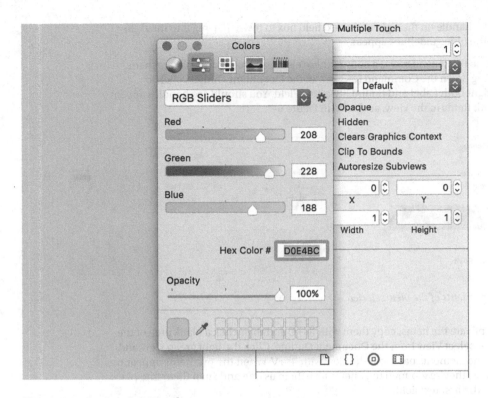

Figure 6-5. *Setting an RGB color*

4. You're ready to add controls to the view. Drag a label and a text field from the Object Library onto the view: put the label in the top-left corner, where it snaps to the blue guidelines, and snap the text field into place directly beneath it, as shown in Figure 6-6.

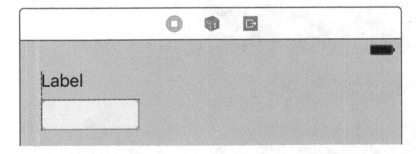

Figure 6-6. *The text field snaps into place below the label*

129

5. Use the handle on the right of the text field box to resize it. Drag it to the right until the blue guidelines appear.

6. Because the second row is a copy of these elements, you can duplicate them. Holding down the Command (⌘) key, in the Document Outline, click to highlight both Label and Round Style Text Field. You should see handles appear on both items in the view, as shown in Figure 6-7.

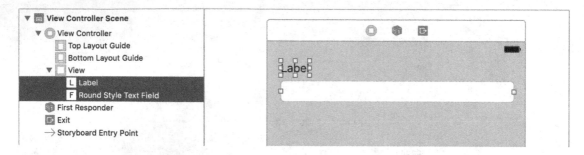

Figure 6-7. *Both elements of the view selected*

7. To duplicate the items, copy them with ⌘+C and then click a blank area of the view or select View from the Document Outline. Click the light green view and paste the elements back into the view with ⌘+V. When the two items appear on the view, they're grouped together: move them as one and snap them into place below the first text field.

8. Drag in a button from the Object Library and position it centrally in the view, a little below the last text field. If everything has gone to plan, your view should resemble that in Figure 6-8.

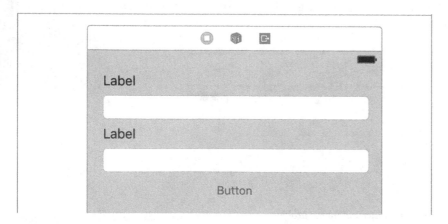

Figure 6-8. *The skeleton of the LoginApp*

9. With the elements all in place, you need to set the titles and text colors of the labels and the button. Select the first label, and from the Attributes Inspector, set Color to Dark Gray Color from the list of presets. Change Text from Label to Email Address. Your attributes for the first label should now resemble those shown in Figure 6-9.

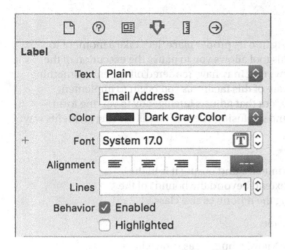

Figure 6-9. *The attributes of the first label*

10. Resize the label to the right just enough to display the full text.

11. Repeat the previous steps on the second label, but set its Title to Password. Then set the button's Title to Log In. When you resize the Password label, drag it to the same width as Email Address. When they're the same size, a blue guideline appears.

Before you go any further, let's run the application as it stands using the iPhone 6s Simulator. The Simulator opens, and the text fields appear perfectly. Rotate the Simulator by selecting Hardware ➤ Rotate Left from the menu bar or pressing ⌘+left arrow. Now the problem is that the fields are too short and aligned on the left rather than spanning the entire view; as you can see in Figure 6-10, the elements stay the same size but also stay in the same position.

Email Address

Password

Log In

Figure 6-10. *The misaligned view, badly needing some constraints*

131

The elements don't move because they have no behaviors applied to them, telling them what to do when the screen rotates or the view is bigger or smaller that the storyboard. In Xcode, these behaviors are called *constraints*.

Debugging Views in Xcode

Before you apply constraints to the view to snap everything into its proper place, let's take a moment to look at Xcode's incredibly useful view-debugging tool. This tool allows you to pause the execution of the application, analyze each control in the view, and see views that may have rendered offscreen—something the Simulator can't help you with. It's important to be aware of this facility as you begin to implement constraints, because in addition to giving you a flexible layout that adjusts intelligently to varying form factors and orientations, they can also have unforeseen and confusing effects, such as moving elements way offscreen when rotated.

Follow these steps:

1. Rerun the application using the iPhone SE Simulator and ensure it is in the standard portrait mode. The fields will now extend beyond the bounds of the view; this is because you designed them using the iPhone 6s size class.

2. Leave the app running and switch back to Xcode.

3. At the bottom of the screen is the icon for the View Debugger, as shown in Figure 6-11. Alternatively, choose Debug ➤ View Debugging ➤ Capture View Hierarchy.

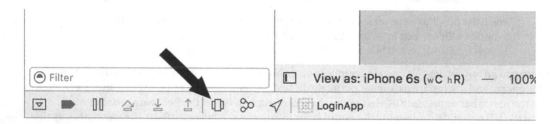

Figure 6-11. *Accessing the View Debugger*

When the View Debugger runs, the view resembles the view shown in the Simulator. Below the view is a series of icons, the first of which is labeled Show Clipped Content; click this and you will see the two fields extending outside the bounds of the view, as shown in Figure 6-12.

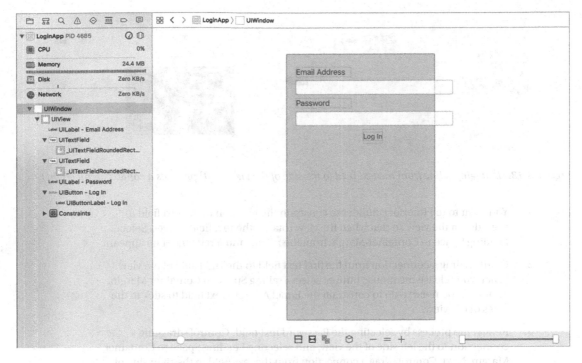

Figure 6-12. *Using the View Debugger in Xcode to view elements outside the bounds of the view*

The View Debugger gives you a huge array of tools to help track down stray elements, but for the most part, you can get everything you need from the basic view hierarchy. Stop the application in the Simulator, and you're returned to the storyboard so that you can begin adding constraints to the view.

Manually Adding Constraints

The first method I'll explain for adding constraints is the manual method, in which you use the familiar Control+click-and-drag technique to specify a constraining relationship between multiple elements. You should be used to holding the Control key while clicking and dragging—you've done it a number of times in previous chapters to create connections to actions and outlets.

■ **Note**   Even though the constraints are being added manually, they're still part of Auto Layout, which is a bit of a contradiction and can be confusing.

Here are the steps:

1. Let's add a number of manual constraints to the layout. Select the first text field, and then, while holding down the Control key, click the text field and drag a line to the left side of the view. When you release the mouse button, a contextual dialog appears, as shown in Figure 6-13.

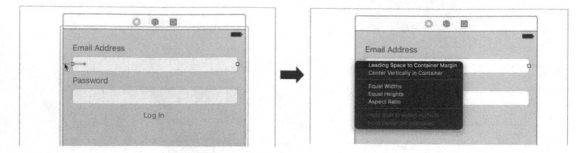

Figure 6-13. *Dragging a line from the text field to the side of the view (left) presents a context menu (right)*

2. You want to tell Interface Builder to constrain the position of the text field to the sides of the view so that when the view rotates, the text field resizes. Select Leading Space to Container Margin from the menu, and a red guideline appears.

3. Control+drag a connection from the first text field to the right side of the view. When you release the mouse button, select Trailing Space to Container Margin. That's all you need to do to constrain the Email Address text field to stick to the sides of the view.

4. Repeat the process by selecting the Password text field, Control+dragging a connection to the left side of the view, and selecting Leading Space to Container Margin. Next, Control+drag a connection from the text field to the right side of the text field and choose Trailing Space to Container Margin.

5. The constraint for the Log In button is slightly different. At this point you're probably happy with the vertical position and size of the button, but to keep it that way, you need to add some constraints. First, you want to constrain the button so that it stays centered horizontally. To do this, select the button and Control+drag a line directly beneath the button, as shown in Figure 6-14.

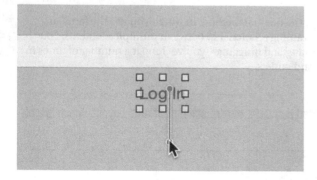

Figure 6-14. *Dragging a connection below the Log In button so that you can constrain it horizontally*

6. When you release the mouse button, the context menu opens again: this time select Center Horizontally In Container. A guideline appears from the top of the view to the bottom.

7. One final lot of constraints: Whatever happens, you want all of the controls to appear below each other as they do now. If you were to run the application, your text fields would bunch up at the top of the page. Start at the top and Control+drag a connection from the Email Address label to the top of the view. Choose Vertical Spacing to Top Layout Guide. This pins the label to the top of the view.

8. Next, Control+drag from the first text field to the Email Address label and choose Vertical Spacing. Repeat this for each element in order until you are dragging a connection from the button to the Password text field and selecting Vertical Spacing again.

That's it! With a few clicks, you've done enough to make your layout respond to changes in orientation and form factor. All that's left to do is to test it in the Simulator. Click the Run button (⌘+R). When the Simulator launches, the elements are aligned nicely in the narrow screen size. Rotate the interface by selecting Hardware ➤ Rotate Left from the menu bar or pressing ⌘+left arrow, as you did earlier. The elements should resize just as you want and exactly as previewed in Figure 6-1, with the button staying in the middle of the view and the text fields resizing because you've constrained them to be a fixed distance from the side of the view.

Even though you've added 12 constraints to this relatively sparse view and the layout is almost satisfactory, Xcode is still displaying a warning triangle. At the top of Xcode, in the Activity Viewer, is a yellow warning triangle. In the Document Outline, next to the View Controller Scene node, is a yellow arrow, as shown in Figure 6-15. Both of these warnings stem from missing constraints within the view.

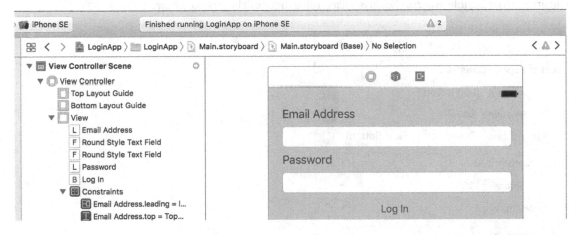

Figure 6-15. *Xcode displaying two separate warnings because of a lack of constraints*

Xcode wants you to specify a minimum number of constraints for every object in the view, including vertical and horizontal positioning, whether in relation to the view itself or to other elements in the view. When you move on to the next segment, you'll find out what constraints you need to add to satisfy Xcode's standards.

Before moving on, let's quickly look at the attributes of a constraint. Back in the Interface Builder, select the Log In button. Now, select one of the constraint guidelines by single-clicking it; it becomes highlighted, as shown in Figure 6-16. Alternatively, with the View item inspected in the Document Outline, you can expand Constraints and select the constraint that starts Log In.top in the list, as shown in Figure 6-16.

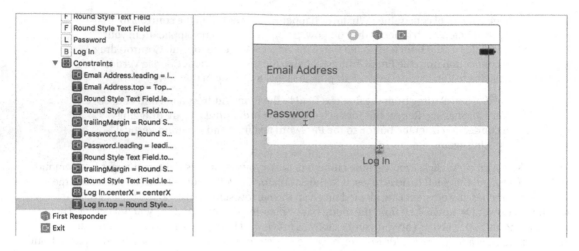

Figure 6-16. *Selecting the constraint for the button's vertical spacing*

If you look at the Attributes Inspector for a moment, as shown in Figure 6-17, you see a variety of ways to fine-tune how a constraint works. First, look at the Relation attribute, which should currently be set to Equal. You can change it to Less Than Or Equal To or More Than Or Equal To. These two options allow the constraint to be flexible, whereas Equal is a fixed value that can't be deviated from.

Figure 6-17. *The attributes of the constraint*

The Constant attribute contains the numerical value assigned to the constraint. Currently, if you positioned your button in the same place as mine, the value is 8. Putting these attributes into plain English, this means the text field will stay a distance *equal to 8* points from the Password text field; increasing or decreasing this value has an impact on the spacing when the application runs. You learn more about customizing these values as the chapter and the book progress. For now; let's move on to look at some other aspects of Auto Layout and constraints.

Specifying Constraints with the Align Menu

The Control+drag method of specifying constraints is best used for precise adjustments and complex layouts. Now, let's look at setting constraints using the Align menu and then the Pin menu. The Align menu is used to specify how controls align to each other and the wider view. Because the constraint you applied to the button is an alignment constraint, you can use the Align menu to constrain it the same way you did earlier with the Control+drag method. The Align button is one of several buttons available at the bottom of Interface Builder. It's the second button in the cluster of buttons at lower right, and it resembles a small box on top of a larger one. Refer back to Chapter 4 if you need to reacquaint yourself with these buttons.

Before you use either the Align menu or the Pin menu, you need to remove the constraints you've applied to your controls. Select the view controller, either from the Document Outline or by clicking a green portion of the view, and then click the Resolve Auto Layout Issues button. Choose Clear Constraints under the All Views In View Controller heading, as shown in Figure 6-18, to remove all the constraints set in this view controller.

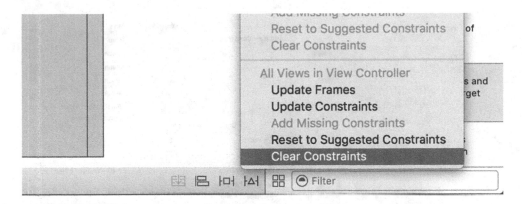

Figure 6-18. *Selecting Clear Constraints from the Resolve Auto Layout Issues menu*

The constraints you applied earlier are removed, and the view is ready for you to reapply them using the Align and Pin menus. First, select just the Log In button, and then click the Align button. In the menu that appears, select the check box next to Horizontal Center In Container, as shown in Figure 6-19.

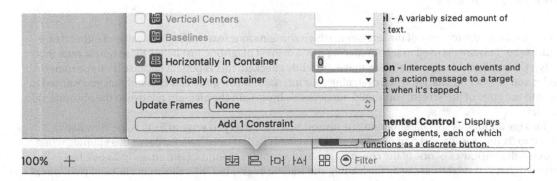

Figure 6-19. *Adding a horizontal alignment constraint using the Align menu*

Clicking the button currently showing Add 1 Constraint, which applies the constraint to the button, exactly the same as when you used the Control+drag method, but without the need to be precise with your mouse movements.

Specifying Constraints with the Pin Menu

So far, you've learned how to center the Log In button using the Align menu. Now it's time to constrain the text fields so that their leading and trailing edges stay fixed to the side of the view's margin at all times. This technique is known as *pinning*, because you're fixing a positional attribute of the control. Therefore, it makes sense to reapply the constraints to the text fields by using the Pin menu. The Pin menu is the second button in the cluster of buttons at lower right in the Interface Builder design area; it sits next to the Align button.

What's great about the Pin menu is that you can apply constraints to both text fields in a single action. Click the Email Address text field to select it, and then hold the ⌘ key and click the Password text field to select it too. Click the Pin button, and a menu appears, as shown in Figure 6-20.

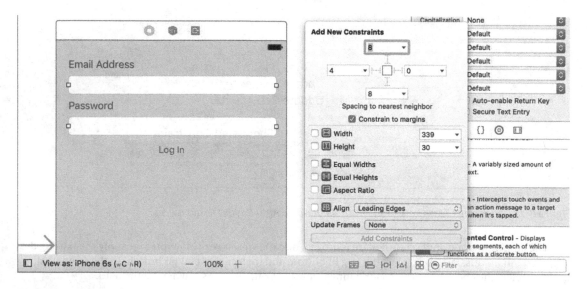

Figure 6-20. *The Pin menu*

Let's focus on the top area of the Pin menu, which contains four text fields with a value of either 8 or 0 in Figure 6-20. This area is used to set the spacing to the nearest neighbor. Just below these boxes, note that there is a Constrain to Margins check box that is currently checked; this is perfect because it's important to consider and respect the margin when designing your interface. If you added an element that you wanted to be fixed to the edge of the screen, you would uncheck this box to pin the element relative to the absolute side of the view.

Thinking about this specific situation, the nearest neighbor that you want to fix to is the view itself; you want to fix the leading and trailing edges of the text fields to that neighbor. Earlier in this chapter, when I discussed the attributes of one of the constraints, it had a value of 8 points. Conveniently, Xcode has anticipated that you might want to fix the leading and trailing edges; but the value in the left and right boxes that control the leading- and trailing-edge constraints is 0. Can that be right? Absolutely: it's 0 because the elements are currently positioned against the left and right margins. The Constrain To Margins check box is selected, so all you need to do here is tell Xcode that you want to apply the constraints.

At this point, it's easy to become confused. The Add Constraints button is grayed out, so how do you set the constraints? Luckily, the answer is easy. At the center of the four text fields in the Pin menu is a square shape with red I-bars going to each of the text fields; click the left and right I-bars and they become bright red. Also notice that the button at the bottom of the Pin menu now says Add 4 Constraints, as shown in Figure 6-21.

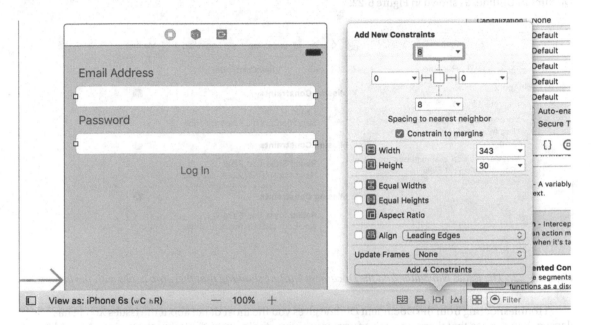

Figure 6-21. Specifying the Pin constraints for the text fields. Note the emphasized left and right I-bars.

Click the Add 4 Constraints button to apply the constraints to your text fields. This is the quickest and most efficient way to add the same set of constraints to a number of controls—and sometimes, being a great developer is as much about knowing the shortcuts in your development environment as it is about knowing the code.

You now know two different ways to use Xcode to manage your layout with constraints. Although next I explain how to automatically set constraints, there will always be a need to override or add constraints manually; the skills you've learned here will be extremely useful when building your own applications.

Automatically Adding Constraints

So far in this chapter, the techniques you've used can definitely be classified as manual, although the process certainly hasn't been complex. Apple has gone to a lot of effort to make managing layouts even easier by providing two great methods for automatically setting constraints. It's not perfect, but it's the quickest way to put the bulk of your constraints in place with the click of a button.

In the previous section, you may have noticed that Xcode isn't happy with the constraints you applied manually in this application, even though the application functions exactly as required. This is because Xcode feels it doesn't have all the information it requires to position the design elements and is making some decisions itself. It would be far happier if you were making all the decisions.

At first, the logic of the situation can be hard to comprehend. Before you added the constraints, there were no warnings, but now that there are five *working* constraints in place, Xcode isn't happy. Fortunately, there are two ways you can find out more about why Xcode is upset, as I indicated back in Figure 6-15: the warning triangle in the Activity Viewer and the red arrow in the Document Outline. Click both now. The Issues Navigator appears in place of the Project Navigator, and a list of all the Auto Layout issues replaces the Document Outline, as shown in Figure 6-22.

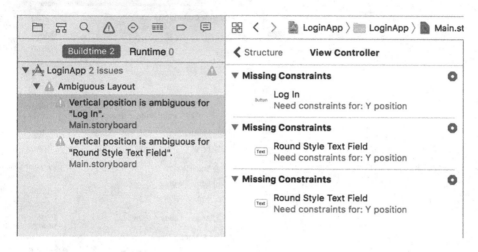

Figure 6-22. *The Issues Navigator and the Document Outline showing that there are issues with the layout*

Troubleshooting from the Document Outline gives you the most detail about the issues Xcode has flagged. You can see that there are a mix of warnings about ambiguity and missing constraints. As you know from previous chapters, Xcode makes it easy to add missing constraints.

Adding Missing Constraints

The Constraint Warning Details view accessed from the Document Outline allows you to automatically resolve layout issues one by one. But in many cases, you just want to let Xcode fix them for you. Let's try both methods.

In the Constraint Warning Details view, click the red dot next to the first constraint warning. As shown in Figure 6-23, you can easily fix the constraint issue with a single click of the Add Missing Constraints button.

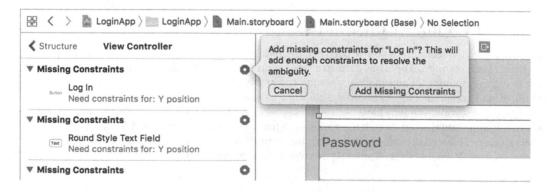

Figure 6-23. *Fixing individual issues with the Constraint Warning Details view*

Ironically, sometimes when you fix this issue this way, the number of issues can go up before it goes down, other times fixing one issue can fix all of them. Keep repeating this step until all the issues are gone. That wasn't too hard, right? In the Document Outline, click the Structure button in the top-left corner to return to the standard Document Outline view. Then expand the Constraints item: Xcode has created a number of constraints, as shown in Figure 6-24, where I have highlighted each constraint so that its position on the view is shown. Finally, run the application just to make sure everything is in place.

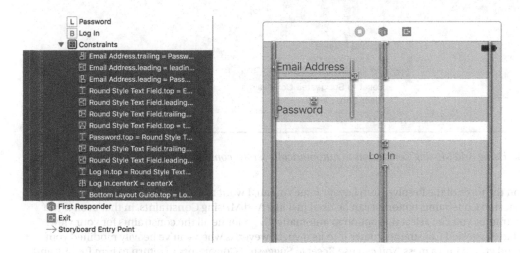

Figure 6-24. *Examining the constraints that Xcode has created*

Back in Interface Builder, note that the previously red guidelines have become blue! The red and orange guidelines are Xcode's way of telling you that there are missing constraints for an object.

Just as you've achieved a perfect set of constraints, you are going to wipe the slate clean and reset all of them so you try fully automated constraint setting. To do this, select View Controller from the Document Outline; then click the Resolve Auto Layout Issues button and choose Clear Constraints under the All Views in View Controller heading to again remove all the constraints that were set in this view controller.

You're back to a clean slate as far as constraints are concerned. Now, reselect the Resolve Auto Layout Issues button and click Add Missing Constraints under the All Views in View Controller heading, as shown in Figure 6-25. This makes Xcode look at every element in the view controller and add the constraints it feels are needed to make the layout adjust to a change in the shape of the view, such as rotating the device or using a different form factor. Because this is a universal app with size classes enabled, the constraints need to be thoroughly tested and customized so your app can be deployed to any iOS device running iOS 10.

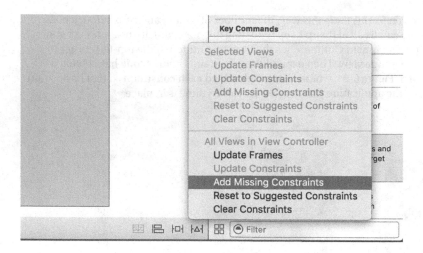

Figure 6-25. *Using Add Missing Constraints to automatically set the constraints for the view*

While on the topic of the Resolve Auto Layout Issues menu, I want to quickly draw your attention to the Reset to Suggested Constraints option. It can be used just like Add Missing Constraints, in that even if you have no constraints, you can select this option to automatically generate all the constraints for your view. Where Reset to Suggested Constraints comes into its own, however, is when you've heavily modified your constraints and gotten into a mess. You can use Reset to Suggested Constraints to return to firm footing and restart the modification process, being more careful to test as you go and ensuring that you use the Preview facility (which I cover shortly).

Updating Constraints

In a short space of time, you've increased your knowledge and now know a number of ways to add constraints to a layout. Adding constraints is well and good, but layouts change, and constraints need updating. There are two ways to do this, depending on the severity of your changes.

In Interface Builder, move the Log In button farther from the Password text field; this causes the blue guideline to turn orange, as shown in Figure 6-26. The constraint is orange because in this example, it was originally set to pin the button 8 points below the Password text field. You moved the button farther from the text field, so the constraint is no longer correct. Interface Builder shows that in this instance, it has moved 49 points farther from the text field, as indicated by the +49 value attached to the now-invalid constraint.

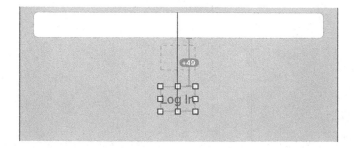

Figure 6-26. *An invalid constraint highlighted in Interface Builder, showing that the constraint is off by 49 points*

These types of minor interface changes happen all the time when you're tweaking your layout to be pixel perfect, and fortunately they're very easy to fix. With the Log In button selected, go back to the Resolve Auto Layout Issues button. This time, select Update Constraints. The constraint guideline turns back to blue, happy that it is now satisfying the attributes of the constraint.

If you're in a situation where you've fine-tuned a number of elements in your layout and want to keep the constraints but with the updated values, go back to your best friend when using Auto Layout: the Resolve Auto Layout Issues button. Select Update Constants under the All Views in View Controller heading, which, as it implies, updates all the altered constraints in your view controller to their correct values.

That's it for the principles of Auto Layout in this chapter. You've learned a lot about how to apply constraints, how to fix issues with your layout, and a lot more. Now let's change pace a little and examine how to preview a layout in Xcode, using size classes to change constraints depending on the form factor, and customizing text fields to create a great user experience.

Previewing Your Layout

As you've gone through this book, you've created a number of small projects that show off particular features of Xcode or iOS. But in the real world, you're potentially creating massive applications, and you may need to go through complex processes to produce a specific layout that you want to test for potential issues in real time without having to rely on the Simulator and repetitively go through the application to get to the view you're working on each time. And when you're facing a tight deadline, you need to get things done as quickly as possible. This is where previewing can come in handy.

The Preview tool provides you with a customizable preview of how the view will look at runtime. This can be configured to show multiple devices and orientations simultaneously.

1. Enable the Assistant Editor in Xcode by clicking the overlapping circles icon.

2. Click Automatic on the jump bar, and then mouse over Preview to expose Main. storyboard (Preview), as shown in Figure 6-27.

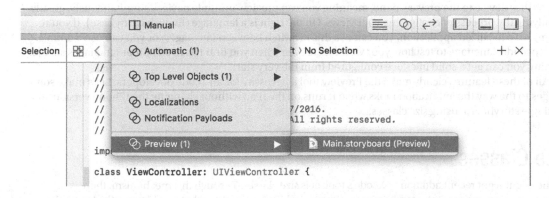

Figure 6-27. Accessing the Preview menu

You may have to resize your windows slightly to accommodate both panes. The result is that you have a preview of your layout on a specific device—in this case, an iPhone 6s, as shown in Figure 6-28.

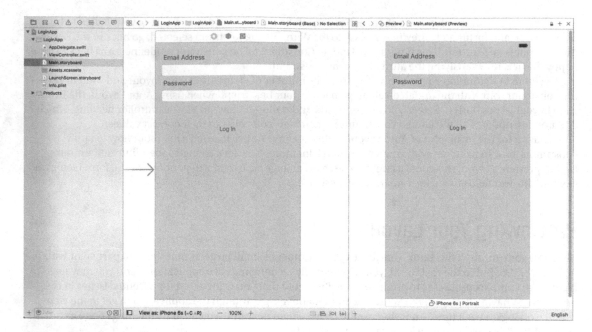

Figure 6-28. *Xcode with the Preview tool enabled*

You can zoom out the preview by using the standard pinch gesture on a multi-touch device or by double-clicking a white area of the Preview background to toggle zoom levels. You can't make any changes to the application in the Preview tool, but anything you change in the Interface Builder is immediately reflected here.

In the bottom corners of preview are two buttons. On the left is a plus symbol: clicking it allows you to add another device to the preview pane, meaning you can preview multiple devices simultaneously, greatly simplifying the process of configuring your views. On the right is a language (English in my case). If you're working on a localized application, you can use this to switch between languages; or you can use a double-length pseudo-language to test how your view reacts even when you don't have any other languages set up, meaning you can get a solid interface configured from the very start.

All of these features clearly make the Preview tool a necessity for all Xcode developers. Let's make some changes to the way the application looks when it runs on the iPad without changing the iPhone version, all in a single storyboard, using size classes.

Size Classes

Another significant recent addition to Xcode's toolset is size classes. Through this mechanism, there is no longer a need to have separate storyboards for iPhone and iPad, something that would typically double the amount of development required for a universal app. In Xcode 8, Apple have moved away from the square layout that resembled no device they make, and gone back to basing the design area on an actual device shape.

Although using size classes isn't mandatory, they're certainly preferable to maintaining two storyboards, although there are instances when you would want to do this such as when the components of the interface are vastly different from one device to the other. One of the first apps I wrote was universal, but the iPhone portion was based around a tab bar controller, whereas the iPad portion adopted a very different dashboard-style approach. This significant difference in styles couldn't have been achieved with size classes, so it's important to remember that although they've become the standard for new iOS applications since Xcode 6, they aren't your only option.

At the bottom of the design area, notice that it says a device name, in my case iPhone 6s, and then wC and hR, as shown in Figure 6-29. The C stands for Compact, and the R for Regular.

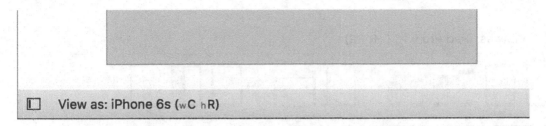

Figure 6-29. *Xcode indicates that the interface being built is for iPhone 6s with compact width and regular height*

To understand a bit better what this means, let's use the Preview tool you just discovered to show what the interface will look like on an iPad as well as an iPhone. If you've closed the preview, reopen it as instructed in the previous section. Then click the + symbol in the bottom-left corner, and select iPad Pro 9.7" | Full Screen. An iPad appears alongside the iPhone. Remember to zoom out to see both devices, as shown in Figure 6-30.

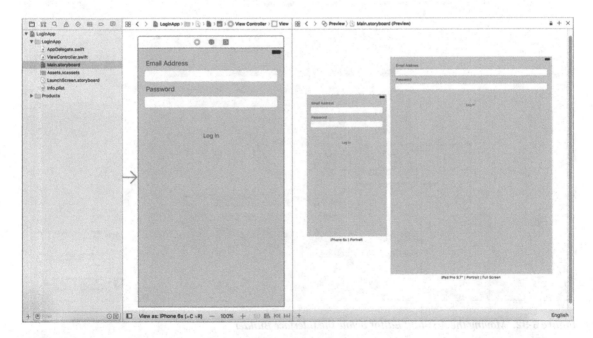

Figure 6-30. *The Preview tool showing an iPhone and an iPad side by side*

Although there is nothing technically wrong with the way the text fields span the view, they're realistically far too big and will add to the impression that the user is running a scaled-up iPhone app, which isn't desirable. To demonstrate the power of size classes, let's alter the layout for iPad by centering the Email Address and Password fields and making them a fixed width.

Click the current device name at the bottom of the design area—mine shows iPhone 6s but yours may be something else—then select the 9.7" iPad, as shown in Figure 6-31. Note that here you can change view orientation from portrait to landscape and can select the split screen view available on the iPad Pro.

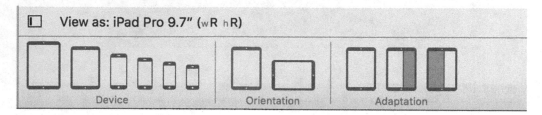

Figure 6-31. *Selecting Regular Width as a size class to develop the iPad layout*

This is where things can get fiddly because of the width of the view and the number of panes. For now, let's experiment with moving the Assistant Editor's location. Go to View ➤ Assistant Editor ➤ Assistant Editors On Bottom. Immediately the preview shifts below the Interface Builder, making it easier to work on this particular iPad layout, as you can see in Figure 6-32.

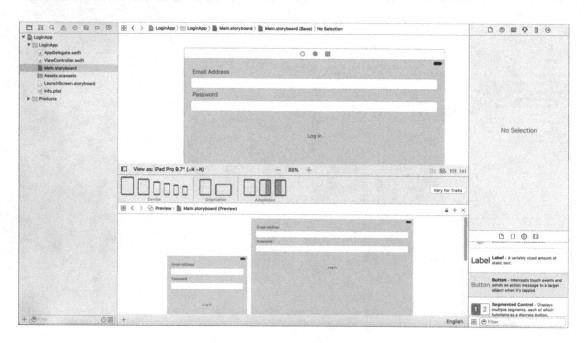

Figure 6-32. *Moving the Assistant Editor below the Interface Builder*

You've probably heard the phrase "It's going to get worse before it gets better," well, that's a good analogy for what you're about to do. Through these next steps, your layout will appear to fall apart before it's finally drawn together in the finished product:

1. Open the Document Outline and expand the Constraints portion for the view. Resize it so that you can see the full text of the constraint names.

2. To achieve the desired effect, you are going to take all of the constraints that are unique to the iPhone view (compact width and regular height) and isolate them so that they don't interfere with your iPad specific constraints. Select the seven constraints that have either `.trailing` = or `.leading` = in them, as shown in Figure 6-33.

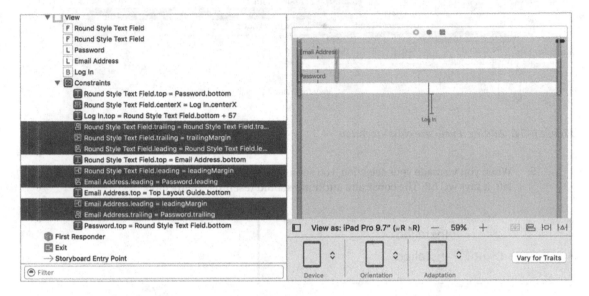

Figure 6-33. *Selecting the iPhone-specific constraints*

3. Open the Attributes Inspector. Notice that the last item in the Attributes Inspector for a constraint is the Installed attribute—uncheck it now. Your view will collapse, but don't worry.

■ **Note**   To left of this attribute is a + symbol. This tiny + symbol appears next to a number of attributes and settings in the different inspectors; it's used when you want to add an exception or customization for a specific size class.

---

4. Click the + symbol next to the Installed attribute and choose Compact Width ➤ Regular Height ➤ Any Gamut, as shown in Figure 6-34.

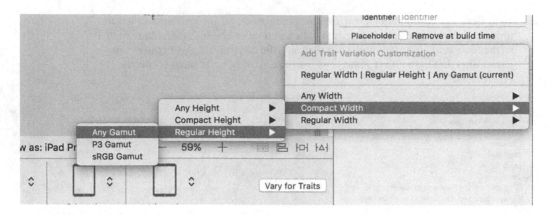

Figure 6-34. *Adding a new size class exception*

5. When you've made your selection, you see a second Installed attribute: to the left, it says wC hR. The constraint attributes should resemble Figure 6-35.

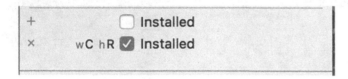

Figure 6-35. *Restricting the constraints for the iPhone portrait size class*

6. Back in the Document Outline or on the view itself, hold down the ⌘ key and click the two labels and the two text fields so they're highlighted as shown in Figure 6-36.

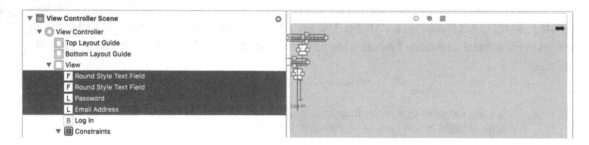

Figure 6-36. *Selecting the labels and text fields in the view*

7. Click the Pin button. Check the Width box and set the value to 400, as shown in Figure 6-37. This makes life easier by locking all four elements to the same width.

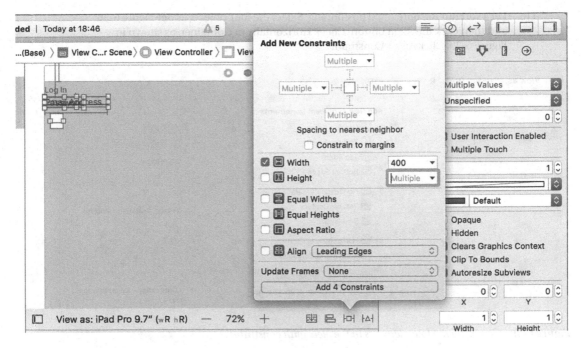

Figure 6-37. *Fixing the width of the labels and text fields to 400 points*

8. Click the Add 4 Constraints button. Xcode now displays a number of red warnings; let's fix these.

9. Now you need to make four changes similar to the beginning of this exercise where you will isolate the fixed width to only the iPad layouts. Start by expanding Round Style Text Field in the Document Outline and then, under constraints, select width = 400.

10. In the Attributes Inspector, click the + symbol next to installed, but this time select Regular Width | Regular Height | Any Gamut (current) and then uncheck the first Installed so that your view matches Figure 6-38. Repeat this step for the three remaining elements in the Document Outline that you fixed to 400.

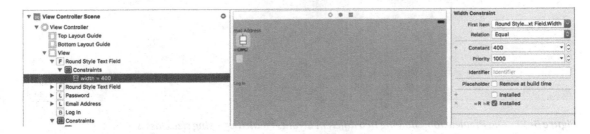

Figure 6-38. *Isolating the width constraint to only the iPad size class*

149

11. Let's sort out the horizontal positioning. Select the four objects as per Figure 6-36 and then click the Align button. Check Horizontally in Container, as shown in Figure 6-39. Click Add 4 Constraints.

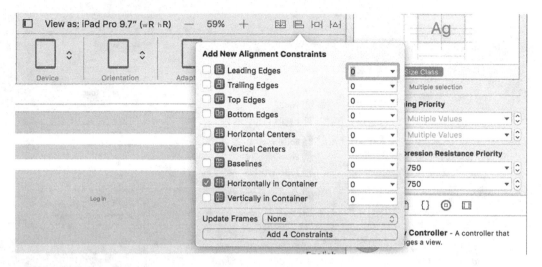

Figure 6-39. *Centering the four elements in the view with constraints*

12. You may have a warning about the object looking different at runtime. Click Resolve Auto Layout Issues and choose Update Frames under All Views In View Controller. This will ensure your design area matches the constraints that have been applied.

13. If everything has worked as planned, your layout for the iPad should snap into place, as shown in Figure 6-40.

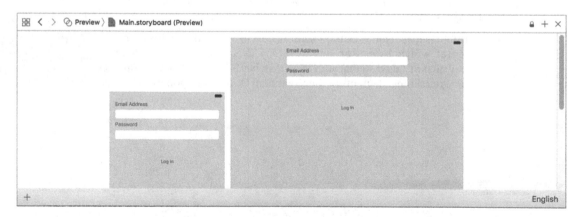

Figure 6-40. *The Preview tool showing two different layouts created by using size classes*

14. Change to the iPad Air Simulator and run the application. Feel free to rotate the virtual device and see how the layout stays true to your constraints, regardless of the orientation. What's more, if you change the size class back to an iPhone 6s, the old layout and constraints are exactly where you left them.

Finishing Touches

You're getting close to the end of this chapter. With the text fields you've added to your view, you have an opportunity to look at how you can use the Interface Builder to create a tailored experience that makes it easy for users to fill out this form.

Customizing Text Fields

Even though you only have a couple of text fields in the view, you can apply a wealth of customizations to make the form fit the purpose. You can also add some neat features so that your users can fly through it in an intuitive manner.

Hiding Passwords

How seriously you take security in your application can make or break it on the App Store, so you need to make sure the basic features a user expects to see in a password-protected application are in place. Therefore, the first customization concerns how to set the Password text field to behave like a typical password field by obscuring the user's password as they type it, which requires absolutely no code at all:

1. Close the Assistant Editor by clicking Standard Editor.

2. Select the Password text field in the Interface Builder and then open the Attributes Inspector.

3. Scroll down the list of attributes until you see the Secure Text Entry check box; select it, as shown in Figure 6-41.

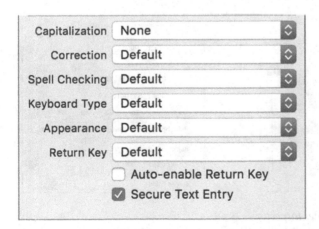

Figure 6-41. Making the Password text field secure

4. Run the application in the Simulator and try typing in the Password field. You see that, as in other applications, the password is obscured as you type it.

5. Another behavior you may want to add to the Password field is automatic clearing of the contents when you tap in the field. This is useful when you can't see what you've typed. Go back to the Interface Builder, and back to the Password field's Attributes Inspector. The Clear Button attribute section has a Clears When Editing Begins check box; select it and change the drop-down option above it from Never Appears to Appears While Editing.

6. Rerun your application in the Simulator. Type in a password, click the Email Address text field, and then click back into the Password field. The contents should be cleared, ready for you to have another go at remembering the password. You can also clear the field while editing.

Optimizing a Text Field for E-Mail Addresses

You have configured the Password field to fit with your users' expectations, but what can you do to make the Email Address field easier to use? Quite a bit, as it happens. Getting the user interface right can go a long way toward making your application a hit on the App Store. These may seem like small changes, but in an oversaturated market, having an immaculate, intuitive interface can make a big difference:

1. Select the Email Address text field and open the Attributes Inspector.

2. The first thing you want to do is emphasize that users should type an e-mail address. You do this by adding placeholder text to guide them. In the Placeholder text field, I typed **E.g. matthewknott@me.com**, but you can type whatever you want.

3. The placeholder text you type is immediately reflected in the text field, as shown in Figure 6-42.

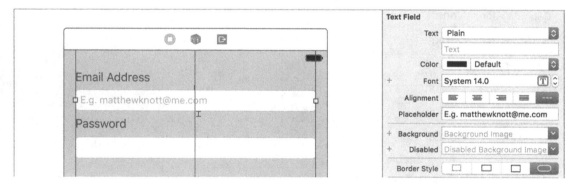

Figure 6-42. *Setting placeholder text in the Attributes Inspector*

4. Think back on how you cleared the Password field when editing. You should make it easier for users to clear the Email Address field, but it shouldn't be the default action. Go to the Clear Button section in Attributes Inspector and change the drop-down option from Never Appears to Appears While Editing. With this option set, the user will be given the opportunity to clear the field whenever they're focused on it.

5. Change the Simulator back to iPhone 6s and run your application in the Simulator. Type something in the Email Address field and as shown in Figure 6-43, the Clear button (an X inside a circle) appears nicely, which is great. What's not so great is that it's suggesting I've misspelled my e-mail address, which is annoying.

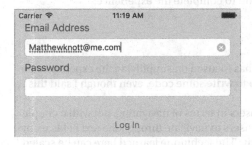

Figure 6-43. *The Clear button appears when the user edits the e-mail address. But, annoyingly, it's reporting spelling errors.*

6. Back in the Attributes Inspector, find the Correction attribute, and select No from the list of options.

7. Below that, change Spell Checking to No as well. Now iOS will ignore the spelling of e-mail addresses.

8. Another common feature that users expect and value when entering an e-mail address is having the keyboard presented in a way that gives priority to common keys such as @ and .com. iOS has a number of options for configuring the keyboard, and all are available from the Keyboard attribute, found directly below the Spell Checking attribute. Figure 6-44 shows the great variety of context-specific keyboard options Apple provides by default, which in turn let you, the developer, make life that much easier for your users. In this case, choose E-Mail Address from the list.

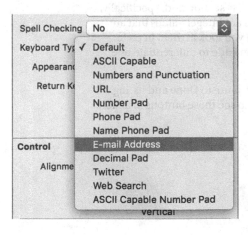

Figure 6-44. *Choosing the E-mail Address keyboard option from a very rich list of context-specific keyboard options*

9. Rerun the application in the Simulator and tap into the Email Address field. The keyboard shown to the user makes it easier to quickly type an e-mail address without having to go hunting for the @ symbol or type the top-level domain.

You've made a number of small but significant tweaks to your interface to make it easier and more intuitive to use, but there is just one more feature you need to add to complete the experience.

Navigating Forms

A lot of what you've looked at regarding customizing text fields has focused on simplifying the experience for the users. This final example is no exception, but it requires you to write some code, even though I said this was a code-free chapter. I lied (sorry!).

The two text fields don't present much of a burden to the users in terms of navigating, but with a couple of lines of code, you can perfect the experience by allowing the users to navigate through the text fields using the keyboard, thus making it easier to complete the fields quickly. The technique learned here can be scaled up to larger forms, where your users will really appreciate it:

1. Open the Assistant Editor and ensure that the `ViewController.swift` file is loaded. If you want the Assistant Editor located back on the right, go to View ➤ Assistant Editor ➤ Assistant Editors On Right.

2. Control+drag a connection from the Email Address text field to just below the class declaration and create an outlet named `usernameField`.

3. Do the same for the Password text field and name this outlet `passwordField`.

4. Switch back to the Standard Editor. You need to make some changes to the interface before moving on to the implementation file.

5. When the user selects the Email Address field, you want them to see a Next button instead of the Return button so that they can tap it to move to the Password field. To set this, select the Email Address text field, and, in the Attributes Inspector, look for the Return Key attribute. Select Next from the list of options.

6. Scroll down the list of attributes until you find the View section and, specifically, the Tag attribute. Enter 1 as the attribute value. Tags are integer values that are used to identify different elements in a layout when you look at them in code. If you have 30 text fields in your view, the best way in code to differentiate one `UITextField` from another is to examine its tag.

7. Select the Password field;; change its Return Key attribute to Done and its Tag attribute to 2. Run the application in the Simulator to see these buttons in action, as shown in Figure 6-45.

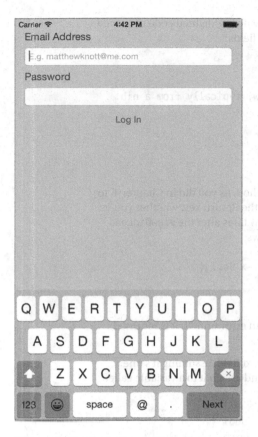

Figure 6-45. *The keyboard changes depending on which field is selected*

8. The buttons look good but don't currently do anything. Open `ViewController.swift` from the Project Navigator, where you add the functionality needed to finish this application.

9. Add the `UITextFieldDelegate` protocol to the class by adding the highlighted code to the class declaration:

```
import UIKit

class ViewController: UIViewController, UITextFieldDelegate {

    @IBOutlet weak var usernameField: UITextField!
    @IBOutlet weak var passwordField: UITextField!
```

10. Go to the viewDidLoad method and add the following highlighted code to specify that the view controller is the delegate for the text fields:

```
override func viewDidLoad() {
    super.viewDidLoad()
    // Do any additional setup after loading the view, typically from a nib.
    usernameField.delegate = self
    passwordField.delegate = self


}
```

11. You need to add the textFieldShouldReturn method, as you did in Chapter 4, to understand what happens when the user presses the Return key, whether you've configured it to say Next or Done. Drop down a few lines after the viewDidLoad method and type the stub for the method as follows:

```
func textFieldShouldReturn(_ textField: UITextField) -> Bool {

}
```

This method returns a Boolean value and shows an error until that is returned; for now, ignore it.

12. You want the method to work out the tag for the next field, assuming it's one more than the current textField.tag property, and assign it to a variable called nextTag for analysis. Add this highlighted code:

```
func textFieldShouldReturn(textField: UITextField) -> Bool {
    let nextTag = textField.tag + 1 as Int
}
```

13. You need to see if there is an element in the view with a tag that matches the nextTag integer value so that you can either move to the Password field or dismiss the keyboard. You do this by creating an instance of the UIResponder class and then set it by going to the current text field's parent view and searching based on the tag. Do that by adding this line of code to your method:

```
func textFieldShouldReturn(textField: UITextField) -> Bool {
    let nextTag = textField.tag + 1 as Int
    let nextField : UIResponder? = textField.superview?.viewWithTag(nextTag)
}
```

14. The following if else statement determines the course of action based on whether the nextField object was found:

```
func textFieldShouldReturn(textField: UITextField) -> Bool {
    let nextTag = textField.tag + 1 as Int
    let nextField : UIResponder? = textField.superview?.viewWithTag(nextTag)
```

```
    if let field : UIResponder = nextField {

    }
    else
    {

    }
}
```

15. If the current field is the Email Address field, the code in the first set of braces is executed. In this case, you want to focus the cursor in the password field so that the users can type their passwords. To do this, make that field the first responder by adding the following highlighted code:

```
func textFieldShouldReturn(textField: UITextField) -> Bool {
    let nextTag = textField.tag + 1 as Int
    let nextField : UIResponder? = textField.superview?.viewWithTag(nextTag)

    if let field : UIResponder = nextField {
        field.becomeFirstResponder()
    }
    else
    {

    }
}
```

16. The else code executes if the current field is the Password field. In many cases you would execute your login routine at this stage, but because you don't have one, let's just dismiss the keyboard by resigning the first-responder state. After the if else statement, you need to return a Boolean value indicating whether the use of the Return key in iOS should insert a line break, which it should not. Type the following highlighted code to complete the method:

```
func textFieldShouldReturn(textField: UITextField) -> Bool {
    let nextTag = textField.tag + 1 as Int
    let nextField : UIResponder? = textField.superview?.viewWithTag(nextTag)

    if let field : UIResponder = nextField {
        field.becomeFirstResponder()
    }
    else
    {
        textField.resignFirstResponder()
    }

    return false
}
```

Run your application in the Simulator. You should be able to tap into the Email Address field and navigate to the Password field using the Next button; then use the Done button to dismiss the keyboard. The great thing is that you can use the same `textFieldShouldReturn` method whether you have two text fields or 30, as long as you make sure each field has a unique tag value that is one more than its predecessor.

Summary

Whatever your feelings were about constraints, Auto Layout and size classes before this chapter, I hope that now you feel at least a bit more confident about how to manipulate them with Xcode. Specifically in this chapter, you did the following:

- Learned about how Auto Layout has changed in Xcode 8

- Manually added constraints with the Control+drag method as well as with the Align and Pin menus

- Learned how to add missing constraints and much more with the Resolve Auto Layout Issues menu

- Added a layer of polish to your text fields with the Secure and Placeholder attributes

- Used a small piece of code to take control of how the Return key works

You've covered a lot this chapter, but hopefully it's all contributing to an application you're working on or giving you the confidence to begin writing that application you've been thinking about for months.

The next chapter focuses on storyboards: the visual approach to building applications through Xcode that lets you create large portions of your application without the need to write a single line of code.

PART II

Diving Deeper

CHAPTER 7

▬ ▬ ▬

Storyboards

Chapter 6 for the most part took a break from writing code to look in detail at Auto Layout, Xcode's system for arranging layouts and specifying how they react to changes in form factor or orientation. It also explained how to craft a tailor-made user experience by customizing keyboards and text fields.

You're now in the second part of this book, "Diving Deeper," and you'll see that demonstrated from the outset as you get into the nitty-gritty of building a complex multi-view application using storyboards. First I present the background of storyboards and the concepts behind them, and then you see the key feature of Xcode storyboards—the segue—and how to make the most of segues when rapidly creating applications.

So far in this book, in every chapter but Chapter 1 you've created an application as a context for your journey through Xcode. The only difference with this chapter's project is that you're building it over this *and* the next chapter. The reason is that you're creating a functional Twitter client for iPad. You begin by laying out and connecting the views using storyboard techniques, but the client is built around customized table views (the subject of Chapter 8). There's a lot to cover, and I rely heavily on two Apple-provided frameworks that take a lot of the pain out of communicating and authenticating with Twitter: the Accounts and Social frameworks.

Although this project won't have all the bells and whistles you might expect from a full Twitter client, you can still choose from multiple accounts, see a full Twitter feed, and compose and post tweets. To get a flavor of what this application will look like, see Figure 7-1.

Figure 7-1. *Some of the key screens in SocialApp, your functional Twitter client*

© Matthew Knott 2016
M. Knott, *Beginning Xcode*, DOI 10.1007/978-1-4302-5005-0_7

A Brief History of Storyboards

Apple introduced the storyboard approach to building iOS apps with iOS 5. Although it was initially seen as a novelty, it has grown to where it is now: the preferred system for application development used with the majority of Xcode's iOS templates.

Storyboards aren't a new concept; they have been used by developers for decades. They're used today as part of the software planning and prototyping process. When my team and I are brainstorming for a particular solution, we storyboard using whiteboards or flip-chart pages because it's a way to rapidly express relationships between web pages or views in a mobile application. It's this system for rapid prototyping that Apple has successfully captured in Xcode—but Apple has taken it to another level, allowing for agile and rapid application development.

Outside of development, storyboards originally came from the world of cinema. They were developed by Walt Disney Studios in the 1930s to plan out animations scene by scene, which is a process that is still used today even in major motion pictures. Although there are parallels in terminology, the major difference between storyboards in animation and storyboards in software development is that in animation, the progress of the story is linear: scene B always follows scene A. But in software development, this is rarely the case: perhaps scene A links to scenes B and C, with scene B linking to scene D and scene C linking to scene E, which links back to scene A. It's because of the complexity of designing a multi-page application's user experience that storyboards are so valuable. The thing that movie storyboards and application storyboards share is their ability to show us the bigger picture without having all the footage—or, in our case, code.

Figure 7-2 shows an overview of the storyboard you will develop for the SocialApp Twitter application.

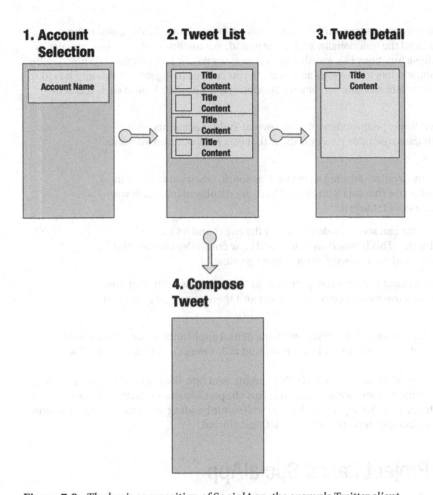

Figure 7-2. The basic composition of SocialApp, the example Twitter client

This is the process that development teams often go through when they start thinking about the composition of an application and the functionality they want to add. We use this storyboarding process to explore ways of assembling those functions in a way that results in an easy-to-use application. When dealing with storyboards in Xcode, Apple refers to the views as *scenes*. As you can see in Figure 7-2, this app has four scenes, and one scene leads to another. Before you begin developing this app, let's look at each scene in more detail:

1. *Account Selection:* Today people often manage several Twitter accounts, so the first scene is a *grouped style* table view controller that lists each account available on the device.

2. *Tweet List:* Once the user has selected a preferred account, you want to show the 20 most recent tweets on that user's timeline. These are displayed in a *plain style* table view with a custom table cell.

3. *Tweet Detail:* The user can see more details about the tweet and its author in the Tweet Detail scene. This is based on a *standard* view controller and lists the user's name, avatar, and the full tweet content in a text view.

4. *Compose Tweet:* Accessed from the compose icon in the Tweet List, this *standard* view controller uses a text view to compose a tweet and then posts it to Twitter on behalf of the user.

If you want to reference the scenes in this storyboard to the actual application screenshots shown in Figure 7-1, the first screenshot is scene 2, Tweet List; the second is 3, Tweet Detail; and the third is 4, Compose Tweet.

Now that you know a little more about storyboards, their origin, and how they're used by developers every day, it's time to begin putting this application together. This chapter focuses on laying out the scenes in the storyboard and putting the connecting segues in place, as well as embedding navigation controllers and creating the custom classes behind the view controllers, so let's get started.

Creating a New Project Called SocialApp

Before I get into adding in the finer details of the interface, you need to create the project and then lay out the views for this application:

1. Open Xcode and create a new project by clicking Create a New Xcode Project from the Welcome screen or going to File ➤ New ➤ Project (⌘+Shift+N). Select the Single View Application template and click Next.

2. Name your project SocialApp and ensure that the targeted device is set to iPad, not iPhone or Universal. Configure the other settings as you've done in previous applications so they match Figure 7-3 (again substituting your name for mine) and click Next.

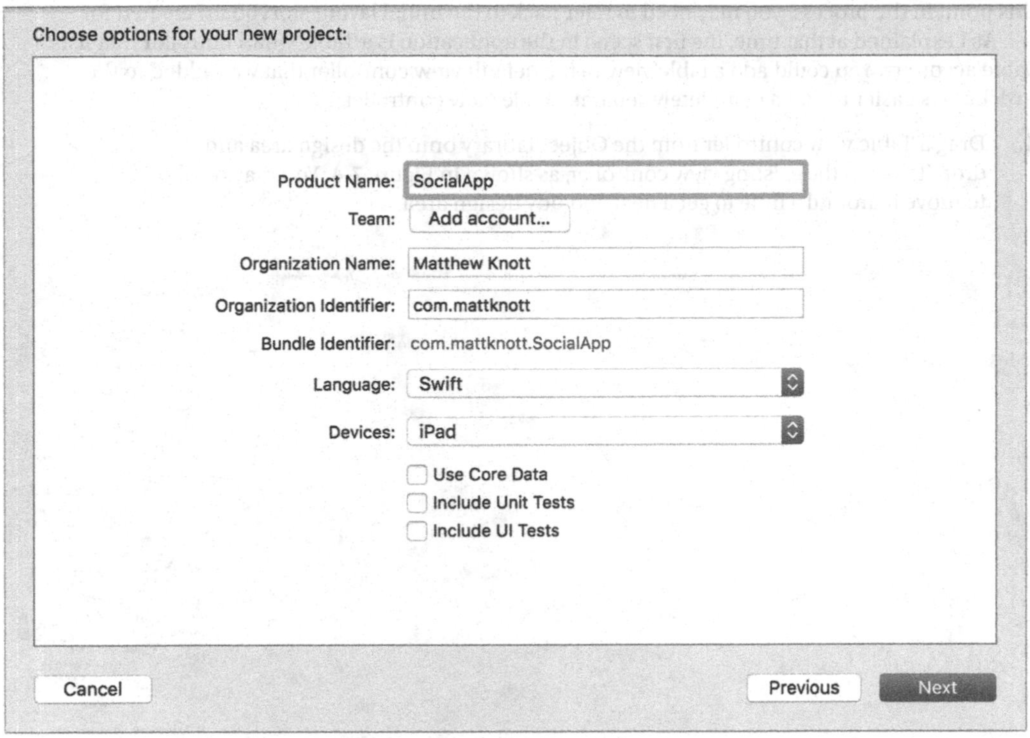

Choose options for your new project:

Product Name:	SocialApp
Team:	Add account...
Organization Name:	Matthew Knott
Organization Identifier:	com.mattknott
Bundle Identifier:	com.mattknott.SocialApp
Language:	Swift
Devices:	iPad

☐ Use Core Data
☐ Include Unit Tests
☐ Include UI Tests

Cancel   Previous   Next

Figure 7-3. Setting the project options

3. You don't need to create a Git repository this time, so leave that option unchecked and make sure your project will be saved in the right place. Then click Create.

4. As should be familiar by now, you're ready to begin your application in earnest. The focus of this chapter is storyboards, so open Main.Storyboard by selecting it from the Project Navigator.

5. If the view is an iPhone view, change it to iPad by clicking the View as: button at the bottom of the design area and select iPad Pro 9.7".

■ **Tip** In previous versions of Xcode, when your zoom level was less than 100%, you could still create segues between scenes and reposition them, but you couldn't add controls to your views. Apple has finally improved on this by allowing you to work more effectively while zoomed out.

At this point in the process, you may need to refer back to the initial layout storyboard created for Figure 7-2. As I explained at that time, the first scene in the application is a Table view controller that lists the available accounts. You could add a table view to the default view controller that was added to the storyboard, but it's easier to add a completely separate Table view controller:

1. Drag a Table view controller from the Object Library onto the design area and drop it next to the existing view controller, as shown in Figure 7-4. You may need to move it around a little to get a neat and tidy design area.

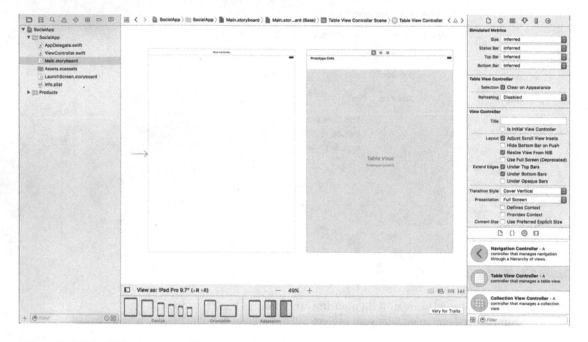

Figure 7-4. *The Table view controller scene, next to the initial scene you started with*

2. Before you add any more scenes, let's run the application in the simulator. Click the Run button on the Toolbar, or press ⌘+R. Notice that the default view controller is loaded instead of the Table view controller, and there is no obvious way of accessing the Table view controller within the application.

3. Quit the simulator and return to Xcode.

4. The initial view controller is the starting point; you can tell this because there is an arrow pointing to the left side of it, known as the storyboard entry point. Drag and drop the starting arrow onto the Table view controller. When the arrow is over the Table view controller, the scene becomes highlighted in blue, as shown in Figure 7-5. The starting arrow now points to the Table view controller, just as it once pointed to the default view controller.

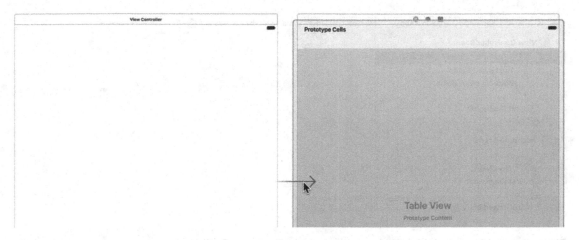

Figure 7-5. *The starting arrow being hovered over the Table view controller*

If you run the application again, you should be greeted with an empty table view. It was that easy to change the starting point for this application! Before storyboards, you had to modify the application delegate to tell it which view controller to start with; now you can just drag and drop a visual aid.

An alternative way to set the initial scene, when you don't want to drag and drop the starting arrow, is to:

1. Select the Table view controller in the design area, either by clicking the scene while zoomed out or by selecting Table View Controller from the Document Outline.

2. Open the Attributes Inspector and look down to the View Controller section. Notice that Is Initial View Controller is selected. Unselect it, and the starting arrow disappears! You'd better bring it back; otherwise the application will run with a black screen.

3. It would be a good idea to set a title while you're here. To do so, click in the Title box and set the title to Accounts.

4. With the initial view controller set, you must now delete the default view controller. Select the blank view by clicking its scene while zoomed out or by selecting View Controller from the Document Outline, as shown in Figure 7-6.

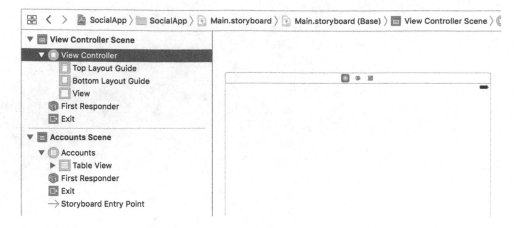

Figure 7-6. *Selecting the initial view controller from the Document Outline*

5. Delete the view controller by pressing the Backspace key or by choosing Edit ➤ Delete.

6. You also need to remove the file that Xcode added for this view controller. Using the Project Navigator, select `ViewController.swift` and, again, press the Backspace key or choose Edit ➤ Delete.

7. You're presented with the dialog shown in Figure 7-7, giving you options for file deletion. The Remove References button removes the files from the project but leaves them in place in the project folder on your Mac. In this case you want to delete the file altogether, so select the Move to Trash option.

Figure 7-7. *The dialog presented by Xcode when removing files via the Project Navigator*

You've removed all the unnecessary files and views from the project. You're now going to step away from the storyboard for a moment to create four custom view controllers for the views by subclassing either `UITableViewController` or `UIViewController`.

Creating View Controllers

You can add as many view controllers to the storyboard as you like. But if you don't tie them to a view controller class file, the application will be extremely limited, because you'll have no way of interacting with the view controllers or controlling them using code. Therefore, let's break away from the application and focus for a moment on the design pattern you're using. It's called model-view-controller, more commonly shortened to MVC.

The Model-View-Controller Design Pattern

Using Xcode with the macOS and iOS SDKs is one of the most natural environments for developing using the MVC principle. First, you don't have to configure Xcode for MVC. Xcode was built from the ground up for MVC, and all the application templates except the Empty Application template are set up using the MVC principle. Second, the semantics of the terminology are completely logical:

> *Model*: An object that stores data in a structured way. Core Data lets you create data models to interface with stored data. You can also create custom classes to represent objects, such as a vehicle class, which might have a type property, a wheels property, a make property, and many more.

> *View*: Unsurprisingly, consists of your views, as laid out in your storyboard (unless you created them programmatically). The view should be all the visual elements of an application, held in isolation from any code.

> *Controller*: The part that manages the views and the models. It acts as an intermediary between the two, taking information from the model and using it to coordinate changes in the view.

SocialApp currently has a view, and you know you're going to add several more. Before you do, let's create all the view controllers so that when you add the views, you can tie them directly to a controller. All your view controllers subclass either UITableViewController or UIViewController to create an individual class file for each view. You've done this in previous chapters, but this time you need to create four view controllers of different types.

Subclassing UIViewController

UIViewController is the class name given to the standard view controller that has been used so far in all the applications in this book. When you declare a class that subclasses UIViewController, you type, for example,

```
class MyCustomViewController: UIViewController
```

This says that the view controller called MyCustomViewController *subclasses* UIViewController. *Subclassing* means taking on all the attributes of another class, but with the ability to add your own methods and properties and override others. Two of your views subclass UIViewController. The two view controllers will be called TweetViewController and ComposeViewController. First, let's create TweetViewController, and then see if you can repeat the process for ComposeViewController:

1. Right-click the SocialApp group in the Project Navigator and select New File, as shown in Figure 7-8; or select the SocialApp group and press ⌘+N.

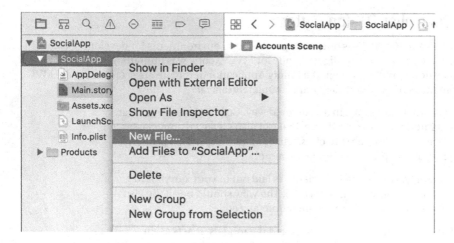

Figure 7-8. *Adding a file to the SocialApp group in the Project Navigator*

2. You're presented with the file template selection screen. Ensure that iOS is selected from the options at the top of the list, then under the Source heading, select Cocoa Touch Class, as shown in Figure 7-9, and click Next.

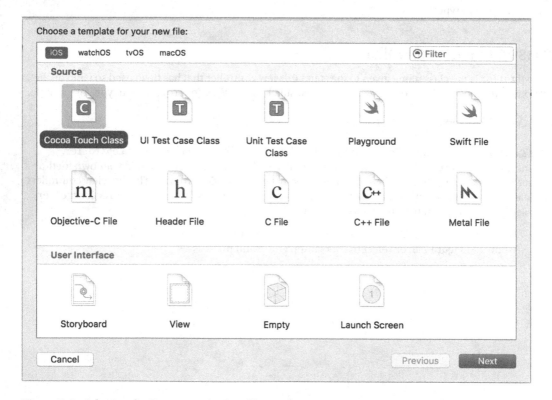

Figure 7-9. *Selecting the Cocoa Touch Class file template*

3. Set the Subclass Of field to UIViewController. This defaults the Class field to ViewController, making it easy for you to change it to TweetViewController. Be sure the Also Create XIB File check box is unchecked, as shown in Figure 7-10, and click Next.

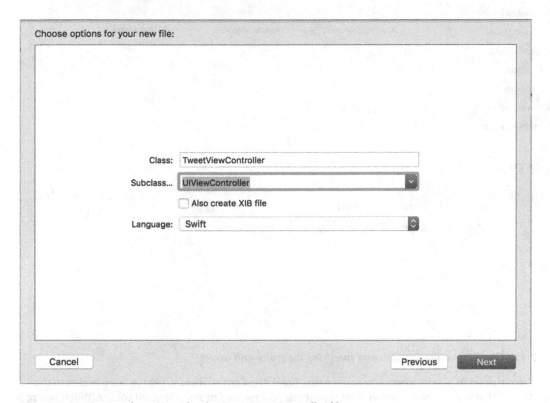

Figure 7-10. Setting the options for the TweetViewController file

4. You need to choose a location to save the file. Xcode automatically suggests the project folder, which is what you want. Be sure the Group option is set to SocialApp and that the SocialApp target is selected, as shown in Figure 7-11. Click Create.

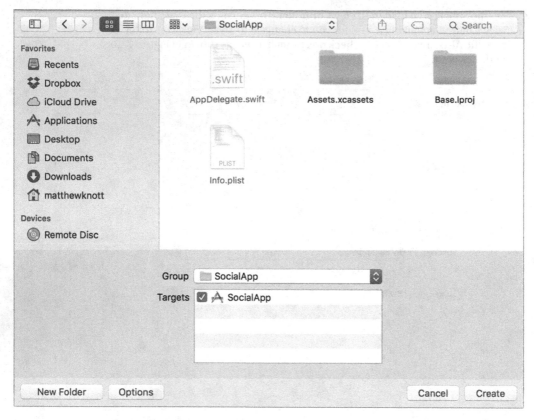

Figure 7-11. *Choosing a save location and specifying the group and target*

You're returned to Xcode, where you can see that `TweetViewController.swift` has been added to the project. Great! That's one view controller; now repeat this process for `ComposeViewController`. When you're done, your Project Navigator should resemble that shown in Figure 7-12.

Figure 7-12. *The growing project in the Project Navigator*

Well done! Creating view controllers and subclassing other classes and objects is an essential task for developing applications, so you're perfecting a valuable skill.

One thing you can foresee, looking at Figure 7-12, is that the file list is growing and you still have three more view controllers to add. You need to tidy up the structure by grouping the view controllers together:

1. At the bottom of the Project Navigator, type View in the Show Files With Matching Name filter to make sure you only see your view controllers.

2. Click the first view controller file (in my case, it's TweetViewController.swift). Holding the Shift key, select the last file (in my case, ComposeViewController. swift). Both view controllers should be selected, as shown on the left in Figure 7-13.

3. Right-click the selected files, and choose New Group from Selection, as shown on the right in Figure 7-13.

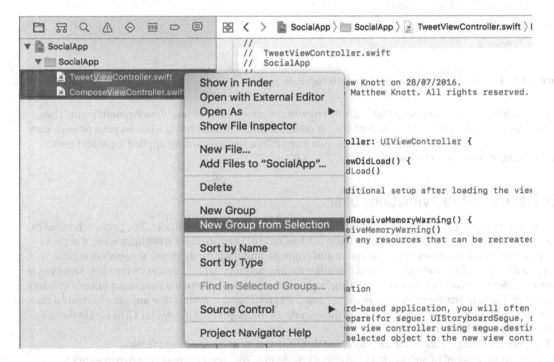

Figure 7-13. *Selecting the view controllers and creating a new group to contain them*

4. When prompted, name your new group View Controllers. Clear the filter by clicking the X at the end of it. You should be left with a neat project, as shown in Figure 7-14.

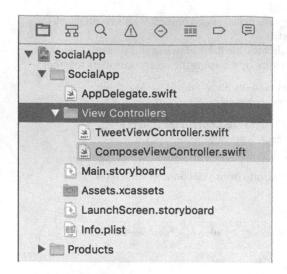

Figure 7-14. *The view controllers grouped neatly together*

Organizing your project neatly and logically ensures the admiration of your development team. They *will* thank you for it. Organizing files in big projects means if someone else has to work on your project, they don't have to hunt for the custom classes or the view controllers, because you've applied logic and good housekeeping to your project structure.

Subclassing UITableViewController

You've created two of the four view controllers, and it's time to create the remainder. The process is more or less the same, but there are some subtle changes. `UIViewControllers` are fairly straightforward: the views themselves are blank canvases, ready for you to add controls; and their methods are also very minimal, giving you just a `viewDidLoad` function and a handler for low memory. `UITableViewController`, however, is a more complex system, designed for displaying large amounts of data through a structured interface. It has a number of intrinsic attributes that result in the code files containing methods that are used to control the number of rows, sections, and more. I explain these in detail in Chapter 8; for now, let's just create them so you can get back to the storyboard.

The process is largely the same as before, but this time you start by selecting the View Controllers group instead of SocialApp in the Project Navigator. You need to create the two instances of `UITableViewController` that this application uses, called `AccountsViewController` and `FeedViewController`:

1. Right-click the View Controllers group and select New File, as shown in Figure 7-15, or press ⌘+N. You're presented with the file template selection screen.

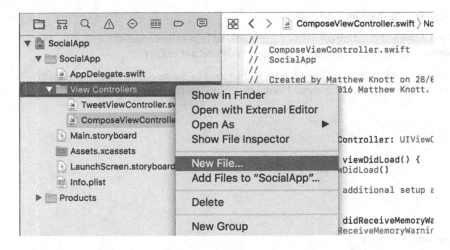

Figure 7-15. *Adding a new file to the View Controllers group*

2. As with the `UIViewControllers`, select the Cocoa Touch Class file template and click Next. Set the Class field to `AccountsViewController` and the Subclass Of field to `UITableViewController`, as shown in Figure 7-16, and click Next.

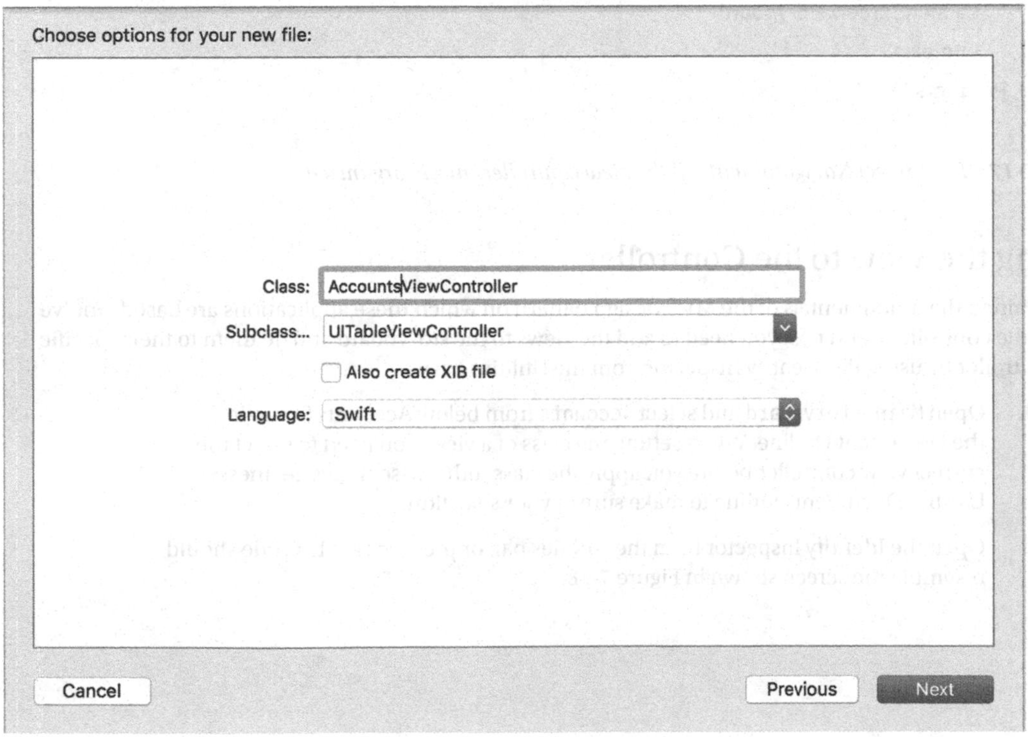

Choose options for your new file:

Class:	AccountsViewController
Subclass...	UITableViewController
	☐ Also create XIB file
Language:	Swift

Cancel   Previous   Next

Figure 7-16. *Specifying the options for the `UITableViewController`*

3. Accept the suggested file location and click Create.

4. You should be a master at creating new view controllers, so repeat these steps and create another UITableViewController called FeedViewController.

You've now created four view controllers. Let's finish adding the views to the storyboard and tie them to their respective controllers. Your Project Navigator should look something like the screen shown in Figure 7-17.

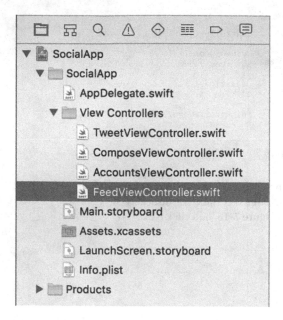

Figure 7-17. *The Project Navigator with all the view controllers nicely organized*

Pairing the View to the Controller

I've explained the fundamentals of the MVC design pattern on which these applications are based. You've created the controllers, and next you need to add the views to the storyboard and tie them to their specific view controller by using the Identity Inspector from the Utilities bar:

1. Open Main.storyboard and select Accounts from below Accounts Scene in the Document Outline. When setting the class of a view, you need to select the correct view controller before you apply the class; otherwise things get messy. Use the Document Outline to make sure of your selection.

2. Open the Identity Inspector from the Utilities bar, or press ⌥+⌘+1. Xcode should resemble the screen shown in Figure 7-18.

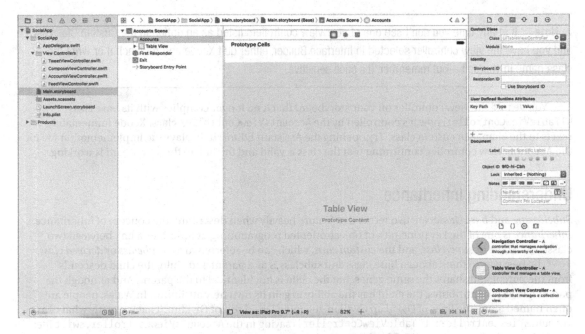

Figure 7-18. *Xcode with the view controller selected and the Identity Inspector open*

3. In the Identity Inspector, look for the Custom Class section. This is where you bind your view controller's visual element to the actual view controller. In the Class field, it currently says that this view controller's class is UITableViewController. It's grayed out because although it knows what its base type is, you haven't yet tied it to a custom view controller.

4. Click the down arrow at the end of the field. You should see three selections: the base class and the two custom view controllers, as shown in Figure 7-19. Select AccountsViewController.

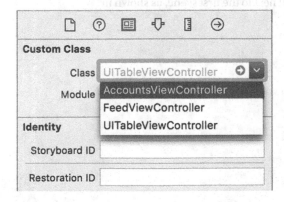

Figure 7-19. *The list of available view controllers*

■ **Note**   If at any time you don't see one of your view controllers listed as an option in the Custom Class list and you have the view controller selected in Interface Builder, either quit Xcode and relaunch it or write the class name in yourself—but remember, it's case sensitive.

You've told the view controller on your storyboard that it no longer complies with its base class UITableViewController; now it's controlled by the AccountsViewController class. Xcode immediately reacts to the change in custom class. Try opening the Assistant Editor: it displays the implementation file for the Accounts view controller, confirming that the class is valid and the link to the storyboard is working.

Understanding Inheritance

Subclassing and *base classes* are two terms that feature heavily when describing the concept of inheritance. *Inheritance* is one of the key principles of object-oriented programming. It describes a link between two classes: the *base* or *superclass*, and the *custom class*, which can be referred to as a *subclass* or *derived class*.

The best way to think about a base class and subclass is as a parent and child; the child descends from the parent and shares the same genes, but the child is not identical to the parent. And although the parent has its own attributes, the child has the ability to gain its own new attributes. In Wales, people are often named along the lines of David ap Gwillim, meaning David son of Gwillim. That is exactly what class AccountsViewController: UITableViewController is saying in the AccountsViewController.swift file: that it descends directly from UITableViewController.

Now that you have a better understanding of inheritance and why you create custom classes, you can finish building the storyboard.

Building Up the Storyboard

With Main.storyboard open, let's get back to the focus of this chapter: storyboards. You've created the first scene for account selection; it's time to create the second scene, which is the list of tweets, more commonly known as the Twitter feed, which is controlled by FeedViewController:

1. This is another UITableViewController class, so you need to drag a Table view controller from the Object Library and drop it next to the first scene, as shown in Figure 7-20.

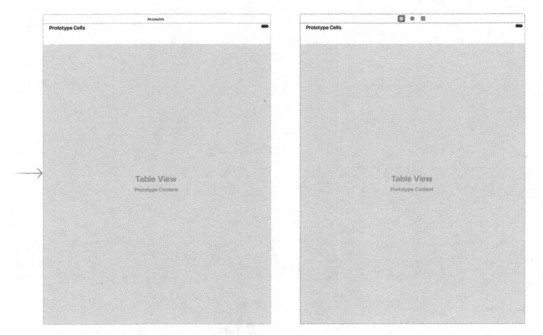

Figure 7-20. *The storyboard with two Table view controllers side by side*

2. Select the new Table view controller and open the Attributes Inspector. Set the Title attribute to Feed; this will help you keep track of your scenes in what will be a full storyboard.

3. Select the Identity Inspector, click the Class drop-down list, and choose FeedViewController.

4. You have two scenes on your storyboard. Let's add the last two so you can move on to a careful examination of one of the key features of any storyboard: segues. The third scene is a regular view controller that is used to show the details of the tweet. Drag a view controller from the Object Library and drop it above and to the right of the Feed view controller.

5. Select the new view controller and open the Attributes Inspector. Set the Title attribute to Tweet.

6. To set the class, open the Identity Inspector and set the Class value to TweetViewController. Your growing storyboard should resemble that shown in Figure 7-21.

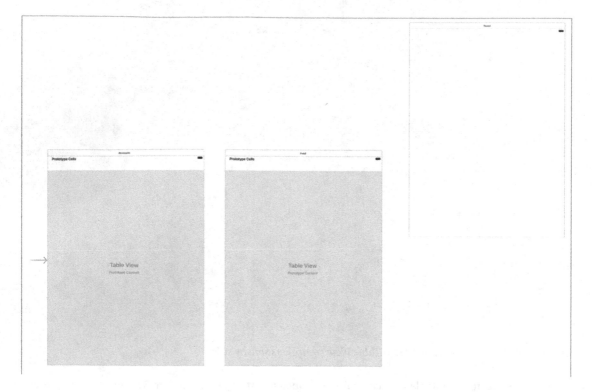

Figure 7-21. *The three scenes, positioned nicely and ready for the fourth*

7. By now you can start to appreciate how it can sometimes be challenging to work on large, multi-view applications using storyboards. This is why it's best to meticulously name every scene as it's created, so you can quickly identify a scene via the Document Outline. The next scene is CompposeViewController, which you will use to write tweets and post them to Twitter. Drag in another view controller and position it directly below the Tweet view controller.

8. Click the new view controller and open the Attributes Inspector. Set the Title attribute to Compose.

9. As you've done previously, open the Identity Inspector and set the Class value to ComposeViewController.

All the scenes of the storyboard are laid out neatly. Each view controller on the storyboard is tied to its respective view controller class. Although you have the basic structure in terms of the scenes, the scenes themselves are largely empty. Let's focus on the individual scenes and begin adding the elements that will make up the interface. Before you move on, check that your interface resembles the one shown in Figure 7-22.

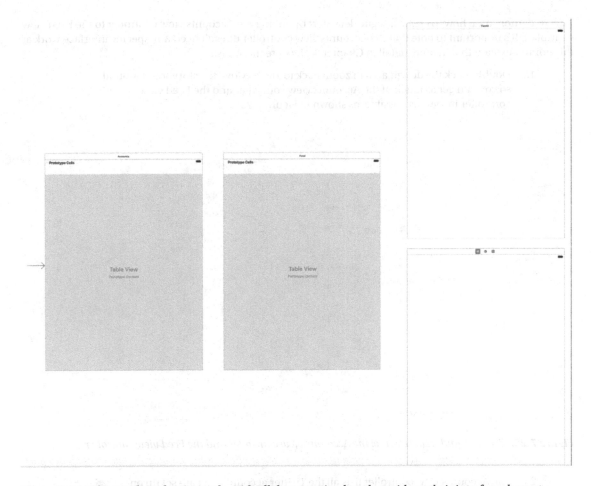

Figure 7-22. The storyboard as it stands, with all the scenes in place, but without their interface elements

Linking Scenes and Building Interfaces

One message that should be coming across in this chapter is that building an application with storyboards is part of a structured process. First you plan your application and its scenes, and then you create the view controllers before tying them into their respective visual counterparts on the storyboard, giving you separate view controllers that have their classes set but are ultimately strangers to one another. To address this issue, you need to progress through each scene from 1 through 4, building and connecting the interface with segues.

What Are Segues?

Just as the concept of storyboards is rooted in the movie industry, so is the term *segue* (pronounced "seg-way"). In a film, a segue is a transition between scenes, so you can immediately see how it's appropriate as a term that describes the mechanism used by Xcode to transition between storyboard scenes.

In Xcode, segues need a starting point and an ending point. Typically, the starting point is a button or a table cell. The ending point is almost always another view controller. Think back to Chapter 3 for a moment; there you wrote several lines of code to push the second view controller onto the screen. With storyboards, a segue allows you to do this with a couple of clicks.

To demonstrate how to create a segue, let's start by linking the Accounts view controller to the Feed view controller. It's important to note that the Accounts view controller doesn't need any specific interface work at this point; I explain that in more detail in Chapter 8. Here are the steps:

1. Double-click the design area to zoom back to 100%. Move the storyboard around so you can get as much of the Accounts view controller and the Feed view controller in view as possible, as shown in Figure 7-23.

Figure 7-23. *Scenes 1 and 2 side by side: the Accounts view controller and the Feed view controller*

2. The Accounts view controller lists all the Twitter accounts that are set up on the device in a table view. Selecting one of the rows takes you to the Feed view controller. To make this happen, you need to create a Show segue from the table cell to the Feed view controller. Highlight the table cell in the Accounts view controller by clicking it, as shown in Figure 7-24.

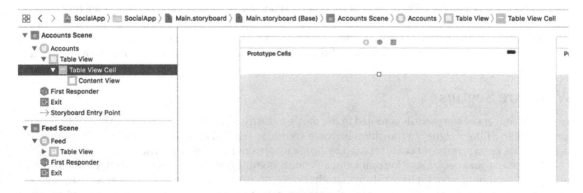

Figure 7-24. *The Accounts view controller table cell selected*

> ■ **Note**   It's not immediately obvious that you've selected the table cell, but if you look at the jump bar above the design area, or in the Document Outline shown in Figure 7-24, you see that it is indeed selected.

3. Hold down the Control key, click the table cell, and drag a connecting line from the cell to the Feed view controller, as shown in Figure 7-25.

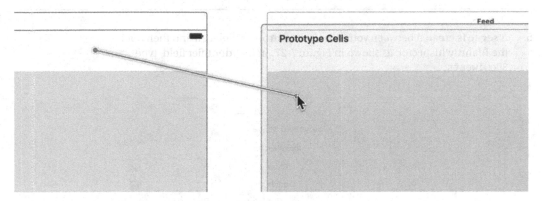

Figure 7-25. *Dragging a connecting line between the table cell and the Feed view controller*

4. When you release the mouse button, you're presented with a contextual dialog asking about the type of segue you want to create, as shown in Figure 7-26. In this instance, you want to create a Show segue from the Selection Segue list of types.

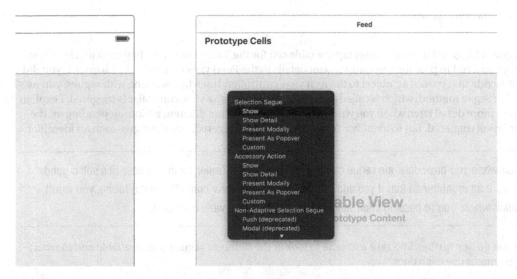

Figure 7-26. *The contextual menu presented when you create a segue from a table cell*

5. A segue is created between your two view controllers. Select it and then open the Identity Inspector, as shown in Figure 7-27. In the Identifier field, type ShowTweets.

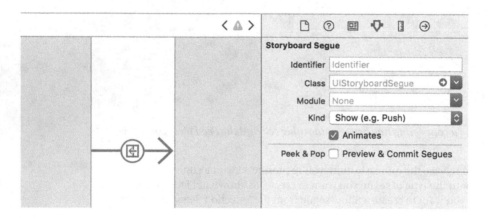

Figure 7-27. *Inspecting the segue*

This segue is triggered when the users tap the table cell for the Twitter account they want to use. When this happens, you need to pass the selected account details to the Feed view controller. In Chapter 3, you did this by writing code that passed an object to the next view controller; but when working with segues, you use the prepareForSegue method, which is called every time a segue on the view controller is triggered. I explain this method in more detail later, when you write the code that performs different actions depending on the segue that is being triggered. But to identify which segue is being triggered, you must give each an identifier.

Before you go any further, let's take a minute to look at the different segue styles available and in what situations you might use each one:

Show: Prior to Xcode 6 and iOS 8, this was referred to as a Push segue. This segue dismisses the current view and pushes the target of the segue onto the screen. Behind the scenes, the Show segue adds the target view controller onto the navigation stack, which is why you always need a navigation controller to be present when using a Show segue. Xcode does all the work of managing the navigation stack for you: when your Show segue is triggered, the view controller that is presented automatically has a button to go back to the previous view controller.

Present Modally: Modal segues are definitely the most interesting and varied type you can use, especially when working with iPad applications. A modal segue presents another view controller without the need of a navigation controller. You can slide these over the top of the view that calls the segue. A number of transition animations and presentation styles are available, some of which I explain later in this chapter. Figure 7-28 shows a modal segue in action, presenting the Tweet view controller from SocialApp modally with the Form Sheet presentation style.

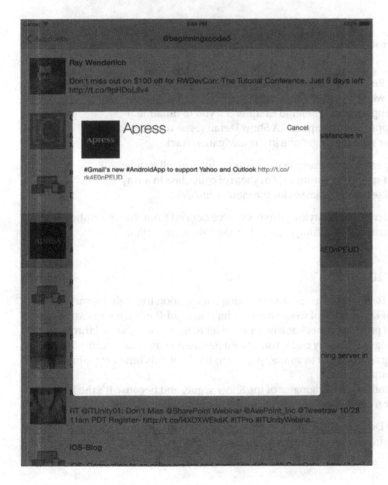

Figure 7-28. *A modal segue in action*

Popover Presentation: Popovers are visually similar to some modal segues in that they cause a view controller to appear above the view controller that originated the segue. These are useful for displaying contextual information; for example, if you created an application for an online store, you could use popover segues to provide a quick view of your products. You can see an example of a popover in Figure 7-29; note that the arrow at the top of the view controller is generated by Xcode and can be configured.

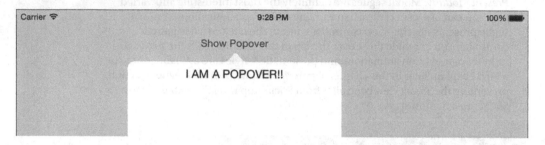

Figure 7-29. *An example of a popover segue presenting another view controller on top of the view*

Show Detail: Known as a Replace segue prior to Xcode 6, this style was previously available only when working with an iPad storyboard. It's mainly used with master-detail applications. (Refer to Chapter 3 if you're unfamiliar with the Master-Detail Application template.) A Show Detail segue replaces the originating view controller with the target one in the navigation stack.

Custom: As you might expect, a custom segue can be anything you tell it to be. With a custom segue, you specify a custom UIStoryboardSegue class in a way similar to how you would set custom classes for the view controllers.

Now that you understand the different segue styles, perhaps you've noticed from the description of the Show segue that your application is missing something essential: a navigation controller.

Adding a Navigation Controller

A navigation controller, or UINavigationController, is used to manage navigation through the various view controllers in your application. It keeps track of where the user has been, adding each successive view controller to the navigation stack, and provides a mechanism for the user to navigate backward through the navigation stack, all without you having to write any code. You first encountered navigation controllers in Chapter 3, where you added one programmatically to your application; however, this time I explain how Xcode makes this possible in just a couple of clicks.

Because the Accounts view controller is the originator of the Show segue, and because it's the initial scene on the storyboard, the navigation controller needs to be added here:

1. Select Accounts from the Document Outline, as shown in Figure 7-30, because you're applying the navigation controller explicitly to the view controller.

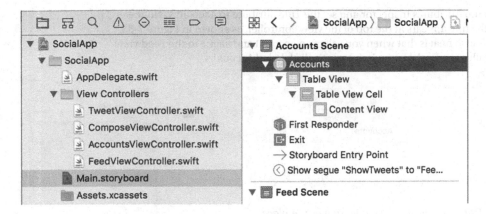

Figure 7-30. *Selecting the Accounts view controller from the Document Outline*

> 2. To add a navigation controller to this view controller, from the menu bar select Editor ➤ Embed In ➤ Navigation Controller. Xcode adds a navigation controller to the storyboard and attaches it to the Accounts view controller for you, as shown in Figure 7-31.

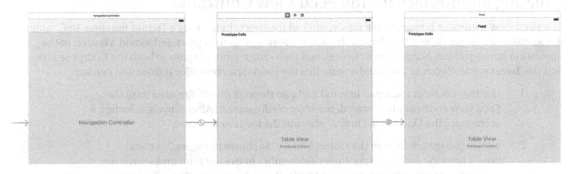

Figure 7-31. *The navigation controller added to the storyboard and linked to the Accounts view controller*

> 3. You can set a title for the view that is visible to the user and provides meaningful text for the Back button. Zoom back in to the storyboard. In Accounts, highlight the navigation bar at the top of the view or select Navigation Item from the Document Outline, as shown in Figure 7-32.

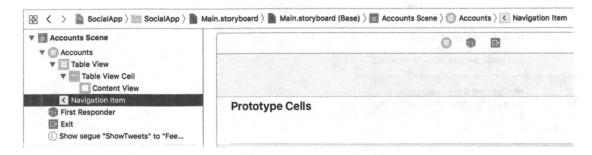

Figure 7-32. *Selecting the Navigation Item from the Document Outline for the Accounts view controller*

4. Open the Attributes Inspector and set the Title attribute to Accounts. Notice how the title appears at the top of the view controller, as shown in Figure 7-33. What's also neat is that when you select an account and segue to the Feed view controller, the Back button is automatically labeled Accounts.

Figure 7-33. *The Title attribute for the navigation bar in place*

With the navigation controller in place and the Accounts view controller complete for now, you're ready to start building the interface on the remaining three scenes. Next up: the Feed view controller.

Creating an Interface for the Feed View Controller

The Feed view controller is responsible for showing all the tweets in the user's Twitter timeline. In Chapter 8, you create a custom table cell to display the actual tweet. But for now you need to add a button to the navigation bar so you can compose new tweets, and then create modal segues to both the Compose scene and the Tweet scene. Zoom to 100% and ensure that the Feed view controller is front and center:

1. Use the mouse or track pad to scroll and pan through the design area until the Feed view controller is centered, ready for configuration. Alternatively selecting a scene from the Document Outline will shift the focus to that item.

2. Locate Navigation Item in the Object Library, as shown in Figure 7-34, and drag it onto the Feed view controller. Remember to use the filter and search for *navigation* to make your search easier. When you do this, the title will change from Feed to Title.

Figure 7-34. *Searching for Navigation Item in the Object Library*

3. You need to add a button to the navigation bar so that you can create a modal segue to the Compose view controller. Search for *button* in the Object Library. You're looking specifically for Bar Button Item, which should be the second item in the Object Library. Drag it onto the right side of the navigation bar, positioning it as shown in Figure 7-35.

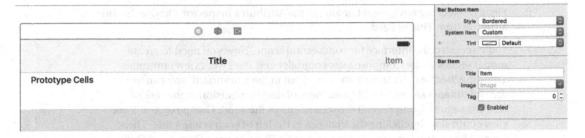

Figure 7-35. *Adding a bar button item to the navigation bar*

4. If you still have the Attributes Inspector open, when you drop the bar button item on the navigation bar, its attributes are displayed. If not, open the Attributes Inspector and select the new button.

5. You could change the Title attribute of this button to read Compose, because that is the scene it will link to. However, Apple provides a standard set of icons you can use for this button by choosing one of the predefined Identifiers. Click the System Item attribute list and select Compose, as shown in Figure 7-36. Your button changes from text to an icon with a pencil in a box.

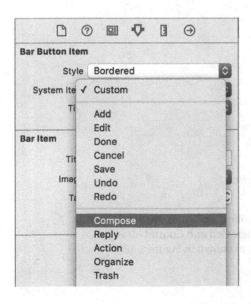

Figure 7-36. *Selecting the Compose identifier for the bar button item*

■ **Note**   Apple provides a number of identifiers that can be used for many common tasks. You should use these whenever possible, to provide users with icons they're familiar with and also to future-proof your application. If Apple updates that identifier in the future, your applications will be easy to update to the new design.

6. Finally, select the navigation bar and, in the Attributes Inspector, change the Title attribute from Title to Feed.

7. You've created the interface for your second scene. Now you need to create modal segues to the Compose view controller and the Tweet view controller. This time, because the scenes are spread out in the storyboard, you can use the Document Outline to add an element of simple precision to the task of creating segues. Compress all the scenes except the Feed, Compose, and Tweet view controllers by clicking the triangles to the left of each scene's title. Then, expand Feed, and beneath that, expand Table View, so your Document Outline resembles that shown in Figure 7-37.

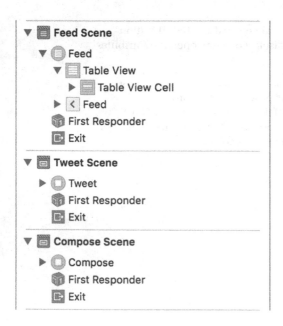

Figure 7-37.   *Preparing to create segues using the Document Outline*

8. The first segue you create is to the Tweet view controller. You get to this scene by selecting one of the table cells, so highlight Table View Cell and Control+drag a connection from there to the Tweet view controller, as shown in Figure 7-38.

190

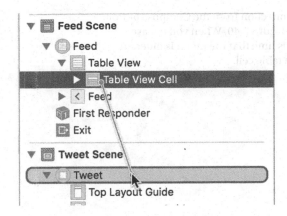

Figure 7-38. *Creating a segue using the Document Outline*

9. When you release the mouse button, the contextual dialog appears, just as it did in Figure 7-26. This time, select Present Modally under the Selection Segue heading. You now have a modal segue connecting the table cell in your scene to the Tweet view controller, but you need to customize it slightly.

10. In the Feed Scene section of the Document Outline, notice the item Present Modally Segue to Tweet. This is the segue: select it to highlight it, and then open the Attributes Inspector.

11. Set the Identifier attribute to ShowTweet, the Presentation attribute to Form Sheet, and the Transition attribute to Cover Vertical.

12. You need to create a modal segue from the Compose bar button item to the Compose view controller. Expand Feed in the Document Outline to reveal Compose, as shown in Figure 7-39.

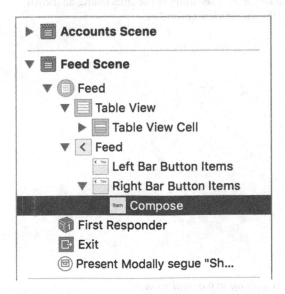

Figure 7-39. *Exposing the bar button item in the Document Outline*

13. In the Document Outline, Control+drag a connection from the Compose button to the Compose view controller, as shown in Figure 7-40. When you release the button, select Present Modally. Notice this time that the menu is different because you're dragging from a button, not a table cell.

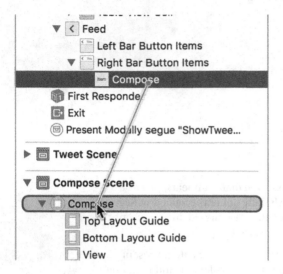

Figure 7-40. *Making a connection between the button and the Compose view controller*

14. Two segues are listed in the Document Outline for your scene. Select the one named Present Modally Segue to Compose. Open the Attributes Inspector and set the Identifier attribute to ComposeTweet, the Presentation attribute to Form Sheet, and Transition to Cover Vertical.

Let's review where you are with the project. Zoom out so you can see more of the storyboard, as shown in Figure 7-41. You're ready to move on to the third scene, the Tweet view controller.

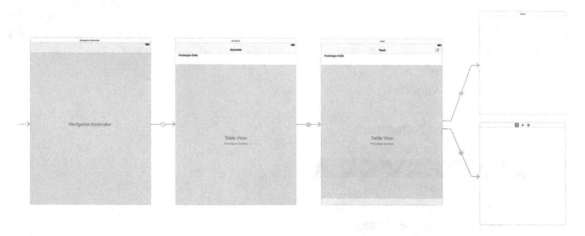

Figure 7-41. *The storyboard changes in appearance after you set up two modal scenes*

Creating an Interface for Tweet View Controller

The purpose of the third scene is to display details about the tweet the user selects from the Twitter feed. You could display all types of information, but for this application you simply display the tweet author's name, the tweet content, and the tweet author's avatar image. Because you've done these steps a few times already in this chapter, I use screenshots at key points in the process so you can verify that you haven't missed anything:

1. Because this is a modal scene, it has no Back button. You need to be able to dismiss the view controller when the user wants to return to the Twitter feed. Add a button at upper right in the view by dragging one from the Object Library. In the Attributes Inspector, set the Title attribute to Cancel.

2. You may need to resize the button slightly to make the text visible. When you're happy with the button's appearance, position it as shown in Figure 7-42. You'll set the auto layout constraints once the view is built.

Figure 7-42. *Placing the button on the Tweet view controller*

3. You need to add an image view from the Object Library to the view controller. Position it somewhere in the view, and then open the Size Inspector. This is a handy tool for gaining pinpoint precision over an object's size and position. Set the X axis value to 20 and the Y axis value to 20; these control where the top-left corner of the image view is positioned relative to the parent view. Set the Width and Height values to 82, as shown in Figure 7-43, to create a square image view.

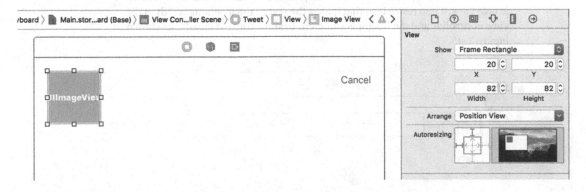

Figure 7-43. *Setting the width, height, and x and y axis positions of the image view*

4. From the Object Library, drag in a label to contain the tweet author's name. Position it loosely between the image view and the Cancel button. You'll adjust the size and the font, so it makes sense not to finalize the position until after you've done that.

5. Open the Attributes Inspector with the label selected. Select the T icon within the Font attribute. Set Font to Custom, Family to Helvetica Neue, Style to Thin, and Size to 34, as shown in Figure 7-44.

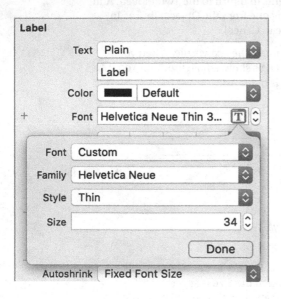

Figure 7-44. *Adjusting the Font attribute for the label that shows the tweet author's name*

6. Notice that you can't see any text in the label, due to its size and shape. Position the left side and top of the label so it snaps into alignment with the top of the image view. Then resize it so that it uses the rest of the available width in the view controller and the height is sufficient to show the text clearly, as shown in Figure 7-45.

Figure 7-45. *Setting the label to fill the remaining width*

7. You need something to show the main content of the selected tweet. Tweets vary in size, so the best choice is a text view. Drag one from the Object Library, snapping it into place below the image view. Resize it to give it a generous size, as shown in Figure 7-46.

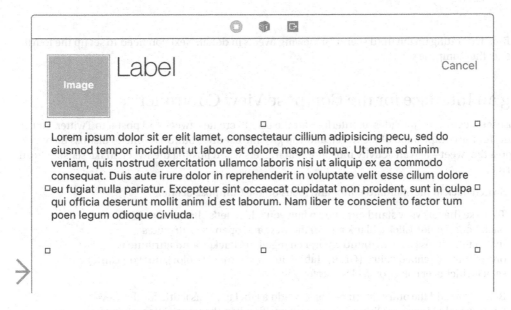

Figure 7-46. *The text view added to the view controller*

8. You don't want this text view to behave like a regular text view, because it shouldn't be editable. Open the Attributes Editor and uncheck the Editable attribute. Leave Selectable checked so the user can copy the tweet text.

9. While the attributes of the text view are open, look at the Data Detectors section. Twitter posts often contain links, so check the Link attribute, which tells Xcode to detect URLs and provide a code-free way of opening the link in Safari.

10. Click the Resolve Auto Layout Issues button. Under the heading All Views in Tweet View Controller, click Add Missing Constraints. This should ensure that your layout adapts correctly.

11. Even though you're using storyboards, you still need to create actions and outlets for the interface objects. Open the Assistant Editor, and be sure it displays TweetViewController.swift in the right pane. If it doesn't, you need to go back and set the class for this view controller to TweetViewController.

12. As you've done numerous times in this book, Control+drag the following outlets: tweetAuthorAvatar for the image view, tweetAuthorName for the author's name label, and tweetText for the text view. Create an action for the Cancel button called dismissView. Your header should contain the following highlighted code:

```
import UIKit

class TweetViewController: UIViewController {
```

```
@IBOutlet weak var tweetAuthorAvatar: UIImageView!
@IBOutlet weak var tweetAuthorName: UILabel!
@IBOutlet weak var tweetText: UITextView!
@IBAction func dismissView(_ sender: AnyObject) {

}
```

You're finished setting up the third scene for viewing tweets in detail. Next you need to set up the fourth and final scene: the Compose scene.

Creating an Interface for the Compose View Controller

The Compose view controller provides an interface for the user to create a tweet and post it to Twitter. You use a text view for the composition of the tweet, and you give the user two buttons—one to dismiss the view and one to post the tweet—and an activity indicator that triggers when posting the tweet. Make sense? Great! Let's get started:

1. Switch back to the Standard editor and focus on the Compose Scene.

2. To make the text view stand out more when you add it, let's change the view's background color. Click a blank area of the view and open the Attributes Inspector. Choose a background color; I changed the Background attribute to one of the predefined colors (Group Table View Background Color), but you can select whichever color you feel works for you.

3. Before you add the other interface objects, add a label to act as a title for the view. Drag in a label from the Object Library and position it in the upper-left corner of the view.

4. In the Attributes Inspector, change the label's Text attribute to Compose a Tweet. You also want to make it stand out, so click the arrow inside the Font attribute and set Font to Custom, Family to Helvetica Neue, Style to Thin, and Size to 32. Resize the Label so that all the text is visible, but don't resize it to fill the width of the view. Reposition the label in the upper-left corner so the guidelines for the margin appear.

5. Drag a button to the upper-right corner of the view; this button will dismiss the view controller. Open the Attributes Inspector and change the button's Title attribute to Cancel. Before you move on, the top of your scene should resemble the one shown in Figure 7-47.

Figure 7-47. *The label and button in position on the Compose scene*

6. Drag in a text view and position it below the label and button. This is where the user composes posts to Twitter, so make it a decent size. Be sure to expand the text view left and right until the margin appears.

7. One downside is that by default, the text view is populated with Lorem Ipsum placeholder text. Open the Attributes Inspector and remove all the default text from the Text attribute. Your scene should be progressing nicely and resemble that shown in Figure 7-48.

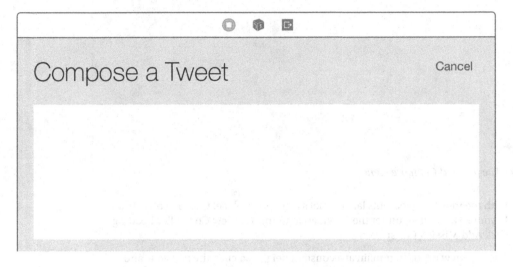

Figure 7-48. The text view in position below the button and label

8. You need to add a second button to allow the user to post the content to Twitter. Drag in a button and position it below to the text view. In the Attributes Inspector, change the Title attribute to Post.

9. Set the Background attribute of the button to White Color. Then make the button a little larger and move it toward the center of the view until the blue guideline appears and it snaps into place, centered horizontally and positioned just below the text view.

10. This is the first time you've dealt with the next object: an activity indicator. Activity indicators are very common in applications that rely on sending or receiving data from the Internet. The control produces the familiar spinning wheel that has become synonymous with data transfer over the past decade; it has long been used with AJAX-based applications on the Web and in iOS applications since iOS 2.0. Drag one in from the Object Library and position it to the left of the Post button.

11. By default, the activity indicator is visible and static; you want it to be hidden until it's told to start animating. Xcode provides a simple attribute to achieve this: open the Attributes Inspector with the activity indicator selected and check the Hides When Stopped attribute. Figure 7-49 shows the finished scene.

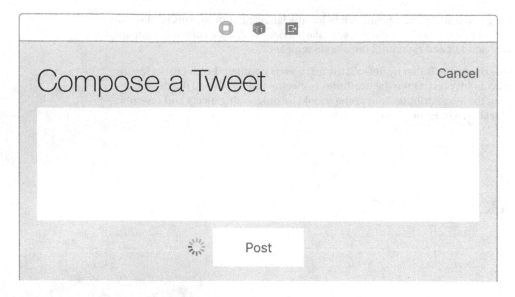

Figure 7-49. *The finished Compose scene*

12. With the interface elements laid out, let's fix them in place. Click Resolve Auto Layout Issues. Then, under the All Views in Compose View Controller heading, click Add Missing Constraints.

13. The text view needs to remain at a constant height, so click the text view and then click Pin. Click the Height check box and be sure the value is around the 170 mark. If you change the value, remember to use the Update Frames function to resolve any issues.

14. If you click the Post button, you see a constraint travelling from it to the bottom of the view. Click the constraint, and then, in the Attributes Editor, change Priority to 250, as shown in Figure 7-50. This change means iOS won't try to stretch your button down to the bottom of the view.

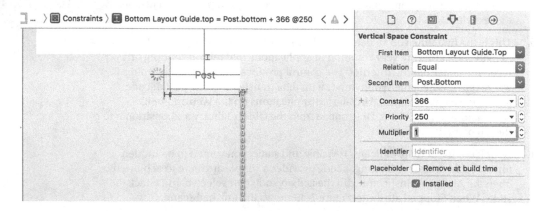

Figure 7-50. *Adjusting the vertical space constraint beneath the Post button*

15. There are no segues from this scene, so all that remains is to create the outlets and actions. Open the Assistant Editor and ensure that `ComposeViewController.swift` is showing on the right.

16. Create an outlet for the text view called `tweetContent`, one for the Post button called `postButton`, and one for the activity indicator called `postActivity`. Create an action for the Cancel button called `dismissView` and one for the Post button called `postToTwitter`.

You should have the following highlighted outlets and actions in your header file:

```
class ComposeViewController: UIViewController {


    @IBOutlet weak var tweetContent: UITextView!
    @IBOutlet weak var postButton: UIButton!
    @IBOutlet weak var postActivity: UIActivityIndicatorView!

    @IBAction func dismissView(_ sender: AnyObject) {
    }

    @IBAction func postToTwitter(_ sender: AnyObject) {
    }
```

That's it for the fourth and final scene—you have all the elements in place for your users to compose messages and post them to Twitter. You've worked really hard getting to this stage in the project, and you've earned a rest before you learn about table and collection views in the next chapter.

Summary

It can be hard going through an entire chapter without having a completed application to show for it at the end; but in any project, you have to do preparation work, which is what you've done here. In the next chapter, you see the application come to life in the first few pages as you configure table views and take the first steps in using the Social and Accounts frameworks.

In this chapter, you've been shown all the skills essential to using Xcode to build an application structure with storyboards. At its core, such an app consists of scenes and segues. But specifically you've learned about the following:

• Organizing files in the Project Navigator using groups

• The model-view-controller design pattern and how Xcode is built around it

• Applying custom view controller classes to view controllers in the storyboard

• The inheritance principle of object-oriented programming

• Different ways of creating segues

• Types of segues

• Specifying identifiers for segues

• Embedding navigation controllers

• Using the Size Inspector to precisely position elements in the view

When you've had a well-deserved rest, move on to the next chapter to finish the SocialApp.

CHAPTER 8

■ ■ ■

Table and Collection Views

In Chapter 7, you began work on SocialApp, a Twitter client; I presented an in-depth look at building an application structure with storyboards, explaining how to tie scenes together with segues. You also learned about the principles of the model-view-controller design pattern, combining the View element with the Controller element. In addition, you learned about subclassing and how inheritance is an import concept of object-oriented programming. Most important, you worked hard preparing the scenes for SocialApp and tying them all together with segues.

In this age of big data, it seems in every facet of our lives we're being bombarded by more and more data, and as developers, we often find ourselves needing a way to display large amounts of data to users in a concise and structured manner. In iOS, Apple has provided the table view and collection view for this purpose.

This chapter focuses on the table view and collection view. You explore how each view is structured and how you can use Xcode to alter their appearance. Additionally, you learn about creating custom cells, where you subclass UITableViewCell to customize the elements in your cells. As in the other chapters in this book, many additional lessons are learned along the way; you see how the segue identifiers specified in Chapter 7 allow you to share data between view controllers, and you learn about a variety of ways to obtain data from the Internet and display that in an application.

Because this chapter is reliant on your having access to at least one Twitter account, if you don't have one, it would be a good idea to register at www.twitter.com. Ensure that you've created the account and that you've "followed" some other Twitter users; whatever your personal feelings are about Twitter, remember that you don't have to use it beyond this chapter, and you can delete your account when you're ready.

After you finish SocialApp, you will enhance the application using collection views, a close cousin of the table view. Collection views have methods and properties similar to those of table views and much of what you learn about table views can be directly applied to collection views.

What Is a Table View?

A table view represents an instance of the UITableView class; it presents the user with a single column of cells listed vertically. Table views provide developers with a great way of displaying a large number of options or data to the user, such as in a Twitter application where you can scroll through potentially hundreds or even thousands of tweets. They can also be used to neatly lay out application settings, exploiting the table view's hierarchical structure to take the user from high-level categories right down to granular details and microsettings. The flexibility of table views means you can find one in nearly every application, but you may not recognize them right away. Figure 8-1 shows some of the table views in use through iOS and the default applications.

© Matthew Knott 2016
M. Knott, *Beginning Xcode*, DOI 10.1007/978-1-4302-5005-0_8

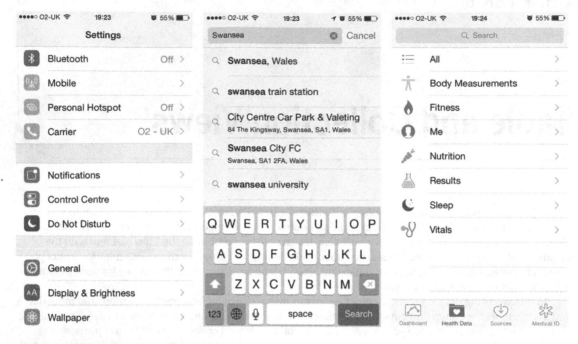

Figure 8-1. *Table views in various iOS apps*

Because of their popularity, Apple spends a lot of time improving the flexibility and feature set of table views with each successive release of iOS. This makes it easy to add features found in many of Apple's own applications such as Pull To Refresh.

Table View Composition

Before you get into the configuration of table views, it's good to have a basic idea of their composition and key components, which are layered on top of each other. Figure 8-2 shows a visual breakdown of the different elements in a table view. Let's examine these components in more detail:

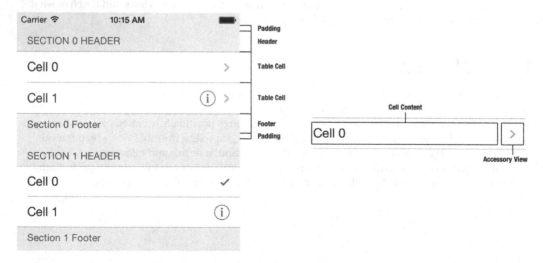

Figure 8-2. *A breakdown of a table view's anatomy*

- *View*: The foundation in the hierarchy of elements. It sits at the bottom of the stack, coordinating all the child components. The `View` element controls the overall look and feel of the table and anchors all the delegate methods together.

- *Section*: The next item in the table view stack. Sections are useful for breaking up tables, grouping cells together, and providing a header and footer for the group.

- *Cell*: Represents a row in the table view and can have varying states, such as when it's being edited, that affects the number of key areas in a cell. The two default areas of a table cell are the cell content and the accessory view. You may think the cell content area is self-explanatory, but it's actually a varied element and, depending on the style of cell, can contain an image, a title, and a subtitle. The accessory view can contain a disclosure indicator, such as an arrow, a detail accessory for providing more information about the row, or both.

Table View Styles

Table views haven't changed visually since they were overhauled in iOS 7. It's worth noting that when Apple released iOS 7, most areas received a visual makeover, but one of the greatest changes was seen in table views. There are two separate styles for table views, but they are no longer as visually distinct as they once were. Figure 8-3 shows a plain style table view on the left and a grouped style table view on the right.

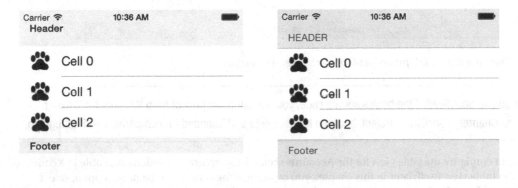

Figure 8-3. *A plain table view (left) and a grouped table view (right)*

In practical terms, you would typically use the plain style to list large amounts of data, usually in a single section with no header or footer. The grouped style is ideal for situations where you have a static list of data and you want to group similar items together, such as the different configuration options in the Settings application in iOS (first image in Figure 8-1).

Configuring the Accounts View

In the Twitter client SocialApp, the Accounts view is one of the simplest to set up, because it uses a plain table view with very little customization. However, you also get your first introduction to the Social and Accounts frameworks, which allow you to access details about accounts set up on the device and then use the account to authorize requests to social media sites such as Twitter or Facebook.

This is the first time you've had to go back to work on an existing project. If you haven't already opened the SocialApp project that you started in Chapter 7, start by opening Xcode and choosing File ➤ Open (⌘+O) to locate SocialApp.xcodeproj in the folder where you created it. Click Open, as shown in Figure 8-4.

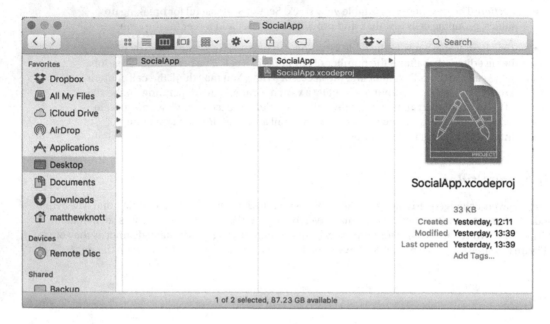

Figure 8-4. *Opening the SocialApp project that you started in Chapter 7*

■ **Note**   If you've downloaded the book's source code, you can open the project from the Chapter 7 folder. Don't open the Chapter 8 SocialApp project, because it's complete and intended for comparison and debugging.

Before you configure the table view for the Accounts scene, let's explore the options available in Xcode for altering the table view itself; later in this chapter, you customize the cells. With the project open, select Main.Storyboard from the Project Navigator and position the storyboard so that you're looking at the Accounts scene, as shown in Figure 8-5.

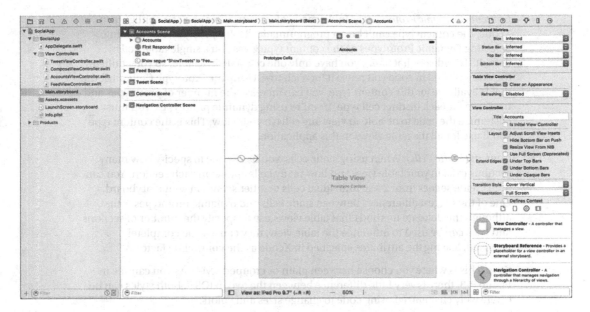

Figure 8-5. *The Accounts scene positioned and ready to go*

The Key Attributes of Table Views

Select the table view in the Accounts scene; you can do this by either clicking the words Table View Prototype Content in the middle of the view or selecting Table View from the Accounts scene in the Document Outline. Now open the Attributes Inspector. If you're looking at the right object, the first segment in the Attributes Inspector is Table View. Figure 8-6 shows the default attributes of a table view in Xcode 8.

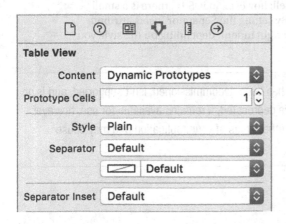

Figure 8-6. *The default attributes of a table view in Xcode 7*

When configuring a table view, most of the time you're after one of these first five attributes, because they have the largest influence on the table view's structure and style. Let's look at these options in more detail.

205

- *Content (Dynamic Prototypes)*: Unlike many of the attributes you can configure in Xcode, the content type can't be set programmatically. It's purely an Xcode thing. Selecting Dynamic Prototypes as the content type gives you a single table cell by default. The idea is that often, you have only one cell style in a table, so you configure the one cell, and in code you reuse it for each row. Using the Prototype Cells attribute that is available for this content type, you can increase the number of prototypes and have one for each distinct cell type. If you're using dynamic prototypes, you must customize the code to be able to view any cells in your view. This is the content type you'll use for all the table views in this application.

- *Content (Static Cells)*: When using static cells, you use Xcode to specify how many sections exist in your table view and how many cells appear in each section. You can then create segues from these individual cells to other scenes in your storyboard. One of the biggest differences between static cells and dynamic prototypes is that, although the delegate methods that table views use to specify the number of sections and cells *can* be used to influence the table view, they can also be completely removed, leaving the attributes specified in Xcode as the controlling factor.

- *Style*: This is where you choose between plain or grouped styles. As you can see in Figure 8-3, there is very little difference between the two in iOS 9. Both styles can be extensively customized using code to change sizes and colors.

- *Separator*: The separator in a table view is the line that appears between cells. This attribute gives you four options to choose from: Default, Single Line, Single Line Etched, and None. In reality, these four options are only two. The Default style is the same as the Single Line style, and Single Line Etched is the same as None, because as it was deemed not compatible with the flat design approach Apple took with iOS 7; effectively, this style and its code equivalent `UITableViewCellSeparatorStyleSingleLineEtched` have been deprecated.

- *Separator Insets*: This was introduced in iOS 7 and Xcode 5. In earlier versions of iOS, the separator spanned the full width of the cell; however, in iOS 10, there is a small indent on the left side of the cell by default. By setting the Separator Insets attribute to Custom, you can specify a custom left and right indent, depending on the style you want to achieve.

■ **Note** In programming, when a class is *deprecated*, it has been decommissioned, isn't supported, and is no longer considered acceptable for use. Often when a class is deprecated, it remains available for use; however, because it's unsupported, it may have consequences with other areas of your application and may cause unexpected issues with other classes.

Manipulating Static Table Views

Let's take a look at how Xcode allows you to manipulate a static layout, before going back and implementing the dynamic prototype system you're using for this scene:

1. Select the Accounts table view and then open the Attributes Inspector. Set the Content attribute to Static Cells; you should notice that the single cell you had becomes three cells, and the second attribute becomes Sections.

2. Let's increase the number of sections so that there are two groups of cells to work with: change the Sections attribute to 2. Your table should now resemble the one shown in Figure 8-7.

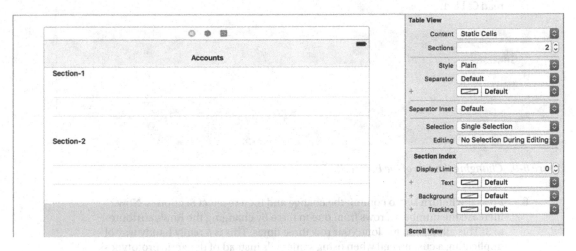

Figure 8-7. *The static layout with two sections*

3. The number of cells in a section is controlled directly by the section attributes. Select the first section by clicking Section-1 in the view or by expanding Table View in the Document Outline and selecting Section-1, as shown in Figure 8-8.

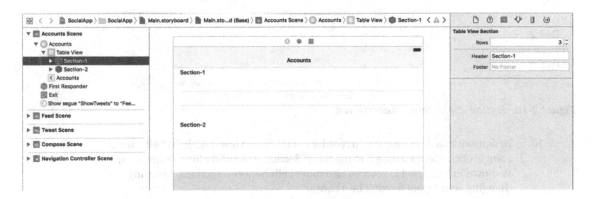

Figure 8-8. *Selecting Section-1 and viewing the section attributes*

4. In the Attributes Inspector, the terminology changes slightly from cells to rows. Looking at the attributes, you can see that here you specify the header and footer value of your section and also the number of rows. Feel free to try setting your own values for these attributes and see how the table changes.

5. You can also delete individual cells and move them around. In Section-2, delete two cells; click the cells individually and then press the Backspace key to remove them. Select the single remaining cell.

6. In the Attributes Inspector, change Style to Basic; doing so adds the word `Title` to the cell.

7. Double-click the word Title to edit it, as shown in Figure 8-9, and change it to read `Cell 1`.

Figure 8-9. *Changing the title of the basic cell*

8. Press the Return key to commit the change and then reselect Section-2. Now increase the number of rows from one to three by changing the Rows attribute to 3. This allows you to clone your row three times. This is a really handy way of duplicating a custom cell when using static cells instead of dynamic prototypes.

9. Rename each of your new cells by double-clicking Cell 1 and changing them to 2 and 3, respectively, so that Section-2 resembles Figure 8-10.

Figure 8-10. *Section-2 with three basic style cells*

10. To demonstrate how easy it is to reorder a static table view, highlight Cell 3 with a single click and then drag it to the top of Section-2. A solid blue line appears, as shown in Figure 8-11. You can also move cells between sections, meaning that changing your layout needn't be a chore.

Figure 8-11. *Selecting the third cell and dragging it to the first position*

11. Now that you've seen the various ways Xcode lets you manipulate static layouts, you're ready to get the Accounts scene built up and working. Reselect the table view, change the Content attribute to Dynamic Prototypes, and ensure that Style is set to Grouped. This will leave you with three cells in the single section.

12. You only want one prototype cell, so delete any excess cells by manually highlighting them and pressing the Backspace key until you're left with a single cell, ready for customizing.

13. Highlight the one remaining cell and go to the Attributes Inspector. The style should currently be set to Custom, which is fine because you'll be setting the content programmatically.

14. Set the Accessory attribute to Disclosure Indicator, which adds the indicator arrow on the right side of the cell.

15. Give your cell an identifier so that you can refer to it in code and reuse it efficiently. Set the Identifier attribute to AccountCell. The cell's attributes should resemble those shown in Figure 8-12.

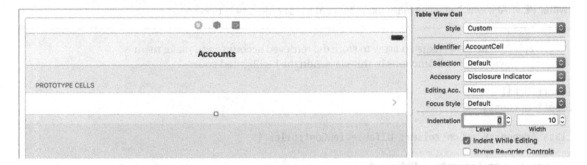

Figure 8-12. *The table cell configured, ready to have its content set*

You're finished with the layout and design of your table view, and it's time to add the code to access the Twitter accounts on the device and display them in the table. To do this, you need to add the Accounts and Social frameworks to the project.

The Accounts and Social Framework

In previous chapters, you took advantage of some of the Apple-provided frameworks, and in this chapter you use two more: Accounts.framework and Social.framework. Like the other frameworks you've used, they make potentially complex and intensive tasks much simpler. Based on the fact that this is the first time you've worked with these two frameworks, it's also worth noting that they work really well together, and you sometimes need to use both in order to make the most of their functionality. Accounts framework classes are prefixed with AC; in this project, you create an instance of the ACAccount class to hold the details of a selected Twitter account. You hand that ACAccount object to other view controllers as you navigate through the project and then combine it with one of the Social framework's classes, SLRequest, which uses the ACAccount object to authenticate requests with Twitter.

If you've worked with Twitter's APIs in the past, you know that authentication involves a process called *three-legged OAuth* that sends a number of requests back and forth with Twitter. The combination of the ACAccount object with the SLRequests means you don't have to do any of that. iOS does all the running around so that you're free to focus on functionality and how you handle the requests to Twitter.

Now that you understand the roles of the frameworks you need to add to the project, you're ready to begin writing the code that will display Twitter accounts in the table view.

Retrieving and Displaying Twitter Accounts

To finish this scene, you need to achieve two objectives: retrieve an array of Twitter accounts registered on the device or in the Simulator and display them for users to choose from. Let's start by setting up the view controller's header, importing the frameworks, and creating the properties that are needed for this scene. As in previous chapters, I explain what needs to be done bit by bit and then review the code at the end of the process:

1. Open AccountsViewController.swift. You first need to import the Accounts framework that is used for this scene. After the line import UIKit, add the following highlighted line:

```
import UIKit
import Accounts
```

■ **Note**   API stands for *application programming interface.* An API is a mechanism that specifies how different pieces of computer software interact with one another. In iOS, Apple uses the term *API* to describe new classes in frameworks. When I talk about the Twitter API, I don't mean classes in the Social framework, but rather the Twitter REST API, which you can learn more about at http://dev.twitter.com.

---

2. You need to create an array to store the retrieved accounts and make them available to all functions in this class. Add the highlighted code:

```
import UIKit
import Accounts

class AccountsViewController: UITableViewController {

    var twitterAccounts : NSArray?
```

3. You need to declare an instance of ACAccountStore. The ACAccountStore class is the gateway to the list of Twitter and other social media accounts stored in iOS; you declare it and then try to get permission from the user to access the Twitter account. If the user grants permission, the object becomes initialized. Add the highlighted code after the NSArray:

```
var twitterAccounts : NSArray?
var accountStore : ACAccountStore?
```

So far, you've added a reference to the Accounts framework, created an array called twitterAccounts, and created an ACAccountStore object to manage the retrieval of Twitter accounts. Your initial code should look like this:

```
import UIKit
import Accounts

class AccountsViewController: UITableViewController {

    var twitterAccounts : Array<Any>?
    var accountStore : ACAccountStore?
```

4. To get into the nitty-gritty, scroll down until you see the `viewDidLoad`
   function. The first thing you want to do when the view loads is initialize the
   `ACAccountStore` instance. That doesn't mean you're accessing the accounts;
   you're just initializing the object so that it can be interacted with. Drop down a
   line after `super.viewDidLoad()` and type the following highlighted line:

```
super.viewDidLoad()
accountStore = ACAccountStore()
```

5. You'll use the `requestAccessToAccountsWithType` method of the `accountStore`
   object. This method needs to be told the type of account to which you're
   requesting access. You do this by creating an `ACAccountType` object and then
   using another `accountStore` method: `accountTypeWithAccountTypeIdentifier`.
   Drop down a line, and add this highlighted code (as a single line):

```
super.viewDidLoad()
accountStore = ACAccountStore()
let accountType : ACAccountType = accountStore!.accountType(withAccountTypeIdentifier:
ACAccountTypeIdentifierTwitter)
```

6. You're at the stage where you want to ask the user for permission
   to use their Twitter accounts in the application using the
   `requestAccessToAccountsWithType` method. When this method is accessed, it
   creates an alert for the users to either grant or deny the request to access their
   Twitter account. Add the following highlighted code:

```
let accountType : ACAccountType = accountStore!.accountType(withAccountTypeIdentifier:
ACAccountTypeIdentifierTwitter)

accountStore?.requestAccessToAccounts(with: accountType, options: nil,
    completion: { granted, error in

})
```

7. Notice that you pass the `accountType` object into the method to specify that it
   wants Twitter account access, and you handle `completion` using a code block
   into which you add the logic as to whether granted returned yes or no. Because
   you only want to look at the accounts available *if* access was granted, that should
   be the next thing you check. To do so, add the highlighted `if` statement in the
   code block, as shown next:

```
let accountType : ACAccountType = accountStore!.accountType(withAccountTypeIdentifier:
ACAccountTypeIdentifierTwitter)

accountStore?.requestAccessToAccounts(with: accountType, options: nil,
    completion: { granted, error in
    if(granted)
    {

    }
})
```

8. With access granted, you need to populate the `twitterAccounts` object with all the available Twitter accounts on the device. Here you use the `accountsWithAccountType` method of the `accountStore` and reuse the `accountType` object to restrict the request to Twitter accounts. In the `if` statement, add the following highlighted code:

```
if(granted)
{
    self.twitterAccounts = self.accountStore!.accounts(with: accountType)
}
```

9. Although the user has granted access, you need to check whether user has added any Twitter accounts to the device. This is done by checking the `twitterAccounts count` property in an `if else` statement. After the previous line, drop down and add this code:

```
if(granted)
{
    self.twitterAccounts = self.accountStore!.accounts(with: accountType)

    if (self.twitterAccounts!.count == 0)
    {

    }
    else
    {

    }
}
```

10. If there are no Twitter accounts stored in iOS, you want to summon an alert view and tell the user that no accounts were found. Because you're running on an arbitrary thread and all interface changes need to be executed on the main thread, you add a Grand Central Dispatch call to execute the display of the alert view. Add the following highlighted code in the first set of braces:

```
if (self.twitterAccounts!.count == 0)
{
    let noAccountsAlert : UIAlertController = UIAlertController(title: "No Accounts Found",
        message: "No Twitter accounts were found.",
        preferredStyle: UIAlertControllerStyle.alert)

    let dismissButton : UIAlertAction = UIAlertAction(title: "Okay",
        style: UIAlertActionStyle.cancel) {
        alert in
        noAccountsAlert.dismiss(animated: true, completion: nil)
    }

    noAccountsAlert.addAction(dismissButton)

    DispatchQueue.main.async() {
```

```
        self.present(noAccountsAlert, animated: true, completion: nil)
    }
}
else
{

}
```

11. If there are Twitter accounts, they're added to the `twitterAccounts` object, and you just need to tell the table view to reload the data shown in the table. This is done by accessing the `reloadData` method. In the second set of braces for the `else` statement, add this highlighted lines of code:

```
else
{

    DispatchQueue.main.async() {
        self.tableView.reloadData()
    }
}
```

You've added the code that pulls together a dataset for the table view in the shape of the `twitterAccounts` array. Now you need to get that data into the cells by using two of the `UITableView` class's delegate methods: `numberOfSectionsInTableView` and `numberOfRowsInSection`. These two methods control the number of sections displayed in the table and also the number of table cells per section by returning an `NSInteger`, a numeric value that the table view interprets. Setting up these two methods is pretty simple in this application: you only ever have one section, and the number of cells is the `count` property from the `twitterAccounts` object. Furthermore, Apple has already added stubs for these two methods.

12. Scroll down until you find the `numberOfSections(in:)` method; or click `AccountsViewController` in the jump bar and select `numberOfSections(in:)`, as shown in Figure 8-13.

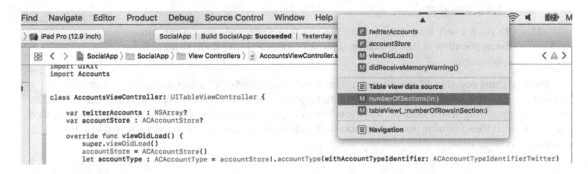

Figure 8-13. *Navigating code using the jump bar*

13. As previously mentioned, the `numberOfSections(in:)` method returns a value that determines how many sections appear in the table view. In this instance, you only want a single section, so change the return value to 1 as shown next:

```
override func numberOfSections(in tableView: UITableView) -> Int {
    return 1
}
```

14. You need to program the tableView(_:numberOfRowsInSection:) method to return the number of items held in the array holding the Twitter accounts configured on this device so that the application knows how many cells to create in the table view, this is done returning the value of cellCount. Because there may be no items in the array, and you don't want an exception, add the highlighted if statement as shown next:

```
override func tableView(_ tableView: UITableView, numberOfRowsInSection section: Int) -> Int
{
    if let cellCount = self.twitterAccounts?.count {
        return cellCount
    }
    else
    {
        return 0
    }
}
```

15. The application will try to create an instance of your prototype cell if there are any Twitter accounts set up in the Simulator, so it's important to set the correct reference name for the cell before trying to run the application. Look for the tableView(_:cellForRowAt:) method: it should be just below the last method you changed. It's commented out by default, so remove the /* from the start and the */ from the end of the method.

16. Within the method you have an object called cell, which is initialized and then before being returned; this object is a UITableViewCell. When initialized, it's passed a value that currently says "reuseIdentifier" but that needs to say "AccountCell", which is the name you gave the table cell when you configured it in the storyboard. Go ahead and change the highlighted value as shown next:

```
let cell = tableView.dequeueReusableCell(withIdentifier: "AccountCell",
        for: indexPath)
```

17. It's been a very long time coming, but you're at a point where you can run the application in the Simulator. Choose Product ➤ Run (⌘+R) to launch the application.

The first thing you should see is a prompt for access to the device's Twitter accounts, as shown in Figure 8-14. It's important to click OK at this point to grant access; you're then presented with one of the two outcomes, depending on the number of Twitter accounts you have. If there are no Twitter accounts installed, you get the alert view warning you that no accounts were found; otherwise, you see a single row with an arrow in your table view.

Figure 8-14. *The security prompt asking for access to the Twitter accounts for the application*

18. If you don't have any Twitter accounts added in iOS and you saw the alert, adding your Twitter account is very easy. In the Simulator, return to the home screen by choosing Hardware ➤ Home (⌘+Shift+H). Navigate to the first page of icons, click the Settings icon, scroll down, and select the Twitter option from the left column, as shown in Figure 8-16.

■ **Note** If you accidentally refuse permission to the application, you can grant permission from the Twitter settings. SocialApp is listed at the bottom of the Twitter settings with a switch beside it, as shown in Figure 8-15. Turn this to the on position, and permission will be granted to access the accounts.

Figure 8-15. *Selecting the Twitter settings and verifying application permissions*

19. Type in your Twitter account name and password and click Sign In. You can repeat this step to add more Twitter accounts if you want. When you're done, go back to Xcode and rerun your application; this time your view should resemble Figure 8-16.

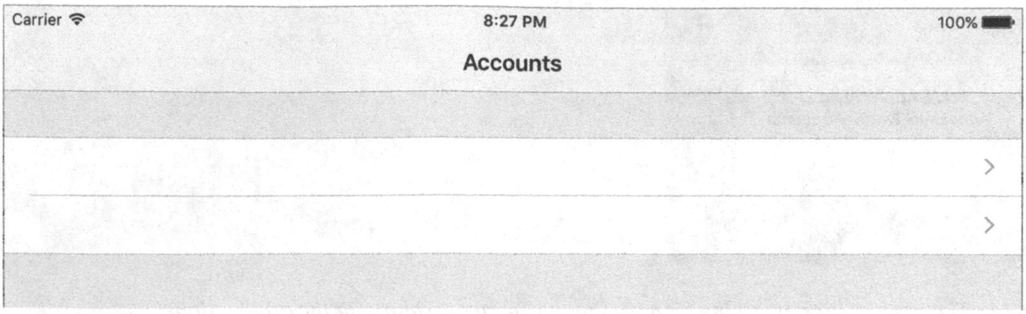

Figure 8-16. *The Accounts view with hopefully one or more rows that will show account details*

Although the application runs, you still have to make the table view display the account name in the cell (currently it's empty); and to do that, you need to add some code to the delegate method tableView(_:cellForRowAt:). This is the method you quickly altered before running the application. All delegate methods are called as the result of an event occurring. In this case, it's the table view responding to the number of rows it has been told to display and then calling the tableView(_:cellForRowAt:) method to allow it to populate the specific cell's contents. To display the correct account information in the cell, the application needs to know which row it's on so that the corresponding entry can be fetched from the array. You can establish this by looking at the method variable indexPath. This object has properties indicating the cell's section and row numbers: both follow the array format for positioning, starting at 0 and incrementing by 1. Because there is only one section, the row value corresponds to the position of elements in the twitterAccounts array. For example, if the indexPath row property is 0, the application will fetch the account at position 0 in the array.

20. Remove the comment // Configure the cell… and in its place create an ACAccount object based on the account stored at the supplied position in the array:

```
if let account : ACAccount = self.twitterAccounts?[indexPath.row] as? ACAccount {

}
```

21. Put a value in the table view cell that shows the name of the account in the array. The table cell is currently the default UITableViewCell, which has three controls that can be manipulated: a label called textLabel, a subtitle label called detailTextLabel, and an image view called imageView. Let's take the accountDescription property of the account object and use it to set the textLabel's Text property, as shown in the highlighted code:

```
if let account : ACAccount = self.twitterAccounts?[indexPath.row] as? ACAccount {
    cell.textLabel!.text = account.accountDescription
}
```

22. The complete method should look like this:

```
override func tableView(_ tableView: UITableView, cellForRowAt indexPath: IndexPath) ->
UITableViewCell {

    let cell = tableView.dequeueReusableCell(withIdentifier: "AccountCell", for: indexPath)
```

```
    if let account : ACAccount = self.twitterAccounts?[indexPath.row] as? ACAccount {
        cell.textLabel!.text = account.accountDescription
    }

    return cell
}
```

23. Run your application again; this time the table view should be populated as shown in Figure 8-17. What's more, if you select an account, you're taken to the FeedViewController scene.

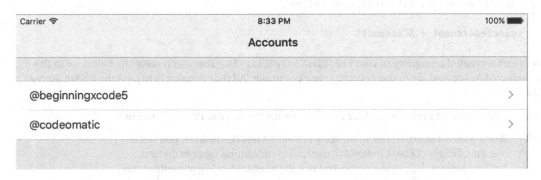

Figure 8-17. *The table view showing a list of Twitter accounts*

■ **Caution**   Clicking the Compose button at this stage will cause the view appear and, while it looks great, you haven't yet written the code to dismiss the view controller and are stuck unless you rerun the application from Xcode.

One great feature to take note of here is that as you show the Feed view controller, you're automatically given a button that takes you back to the Accounts view controller without having to write any code.

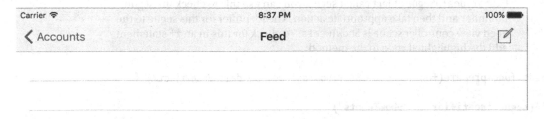

Figure 8-18. *The navigation controller allows you to navigate back to the Accounts view without adding any code*

Before you focus on the next scene—the Feed view controller—you need to think ahead slightly. When an account is selected, that selection made in the Accounts view controller needs to be passed on, a bit like a baton in a relay, to the Feed view controller when the segue is triggered. To do this, you need to create a custom initializer in the Feed view controller to receive the selected ACAccount object.

24. Open FeedViewController.swift from the Project Navigator. Because you need to refer to both the Accounts *and* the Social framework in this view controller, add the following two highlighted import statements after import UIKit:

```
import UIKit
import Accounts
import Social
```

25. Right after the class definition, type the following highlighted line:

```
class FeedViewController: UITableViewController {

    var selectedAccount : ACAccount!
```

You've now created a property in your FeedViewController class that can receive the baton, or in this case the selected ACAccount, from the Accounts view controller. All that remains is to pass the object across when the segue is called.

26. Open AccountsViewController.swift once more from the Project Navigator.

27. If you weren't using segues to navigate between view controllers, you would use the didSelectRowAtIndexPath method to determine what to do next; but because you're using a segue, you use the prepareForSegue method. Yet again, the good folks at Apple have already written a basic implementation of the method for you, but it's currently commented out. At the bottom of the AccountsViewController.swift file, you should see the method you need, commented out in green (assuming you haven't deviated from the default color scheme). Before the line // MARK: - Navigation are the characters /* that index the start of a commented block of code; remove them. Next, look for */ just before the last }; this signifies the end of the comment block. Remove it as well. The method is now uncommented and ready for use.

28. The prepare(for:sender:) method is called when a segue is about to be triggered. It gives you a chance to perform any actions that need to be processed before the view changes. One of the parameters passed to this method is a UIStoryboardSegue object called segue; you can use this to check the segue identifier and then take appropriate action. The identifier for this segue to the Feed view controller scene is ShowTweets. To check for this in an if statement, add the highlighted code to the method:

```
override func prepare(for segue: UIStoryboardSegue, sender: AnyObject?) {

    if(segue.identifier == "ShowTweets")
    {

    }
}
```

29. You need to find out which account was selected. Create an ACAccount object from the selection and pass that to the Feed view controller's selected account property. The first task is to determine which row was selected. You do this by creating an NSIndexPath object called path based on the result of the indexPathForSelectedRow property. Add the following highlighted line to your if statement:

```
if(segue.identifier == "ShowTweets")
{
    if let path : IndexPath = self.tableView.indexPathForSelectedRow {

    }
}
```

30. Create the ACAccount object, called account. This is almost an exact duplicate of when you instantiated an ACAccount object in the cellForRowAtIndexPath method, as the highlighted code shows:

```
if(segue.identifier == "ShowTweets")
{
    if let path : IndexPath = self.tableView.indexPathForSelectedRow {

        if let account : ACAccount = self.twitterAccounts![path.row] as? ACAccount {
        }
    }
}
```

31. Pass the account object to the Feed view controller. When a segue is triggered and this method is called, the destination view controller is stored in a property of the segue object called destinationViewController. Because you know that the destination view controller is a Feed view controller, you cast destinationViewController from a generic AnyObject type to be a FeedViewController type. Once you've created a FeedViewController object, you simply take the account object and give it to selectedAccount. All of these actions are done in the following highlighted code:

```
if(segue.identifier == "ShowTweets")
{
    if let path : IndexPath = self.tableView.indexPathForSelectedRow {

        if let account : ACAccount = self.twitterAccounts![path.row] as? ACAccount {
            let targetController = segue.destination as! FeedViewController
            targetController.selectedAccount = account
        }
    }
}
```

That's it! You've finished writing the code for the Accounts view controller and even added a bit to the Feed view controller. That's one down and five to go. Let's move on to the Feed view controller, where you build on your table view skills and learn about creating custom cells and subclassing UITableViewCell to take customizations to another level.

Configuring the Feed View

The Feed view is the center point of SocialApp; it lists the 20 latest tweets using some of the methods and classes used in the previous Accounts view, along with many that haven't been encountered in the app so far. In the sections that follow, you learn how to:

- Use the `SLRequest` class to fetch the JSON-formatted data from the Internet

- Use an `NSCache` object to handle some basic caching

- Use an `NSOperationQueue` to streamline the retrieval of Twitter avatar images

- Subclass `UITableViewCell` to create a custom class for the cells in the table view

Because I really want to focus on the table view and how to populate it, I won't go into much detail about the code used for retrieving the data from the Twitter API or processing it. You've already learned how to access the documentation for different classes, so if you want to know more, I encourage you to look at the documentation and then branch out onto the Internet if you want to know more.

Figure 8-19 shows what the rows in the finished table view will look like. Before I get into the code, you need to build the cell's interface and link it to a custom `UITableViewCell` class. Here are the steps:

1. You subclass `UITableViewCell` the same way you did `UITableViewController`. Right-click the SocialApp group in the Project Navigator and choose New File (⌘+N), as shown in Figure 8-20.

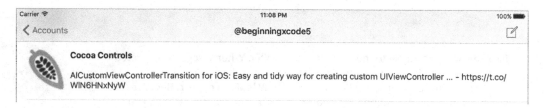

Figure 8-19. A look ahead at a row from the finished Feed view

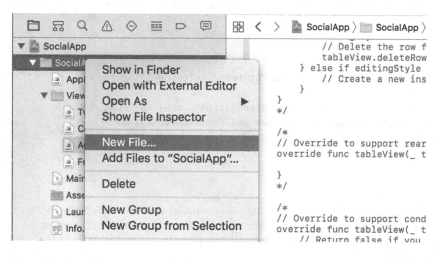

Figure 8-20. Adding a new file to the SocialApp group in the Project Navigator

2. Select the Cocoa Touch Class option, which should be selected by default, and click Next. Set the Subclass… value to UITableViewCell and the Class value to TweetCell. There is no need to create an XIB file, so leave that unchecked and click Next. As always, you want to save the file in the project folder. Click Create to create the file and add it to the project. You're now ready to set up the visual elements of the table view.

3. Open Main.storyboard from the Project Navigator and arrange the view so you can see the Feed scene, as shown in Figure 8-21.

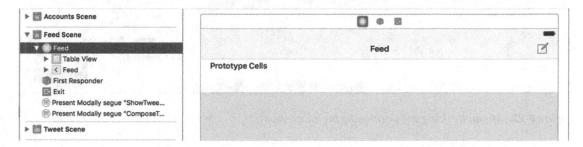

Figure 8-21. *The storyboard file, open and ready for you to build the interface*

4. The default row height of the cell is far too small to display everything nicely. To resize the cell, select the table view as you did in the previous scene by clicking the view where it says Table View Prototype Content or by selecting Table View from the Feed view controller scene in the Document Outline. Next, open the Size Inspector and set the Row Height value to 120, as shown in Figure 8-22.

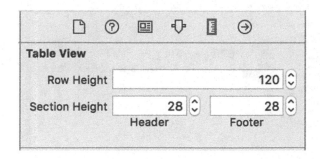

Figure 8-22. *Adjusting the height of the row in the Size Inspector*

5. Before you start creating the interface of the cell, you need to specify that the cell is controlled by the new TweetCell class. Select the cell, open the Identity Inspector, and, from the Class drop-down list, select TweetCell.

6. Open the Attributes Inspector for the cell. You need to specify a reuse identifier here, so in the Identifier attribute, type TweetCell.

7. Now that there is plenty of room to work, you can add the controls: an image view and two labels. Start by dragging in an image view from the Object Library onto the cell. It tries to fill the view, but don't worry; put it anywhere and go back the Size Inspector. Set the X and Y values to 20 and the Height and Width values to 79. The view should resemble that shown in Figure 8-23.

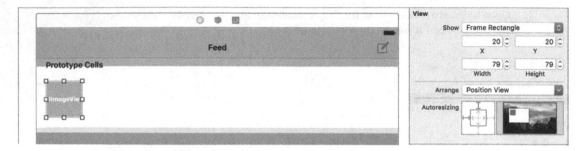

Figure 8-23. *Manually sizing and positioning the image view*

8. This image view will display the Twitter photo of the tweet's author. Before you leave the image view, you need to set a default image to act as a placeholder while the image is downloading from the Internet. Open `Assets.xcassets` from the Project Navigator: in the project files for this chapter is a folder called `images` that contains a file called `camera.png`. Drag that file from Finder to the Asset Catalog sidebar, as shown in Figure 8-24.

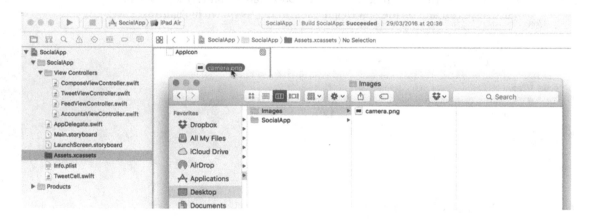

Figure 8-24. *Dragging in* `camera.png`

9. When you release the file, it automatically creates an image set named `camera`. Switch back to the storyboard, select the image view if it isn't already selected, and open the Attributes Inspector.

10. Set the Image attribute to `camera`, which should be shown in the list of available images. Your image view should now resemble Figure 8-25.

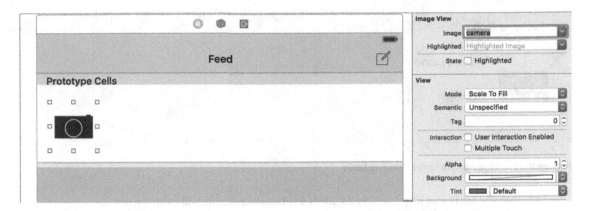

Figure 8-25. *Setting the attributes of the image view so that it has a placeholder image*

11. Add a label for the username of the author of the tweet. To do so, drag in a label from the Object Library and align it with the top of the image view. In the Attributes Inspector, change the Text attribute to User Name. Using the arrow icon, change the Font attribute to System, Style to Bold and Size to 17.

12. With the font and the placeholder text set correctly, size the label appropriately. Keep it at a single-line height, but increase the width to the right until the blue margin appears. It should resemble Figure 8-26.

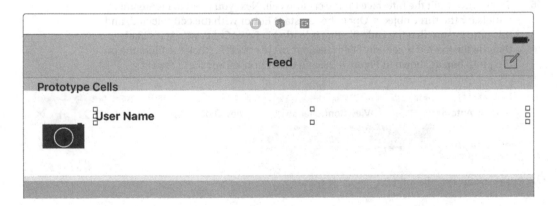

Figure 8-26. *Aligning the User Name label*

13. The final object that needs to be added to the cell is a label for the tweet content. Drag in a label and position it just below the User Name label. Make it the same width as the User Name label and then increase the height until the margin guidelines at the bottom of the cell appear. Change the default text to read Content. Your cell should resemble Figure 8-27.

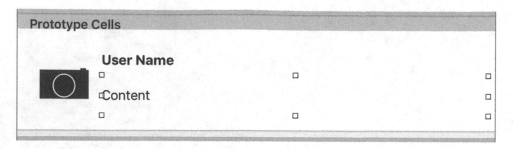

Figure 8-27. Aligning the tweet Content label

14. In the Attributes Inspector, set the Lines attribute to 2. Xcode will wrap the text onto a second line if needed.

■ **Note** If the text length exceeds what will fit on two lines, the Line Breaks attribute will determine what will happen. The default option is Truncate Tail, which cuts the text short and appends an ellipsis (or …) to the end of the text.

---

15. To align the interface elements, click the Resolve Auto Layout Issues button. Under All Views in TweetCell, choose Add Missing Constraints.

16. You've now built the interface for the custom cell. Next you need to create the outlets for the three objects. Open the Assistant Editor with the cell selected, and this time ensure that the code file that is loaded is TweetCell.swift; it's likely that the file loaded is actually FeedViewController.swift. Click the filename on the jump bar, as shown in Figure 8-28. and then choose TweetCell.swift.

Figure 8-28. Ensuring that TweetCell.swift is loaded before creating the outlet

17. Control+drag a connection from the image view to just below class TweetCell and release the mouse. Name this outlet tweetUserAvatar, as shown in Figure 8-29.

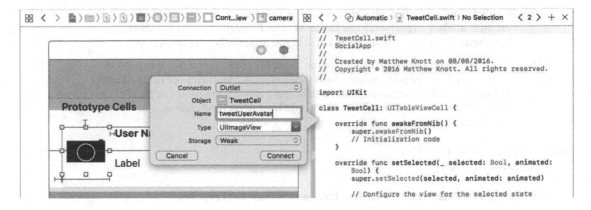

Figure 8-29. *Creating an outlet for the image view called* `tweetUserAvatar`

18. Create an outlet in the same way for the User Name label, naming it
     tweetUserName. Finally, create an outlet for the Content label named
     tweetContent. The start of your custom UITableViewCell class should resemble
     the following code:

```
import UIKit

class TweetCell: UITableViewCell {
    @IBOutlet weak var tweetUserAvatar: UIImageView!
    @IBOutlet weak var tweetUserName: UILabel!
    @IBOutlet weak var tweetContent: UILabel!
```

Now that you've created the interface and the outlets for the objects in the cell's view, you can begin to
bring all the different elements and classes together in the Feed view controller. Here you write the code that
fetches the Twitter feed and then parses the returned data before displaying it in the custom table cell:

1. To get started, prepare the header file. Switch back to the Standard Editor and
    then open FeedViewController.swift from the Project Navigator. You need to
    create some instance variables, just as you did for AccountsViewController, but
    this time you're creating three. After var selectedAccount : ACAccount!, add
    the following highlighted code:

```
class FeedViewController: UITableViewController {

    var selectedAccount : ACAccount!
    var tweets : NSMutableArray?
    var imageCache : NSCache<AnyObject, AnyObject>?
```

___

■ **Note** You have a lot of code to get through for this view controller. As I already mentioned, I won't be going
into a huge amount of detail, but be assured that much of the code you're writing in this chapter is reusable for
any kind of application that fetches data from the Internet.

___

2. Scroll down to the viewDidLoad method. Because this method is called when the view loads, you perform a few key tasks here. First, clear out all the green commented lines of code so you're left with just super.viewDidLoad().

3. You need to set the title of the view to the Twitter account name that was passed to the view from the previous Accounts view controller, initialize OperationQueue and configure its basic settings, and finally add a call to a function that hasn't been written yet called retrieveTweets. Add the highlighted code to your viewDidLoad method:

```
override func viewDidLoad() {
    super.viewDidLoad()

    self.navigationItem.title = selectedAccount.accountDescription

    retrieveTweets()
}
```

4. Xcode correctly flags the last line of the viewDidLoad method as being in error. This is because you haven't written that function yet. Drop down a few lines after the viewDidLoad method and declare the function stub as shown next:

```
func retrieveTweets() {

}
```

5. Xcode is happy that everything is back in order. You still need to write this method's substantial code. I'll take you through each major block of code and explain the function as I go, as opposed to going line by line as I have in the past. First you need to clear the tweets array to remove any previously stored tweets. Add the highlighted code to start the function:

```
func retrieveTweets() {
    tweets?.removeAllObjects()
}
```

6. You need to check that you do indeed have a valid ACAccount object. If so, you declare and initialize an SLRequest object with the URL to the Twitter API that provides the home timeline data you want to display in the table view. You then authenticate the request using the selectedAccount ACAccount object. Drop down a line and add this highlighted code:

```
func retrieveTweets() {
    tweets?.removeAllObjects()

    if let account = selectedAccount {
        let requestURL =
            URL(string: "https://api.twitter.com/1.1/statuses/home_timeline.json")

        if let request = SLRequest(forServiceType: SLServiceTypeTwitter,
            requestMethod: SLRequestMethod.GET,
            url: requestURL,
```

```
        parameters: [:]) {

        request.account = account
    }
}
}
```

7. For the final block of this method, you've given the `request` object all the parameters it needs, and now you execute the `performRequestWithHandler` method. This method accesses the supplied URL and returns the response from the request to a code block. If the request is successful, it returns a status code of 200. When this happens, you parse the JSON code into an array and use that as the contents of the `tweets` array. Finally, you call the `reloadData` method of the table view to update the information shown on the screen. Add the highlighted code after the last line you wrote:

```
request.account = account
request.perform()
{
    responseData, urlResponse, error in

    if(urlResponse?.statusCode == 200)
    {
        if(urlResponse?.statusCode == 200)
        {
            do {
                self.tweets = try JSONSerialization.jsonObject(with: responseData!,
                    options: JSONSerialization.ReadingOptions.mutableContainers) as?
                    NSMutableArray
            }
            catch let error as NSError {
                print("json error: \(error.localizedDescription)")
            }
        }
    }

    DispatchQueue.main.async() {
        self.tableView.reloadData()
    }
}
```

■ **Note** If you aren't familiar with `http response` codes, it may be worth looking up the common codes online. Even if you've never heard the term before, you've almost certainly come across them while browsing the Internet. Errors 404 and 500 are two of the more visible error codes that you may have seen on a web site in the past, but there are many others, and it's worth doing some research on them if you intend to use web APIs to get data into your application.

---

8. The completed code for the retrieveTweets method should look like this:

```
func retrieveTweets() {
    tweets?.removeAllObjects()

    if let account = selectedAccount {
        let requestURL =
            URL(string: "https://api.twitter.com/1.1/statuses/home_timeline.json")

        if let request = SLRequest(forServiceType: SLServiceTypeTwitter,
                            requestMethod: SLRequestMethod.GET,
                            url: requestURL,
                            parameters: [:]) {

            request.account = account
            request.perform()
                {
                    responseData, urlResponse, error in

                    if(urlResponse?.statusCode == 200)
                    {
                        if(urlResponse?.statusCode == 200)
                        {
                            do {
                                self.tweets = try JSONSerialization.jsonObject(with:
                                responseData!, options: JSONSerialization.ReadingOptions.
                                mutableContainers) as? NSMutableArray
                            }
                            catch let error as NSError {
                                print("json error: \(error.localizedDescription)")
                            }
                        }
                    }

                    DispatchQueue.main.async() {
                        self.tableView.reloadData()
                    }
                }
        }
    }
}
```

9. This is a good point at which to run your application to check for errors. The application should compile and allow you to select a Twitter account. On the feed screen, you don't see anything yet; but more importantly, you shouldn't see any errors. If you do, check things such as the correctness of the name of the segue in the storyboard and whether you typed the URL correctly.

10. Back in FeedViewController.swift, it's time to look at the table view delegate methods. Starting with numberOfSections(in:) and tableView(_:numberOf RowsInSection:), you need to return 1 for the single section you want to have and the number of tweets in the array to set the number of rows in the table. The completed methods should look like this:

```
override func numberOfSectionsInTableView(tableView: UITableView) -> Int {
    return 1
}

override func tableView(_ tableView: UITableView, numberOfRowsInSection section: Int) -> Int
{
    // Return the number of rows in the section.

    if let tweetCount = self.tweets?.count {
        return tweetCount
    }
    else
    {
        return 0
    }
}
```

11. It's time to pair the data you've received and stored in the array with the custom TweetCell table cell using the tableView(_:cellForRowAt:) method. Delete the comments surrounding the method so you're left with just the stub and change the highlighted values:

```
override func tableView(_ tableView: UITableView, cellForRowAt indexPath: IndexPath) ->
UITableViewCell {
    let cell = tableView.dequeueReusableCell(withIdentifier: "TweetCell",
        for: indexPath) as! TweetCell

    // Configure the cell...

    return cell
}
```

12. You need to create two NSDictionary objects to store different parts of the Twitter feed data. One stores the main message data; the other stores the portion that relates directly to the user who created the tweet. An NSDictionary is a type of array that uses a key-value pairing system to store and access data. This means instead of asking for the value at position 0, as you would with an array, you ask for the value that corresponds to "name." Add the following highlighted code into your method:

```
let cell = tableView.dequeueReusableCell(withIdentifier: "TweetCell", for: indexPath) as!
TweetCell

let tweetData = tweets?.object(at: indexPath.row) as! NSDictionary
let userData = tweetData.object (forKey: "user") as! NSDictionary

return cell
```

13. Let's take data from those NSDictionary objects and populate the interface. Add the following highlighted code to set the values of the two labels and then return the cell object to stop the error from being reported in Xcode:

```
let tweetData = tweets?.object(at: indexPath.row) as! NSDictionary
let userData = tweetData.object(forKey: "user") as! NSDictionary
```

```
cell.tweetContent.text? = tweetData.object(forKey: "text") as! String
cell.tweetUserName.text? = userData.object(forKey: "name") as! String
```

```
return cell
```

14. Because you returned the `cell` object, you're now error free and can run the application. You haven't set the image yet, but you should be able to select your Twitter account and see the user and content values in each cell, as shown in Figure 8-30. If you get an exception when you go to the Feed view controller, check that you specified the correct reuse identifier on the cell in the storyboard as well as in the code.

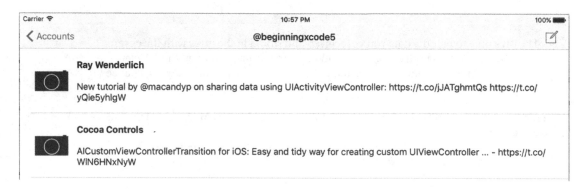

Figure 8-30. *The avatar-less Twitter feed being displayed*

15. I hope you have a huge sense of satisfaction at seeing your application finally come to life as it reads live data from the Internet. There is one final block of code for this method, which focuses on retrieving, caching, and displaying Twitter users' avatars. First you try to retrieve the image from the cache; if that fails, you create an operation for the `OperationQueue` queue object to fetch the image's data and create an image from it before displaying it and then caching it for future use. Add the following highlighted code:

```
cell.tweetUserName.text? = userData.object(forKey: "name") as! String
```

```
let operationQueue = OperationQueue.main
operationQueue.maxConcurrentOperationCount = 4
```

```
let imageURLString = userData.object(forKey: "profile_image_url_https") as! String
let image = imageCache?.object(forKey: imageURLString as AnyObject) as? UIImage
```

```
if let cachedImage = image {
    cell.tweetUserAvatar.image = cachedImage
}
```

```
else
{
    cell.tweetUserAvatar.image = UIImage(named: "camera.png")

    operationQueue.addOperation() {
        let imageURL = URL(string: imageURLString)
        do {
            if let imageData : Data = try Data(contentsOf: imageURL!) {

                let image = UIImage(data: imageData) as UIImage?

                if let downloadedImage = image {
                    OperationQueue.main.addOperation(){
                        let cell = tableView.cellForRow(at: indexPath) as! TweetCell

                        cell.tweetUserAvatar.image = downloadedImage

                    }

                    self.imageCache?.setObject(downloadedImage, forKey: imageURLString as
                    AnyObject)
                }
            }
        }
        catch let error as NSError {
            print("parse error: \(error.localizedDescription)")
        }
    }
}

return cell
```

16. Finally, open the info.plist file from the Project Navigator. Hover over the first
    line information property list and click the plus symbol. In the row that
    appears, choose App Transport Security Settings. Next mouse over the row
    you just added and click the plus icon, this time select Allow Arbitrary Loads
    and change its value from No to Yes. Your info.plist should resemble Figure 8-31.

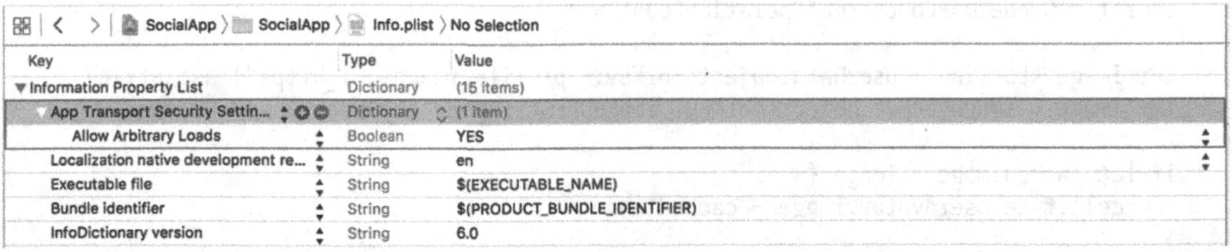

Key	Type	Value
▼ Information Property List	Dictionary	(15 items)
▶ App Transport Security Settin... ⬍ ⊕ ⊖	Dictionary ⬍	(1 item)
Allow Arbitrary Loads ⬍	Boolean	YES
Localization native development re... ⬍	String	en
Executable file ⬍	String	$(EXECUTABLE_NAME)
Bundle identifier ⬍	String	$(PRODUCT_BUNDLE_IDENTIFIER)
InfoDictionary version ⬍	String	6.0

Figure 8-31. Changing the info.plist settings for the application

17. Take this opportunity to rerun the application. This time, after a brief delay,
    images should appear instead of the placeholder camera.png image, as shown in
    Figure 8-32.

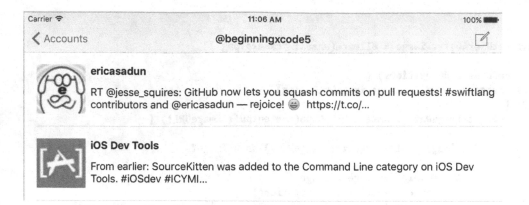

Figure 8-32. *The Twitter feed, with avatar images included this time*

> ■ **Note**   There is always a delay when fetching data from the Internet. But because you're using the `OperationQueue` object and efficiently switched between the main and arbitrary threads, there is no slowdown in the application, which would have guaranteed you negative app store reviews. Notice how quickly you can scroll up and down the list of tweets, all because the NSCache stores them for later use.

Before moving on, here is the full code for the `tableView(_:cellForRowAt:)` method:

```
override func tableView(_ tableView: UITableView, cellForRowAt indexPath: IndexPath) ->
UITableViewCell {
    let cell = tableView.dequeueReusableCell(withIdentifier: "TweetCell", for: indexPath)
    as! TweetCell

    let tweetData = tweets?.object(at: indexPath.row) as! NSDictionary
    let userData = tweetData.object(forKey: "user") as! NSDictionary

    cell.tweetContent.text? = tweetData.object(forKey: "text") as! String
    cell.tweetUserName.text? = userData.object(forKey: "name") as! String

    let operationQueue = OperationQueue.main
    operationQueue.maxConcurrentOperationCount = 4

    let imageURLString = userData.object(forKey: "profile_image_url_https") as! String
    let image = imageCache?.object(forKey: imageURLString as AnyObject) as? UIImage

    if let cachedImage = image {
        cell.tweetUserAvatar.image = cachedImage
    }
    else
    {
        cell.tweetUserAvatar.image = UIImage(named: "camera.png")

        operationQueue.addOperation() {
```

```
            let imageURL = URL(string: imageURLString)
            do {
                if let imageData : Data = try Data(contentsOf: imageURL!) {

                    let image = UIImage(data: imageData) as UIImage?

                    if let downloadedImage = image {
                        OperationQueue.main.addOperation(){
                            let cell = tableView.cellForRow(at: indexPath) as! TweetCell

                            cell.tweetUserAvatar.image = downloadedImage

                        }

                        self.imageCache?.setObject(downloadedImage, forKey: imageURLString
                        as AnyObject)
                    }
                }
            }
        catch let error as NSError {
            print("parse error: \(error.localizedDescription)")
        }
    }
}

return cell
}
```

18. Next let's create the stubs for the two segues away from this view controller:
     ComposeTweet and ShowTweet. Scroll down to the bottom of the file and
     uncomment the prepare(for:sender:) method.

19. Handle the two possible segues by adding the following highlighted code:

```
override func prepare(for segue: UIStoryboardSegue, sender: Any?) {
    if(segue.identifier == "ComposeTweet")
    {

    }
    else if(segue.identifier == "ShowTweet")
    {

    }
}
```

That's it for the Feed view controller for now. Once the other views have been configured, you'll come back to this file and add the code to pass the baton when the segue is triggered. For now, let's move on to the third view controller: Tweet view controller.

Because the final two views in the application subclass the UIViewController, in the following section I only focus on adding the code. This is mainly so that you can see how the application builds up in stages and that it's rarely spit into neat chunks. But this will also give you the satisfaction of building your own working Twitter client.

Configuring the Tweet View

The Tweet view controller allows users to see the full text of the tweet they selected from the Twitter feed, as well as any associated metadata. This is useful if the text in the table view cell has been truncated. If you were making a complete Twitter client, you would have to add numerous bits of additional information, such as how many times the tweet has become a favorite or been retweeted. For SocialApp, however, you configure the Feed view controller to pass across an NSDictionary object containing the data of the selected tweet; you then pick relevant information from that object to be displayed in the view.

First, as you did with the Feed view controller, let's configure the Tweet view controller to receive the NSDictionary. Because you're just pulling information from an NSDictionary object and not interacting with Twitter or the Internet, you don't need the Accounts or Social framework in this view controller. Follow these steps:

1. Open TweetViewController.swift from the Project Navigator. After the
    @IBOutlets and @IBActions, create an NSDictionary property called
    selectedTweet with this line of code:

```
var selectedTweet : NSDictionary?
```

This creates the global property that will be set when the view is initialized—or, to think of it another way, it's a runner on the track waiting to receive the NSDictionary baton from the runner or view controller before it. Now you need to go back to Feed view controller and pass across an NSDictionary of tweet data.

2. Back in FeedViewController.swift, scroll down to the prepareForSegue
    method. You've already created the if statement that checks for the ShowTweet
    segue, but in that if statement you need to determine the selected row's index,
    retrieve the relevant entry from the tweets array , and pass it to the Tweet view
    controller by setting its selectedTweet property. Following is the if statement
    and all the required highlighted code:

```
else if(segue.identifier == "ShowTweet")
{
    if let path : IndexPath = self.tableView.indexPathForSelectedRow {

        if let tweetData = self.tweets?.object(at: path.row) {

            let targetController = segue.destination as! TweetViewController
            targetController.selectedTweet = tweetData as? NSDictionary
        }
    }
}
```

3. Now that the information is being passed across, it's easy to access the
    information you want to display. Open TweetViewController.swift again.

4. All the processing of data is done in the viewDidLoad method. You fetch the user's avatar directly from the Internet, rather than from the cache. You should be familiar with the rest of the code from the previous view controller. Add the highlighted code to the viewDidLoad method:

```
override func viewDidLoad() {
    super.viewDidLoad()

    let userData = selectedTweet?.object(forKey: "user") as! NSDictionary

    tweetText.text? = selectedTweet?.object(forKey: "text") as! String
    tweetAuthorName.text? = userData.object(forKey: "name") as! String

    let imageURLString = userData.object(forKey: "profile_image_url_https") as! String
    let imageURL = URL(string: imageURLString)
    if let imageData = NSData(contentsOf: imageURL!) {

        DispatchQueue.main.async {
            self.tweetAuthorAvatar.image = UIImage(data: imageData as Data)
        }
    }
}
```

5. To make the tweet close with the Cancel button, you implement the dismissView method, which uses the UIViewController method of dismiss. Because it's a UIViewController method and this is the implementation file for a class that subclasses UIViewController, you access your base class methods by using self, although it isn't always necessary with Swift. Add the highlighted line of code to your action:

```
@IBAction func dismissView(sender: AnyObject) {
    self.dismiss(animated: true, completion: nil)
}
```

That's it! Go ahead and run your application. Select a tweet from the feed, and the tweet should be expanded in the modal dialog. For the first time, you can see the form sheet presentation style in effect, as shown in Figure 8-33. Now let's move on to the final view controller in this application: the Compose view controller.

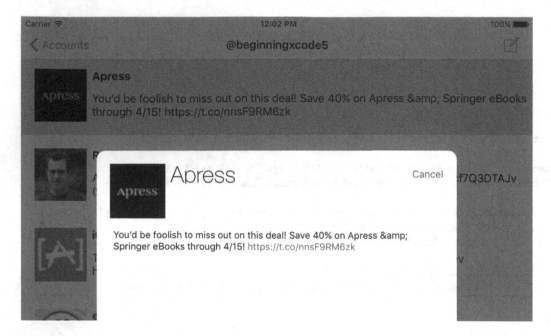

Figure 8-33. *The Tweet view controller showing the data that was passed to it along with an image pulled directly from the Internet. Notice the link detection in effect.*

Configuring the Compose View

The final view for this application is the Compose view controller. This is where the user can compose a message and post it to Twitter. Let's enforce the 140-character limit for tweets by using a `UITextView` delegate method and then animate the activity indicator when it's sending the tweet data to Twitter. Here are the steps:

1. You've created the visual element and set up the outlets, so open `ComposeViewController.swift`. As previously mentioned, you're using a `UITextView` delegate method, so the first thing you need to do is implement the `UITextViewDelegate` protocol. Add the highlighted code to the `class` line so that it looks like this:

```
class ComposeViewController: UIViewController, UITextViewDelegate {
```

2. You need the Social and Accounts frameworks for this view controller, so add their `import` statements beneath the line that says `import UIKit`:

```
import UIKit
import Accounts
import Social
```

3. To create a property to receive the `ACAccount` object for the selected account from the Feed view controller, after the `class` line, add the following highlighted code:

```
class ComposeViewController: UIViewController, UITextViewDelegate {
    var selectedAccount : ACAccount!
```

4. Go back to FeedViewController.swift to pass the selected account details over to your newly created property.

5. Scroll down until you see the prepareForSegue method. You have an empty if statement set up for the ComposeTweet segue; modify it so that it passes the selectedAccount object to the Compose view controller, as shown next:

```
if(segue.identifier == "ComposeTweet")
{
    let targetController = segue.destination as! ComposeViewController
    targetController.selectedAccount = selectedAccount
}
```

6. Switch back to ComposeViewController.swift.

7. You need to create a custom function and a delegate method as well as two actions in this view controller. The good news is that none of them require a great deal of code. Scroll down until you see the viewDidLoad method. All you need to do here is specify the delegate property of the text view, which as I've mentioned previously is this view controller, so it's set to self. Although you can add this in the storyboard, let's do it here for the sake of variety. After the super.viewDidLoad() line, add the following code:

```
override func viewDidLoad() {
    super.viewDidLoad()
    self.tweetContent.delegate = self
}
```

8. You need to create a function called postContent to handle the transmission of the tweet text to the chosen Twitter account. Create the function stub just below the viewDidLoad method:

```
func postContent(post : String) {

}
```

9. As you can see, the function takes one parameter, a String object called post. The first thing you want to do when this function is called is to start animating the postActivity activity indicator. You do this by sending the startAnimating message. Due to the way the activity indicator was configured in Chapter 7, it's at this point that it appears and begins its animation:

```
func postContent(post : String){
    postActivity.startAnimating()

}
```

10. You're ready to prepare the Twitter request. Just as you did in the Feed view controller, let's create an NSURL object with the appropriate API URL for the type of request you want to make, which is used when instantiating the SLRequest object. A key difference this time is that you use a different HTTP method. You no longer issue a get request but instead issue a post request. When a post request is made with the SLRequest object, you supply the required parameters in an NSDictionary object. If you refer to the Twitter documentation for the status update API at https://dev.twitter.com/docs/api/1.1/post/statuses/update, you see that the only required parameter is called status. The status parameter should be the textual content of the status update, which is the contents of the post parameter the function is supplied with. Drop down a line in the function and add the following code:

```
func postContent(post : String){
    postActivity.startAnimating()

    if let account = selectedAccount {
        let requestURL = URL(string: "https://api.twitter.com/1.1/statuses/update.json")
        if let request = SLRequest(forServiceType: SLServiceTypeTwitter,
                                requestMethod: SLRequestMethod.POST,
                                url: requestURL,
                                parameters: NSDictionary(object: post, forKey: "status" as
                                NSString) as [NSObject : AnyObject]) {

            request.account = account
        }
    }
}
```

11. Access the perform method of the SLRequest object just as you did in the Feed view controller. This time, however, when you receive a successful response code, you want to stop animating the activity indicator and dismiss the view controller. Drop down a line and add the following highlighted code to complete the method:

```
request.account = account
request.perform()
{
    responseData, urlResponse, error in

    if(urlResponse?.statusCode == 200)
    {
        print("Status Posted")

        DispatchQueue.main.async
        {
            self.postActivity.stopAnimating()
            self.dismiss(animated: true, completion: nil)
        }
    }
}
```

Your finished method code should look like this:

```
func postContent(post : String) {
    postActivity.startAnimating()

    if let account = selectedAccount {
        let requestURL = URL(string: "https://api.twitter.com/1.1/statuses/update.json")
        if let request = SLRequest(forServiceType: SLServiceTypeTwitter,
                        requestMethod: SLRequestMethod.POST,
                        url: requestURL,
                        parameters: NSDictionary(object: post, forKey: "status") as
                        [NSObject : AnyObject]) {

            request.account = account

            request.perform()
            {
                responseData, urlResponse, error in

                if(urlResponse?.statusCode == 200)
                {
                    print("Status Posted")

                    DispatchQueue.main.async
                    {
                        self.postActivity.stopAnimating()
                        self.dismiss(animated: true, completion: nil)
                    }
                }
            }
        }
    }
}
```

12. It's time to address the two action methods: dismissView and postToTwitter. These are both one-liners; dismissView is a duplicate of the method used in the Tweet view controller, and postToTwitter simply calls the postContent method you just finished writing. Implement them both as follows:

```
@IBAction func dismissView(_ sender: AnyObject) {
    dismiss(animated: true, completion: nil)
}


@IBAction func postToTwitter(_ sender: AnyObject) {
    postContent(post: self.tweetContent.text)
}
```

13. You need to implement a UITextView delegate method that restricts the text view's content to 140 characters. This is done by using the textView(_:should ChangeTextIn:) method, which is called every time a character is typed. The method checks that the text view's content isn't greater than 140 characters and that it won't exceed 140 characters if someone pastes in some text. If the content is too large, the method returns false, and no more text can be typed. Add the following method just below viewDidLoad:

```
func textView(_ textView: UITextView,
              shouldChangeTextIn range: NSRange,
              replacementText text: String) -> Bool {
    let targetlength : Int = 140
    return textView.text.characters.count <= targetlength
}
```

That was the last line of code for this application! Go ahead and run it and see how all the hard work you've put in over these two chapters has finally paid off. You should be able to successfully access your Twitter accounts, view the Twitter feed, see a tweet in detail, and even post your own.

Importantly, in this chapter, you've learned all about configuring table views and the different methods and properties of the UITableView class, which you no doubt will use heavily in your own applications.

Discovering the Collection View

A collection view is a fantastic class that Apple introduced in iOS 6 and is relatively new (compared to most other objects, which have existed since the first version). Collection views offer developers a flexible way to display large amounts of data just like their cousin the table view, with the difference being that you can display data in columns as well as rows. Another neat feature is that collection views can scroll either vertically or horizontally, giving you that extra dimension as a developer.

Although structurally they're quite similar, one of the largest differences between the collection view and the table view is that the collection view's layout is completely separate from the view. It can be set to either a default or a custom UICollectionViewLayout, giving you a massive amount of flexibility over your design.

To demonstrate the implementation and configuration of a collection view, let's make some pretty drastic changes to SocialApp. First, let's turn it into a tabbed application, and then look at storing user preferences to automate account selection.

Embedding a Tab Bar Controller

The change I'm aiming for here is to have a Feed tab and a Following tab in the application, with the Feed tab obviously being the Feed view controller. Let's create the Following view controller, which is a collection view controller that shows the avatars of all the users that the selected Twitter account follows. To turn SocialApp into a tabbed application, you need to add a tab bar controller between the Accounts view and the Feed view:

1. Open Main.storyboard from the Project Navigator. Navigate around the storyboard until you're able to see the segue connection from the Accounts scene to the Feed scene. Highlight the segue and delete it, as shown in Figure 8-34.

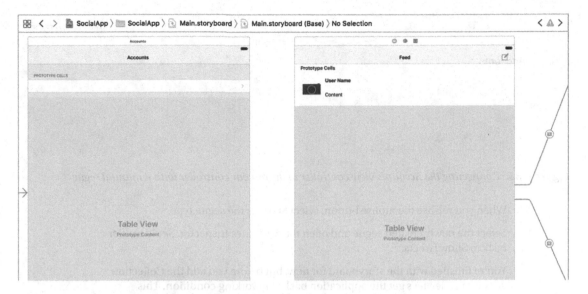

Figure 8-34. The SocialApp storyboard with the ShowTweets segue removed

2. Add a tab bar controller, with the Feed scene as one of the tabs. You could drag in a tab bar controller and manually link it up, but instead let's allow Xcode do the hard work for you. Select the Feed view controller either by clicking it directly in the storyboard or by selecting Feed from beneath Feed Scene in the Document Outline.

3. From the menu bar, choose Editor ➤ Embed In ➤ Tab Bar Controller. This adds a tab bar controller to your storyboard, sets the Feed scene as the first tab, and arranges the views to suit your needs.

4. You need to recreate the ShowTweets segue, but this time you're doing things differently by linking from the Accounts view controller rather than the table cell to the tab bar controller. This is called a *manual* segue because it isn't tied directly to an object that can be triggered by the user. Instead, the segue is triggered programmatically, because it's not possible to segue from a table cell to a tab bar controller and then on to the default view controller. Zoom out and Control+drag a connection from the yellow Accounts icon to the tab bar controller, as shown in Figure 8-35.

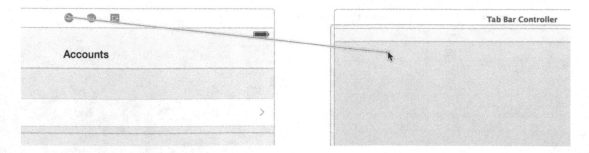

Figure 8-35. *Connecting the Accounts view controller to the tab bar controller with a manual segue*

5. When you release the mouse button, select Show as the segue type.

6. Select the newly created segue and open the Attributes Inspector. Set Identifier back to ShowTweets.

   You're finished with the storyboard for now, but before you add the Collection view controller, let's get the application back to a working condition. This involves executing a manual segue and storing the user's account selection so that whenever the application runs in the future, it will default to the account that the user selected and go straight to the feed.

Persisting User Preferences with UserDefaults

In a real-world scenario, a user picking up SocialApp would find it slightly annoying to have to select their account every time the application runs. Fortunately, iOS gives you a number of ways to persist user preferences, including iCloud and Core Data. In this instance, you're using the incredibly handy UserDefaults class.

UserDefaults allows the app to store values or certain types of objects against a textual key and can't be accessed from other applications. Whenever the application is closed and rerun, the preferences stored in UserDefaults are preserved, but the user can access and change the saved preferences to their heart's content. The UserDefaults class has methods that make it easy to both store and access a range of common types such as Booleans, floats, integers, doubles, and URLs, and it also supports the storage of the following objects:

- Data
- String
- Number
- Date
- Array
- Dictionary

The object you want to store here is an ACAccount, so you have to convert it to a Data object, but I'll get to that in a moment. Follow these steps:

1. Open AccountsViewController.swift from the Project Navigator. You need to create a UserDefaults instance variable to allow you to access the preferences from different methods without having to instantiate the method each time. After the line var accountStore : ACAccountStore?, drop down a line and add the highlighted code:

```
import UIKit
import Accounts

class AccountsViewController: UITableViewController {

    var twitterAccounts : NSArray?
    var accountStore : ACAccountStore?
    var userDefaults : UserDefaults?
```

2. Scroll down to the viewDidLoad method. The first thing you need to do when the view loads is to initialize the userDefaults object and then determine whether a preference called selectedAccount has already been saved; if so, you execute the manual segue with the perform method and go straight to the Feed view controller. After the line accountStore = ACAccountStore(), add the highlighted code:

```
override func viewDidLoad() {
    super.viewDidLoad()
    accountStore = ACAccountStore()

    userDefaults = UserDefaults.standard

    if (userDefaults?.object(forKey: "selectedAccount") != nil) {
        performSegue(withIdentifier: "ShowTweets", sender: self)
    }

    let accountType : ACAccountType = accountStore!.accountType(withAccountTypeIdentifier:
ACAccountTypeIdentifierTwitter)
```

3. That's it for the viewDidLoad method. It's time to address what happens when you tap on a cell. In the past, the segue from the cell was triggered, and the prepare method then passed the selected account across to the feed. This time, however, the application is going to save the selection before moving away. To do this, you use another commonly used UITableView method called didSelectRowAt, which is triggered every time a table cell is selected. Before you implement this method, *delete the entire* prepareForSegue *method;* there is no longer a segue associated with the cell, and the method won't be needed from here on out.

4. To create the didSelectRowAt method stub, after the cellForRowAt method, type the following highlighted code:

```
    return cell
}

override func tableView(_ tableView: UITableView, didSelectRowAt indexPath: IndexPath) {

}
```

5. In this method, you use the indexPath object to allocate an ACAccount object from twitterAccounts array based on the selected cell's index. Add the following highlighted code to the didSelectRowAt method:

```
override func tableView(_ tableView: UITableView, didSelectRowAt indexPath: IndexPath) {

    if let account : ACAccount = self.twitterAccounts![indexPath.row] as? ACAccount {

    }
```

6. As mentioned previously, you need to convert the account object into something that can be stored in the NSUserPreferences; in this case, it will be converted to an NSData object using the NSKeyedArchiver class. After the previous line, add the following highlighted code:

```
override func tableView(tableView: UITableView, didSelectRowAtIndexPath indexPath:
NSIndexPath) {
    if let account : ACAccount = self.twitterAccounts![indexPath.row] as? ACAccount {

        let accountData = NSKeyedArchiver.archivedData(withRootObject: account) as Data
```

7. The selected account is in a compatible format, so it can be saved to the NSUserPreferences instance, userDefaults. The process for saving a preference comes in two parts: first, use the setObject: forKey: method, which associates the accountData object with a key; then, call the synchronize method, which saves the preference to the system. Add the following code to the method:

```
let accountData = NSKeyedArchiver.archivedData(withRootObject: account) as Data
userDefaults?.set(accountData, forKey: "selectedAccount")
userDefaults?.synchronize()
```

8. Now that you've saved the user's selection, you can manually trigger the segue. Just as you did in the viewDidLoad method, you need to call the performSegueWithIdentifier method. Add this code to complete the method:

```
override func tableView(tableView: UITableView, didSelectRowAtIndexPath indexPath:
NSIndexPath) {
    if let account : ACAccount = self.twitterAccounts!.object(at: indexPath.row) as? ACAccount {
        let accountData = NSKeyedArchiver.archivedData(withRootObject: account) as Data
        userDefaults?.set(accountData, forKey: "selectedAccount")
        userDefaults?.synchronize()

        performSegue(withIdentifier: "ShowTweets", sender: self)
    }
}
```

That's it for the Accounts view controller. You've removed the previous mechanisms for selecting an account, considered the overall user experience, and replaced those mechanisms with something that will be much more user friendly.

Now that you've saved the user's selection, you need to implement the retrieval of that selection when the application moves to the Feed view controller:

1. Open FeedViewController.swift and scroll down to the viewDidLoad method.

2. When the view loads, you create an instance of NSUserDefaults; there is no point in creating an instance variable, because this is the only time you need to access it in this file. You then retrieve the selected account from the preferences using the object(forKey:) method, which retrieves the object associated with the key that is supplied: in this case, selectedAccount. Finally, you reverse the conversion process with the NSKeyedUnarchiver class, which allows the conversion of the Data object back into an ACAccount object. After the line super.viewDidLoad(), add the following highlighted code:

```
override func viewDidLoad() {
    super.viewDidLoad()

    let userDefaults = UserDefaults.standard
    let accountData = userDefaults.object(forKey: "selectedAccount") as! Data
    selectedAccount = NSKeyedUnarchiver.unarchiveObject(with: accountData) as! ACAccount

    self.navigationItem.title = selectedAccount.accountDescription

    retrieveTweets()
}
```

3. Run the application in the Simulator. Select an account, and you segue across to the newly tabbed Feed view. Quit the Simulator and then rerun the application. If everything has been done correctly, you should start facing the Feed view instead of the Accounts view! As a user, this is a much more favorable situation to be in. There is, however, one small issue you need to address: after embedding a tab bar controller, the table view positioning changed, and now the first row renders underneath the navigation bar and the title has vanished, as shown in Figure 8-36. This is far from ideal, and unfortunately Xcode doesn't give you an easy way to fix this; it has to be done in code.

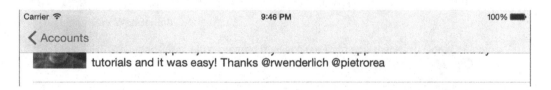

Figure 8-36. The first table row obscured by the navigation bar

4. The title no longer applies itself because when you embedded the tab bar controller, you effectively inserted another level between the view and the navigation bar controller. Ensure that you still have FeedViewController.swift open. Then, in the viewDidLoad method, add the highlighted code below:

```
self.tabBarController?.navigationItem.title = selectedAccount.accountDescription
```

5. Drop down another line and add the following highlighted code to resolve the positioning issue:

```
self.tabBarController?.navigationItem.title = selectedAccount.accountDescription
self.tabBarController?.edgesForExtendedLayout = []
```

6. Rerun the application; it should function perfectly! You've successfully implemented a user preferences system that will make life much easier for your users. You're now ready to start creating the Collection view controller.

Adding a Collection View Controller

You've successfully pulled apart and reassembled your application. It's time to turn your attention back to the storyboard and, in particular, to add a Collection view controller to the application:

1. Open Main.storyboard from the Project Navigator and position the scenes as shown in Figure 8-37.

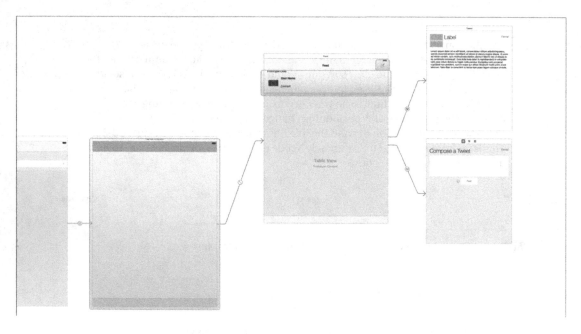

Figure 8-37. *Arranging the storyboard in anticipation of the Collection view controller*

2. Drag in a Collection view controller from the Object Library and position it below the Feed scene, as shown in Figure 8-38.

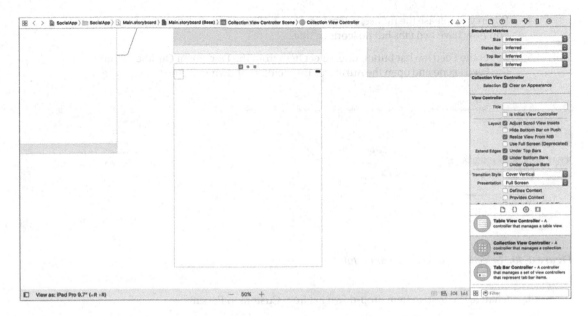

Figure 8-38. *Dragging in a Collection view controller from the Object Library*

3.   Create a relationship between the tab bar controller and the Collection view controller. To do this, select the tab bar controller and then Control+drag a connection to the Collection view controller, as shown in Figure 8-39.

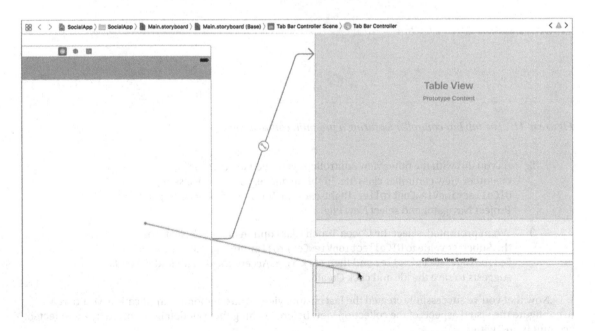

Figure 8-39. *Control+dragging a connection from the tab bar controller to the Collection view controller*

4. When you release the mouse, select View Controllers under Relationship Segues. You now have two tabs but no icons or title.

5. To set the Feed tab bar button title, select Item from the Document Outline within the Feed scene and open the Attributes Inspector, as shown in Figure 8-40.

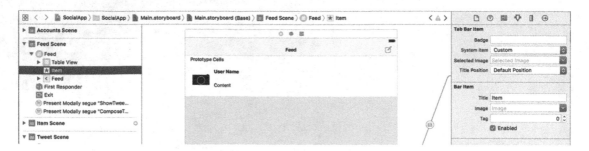

Figure 8-40. *Selecting the Feed tab bar button*

6. Change the System Item drop-down list from Custom to Recents.

7. Next, expand the Collection View Controller Scene in the Document Outline, again select Item and, in the Attributes Inspector, change System Item from Custom to Contacts. Your tab bar for the collection view should now look like the one shown in Figure 8-41.

Figure 8-41. *The tab bar controller featuring a pre-built contacts tab*

8. As you did with the other view controllers, you need to create a customer view controller class file. In this instance, you're subclassing `UICollectionViewController`. Right-click the View Controllers group in the Project Navigator and select New File.

9. When prompted, select the Cocoa Touch Class option and click Next. Set the Subclass value to `UICollectionViewController` and the Class value to `FollowingViewController` and then click Next. Accept the default folder Xcode suggests to save the file and click Create.

Now that you've successfully created the last custom view controller for this application, you're ready to configure the visual aspects of the collection view before fetching the user details followed by the selected account from Twitter.

Configuring a Collection View

I've already mentioned that the UICollectionView class is very similar to the UITableView class in terms of methods and the fact that they both use cells to present large amounts of data to the users. They also have sections with independent headers and footers. Yet despite these similarities, the collection-view configuration in Xcode is significantly different from that of the table view.

To begin, open Main.storyboard from the Project Navigator and position the storyboard so that you can see the collection view, as shown in Figure 8-42. Structurally, what you're looking at isn't really any different from what you started with in the table view, as shown in Figure 8-21. The white-bordered box in the top-left corner of the view is the prototype cell.

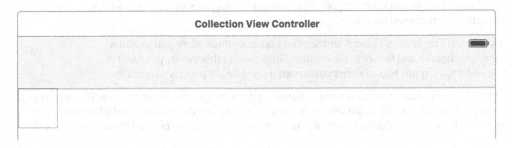

Figure 8-42. *The top of the Collection view controller showing the prototype cell*

Select the collection view so that you can look at the key attributes in the Attributes Inspector. To do this, click the main area of the collection view or select Collection View from the Document Outline, as shown in Figure 8-43.

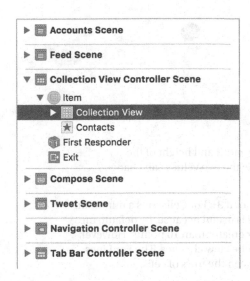

Figure 8-43. *Selecting the collection view from the Document Outline*

Open the Attributes Inspector. Let's take a closer look at the key options available to you:

- *Items*: Unlike the table view, collection views don't have a static mode. The Items attribute increases and decreases the number of prototype cells. No matter how many items you have to display, if they have a single type of appearance, then you only need one cell, which you reuse.

- *Layout*: In a collection view, the layout is a separate entity from the view. The default layout is Flow, which provides a grid of items continuing uninterrupted in a fixed direction. Changing the attribute to Custom exposes a class selector whereby you can specify a custom UICollectionViewLayout.

- *Scroll Direction*: As you might expect, this attribute controls the direction in which the cells are positioned for scrolling.

- *Accessories:* The Section Header and Section Footer options allow you to add a prototype header and footer to the section. Unlike with table views, you can't manually specify any text in either container; it must be set programmatically.

Unlike in other views, much in collection views depends on the settings of the Size Inspector. When you open the Size Inspector, you see many configurable values; Figure 8-44 shows the different sizes and where they take effect. In this example, the number of items is set to 8 to help you visualize how the cells react to one another.

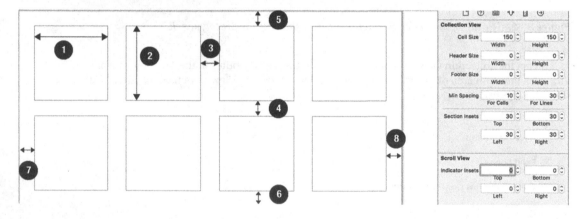

Figure 8-44. *The different sizes you can alter in a collection view*

- *Cell Width and Height*: Points 1 and 2 represent the width and height of the cell, respectively. The cell doesn't have to be square; the two values can change independently of each other.

- *Minimum Spacing*: The first value (highlighted by point 3), For Cells, sets a minimum value for the horizontal spacing between cells. This is useful because, by default, the cells are spaced nicely, and the horizontal gap is far greater than 10 points. However, you know it won't slip below 10 points if the size of the view changes. The For Lines value shown by point 4 sets a minimum width between the rows of cells.

- *Section Insets*: These four values control the spacing around the outside of the section of cells, so the cells function as a collective entity. When you increase the value of any of the sizes illustrated by points 5–8, you move the cells farther from that side of the view. By default, the Section Insets values are set to 0, which can leave content feeling squashed; set a nice inset value to bring the cells in from the edge, which is more visually appealing.

Follow these steps:

1. For the Followers collection view, set the Cell Size Width and Height values to 75, set Minimum Spacing to 10 For Cells and 30 For Lines, and set all Section Insets to 30.

2. Before you start adding code to the Followers view controller, you need to specify the class the view controller uses. Select the Collection view controller by either clicking the top bar of the view controller or selecting Item under Collection View Controller Scene in the Document Outline.

3. Open the Identity Inspector and set the class to FollowingViewController, as shown in Figure 8-45.

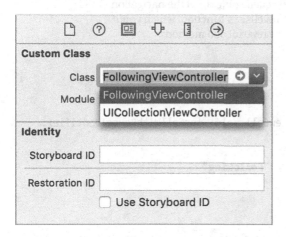

Figure 8-45. Setting Class to FollowingViewController

4. Select the single cell in the Following view controller. Open the Attributes Inspector and set the Identifier value to FollowerCell.

Displaying Items in a Collection View

You've configured the collection view in Xcode, but to finish the view you need to write the code that retrieves the list of users the app follows. I won't focus too much on the code for retrieving the list of followed users, but rather on the key methods of the UICollectionViewController class:

1. Open FollowingViewController.swift from the Project Navigator. The first thing you need to do is import the Social and Accounts frameworks. After the line import UIKit, add the following highlighted import statements:

```
import UIKit
import Accounts
import Social
```

2. Set the reuse identifier and declare a number of instance variables, just as you did with the Feed view controller. You need an NSMutableArray instance called following to store the details of each user the account follows and an NSCache object called imageCache. The start of your file, with these items added, should look like this:

```
import UIKit
import Accounts
import Social

private let reuseIdentifier = "FollowerCell"

class FollowingViewController: UICollectionViewController {

    var following : NSMutableArray?
    var imageCache : NSCache<AnyObject, AnyObject>?
```

3. Move down to the viewDidLoad method; in this method, just as you did with the Feed view controller, you want to initialize the queue object, set the navigation bar title to Following, and then call the retrieveUsers function, which you'll add shortly. Add the highlighted code to your viewDidLoad method:

```
override func viewDidLoad() {
    super.viewDidLoad()

    // Register cell classes
    self.collectionView!.register(UICollectionViewCell.self, forCellWithReuseIdentifier:
    reuseIdentifier)

    self.tabBarController?.navigationItem.title = "Following"

    retrieveUsers()
}
```

4. Look at the retrieveUsers function. Create a stub for the function below the viewDidLoad method, as shown next:

```
    retrieveUsers()
}

func retrieveUsers() {

}
```

5. Much of this code is the same as that used in the Feed view controller, so I don't present the code in any detail. Clear the following array and then retrieve selectAccount from the stored user preferences, as shown next:

```
func retrieveUsers() {
    following?.removeAllObjects()

    let userDefaults = UserDefaults.standard
    let accountData = userDefaults.object(forKey: "selectedAccount") as! Data
    let selectedAccount = NSKeyedUnarchiver.unarchiveObject(with: accountData) as! ACAccount
}
```

6. Declare an SLRequest object and instantiate it using the URL specified by the Twitter API for retrieving a list of "friends," as Twitter refers to the API that returns "up to 200 users," followed by the supplied account:

```
let accountData = userDefaults.object(forKey: "selectedAccount") as! Data
let selectedAccount = NSKeyedUnarchiver.unarchiveObject(with: accountData) as! ACAccount

let requestURL = URL(string: "https://api.twitter.com/1.1/friends/list.json?count=200")

if let request = SLRequest(forServiceType: SLServiceTypeTwitter,
                           requestMethod: SLRequestMethod.GET,
                           url: requestURL,
                           parameters: nil) {

    request.account = selectedAccount
}
```

■ **Note**   For more information on configuring the Twitter Friends/List API, visit `https://dev.twitter.com/docs/api/1.1/get/friends/list`.

---

7. You need to call the performRequestWithHandler method of the SLRequest. Just as before, you check for a valid status code and parse the JSON response before picking the "users" array from the parsed code and assigning it to the following array. Calling the UICollectionView method reloadData causes three methods to be called. Add the following code to complete this method:

```
request.account = selectedAccount

request.perform()
{
    responseData, urlResponse, error in

    if(urlResponse?.statusCode == 200)
    {
        do {
            let followingData = try JSONSerialization.jsonObject(with: responseData!,
                                                                 options:
JSONSerialization.ReadingOptions.mutableContainers) as! NSDictionary

            self.following = followingData.object(forKey: "users") as? NSMutableArray
        }
        catch let error as NSError {
            print("json error: \(error.localizedDescription)")
        }
    }

    DispatchQueue.main.async {
        self.collectionView!.reloadData()
    }
}
```

8. On to the delegate methods. Just as with the table view, you have to specify the number of sections via the numberOfSections(:in:) method. Set it to return 1, as shown next:

```
override func numberOfSections(in collectionView: UICollectionView) -> Int {
    return 1
}
```

9. You need to specify how many of the potential 200 cells to render should appear via the collectionView(_ :numberOfItemsInSection:) method, which returns the number of rows in the following array:

```
override func collectionView(_ collectionView: UICollectionView, numberOfItemsInSection
section: Int) -> Int {
    if let followCount = following?.count {
        return followCount
    }
    else
    {
        return 0
    }
}
```

10. Scroll down and locate the cellForItemAtIndexPath method. It's used to initialize the cell and set its content, just as its UITableView equivalent does.

11. Use the highlighted code to pull the relevant data for the current index from the following array and store it in an NSDictionary object before extracting the URL for the user's profile image, as you did in the Feed view controller:

```
override func collectionView(_ collectionView: UICollectionView, cellForItemAt indexPath:
IndexPath) -> UICollectionViewCell {
    let cell = collectionView.dequeueReusableCell(withReuseIdentifier: reuseIdentifier, for:
    indexPath)

    let userData = following?.object(at: indexPath.row) as! NSDictionary
    let imageURLString = userData.object(forKey: "profile_image_url") as! String

    return cell
}
```

12. You need to set up the image that is programmatically added to the cell using the addSubview method, because no UIImageView exists in the cell, and then return the cell object. Complete the method with this highlighted code:

```
override func collectionView(_ collectionView: UICollectionView, cellForItemAt indexPath:
IndexPath) -> UICollectionViewCell {
    let cell = collectionView.dequeueReusableCell(withReuseIdentifier: reuseIdentifier, for:
    indexPath)

    let userData = following?.object(at: indexPath.row) as! NSDictionary
    let imageURLString = userData.object(forKey: "profile_image_url") as! String
```

```
let operationQueue = OperationQueue.main
operationQueue.maxConcurrentOperationCount = 4

if let image = imageCache?.object(forKey: imageURLString as AnyObject) as? UIImage {
    let imageView = UIImageView(image: image) as UIImageView
    imageView.bounds = cell.frame
    cell.addSubview(imageView)
}
else
{
    operationQueue.addOperation() {
        let imageURL = URL(string: imageURLString)

        do {
            if let imageData : Data = try Data(contentsOf: imageURL!) {

                let image = UIImage(data: imageData) as UIImage?

                if let downloadedImage = image {
                    OperationQueue.main.addOperation(){
                        let imageView = UIImageView(image: downloadedImage)
                        imageView.bounds = cell.frame

                        if let cell = self.collectionView!.cellForItem(at: indexPath) as
                        UICollectionViewCell! {
                            cell.addSubview(imageView)
                        }
                    }

                    self.imageCache?.setObject(downloadedImage, forKey: imageURLString
                    as AnyObject)
                }
            }
        }
        catch let error as NSError {
            print("parse error: \(error.localizedDescription)")
        }
    }

}

return cell
}
```

That completes the collection view and the chapter! Go ahead and run your application. As long as you're following some other Twitter users, your collection view should populate with user avatars, as shown in Figure 8-46. Note that I've used the Xcode logo instead of some of the faces, for privacy reasons.

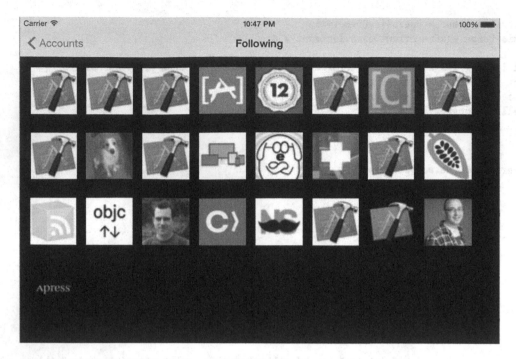

Figure 8-46. *The finished collection view showing the avatars of users you follow*

Summary

There's no doubt that you covered a lot in this chapter. Most important, you've taken SocialApp from the shell it was at the end of Chapter 7 and created a working Twitter client. This was no mean feat, and hopefully you're feeling really pleased with yourself. Take a break and reflect on all the things you learned in this chapter:

- The difference between static and prototype table cells
- When to use a grouped or a plain style table view
- How to create a custom table cell
- How to fetch data from the Internet
- How to parse JSON data
- How to embed a tab bar controller into your application
- How to persist user preferences even when the application has closed

The next chapter looks at other ways you can use frameworks in Xcode, as well as libraries and how Xcode lets you create different applications with the same code using targets.

CHAPTER 9

■ ■ ■

Frameworks, Libraries, and Targets

In Chapter 8, you learned about how to configure and implement table and collection views as you completed a Twitter client, SocialApp. You also used two frameworks, Social and Accounts, to access the Twitter API; frameworks are a topic I explain in more detail in this chapter. You also parsed the JSON-formatted data and looked at NSDictionaries in action. The chapter covered many important aspects of Xcode application development, and I hope you found the project useful and enjoyable—maybe even a bit exciting!

Chapter 8 had a lot of code to go through as you subclassed cells and view controllers, but in this chapter you see how a little code can go a long way. This chapter explains how Xcode uses frameworks to add functionality; libraries to encapsulate lots of classes, methods, and resources neatly; and targets to create different versions of your application in a single project.

The project for this chapter is an application based on the Map Kit framework that displays pushpins on a map. You create two versions of the application by using targets: both use the same base code, but the output changes based on the version.

Map Kit is a framework provided by Apple that renders an interactive map. It has numerous classes for modifying and complementing the map. Whether you're adding pushpins or custom markers, plotting routes, or outlining areas, the Map Kit framework has everything you need to create a rich, map-based application.

Understanding Frameworks

Chapter 7 introduced inheritance as being one of the core principles of object-oriented programming. Frameworks embody another of these core principles: encapsulation. Encapsulation is usually defined as one of two things:

- A mechanism by which information (code) is hidden

- A construct for bundling data together

A framework groups classes, resources, interface files, and more together in a hierarchical package. Although you can view some of the resources in the framework, the implementation of the classes—the key code—is hidden. Figure 9-1 shows the Map Kit framework you're working with in this chapter.

© Matthew Knott 2016
M. Knott, *Beginning Xcode*, DOI 10.1007/978-1-4302-5005-0_9

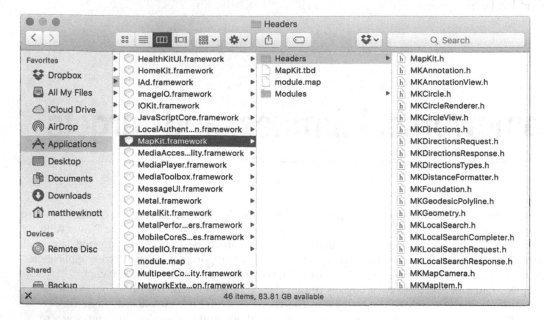

Figure 9-1. *A look at the large number of class headers held in* `MapKit.framework`

As you learn later in this chapter, frameworks don't differ greatly from libraries in terms of definition: the key difference is in how you define their purpose. Frameworks encapsulate a wide range of functions; Map Kit has a mass of classes and different resources. Libraries, on the other hand, are intended to fulfill smaller, more specific tasks, such as caching images or grouping code you may use often for a specific type of project, such as with Map Kit applications. Frameworks provide a way to unlock the features and functions of the operating system and the hardware.

Creating the Project

The project for this chapter is called `MapPin`; it shows a number of pushpins on a map with a textual annotation. Many applications use the Apple-provided Map Kit to display information in really interesting ways, and if this is something you want to add to your own applications, hopefully you'll be encouraged by how easy it is to add a map view to your application and to make it display information with just a few lines of code:

1. Open Xcode and create a new project by clicking Create A New Xcode Project from the Welcome screen or by choosing File ➤ New ➤ Project (⌘+Shift+N). Select the Single View Application template and click Next.

2. Name your project `MapPin` and ensure that Language is set to Swift and Devices is set to iPhone, not iPad or Universal. Configure the other values to your own preferences; mine are shown in Figure 9-2. Click Next.

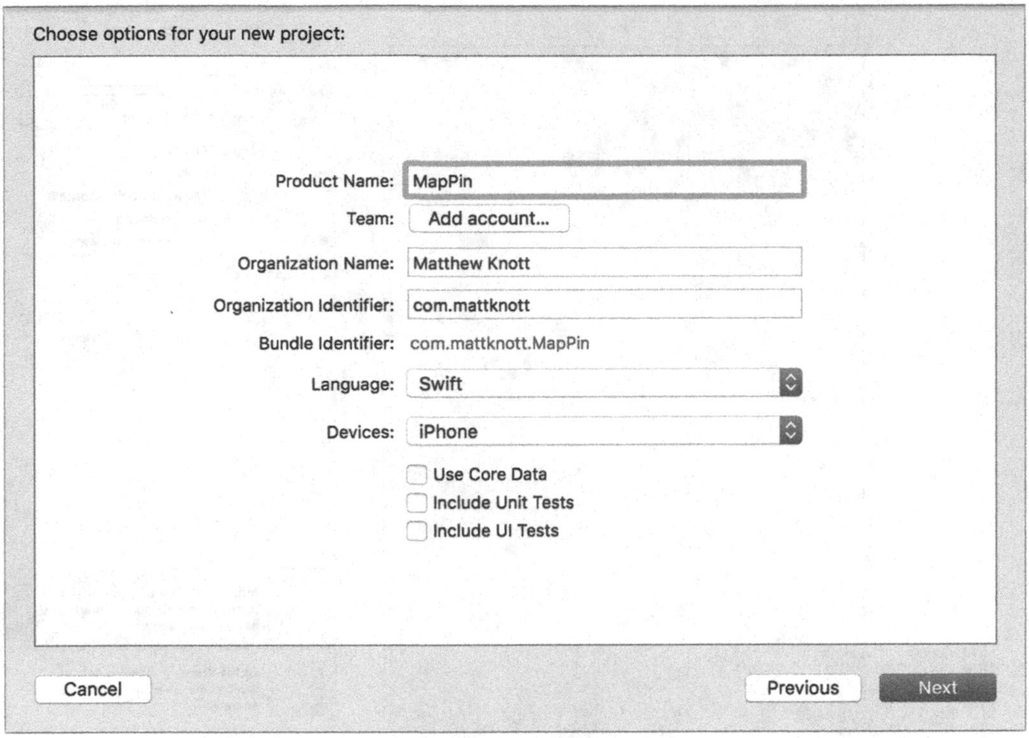

Choose options for your new project:

Product Name:	MapPin
Team:	Add account...
Organization Name:	Matthew Knott
Organization Identifier:	com.mattknott
Bundle Identifier:	com.mattknott.MapPin
Language:	Swift
Devices:	iPhone

☐ Use Core Data
☐ Include Unit Tests
☐ Include UI Tests

Cancel   Previous   Next

Figure 9-2. *The initial settings for the MapPin project*

3. You don't want to create a Git repository, so leave that option unchecked. You also don't want to add this to another project. With those options set, click Create.

4. You now have a blank project—a fresh canvas to which you need to add a map view. Open Main.storyboard and locate a map view object in the Object Library. Drag it onto the view controller in the design area, as shown in Figure 9-3.

5. Drag the corners of the map view until it fills the entire view.

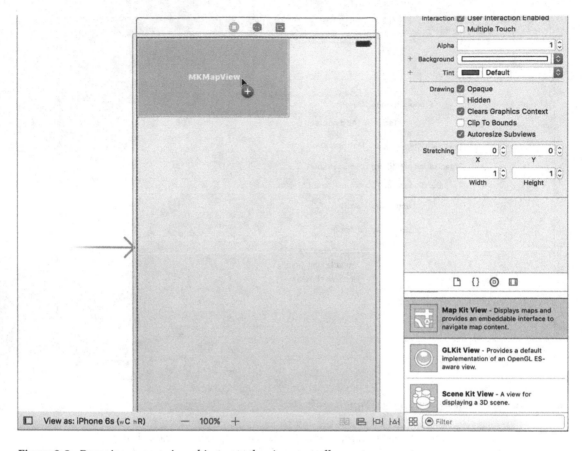

Figure 9-3. *Dragging a map view object onto the view controller*

The map view represents an MKMapView object and is the only object needed to display maps in your application. Go ahead and run the application to see what happens after you add the object to the view controller. The application builds successfully and launches in the simulator; then it drops back to Xcode with an exception, as shown in Figure 9-4, because the application has no knowledge of the MKMapView class. A prerequisite for adding a map view to your applications is that you also need to add the Map Kit framework.

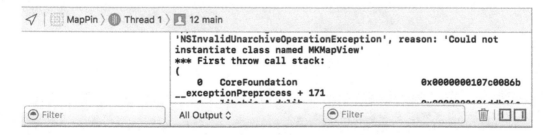

Figure 9-4. *The exception shown in the debug area when you add a map view without the Map Kit framework*

Adding a Framework

Back as early as Chapter 4, in the Showcase application, you first encountered frameworks. At that point I gave a very brief explanation of how to import one and how the modules concept works. Let's recap.

With iOS 7 and Xcode 5, before Swift came along, Apple gave developers a new alternative called *modules* for manually adding frameworks to a project. The concept behind modules is that instead of going through Xcode to find and add a selected framework to physically integrate into a project and *then* go on to reference it in code with an #import statement, you can simply reference it with a single line of code using the @import statement. Xcode automatically identifies the framework and links the frameworks headers at build time behind the scenes.

As you can imagine, not having to go through the time-consuming process of locating and adding frameworks was a big hit with developers, and with Swift, Apple has kept this functionality and made it the default approach. You rarely need to manually import a framework in a Swift application.

The only downside is that before you add a framework, you need to know its name. To help you, Table 9-1 lists some of the more important frameworks available in iOS 10 that you haven't come across yet and lists some of the functionality they unlock.

Table 9-1. *Key Frameworks for iOS 8*

Framework	Purpose
Core Data	An object persistence engine that allows flexible management of data. Creates sophisticated queries so you quickly retrieve data for your application.
Local Authentication	Provides access to the Touch ID API for devices with a fingerprint reader.
HealthKit	Provides numerous APIs to access the M7 motion chip's functions, such as the pedometer.
Web Kit	Allows you to use much more Safari-level functionality for your web view and is highly customizable.
Notification Center	Lets you add your own custom widgets to the notification center in iOS. This is a great way to extend your app's functionality.
Photos and Photos UI	Two new frameworks that allow you to manipulate photos and add custom functionality to the iOS Photos app.
Message UI	Allows you to create e-mails and text messages programmatically.

These are just a few examples of the dozens and dozens of frameworks available to you with iOS 10. I mentioned that you rarely have to add a framework to a project. However, this is one of those occasions when you do have to perform this task, because you're using the Map Kit framework:

1. Adding a framework to the project is a breeze. Start by selecting the MapPin project in the Project Navigator and select the MapPin target, as shown in Figure 9-5.

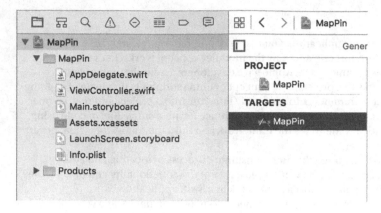

Figure 9-5. *Selecting the MapPin project from the Project Navigator*

2. Click the General tab. Scroll down to the Linked Frameworks And Libraries section, as shown in Figure 9-6.

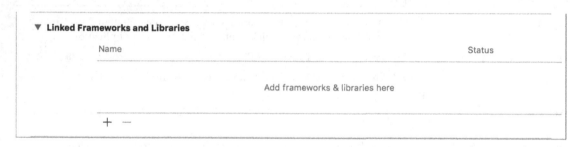

Figure 9-6. *The Linked Frameworks and Libraries area of your project's settings*

3. You can display a list of available frameworks, as shown in Figure 9-7, by clicking the + symbol at the bottom of the section, below Add Frameworks & Libraries Here.

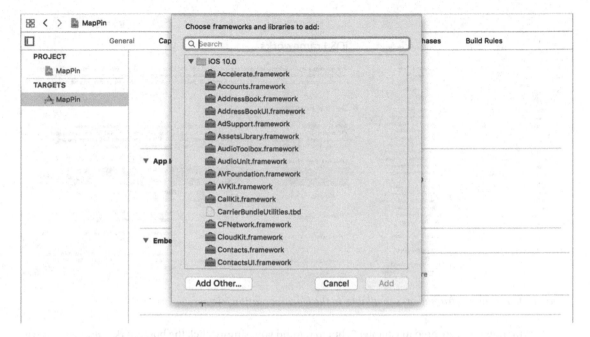

Figure 9-7. *The list of iOS frameworks and libraries available with the SDK in Xcode 8*

4. Scroll through the list until you see `MapKit.framework`, or use the filter bar and type `map` to narrow the list substantially.

5. Select the Map Kit framework and click the Add button. You return to Xcode, and the Map Kit framework is added to the project.

It's important to be aware of the APIs available for your development platform, so you can create the best, most functional and integrated application. Also, frameworks become deprecated between releases of iOS and are replaced with new classes and methods. Fortunately, the documentation in Xcode lists all the frameworks and describes their purpose.

To see this, open the Documentation Viewer by going to Help ➤ Documentation and API Reference (⌥+⌘+0). Search for `Device Frameworks` and open the document. As you can see in Figure 9-8, the document contains a table listing all the available frameworks and the version of iOS in which they were introduced. This page is updated with each iOS release, so it makes sense to bookmark it.

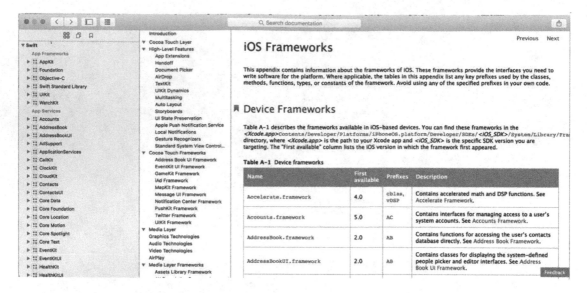

Figure 9-8. *Listing the frameworks available, in the Documentation Viewer*

Bookmarking was covered in Chapter 5, but to remind you, simply click the bookmark symbol as shown in Figure 9-9. This section will now be quickly accessible in future updates.

Figure 9-9. *Bookmarking the Device Frameworks document*

Now that you've added the prerequisite framework for using a map view, you're in a position to run the application again. Run it; you should be greeted by a map showing an area of the world, as shown in Figure 9-10.

Figure 9-10. *The MapPin application displays an interactive map without you writing a line of code*

Manipulating a Map View

You haven't written a single line of code, but already what the application does is fairly impressive; you can pan and zoom the map. Although this is initially fun, it's not very useful. If you're writing a Map Kit–based application, you'll instinctively want to add your own touches, setting the initial position of the map and adding some landmarks, as I now explain.

In this application, you set the region property of the map view to show a map of Wales in the UK, and then you add points of interest that display as pushpins. But the first thing to do is to align the map correctly using constraints and then create an outlet for the map view:

1. Open Main.storyboard from the Project Navigator.

2. Select the map view and click the Pin icon.

3. Uncheck Constrain to Margins if it is checked, and then click the four bars at value 0 to lock the map view to the screen edges, as shown in Figure 9-11. Click Add 4 Constraints.

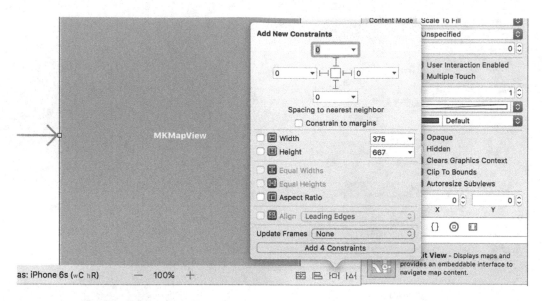

Figure 9-11. *Pinning the map view in place*

4. Now that the view is pinned in place, enable the Assistant Editor so you can create an outlet. Make sure the file displayed in the code editor is ViewController.swift.

5. Control+drag a connection from the map view to the view controller just below the class declaration, as shown in Figure 9-12.

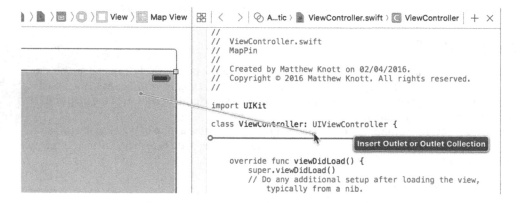

Figure 9-12. *Dragging a connection from the map view for an outlet*

6. Name the outlet mapView and then click Connect. You see an error and a warning for the outlet because the import reference for the Map Kit framework hasn't been added to the view controller's header file.

7. From the Project Navigator, open `ViewController.swift`. Switch back to the Standard Editor. Import the Map Kit framework so you have access to the map view class and its associated classes. To do this, add the following code after the `import UIKit` line (remember, it's case sensitive):

```
import MapKit
```

8. In order to manipulate the map view from the view controller, you need to set it up as the delegate. Therefore, the next thing to do is add the `MKMapViewDelegate` protocol to the view controller. Amend the `class ViewController: UIViewController` line with the highlighted code as follows:

```
class ViewController: UIViewController, MKMapViewDelegate {
```

9. Before moving on, check that the beginning of your view controller matches that shown here:

```
import UIKit
import MapKit

class ViewController: UIViewController, MKMapViewDelegate {

    @IBOutlet weak var mapView: MKMapView!
```

10. Scroll down to the `viewDidLoad` method.

11. You need to tell the map view that the view controller will be its delegate, so it obeys the instructions you send it. To do this, you use the `delegate` property of the mapView object and set it to `self`. In the `viewDidLoad` function, after the `super.viewDidLoad()` line, add the following statement:

```
mapView.delegate = self
```

12. To position the map view in a specific position, you need to create a region, represented by `MKCoordinateRegion`. Think of a region as an invisible window that can be set at a specific location and that shows a specific amount of the map. To create your region, you need two sets of values: the latitude and longitude for the center point of the region, and the north-to-south and east-to-west span values. Start by adding a new function below `viewDidLoad` called `viewDidAppear`:

```
override func viewDidAppear(_ animated: Bool) {

}
```

13. Drop down a line and add the following three lines of highlighted code:

```
override func viewDidAppear(_ animated: Bool) {
    let centerPoint = CLLocationCoordinate2D(latitude: 52.011937, longitude: -3.713379)
    let coordinateSpan = MKCoordinateSpanMake(3.5, 3.5)
    let coordinateRegion = MKCoordinateRegionMake(centerPoint, coordinateSpan)
}
```

■ **Note**   You're probably familiar with longitude and latitude, but the *span* is a concept that is unique to Apple Maps. It consists of a *latitude delta*, which is a measurement in degrees north to south that equates to roughly 111 kilometers; *longitude delta*, which is also measured in degrees but, unlike the latitude, equates to a distance that varies from 111 kilometers at the equator to 0 at either pole. If you want to show a fixed zoom level where the location can't be guaranteed, you'll get more consistent results with the MKCoordinateRegionMakeWithDistance method.

---

14.   You need to apply this region to the mapView object. Do this by calling two methods that apply the region in a way that ensures the map displays properly. Drop down a line and add the following code:

```
let centerPoint = CLLocationCoordinate2D(latitude: 52.011937, longitude: -3.713379)
let coordinateSpan = MKCoordinateSpanMake(3.5, 3.5)
let coordinateRegion = MKCoordinateRegionMake(centerPoint, coordinateSpan)

mapView.setRegion(coordinateRegion, animated: false)
mapView.regionThatFits(coordinateRegion)
```

15.   Run the application. When the map loads, it should be focused over the country of Wales, as shown in Figure 9-13. If your view doesn't match the figure, check that you set the delegate correctly and that your latitude and longitude values are spot on.

Figure 9-13.   The map view now that you've specified a region to display

Knowing how to move the map where you want it to be and setting the correct region to view are basic but essential skills when working with a map view. Another common requirement in a Map Kit application is marking locations on the map using pushpins.

You do this by creating instances of the `MKPointAnnotation` class and adding them to the map individually using the `addAnnotation` method. To instantiate an `MKPointAnnotation`, you set three attributes—`title`, `subtitle`, and `coordinates`—as follows:

1. Drop down a line in the `viewDidAppear` method and add the following highlighted code:

```
mapView.setRegion(coordinateRegion, animated: false)
mapView.regionThatFits(coordinateRegion)

let annotation1 = MKPointAnnotation()
annotation1.title = "Swansea Bay"
annotation1.subtitle = "Beautiful Beaches"
annotation1.coordinate = CLLocationCoordinate2DMake(51.587736,-3.90152)

let annotation2 = MKPointAnnotation()
annotation2.title = "Menai Bridge"
annotation2.subtitle = "Fantastic Engineering"
annotation2.coordinate = CLLocationCoordinate2DMake(53.220527,-4.163561)

let annotation3 = MKPointAnnotation()
annotation3.title = "Parc Y Scarlets"
annotation3.subtitle = "Oh Dear"
annotation3.coordinate = CLLocationCoordinate2DMake(51.678809,-4.127469)

let annotation4 = MKPointAnnotation()
annotation4.title = "Castell Coch"
annotation4.subtitle = "A Fairytale Castle"
annotation4.coordinate = CLLocationCoordinate2DMake(51.535819,-3.2547)

let annotation5 = MKPointAnnotation()
annotation5.title = "Arthur's Stone"
annotation5.subtitle = "Rock Of Legend"
annotation5.coordinate = CLLocationCoordinate2DMake(51.593735,-4.179525)

mapView.addAnnotation(annotation1)
mapView.addAnnotation(annotation2)
mapView.addAnnotation(annotation3)
mapView.addAnnotation(annotation4)
mapView.addAnnotation(annotation5)
```

2. Rerun the application. You should see five annotations. Tap an annotation, as shown in Figure 9-14, to display the text associated with that pushpin.

Figure 9-14. *The map view, now with five annotations showing various attractions in Wales*

With very little code, you've made a really useful and interactive application! You could make endless customizations, such as replacing the pushpins with an image or adding controls to the callout that display the annotation text. I won't explain how to customize the pushpins any further, because the focus of this book is Xcode. However, I'll show you one of the key steps you typically perform before any customization of a class's behavior: subclassing the MKPointAnnotation class and then creating a custom initializer to simplify creation of the annotations.

Subclassing MKPointAnnotation

Because this code is reusable in different projects, you create it in a separate class file. You're working with annotations, so it probably comes as no surprise that you subclass the MKPointAnnotation class and replace the pushpin objects you just created with this new class, MyPin:

1. To create the new class, choose File ➤ New ➤ File (⌘+N). Choose Cocoa Touch from the left menu, and then select the Cocoa Touch Class template, as shown in Figure 9-15. Click Next.

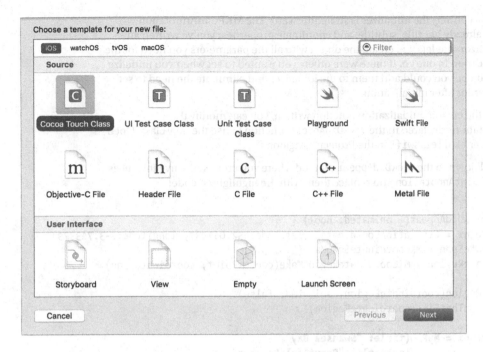

Figure 9-15. Creating a new Swift class

2. Name the class MyPin and set Subclass Of to MKPointAnnotation. Click Next. Then accept the default save location and click Create.

3. You have successfully created your custom class, but to make it work you need to make some modifications. Open MyPin.swift in the Project Navigator.

4. You can add a custom initializer to simplify the process of creating the annotation. The initializer takes the three parameters that are required: title, subtitle, and coordinate. Add the following highlighted code:

```
import UIKit
import MapKit

class MyPin: MKPointAnnotation {

    init(title : String, subtitle : String, coordinate : CLLocationCoordinate2D) {
        super.init()
        self.title = title
        self.subtitle = subtitle
        self.coordinate = coordinate
    }
}
```

As you can see, the initializer is straightforward. The MKPointAnnotation class already has title, subtitle, and coordinate properties; you've written an initializer that lets you create the object with all the parameters you need for the application in one go. If there were others you wanted to set when you initialize the object, you could add them to the initializer and eliminate the need to set properties after initialization.

5. With the custom initialization function written, you can modify the annotations declared in the viewDidAppear function to use the new class. Open ViewController.swift in the Project Navigator.

6. Scroll down to the viewDidAppear method where you created the five instances of MKPointAnnotation and replace them with the highlighted code:

```swift
override func viewDidAppear(_ animated: Bool) {
    let centerPoint = CLLocationCoordinate2D(latitude: 52.011937, longitude: -3.713379)
    let coordinateSpan = MKCoordinateSpanMake(3.5, 3.5)
    let coordinateRegion = MKCoordinateRegionMake(centerPoint, coordinateSpan)

    mapView.setRegion(coordinateRegion, animated: false)
    mapView.regionThatFits(coordinateRegion)

    let annotation1 = MyPin(title: "Swansea Bay",
                            subtitle: "Beautiful Beaches",
                            coordinate: CLLocationCoordinate2DMake(51.587736,-3.90152))

    let annotation2 = MyPin(title: "Menai Bridge",
                            subtitle: "Fantastic Engineering",
                            coordinate: CLLocationCoordinate2DMake(53.220527,-4.163561))

    let annotation3 = MyPin(title: "Parc Y Scarlets",
                            subtitle: "Oh Dear",
                            coordinate: CLLocationCoordinate2DMake(51.678809,-4.127469))

    let annotation4 = MyPin(title: "Castell Coch",
                            subtitle: "A Fairytale Castle",
                            coordinate: CLLocationCoordinate2DMake(51.535819,-3.2547))

    let annotation5 = MyPin(title: "Arthur's Stone",
                            subtitle: "Rock Of Legend",
                            coordinate: CLLocationCoordinate2DMake(51.593735,-4.179525))

    mapView.addAnnotation(annotation1)
    mapView.addAnnotation(annotation2)
    mapView.addAnnotation(annotation3)
    mapView.addAnnotation(annotation4)
    mapView.addAnnotation(annotation5)

}
```

■ **Note**   In Objective-C, you had to declare the initializer in the class header, implement the initializer in the implementation file, and then import the header into the view controller in order to use the class. Swift has changed all of that and created something far more straightforward.

Go ahead and rerun your application. The pushpins are still in place, but you did this with a fraction of the code.

Static Libraries, Frameworks, and Swift

In the first release of Swift, the language and syntax was changing constantly, meaning that releasing your own frameworks was impractical because you would be constantly re-releasing them on a frequent basis. The developers using those frameworks would also find that as soon as they started working with the framework, there was a good chance it would become invalid.

Thankfully, things have moved on since then and Apple now supports the creation of Cocoa Touch Frameworks written in Swift. Although it's not covered in this book, it is now possible to create redistribute frameworks, although some complex steps are involved. If you're interested on reading more on the topic, I recommend this blog post on Kodmunki at `https://kodmunki.wordpress.com/2015/09/22/ios-9-universal-cocoa-touch-frameworks/`.

At this time, static libraries can be created but cannot use Swift, only Objective-C.

Working with Multiple Targets

I hope that when you finish this book, you'll feel ready to start writing your own applications for the App Store. When you create an application that you want to charge for, it's possible that you may also want to create a free "lite" version with fewer features to tempt users into upgrading to the full version. You can create a new project and copy all your code over to it, but then you've fallen into the snare of having to maintain two versions of the same code.

By using different targets, Xcode allows you to maintain multiple versions of the same application in the same project and then, in the code, identify which version of the application is running and adjust the functionality to suit. For this example, you will create another target called `MapPinSatellite` that displays the map in satellite mode instead of the default standard mode.

Rather than create a new target and apply a lot of settings, you can duplicate the existing `MapPin` target:

1.   Select the `MapPin` project from the Project Navigator. When the project settings load, select the `MapPin` target and press ⌘+D, or right-click the `MapPin` target and click Duplicate, as shown in Figure 9-16.

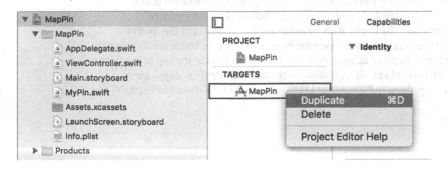

Figure 9-16. *Duplicating the MapPin target*

2. Xcode detects that you're duplicating an iPhone-specific target and asks if you want to convert it for use with an iPad, as shown in Figure 9-17. In this instance, you just want to duplicate the target, so click the Duplicate Only button.

Duplicate iPhone Target

The selected target is an iPhone target, you can duplicate and transition it to an iPad target at the same time. The user interface used for running on iPhone can be used as a starting point for iPad development. Would you like to duplicate the iPhone target and transition the new target for running on iPad?

Cancel   Duplicate Only   Duplicate and Transition to iPad

Figure 9-17. *Xcode prompts you if you try to duplicate an iPhone-specific target*

3. Xcode duplicates the target and names it MapPin Copy. This is great but not really what you want your target to be named. Click the MapPin Copy target and then click it again so you can edit its name. Change the name to MapPinSatellite, as shown in Figure 9-18.

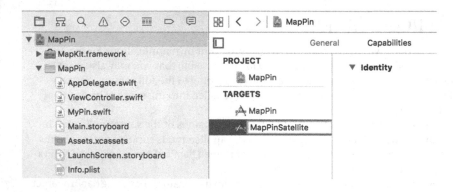

Figure 9-18. *Renaming the new target*

4. Xcode has improved over previous versions and now renames many of the attributes of the new target automatically when you change the target name; however, there is one attribute within the target that needs to be updated. When you duplicated the target, it also duplicated the info.plist file. With the MapPinSatellite target selected, open the Build Settings tab. There are dozens of settings in this list! To make things easier, use the search filter at the top of the page. First search for info.plist File, double-click the words MapPin copy-info. plist and change them to MapPinSatellite-info.plist, as shown in Figure 9-19.

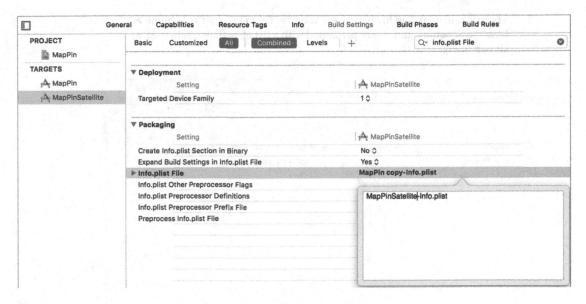

Figure 9-19. *Changing the info.plist file setting to MapPinSatellite-info.plist*

5. Next search for Product Bundle Identifier and change the name from com.
    yourname.MapPin to com.yourname.MapPinSatellite to distinguish the two
    products.

6. When you duplicated the target, Xcode actually duplicated three things: the
    target, the info.plist file, and the targets scheme. You've just named the info.
    plist file in the settings for your target, so you should change the info.plist file
    name next. In the Project Navigator, notice that at the bottom of the project there
    is now a plist file named MapPin copy-Info.plist. Highlight the file, press
    Return to begin editing, and change the name to MapPinSatellite-Info.plist.
    Your Product Navigator should resemble Figure 9-20.

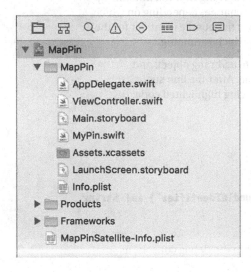

Figure 9-20. *The Project Navigator after renaming the file*

7. There is one final item to change: the scheme. Go to Product ➤ Scheme ➤ Manage Schemes, and you're presented with a list of available schemes, as shown in Figure 9-21.

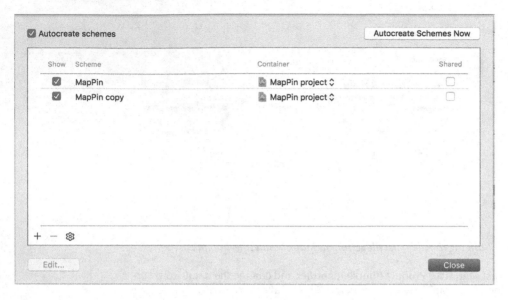

Figure 9-21. *Xcode's Manage Schemes view, listing the available schemes*

8. Highlight the bottom scheme named MapPin Copy and press Return. Change the scheme name to MapPinSatellite. You've now updated everything required to start taking advantage of your new target. Click OK to close the window.

9. Open ViewController.swift from the Project Navigator and scroll down to the viewDidLoad function. To separate functionality based on the active target, you first need to identify which version of the application is being run. You find this by examining the application's bundle identifier, which changes depending on which target scheme is being run. You have already changed the bundle identifier for the target, but can retrieve it programmatically to verify which is running.

10. You need to retrieve the bundle identifier, assign it to a String object, and then use print to output the identifier to the console. After the line super. viewDidLoad(), drop down a line and add the following highlighted code:

```
override func viewDidLoad() {
    super.viewDidLoad()
    mapView.delegate = self

    let currentBundle : String =
        Bundle.main.object(forInfoDictionaryKey: "CFBundleIdentifier") as! String
    print(currentBundle)
```

11. Run the application. You'll see the bundle identifier in the debug console, as shown in Figure 9-22.

Figure 9-22. *The bundle identifier shown in the debug console*

12. To change the scheme for this project from MapPin to MapPinSatellite, select the MapPin scheme next to the Run and Stop buttons in the Toolbar area and select MapPinSatellite, as shown in Figure 9-23.

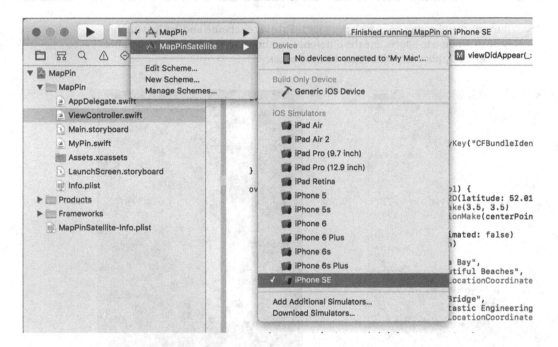

Figure 9-23. *Changing to the MapPinSatellite scheme*

13. If the Stop button is active, click it to terminate the application running under the other scheme; otherwise Xcode will throw an error about the simulator being in use. Run the application again with the new scheme: the bundle identifier in the debug area changes to match the product name specified for this scheme, which ends with MapPinSatellite. You now have two distinct values that let you implement different functionalities.

14. The different functionality in this project is that the original target runs using the standard map type, but the satellite version runs with the satellite map type. In the ViewController.swift file, after the line print(currentBundle) line, add the following highlighted code, remembering that MapPinSatellite is case sensitive and must match what you've written as a bundle identifier:

277

```
mapView.delegate = self

let currentBundle : String =
    Bundle.main.object(forInfoDictionaryKey: "CFBundleIdentifier") as! String
print(currentBundle)

if currentBundle.hasSuffix("MapPinSatellite")
{
    mapView.mapType = MKMapType.satellite
}
```

■ **Note**   hasSuffix is a helper function that examines the end of the string to see if it matches the string it is compared against. This is quicker than typing the full string for comparison and reduces the chance of a typo.

---

15.   Run your application once with the MapPinSatelite scheme and again with the MapPin scheme to appreciate the difference, as shown in Figure 9-24. Remember to stop the application when switching schemes.

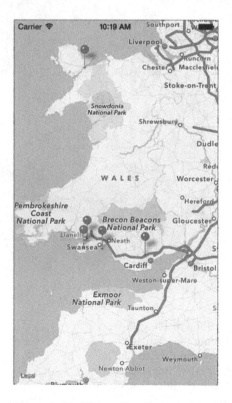

Figure 9-24. *The application running under both schemes*

Summary

As you get further into this book, the topics become more advanced. If you're serious about becoming an iOS or macOS developer, then the skills you've learned in this chapter will help you do super-efficient work, using frameworks and custom initializers to good effect.

This chapter combined your knowledge of frameworks and targets to create a Map Kit–based application that shows just a few of the many hundreds of points of interest in Wales. You learned how to add annotations to the map view and then subclassed `MKPointAnnotation` to create a one-hit initializer for the annotation object.

Specifically, in this chapter you have done the following:

- Learned more about modules, which are an efficient way to expose new APIs in your project

- Learned about manually adding frameworks to a project

- Looked at the Device Frameworks section in the help documentation and bookmarked it for future reference

- Discovered how to use map views and manipulate them in code

- Duplicated a target to create different sets of features from the same code

- Learned about Swift and its support for native libraries and frameworks

In the next chapter, you learn how to mold Xcode into a more personalized development environment and how to get more out of Xcode as you explore new customizations that will make you a better and more efficient developer.

CHAPTER 10

■ ■ ■

Advanced Editing

Chapter 9 looked at how to add frameworks to a project and efficient ways of managing code through the use of libraries, as well as using multiple targets and aggregate targets. These skills were combined and developed as you created a basic Map Kit application that showed a selection of interesting points on a map of Wales, the country I live in. If you want to become an accomplished iOS or Xcode developer, either on your own or in a team of developers, then learning how to efficiently reuse code is essential.

This chapter maintains the efficiency theme and focuses on the code editor while you create a fun SpriteKit–based application called AlienDev that shows our hero, the alien dev (Alien Cyborg Dev, to give him his full name) surrounded by an increasing numbers of bugs (evil ones). I explain how small bits of reusable code can be saved as snippets, readily available to be dropped into your application, as well as look at the many ways you can customize Xcode to work for you. It's a cliché, but everyone is different, and developers are no exception. Xcode is hugely customizable, from the font and colors used in the code editor to the wayXcode reacts to different events. There are many ways you can tweak the IDE to be a better environment for you to code in. I also discuss how to work with large implementation files by using code folding and some of the subtle ways you can efficiently navigate your code using the jump bar and its pragma marks to bring order to your jump bar hierarchy.

Without further ado, let's get started on the project, and let the bug wars commence!

Getting Started

The project for this chapter is created using the SpriteKit application template. As mentioned in Chapter 3, SpriteKit is an exciting framework that Apple introduced with Xcode 5 and iOS 7 to let developers easily create 2D animations and even games without having to use a third-party system such as Cocos2D or Unity.

■ **Note**   I recommend that you download the resources for this project and all the others in the book from the Apress web site at www.apress.com. Alternatively, if you're feeling adventurous, you can create your own characters.

Follow these steps:

1. Open Xcode and create a new project by clicking Create A New Xcode Project on the Welcome screen or choosing File ➤ New ➤ Project (➤+Shift+N). Select the Game template and click Next.

2. Name your project AlienDev. Be sure Game Technology is set to SpriteKit and Devices is set to iPhone. Configure the other values to your own preference; mine are shown in Figure 10-1. Click Next.

© Matthew Knott 2016
M. Knott, *Beginning Xcode*, DOI 10.1007/978-1-4302-5005-0_10

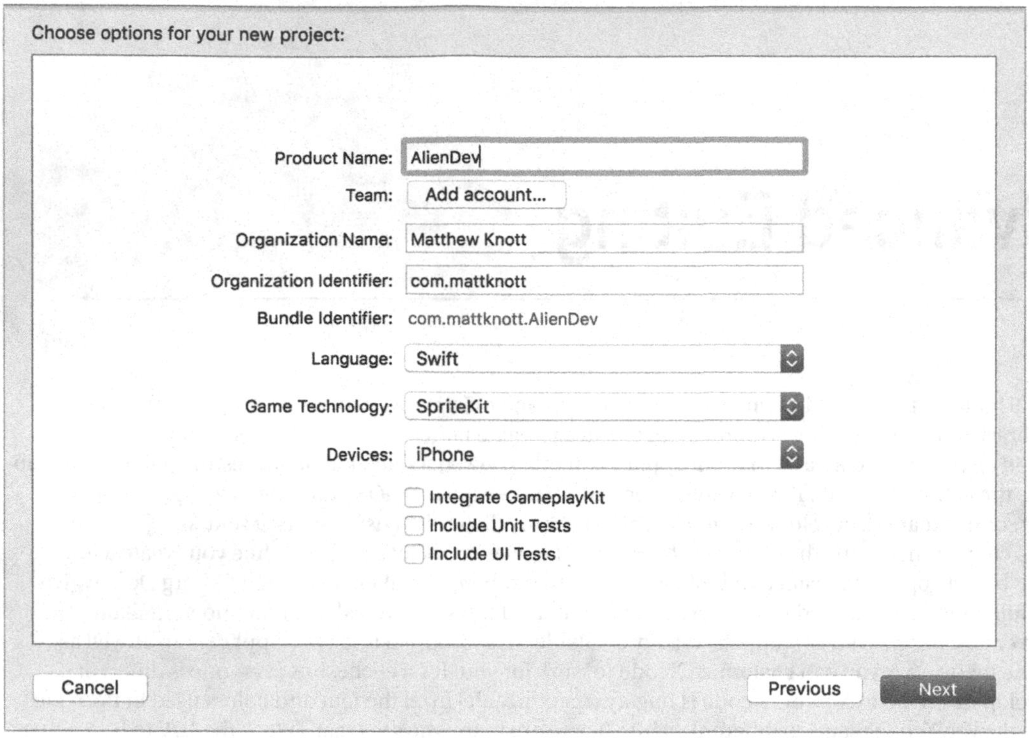

Choose options for your new project:

Product Name: AlienDev

Team: Add account...

Organization Name: Matthew Knott

Organization Identifier: com.mattknott

Bundle Identifier: com.mattknott.AlienDev

Language: Swift

Game Technology: SpriteKit

Devices: iPhone

☐ Integrate GameplayKit
☐ Include Unit Tests
☐ Include UI Tests

Cancel   Previous   Next

Figure 10-1. Setting up the initial project

3. By now you should be familiar with the process: you want to save in the default location, and you don't want to create a Git repository, so go ahead and click Create.

4. Xcode takes you straight into the project settings. You want the application to run in landscape mode only, so scroll down to the Deployment Info section. The default-supported orientations for an iPhone application are Portrait, Landscape Left, and Landscape Right; you need to uncheck Portrait so that only the landscape options remain, as shown in Figure 10-2.

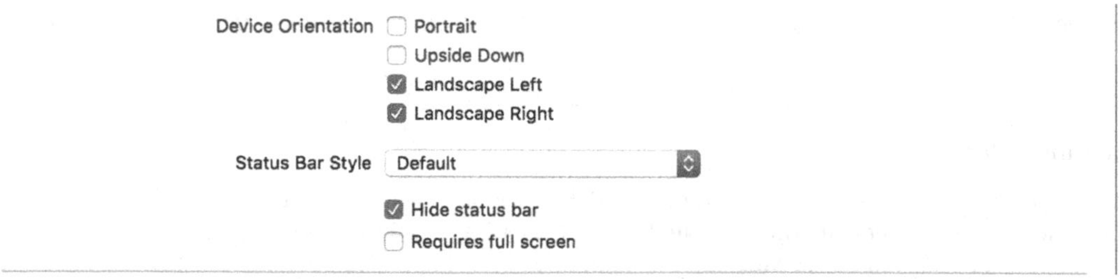

Device Orientation ☐ Portrait
☐ Upside Down
☑ Landscape Left
☑ Landscape Right

Status Bar Style Default

☑ Hide status bar
☐ Requires full screen

Figure 10-2. Restricting device orientation to landscape

5.   Before you go any further, let's stop to take a look at the assets for the application. Figure 10-3 shows the two characters you use: the hero—the alien dev—on the left and the villainous bug on the right. One thing you should be able to gather is that I am *not* a graphic artist. Each character is represented by a single high-resolution image: Dev.png and Bug.png. Both are transparent PNG images, which means the background appears in the whitespace behind them. Downloaded these images or create your own with the same names.

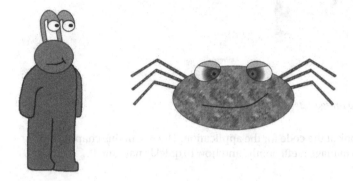

Figure 10-3. The hero and villain for this application

6.   Open Assets.xcassets from the Project Navigator and drag the files from the Finder into the sidebar of the asset catalog in Xcode, as shown in Figure 10-4.

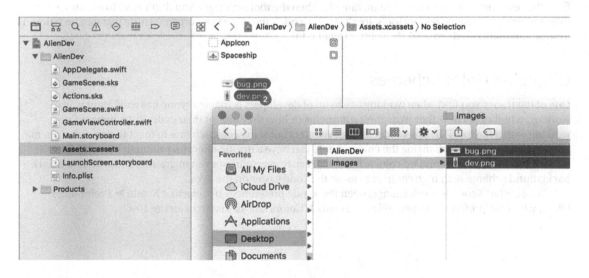

Figure 10-4. Dragging the image files into the Assets Catalog

7. When you release the files, image sets are created automatically for each file. Highlight the `spaceship` image set and remove it with the Backspace key so that your asset catalog resembles Figure 10-5.

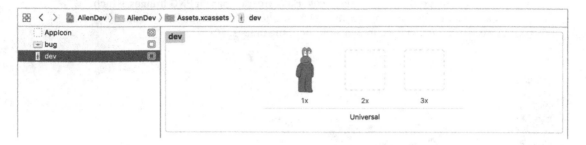

Figure 10-5. *The asset catalog with the new image sets*

With the assets in place, let's start to look at the code for the application. The rest of this chapter is dedicated to code: how to look at it, how to manage it efficiently, and how to quickly navigate it.

Efficient Editing

A good developer can be compared to a master craftsman, except that instead of a hammer and chisel, developers have IDEs and compilers. Like a master craftsman, good developers take pride in their work, taking time to achieve perfection and adding the painstakingly small touches that set their product apart from the rest. Unlike a master craftsman, though, when the tool isn't right, you don't have to pick up a different one, because developer tools aren't static; Xcode's interface is an organic entity that can be tailored to your needs and made to work the way you want it to.

Changing Color Schemes

One of the things you find when working in a team of developers is that everyone has a different way of working, whether it's how they write their comments or how they indent their code. But when you're working with a flexible IDE like Xcode, most developers tailor the color scheme to meet their needs. You may not have realized it, but changing the color scheme can have a drastic effect on productivity; sometimes I find the lightness of the standard color scheme can cause eyestrain or even migraines, so I switch to a dark background scheme with high contrast to make the code easier on the eyes.

To see what Xcode lets you change, open the Xcode preferences by selecting Xcode ➤ Preferences (⌘+,); when the preferences open, select theFonts & Colors tab, as shown in Figure 10-6.

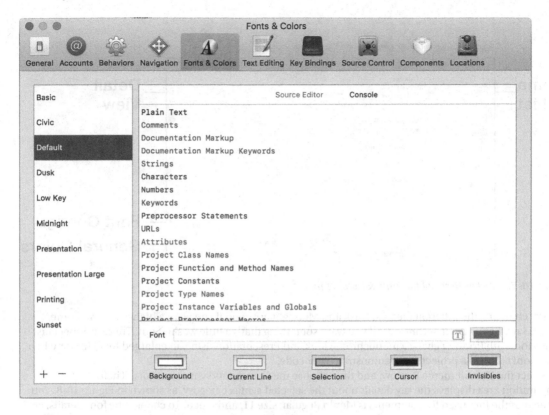

Figure 10-6. *The Fonts & Colors tab in Xcode's preferences*

The Fonts & Colors tab is divided into four key areas, as highlighted in Figure 10-7.

- *Theme list*: This area lists the preset themes Xcode makes available. A *theme* is a predetermined combination of fonts and colors.

- *Detail view*: The items listed in the detail view are known as *syntax categories*. These represent all the conceivably customizable elements of code in either the source editor or console, depending on which tab is selected at the top of the detail view.

- *Font configuration*: This area allows you to customize the font and color for the selected syntax category.

- *General colors*: The general colors control the background color; the selection color, which is used when highlighting text; the cursor color; and the "invisibles" color or the instruction pointer if you're looking at the Console tab.

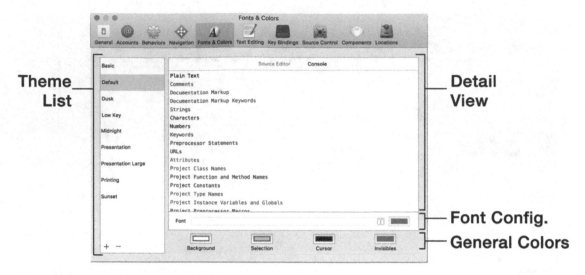

Figure 10-7. *The key areas of theFonts & Colors tab*

Try changing the different themes: Dusk and Midnight are good if you want a high-contrast theme, whereas Low Key and Sunset are great if you want something that's a little washed out. There are specialist themes too, with Printing giving a monochrome look and Presentation using an enlarged font size for when you're hooked up to a projector to demonstrate your code.

Select the Default theme for now, and then choose the Comments syntax category. Thefont configuration area displays the key details about the selected syntax category, as shown in Figure 10-8. You can see that the font used for comments is Menlo Regular, size 11, and green. To change the font details, click the T icon as you would when setting font information for labels and text fields in Interface Builder. Unlike in Interface Builder, however, you're presented with the standard font selection dialog that will be familiar to anyone who has used macOS for a while; this is shown in Figure 10-9.

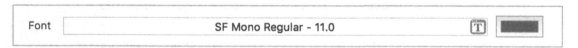

Figure 10-8. *The font configuration details*

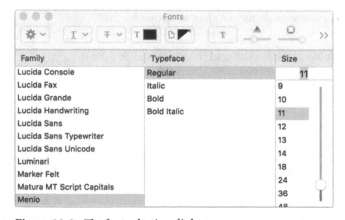

Figure 10-9. *The font selection dialog*

Creating a New Theme

Although it's easy to modify a theme, there is no Reset button to revert your changes to the theme's original settings. If you modify a theme and want to get it back to its original state, the best way is to start over and create a new theme based on one of the preset themes. This may sound drastic, but it's perfectly all right; all the themes that come with Xcode by default are stored as templates in Xcode that can be re-created in a couple of clicks.

First, let's examine the Add button at the bottom of the theme list. Click the + symbol, as shown in Figure 10-10. You're presented with a popup menu that effectively gives you two choices: you can either duplicate your current theme or create a new theme from one of the default templates.

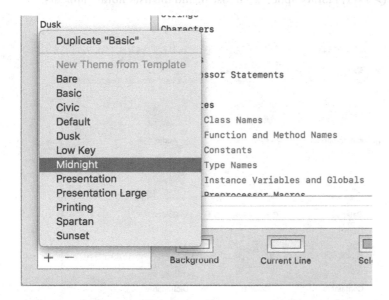

Figure 10-10. *The Add menu in the themes list*

Select Midnight, and a new version of the Midnight theme is added to your themes list, as shown in Figure 10-11. At this point you can change the name of the theme to anything you want. I'll name my theme `Matt's Midnight`; call your theme whatever suits your fancy.

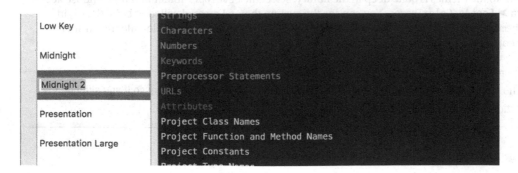

Figure 10-11. *The new theme, ready to be customized*

There may be a time where you get bored with your theme and want to remove it; you do this by clicking the minus symbol next to the + symbol in the themes list.

Sharing or Importing a Theme

You've spent hours customizing your theme to suit your preferences, fine-tuning every syntax category until the color and tone are perfect, and now you want to share it with the world. The good news is that this is really easy to do!

All the themes you create are stored on your computer in a dvtcolortheme file format. To locate these files, open the Finder, and then select Go from the menu bar. The Library option is hidden by default, but if you press the Option (➤) key, Library appears; choose it, and the user library appears, as shown in Figure 10-12.

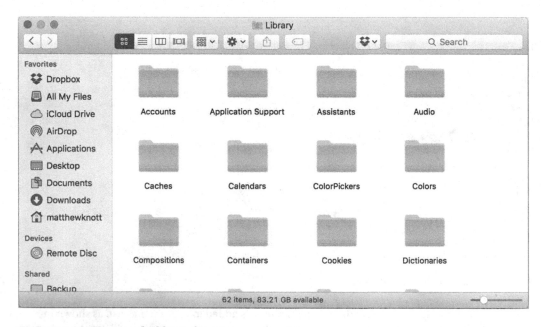

Figure 10-12. *Viewing the library for my user account*

The path to the themes is quite deep in the library: select the Developer folder and then choose Xcode ➤ UserData ➤ FontAndColorThemes. You can see the custom theme I created called Matt's Midnight. dvtcolortheme, as shown in Figure 10-13. From here, you can add themes you've downloaded from the Internet or copy them to share online.

■ **Note** The FontAndColorThemes folder is only visible if you've duplicated a theme, so if you skipped the previous section, you may not see this folder.

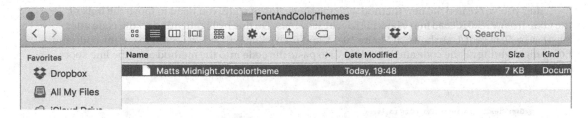

Figure 10-13. The contents of my FontsAndColorThemes folder

■ **Note** Whenever you make changes in this folder, you must restart Xcode for those changes to take effect.

Back in Xcode, choose the theme you're happiest with and close the preferences by clicking the red ball in the top-left corner. You now know everything there is to know about themes in Xcode! Next, I delve into the code for AlienDev and show you how to make dealing with large amounts of code less of a chore.

Organizing and Navigating Code

You've learned how to alter the visual appearance of code, so it's time to go a bit deeper and look at the fantastic shortcuts Xcode provides to help you be super-efficient in how you code. In order to see some of the finer points of organizing and navigating through code, you first need to add that code. At this point, you've added the assets to display in the SpriteKit scene, but if you were to run the application, it would still have all the behaviors of the default SpriteKit template. The first thing you need to do is make some modifications toGameViewController.swift so that the stage is set for adding the hero and the villainous bugs.

Start by opening GameViewController.swift from the Project Navigator. Because you're using a landscape-only orientation, and because of the point at which viewDidLoad is called, you need to create a method that performs the initialization once the view has been added to the stack. This method is called viewWillLayoutSubviews, and you need to add it just after viewDidLoad, as shown highlighted here:

```
override func viewDidLoad() {
    super.viewDidLoad()

    if let view = self.view as! SKView? {
        // Load the SKScene from 'GameScene.sks'
        if let scene = SKScene(fileNamed: "GameScene") {
            // Set the scale mode to scale to fit the window
            scene.scaleMode = .aspectFill

            // Present the scene
            view.presentScene(scene)
        }

        view.ignoresSiblingOrder = true

        view.showsFPS = true
        view.showsNodeCount = true
    }
}

override func viewWillLayoutSubviews() {
    super.viewWillLayoutSubviews()
}
```

After you've created the new method with the single line of code, you need to move the bulk of the code from viewDidLoad into viewWillLayoutSubviews. Do this by highlighting all the code after super.viewDidLoad(), as shown in Figure 10-14, and then using Edit ➤ Cut (⌘+X) to cut the code and Edit y highlighting all the code afte Paste (⌘+V) to paste the code into the method after the line super. viewWillLayoutSubviews().

```
class GameViewController: UIViewController {

    override func viewDidLoad() {
        super.viewDidLoad()

        if let view = self.view as! SKView? {
            // Load the SKScene from 'GameScene.sks'
            if let scene = SKScene(fileNamed: "GameScene") {
                // Set the scale mode to scale to fit the window
                scene.scaleMode = .aspectFill

                // Present the scene
                view.presentScene(scene)
            }

            view.ignoresSiblingOrder = true

            view.showsFPS = true
            view.showsNodeCount = true
        }
    }

    override func viewWillLayoutSubviews() {
        super.viewWillLayoutSubviews()
    }
}
```

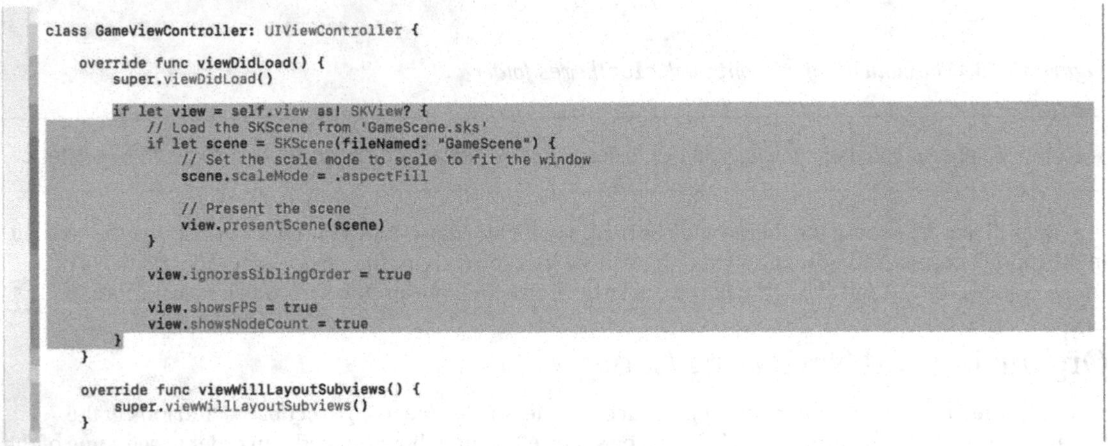

Figure 10-14. *Highlighting the code in the*viewDidLoad *method that needs to be moved*

After you move the code, the finished structure of the two methods should resemble the code shown next:

```
override func viewDidLoad() {
    super.viewDidLoad()
}

override func viewWillLayoutSubviews() {
    super.viewWillLayoutSubviews()

    if let scene = GameScene(fileNamed:"GameScene") {
        // Configure the view.
        let skView = self.view as! SKView
        skView.showsFPS = true
        skView.showsNodeCount = true

        /* SpriteKit applies additional optimizations to improve rendering performance */
        skView.ignoresSiblingOrder = true

        /* Set the scale mode to scale to fit the window */
        scene.scaleMode = .AspectFill

        skView.presentScene(scene)
    }

}
```

The outcome of any code tutorial is usually a known quantity, but in this case let's pretend you don't know what's going to happen as you develop this application. You've emptied all the code from the override of the viewDidLoad method, because it was effectively just taking up space at this point, but you *might* need it in the future. So let's set a reminder to clean up the method if it doesn't get used.

Creating Code Reminders

Xcode provides several handy tags that can be used in code comments to help you remember to deal with different tasks such as adding code to a method, fixing something that isn't quite right but doesn't break the compiler, and adding a general reminder to either research something further or double-check whether you've added all the required elements to a view.

In Swift, you comment a single line of code by prefixing it with two forward slashes (//). If you then start your comment in one of the following two ways, Xcode detects it and displays it in the jump bar, which I'll explain shortly:

> // TODO: TODO reminders should be used when you want to create a quick reminder about a piece of work you haven't done. This can be great when you're writing a large method and you want to focus on the key functionality, but you know you need to come back later and write the error checking.

> // FIXME: I use FIXME mainly when transitioning code between two versions of iOS. When iOS 8 came out, some of my iOS 7 applications developed small code glitches. I pinpointed these glitches in one go, adding FIXME comments to the errors of concern so that I could work through them one by one, checking them off.

Because this is something you want to look at later on, let's use the TODO mark to set a reminder. After the line super.viewDidLoad(); add your TODO comment so the method looks like this:

```
override func viewDidLoad() {
    super.viewDidLoad()

    //TODO: Remove if not used
}
```

■ **Note** These code words are case-sensitive. If you use any lowercase characters or fail to use the colon correctly, they won't display in the jump bar.

That's it: you've added a handy reference that will stand out in the jump bar like a sore thumb and remind you to tidy up your code when you finish the application.

Using the Jump Bar

I've mentioned the jump bar several times, so let's take a closer look at it. The *jump bar* is the series of items at the top of the code view, as shown in Figure 10-15. It's called the jump bar because, depending on which part you choose, it allows you to jump quickly between files, folders, and different areas of a code file.

The very last block of the jump bar, which in Figure 10-15 says viewDidLoad(), is by far the most commonly used part. For many developers, this *is* the jump bar, and it's the only part of it they ever use. Select this block of the jump bar, and you should see the effect of the added TODO comment, as shown in Figure 10-16. Although there are many comments in the code, the only one that appears in the jump view among the methods is the cleanup message.

Figure 10-15. *The jump bar is located at the top of the code window*

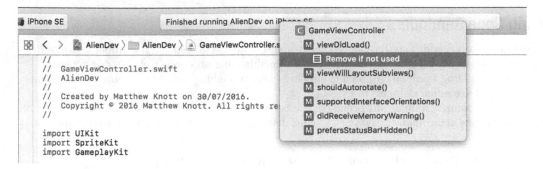

Figure 10-16. *The structure of the code outlined in the jump view*

Notice in the jump bar that each of the methods is listed, as well as the class implementation. Selecting any of these takes you directly to the relevant portion of code.

Organizing Code with Pragma Marks

If you have any experience programming with a C-based language, you're probably familiar with the `#pragma` directive. Traditionally it's used to provide additional information to the compiler in addition to what the language itself can express. You can also provide additional information to the IDE by using the `#pragma mark` directive to create sections for the methods in the jump bar. In Swift, the pragma mark has been streamlined to fit the same format as the other bookmarking tags and is now written `// MARK:`, as you may have noticed in previous chapters.

Let's say you want to isolate the bottom three methods in the `GameViewController.swift` file. You can add a directive to indicate that these methods are not to be touched. Before the `override func shouldAutorotate()` method, type the following code:

```
//MARK: Standard Methods : Ignore
```

Now go back and look at what the jump view shows for the code file. As shown in Figure 10-17, the mark has been added to the hierarchy and now provides a heading for the bottom four methods.

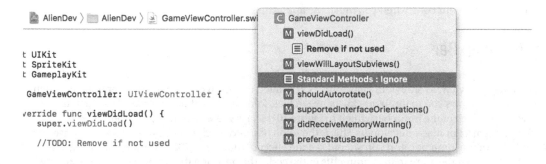

Figure 10-17. *The mark appearing in the jump bar to isolate the standard methods*

These marks are incredibly useful, especially when you're working with dozens of methods. Grouping your methods together by area of function makes your life easier and also that of anyone else who needs to look at your code.

Building the Scene

Unlike other applications you've built so far in this book, a SpriteKit application doesn't need much work in the view controller, which initializes the environment. All the logic that controls what you see on the screen comes from the scene. By default, the SpriteKit application comes with two custom classes: GameViewController and GameScene. Open GameScene.swift, and you see that it subclasses SKScene.

In a SpriteKit application, the scene is responsible for calculating what is shown onscreen in each frame. First you need to prepare the SpriteKit Scene file GameScene.sks. There are some boilerplate items to remove from this file.

1. Open GameScene.sks from the Project Navigator.

2. In the Attributes Inspector, set the Size to iPhone SE and ensure the orientation is set to Landscape.

3. Next, set the Scale attribute to 2 and both Anchor Point values to 0.

4. Finally, select the boilerplate Hello World text in the scene and delete it using the Backspace key.

Now that the scene file is prepared, let's modify GameScene.swift to add the alien dev hero to the screen, before swamping him with bugs:

1. If you haven't already, open GameScene.swift. Create an SKSpriteNode variable called alienDev to hold all the information for the alien dev's character in the scene. Add the following highlighted code:

```
import SpriteKit
import GameplayKit

class GameScene: SKScene {

    var alienDev : SKSpriteNode?
```

2. Let's clean up this file a little. Start by removing the two private variables beneath your new alienDev variable. Scroll down and remove the touchdown, touchMoved, touchup, touchesMoved, touchesBegan, touchesEnded, and touchesCancelled methods.

3. Remove all the code in the didMove method. The entire file should now look like this:

```
import SpriteKit
import GameplayKit

class GameScene: SKScene {

    var alienDev : SKSpriteNode?

    override func didMove(to view: SKView) {

    }
```

```
    override func update(_ currentTime: TimeInterval) {
        // Called before each frame is rendered
    }
}
```

4. Let's set the scene for the application by choosing the background color and initializing and adding the alienDev object. TheSKScene object is always the root node in the hierarchy of SpriteKit nodes; so you need to add the sprites to the scene to begin creating the hierarchy. In the didMove method, add the following highlighted code:

```
override func didMove(to view: SKView) {
    self.backgroundColor = SKColor.white
    alienDev = SKSpriteNode(imageNamed: "dev")
    alienDev!.position = CGPoint(x: self.frame.midX, y: self.frame.midY)
    alienDev!.size = CGSize(width: 120, height: 220)

    self.addChild(alienDev!)
}
```

5. Run the application. If everything works as it should, the hero stands alone in the middle of the screen, as shown in Figure 10-18, along with the node and frames per second (fps) counts. These two values are great for debugging poor performance in your animation and can help to identify choke points where you may have too many sprites (nodes) on the screen at any one time. They can also help you scale your application for different devices; more capable hardware can handle more sprites without a drop in performance, whereas an older device may need to have lower-quality images and fewer sprites. When you're finished with them, you can disable them by changing the showsFPS and showsNodeCount properties of SKView to false in GameViewController.swift.

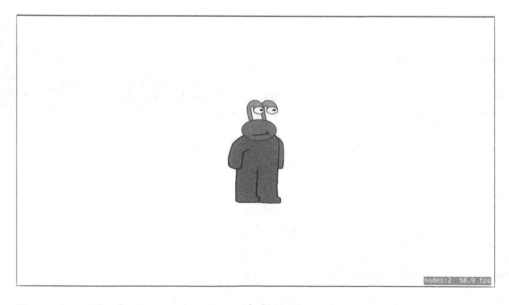

Figure 10-18. TheAlienDev app in action, with the single, static sprite

6. The hero is a bit lonely on the screen, which looks quite sparse. Before you add every developer's nemesis, the bug, let's add a title to the scene as another node. It's an instance of theSKLabelNode class. Although this will be the only text you add, adding text nodes to the scene is a common requirement, so let's be efficient and create a function that adds to the scene whatever text you send it. Drop down a few lines after the didMove method and add the following function stub:

```
func createTextNode(text: String, nodeName: String, position: CGPoint) -> SKLabelNode {

}
```

7. The function returns an SKLabelNode object, so you need to declare and initialize an object of this class and return it. In the function, add the following lines of highlighted code:

```
func createTextNode(text: String, nodeName: String, position: CGPoint) -> SKLabelNode {
    let labelNode = SKLabelNode(fontNamed: "Futura")

    return labelNode
}
```

8. Set the attributes of thelabelNode object to specify the text, size, color, and position of the label, as well as give it a name as an identifier. Once the attributes are set, return the label. To do so, add the following highlighted code:

```
func createTextNode(text: String, nodeName: String, position: CGPoint) -> SKLabelNode {
    let labelNode = SKLabelNode(fontNamed: "Futura")
    labelNode.name = nodeName
    labelNode.text = text
    labelNode.fontSize = 30
    labelNode.fontColor = SKColor.black
    labelNode.position = position
    return labelNode
}
```

■ **Note** SpriteKit applications don't use UIKit like the other solutions have, so in this instance you use SKColor to set the color rather than UIColor. They're separate classes in separate frameworks but perform largely the same function with almost identical syntax.

9. Now that you have a function for generating labels, let's give the application a title. Go back to the didMove method and, after the line self. addChild(alienDev!), add the following code:

```
self.addChild(alienDev!)

let title = createTextNode("Welcome to Alien Dev",
                           nodeName: "titleNode",
                           position: CGPoint(x: self.frame.midX, y: self.frame.midY+150))
self.addChild(title)
```

10. Run the application again. This time it looks a little less sparse, as you can see in Figure 10-19.

Figure 10-19. *The application, now with two nodes: the dev and the title*

11. You have everything in this scene except the bugs that plague the hero. In this application, the bugs appear from the top of the screen and slide down toward the hero—the alien dev. To achieve this, let's create a function that adds a bug at a random position offscreen. This is called by the SKScene update method at regular intervals. Add the stub for this function beneath the createTextNode function:

```
func createBug() {

}
```

12. This will be a particularly large function. As in previous chapters, I won't dwell too much on the actual code—just how Xcode ultimately makes it easy to manage and interact with this code. In pseudo-code, let's create an SKSpriteNode as you did when you initialized the dev character. You set the bug to appear just offscreen above the top of the screen, but then randomly determine where it "spawns" on the x (horizontal) axis. After adding the bug to the scene, you indicate how long it should appear and then send it down the screen before it disappears and is removed from the scene. Add the following highlighted code in the createBug function:

```
func createBug() {
    let evilBug = SKSpriteNode(imageNamed: "bug")
    evilBug.size = CGSize(width:220, height:120)
```

```
let minX = (evilBug.size.width / 2)
let maxX = (self.frame.size.width - evilBug.size.width)
let rangeX = UInt32(maxX - minX)

let finalX = Int(arc4random() % rangeX) + Int(minX)
let startPos = CGPoint(x:CGFloat(finalX),
                           y:self.frame.size.height + evilBug.size.height/2)
let endPos = CGPoint(x:CGFloat(finalX),
                       y:evilBug.size.height/2)

evilBug.position = startPos
self.addChild(evilBug)

let minDuration : Int = 3
let maxDuration : Int = 8
let rangeDuration : UInt32 = UInt32(maxDuration - minDuration)
let finalDuration = Int(arc4random() % rangeDuration) + minDuration

let actionMove = SKAction.move(to: endPos, duration:TimeInterval(finalDuration))
let actionMoveDone = SKAction.removeFromParent()

evilBug.run(SKAction.sequence([actionMove, actionMoveDone]))
}
```

Folding Code

The GameScene.swift file is really starting to fill out now, but there are still two methods and some instance variables to add so that you can see the application in all its glory. Xcode kindly provides a way to make this file easier to navigate and modify, in the shape of *code folding*.

Code folding is the concept of compressing code that is encapsulated by brackets—such as in methods, if statements, and other logical structures—into a single line, thus hiding the code from view and allowing you to focus on a specific segment of code. You can fold code in the editor as well as through menus and key combinations. Code folding isn't unique to Xcode—the concept exists in many popular IDEs and code editors—but it's not as obvious how to access it in Xcode as it is in those other systems.

First, let's ensure code folding is enabled; open the Xcode preferences by choosing Xcode ➤ Preferences (⌘+,); when the preferences open, click the Text Editing tab and choose the code folding ribbon. Ensure the code folding Ribbon and Focus Code Blocks On Hover are both checked.

Now scroll to the top of the GameScene.swift file, to the start of the didMove method. Move your mouse cursor to the gutter next to the code just adjacent to the start of the method, as shown in Figure 10-20.

```
    var alienDev : SKSpriteNode?

▼   override func didMove(to view: SKView) {
        self.backgroundColor = SKColor.white()
        alienDev = SKSpriteNode(imageNamed: "dev")
        alienDev!.position = CGPoint(x: self.frame.midX, y: self.frame.midY)
        alienDev!.size = CGSize(width: 120, height: 220)

        self.addChild(alienDev!)

        let title = createTextNode("Welcome to Alien Dev",
                                    nodeName: "titleNode",
                                    position: CGPoint(x: self.frame.midX, y: se
        self.addChild(title)
    }
```

Figure 10-20. *Exposing the fold toggle in the code editor*

Notice that a downward-pointing arrow appears: Xcode highlights all the code that will be hidden if you click the mouse on that area of the gutter. Click the arrow, and the entire method is compressed, as shown in Figure 10-21. As you can see, the code shrinks to a single line, greatly reducing the visual clutter. There is now a right-pointing arrow in the gutter: click it, and your method is restored.

```
    var alienDev : SKSpriteNode?

▶   override func didMove(to view: SKView) {⋯}

    func createTextNode(_ text: String, nodeName: String, position: CGPoint) -> SKLabelNode {
        let labelNode = SKLabelNode(fontNamed: "Futura")
        labelNode.name = nodeName
        labelNode.text = text
        labelNode.fontSize = 30
        labelNode.fontColor = SKColor.black()
        labelNode.position = position

        return labelNode
    }
```

Figure 10-21. *The "folded"* didMove *method*

Folding one method at a time can be time consuming, which is where the menu options come into play. From the menu bar, select Editor ➤ Code Folding. As you can see in Figure 10-22, Xcode gives you a number of options for folding the code in this file: Fold, Unfold, and Unfold All. In addition, Xcode separates itself from other, lesser IDEs by giving you the option to specifically Fold Methods & Functions or Fold Comment Blocks. This fine level of control is really satisfying for developers who like to fold methods but not comments, rather than folding everything that could possibly be folded.

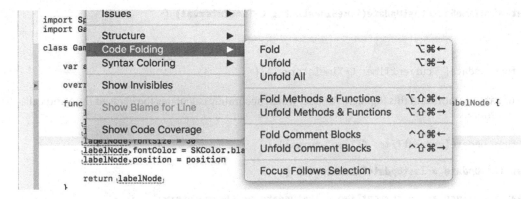

Figure 10-22. *Options offered inXcode's Editor tab*

Select the Fold Methods & Functions option. Instantly, the implementation is compressed from 60 lines to just a handful, as shown in Figure 10-23!

```
import SpriteKit
import GameplayKit

class GameScene: SKScene {

    var alienDev : SKSpriteNode?

    override func didMove(to view: SKView) {⬚}

    func createTextNode(_ text: String, nodeName: String, position: CGPoint) -> SKLabelNode {⬚}

    func createBug() {⬚}

    override func update(_ currentTime: TimeInterval) {⬚}
}
```

Figure 10-23. *The neatly foldedimplementation file*

Now that there is some room to breathe in the file, you can add the remaining two methods and the instance variables. This code is provided by Apple as part of its SpriteKit adventure template, and it allows you to call thecreateBug method at regular intervals. At the top of GameScene.swift, add the two instance variables as follows:

```
class GameScene: SKScene {

    var alienDev : SKSpriteNode?
    var lastSpawnTimeInterval : CFTimeInterval?
    var lastUpdateTimeInterval : CFTimeInterval?
```

These variables are used to calculate the time elapsed between frames. Next, you need to create one function stub and use an existing one to handle the updates: updateWithTimeSinceLastUpdate and update. The update method is aclass method that is called each frame, and updateWithTimeSinceLastUpdate is a custom function that ensures that bugs are added at a constant rate. Add the updateWithTimeSinceLastUpdate function stub before the update method in the implementation file, as shown in the following highlighted code:

```
func updateWithTimeSinceLastUpdate(timeSinceLast : CFTimeInterval) {

}

override func update(_ currentTime: CFTimeInterval) {
```

In the update method, add this highlighted code, which accurately calculates the elapsed time and calls the custom method:

```
override func update(currentTime: CFTimeInterval) {

    if let lastUpdate = lastUpdateTimeInterval {

        var timeSinceLast = currentTime - lastUpdate as CFTimeInterval

        lastUpdateTimeInterval = currentTime
        if (timeSinceLast > 1) {
            timeSinceLast = 1.0 / 60.0
            lastUpdateTimeInterval = currentTime
        }

        updateWithTimeSinceLastUpdate(timeSinceLast: timeSinceLast)
    }
    else
    {
        lastUpdateTimeInterval = currentTime
    }
}
```

For the last method in this implementation file, let's look at another weapon in the efficient developer's arsenal: code snippets.

The Code Sni⌐ppet Library

The Code Snippet library is a collection of small pieces of code, like microtemplates, that allow you to quickly create commonly written blocks of code by simply dragging and dropping the code into the code editor. The concept of code snippets, like code folding, is not unique to Xcode; but like code folding, it's implemented in a clear and intuitive manner. The Code Snippet library, shown in Figure 10-24, is located in theutilities bar and is accessed by clicking the { } icon (Control+⌥+⌘⌥+2).

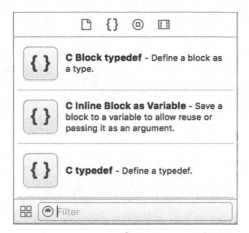

Figure 10-24. *The Code Snippet library*

Using Code Snippets

I'll explain how to create an if statement using a code snippet, but before you can do that, you need to add a line of code to the updateWithTimeSinceLastUpdate function. The following highlighted lines update the lastSpawnTimeInterval object:

```
func updateWithTimeSinceLastUpdate(timeSinceLast : CFTimeInterval) {
    if lastSpawnTimeInterval != nil {
        lastSpawnTimeInterval! += timeSinceLast
    }
    else
    {
        lastSpawnTimeInterval = 0
    }
}
```

You want to spawn a bug every 1 second, so you need an if statement to check that the lastSpawnTimeInterval object, which counts in milliseconds, is greater than 1. Look in the Code Snippet library for Swift If Statement, or type swift if state in the filter box, as shown in Figure 10-25.

Figure 10-25. *Filtering theCode Snippet library for an* if *statement*

Create an empty line under the last line of code you added, and then drag the if statement from the Code Snippet library. Position it just below that last line of code, as shown in Figure 10-26.

```
func updateWithTimeSinceLastUpdate(timeSinceLast : CFTimeInterval) {
    if lastSpawnTimeInterval != nil {
        lastSpawnTimeInterval! += timeSinceLast
        |          {˙}
    }                 +
    else
    {
        lastSpawnTimeInterval = 0
    }

}
```

Figure 10-26. *Dragging an* if *statement from the Code Snippet library*

When you release the snippet, it creates the outline of the if statement exactly as it does when you use the code-completion method for creating if statements. Change the condition placeholder to say lastSpawnTimeInterval! > 1 and the statements to lastSpawnTimeInterval! = 0 and, below that, createBug(). Thefinished method code looks like this:

```
func updateWithTimeSinceLastUpdate(timeSinceLast : CFTimeInterval) {
    if lastSpawnTimeInterval != nil {
        lastSpawnTimeInterval! += timeSinceLast
        if lastSpawnTimeInterval! > 1 {
            lastSpawnTimeInterval! = 0
            createBug()
        }
    }
    else
    {
        lastSpawnTimeInterval = 0
    }
}
```

> ■ **Tip** If your code is a bit messy after dragging in the code snippet, highlight the whole function and choose Editor ➤ Structure ➤ Re-Indent (Ctrl+I) to fix the indenting.

Using code snippets to create an `if` statement isn't the most efficient way to use them, but look through the list of snippets—there are dozens of premade snippets for a wide range of scenarios.

Creating Code Snippets

Where code snippets come into their own is when you create them from your own code. You know better than anyone else the code you type time and again—whether it's a template for a web request or a pattern you use for error handling—so creating code snippets is a great way to simplify code reuse.

Now for the paradox of creating code snippets—it's as easy as drag and drop, but *this* drag and drop isn't necessarily easy. To explain, you create a code snippet by highlighting the code you wish to save and dragging it into the Code Snippet library. Unfortunately, if you try this, you probably find you just end up selecting even more code when you try to drag; this is where the art of dragging code in Xcode comes into play.

Let's say you want to save the last two methods you created as they're the best way to perform a SpriteKit action at a regular interval. Start by highlighting the code, as shown in Figure 10-27.

Figure 10-27.   Thehighlighted code that you want to create a snippet from

Now, the technique—click and *hold* the mouse pointer in place until it changes from a bar to a normal mouse cursor anddrag the code to the Code Snippet library, as shown in Figure 10-28.

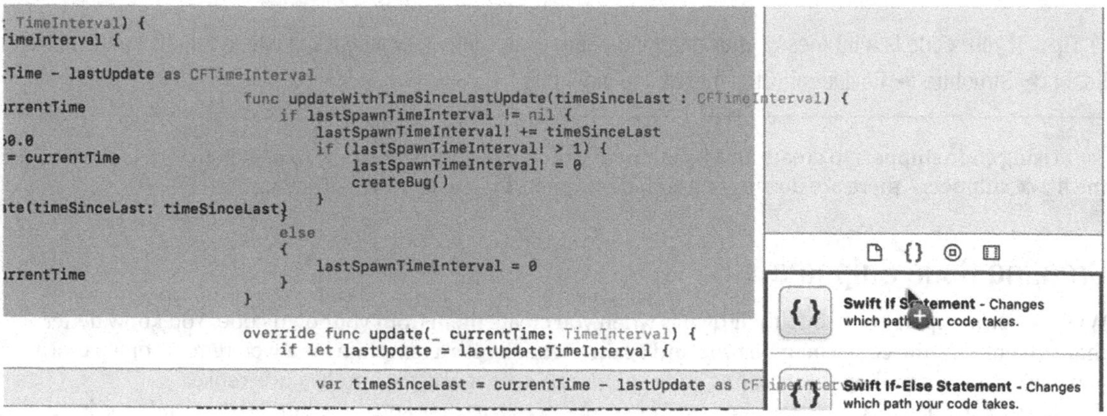

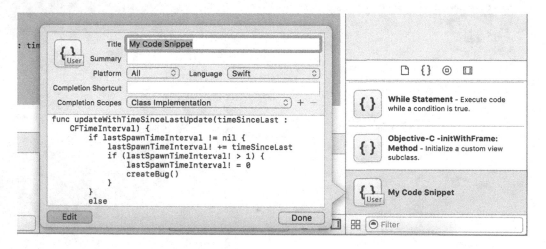

Figure 10-28. *Dragging the code to the Code Snippet library*

When you release the mouse, it will create an entry in the library called My Code Snippet. To save it from getting lost, it's important to name the snippet and set its attributes before you forget why you created it. Double-click the snippet to see a preview of the code, as shown in Figure 10-29. Click the Edit button.

Figure 10-29. *Previewing the code snippet you created*

You can see that you can now edit the entire code snippet here, but what you need to do is set the Title to SKScene Update Functions, the Platform to iOS, and the Completion Shortcut to SKU, as shown in Figure 10-30. Then click Done.

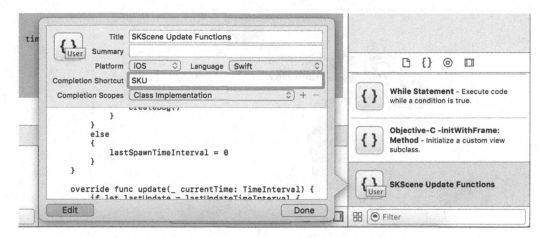

Figure 10-30. *Setting theproperties of the snippet*

You can see as soon as the Title property is set, it's updated in the library. One important value you set is the Completion Shortcut. I mentioned earlier that an if statement isn't the most efficient use of a code snippet, but in fact the drag and drop of the code snippet wasn't efficient because you've learned that when you type if in the code editor, you can press the Tab key to complete the entire statement, which is faster than dragging the snippet. All that actually happens is when you type if, it sees that you have a snippet in your library with a completion shortcut of if.

Go to your code editor and after the last method, type SKU. You see that you can now quickly create the twoupdate methods in your snippet simply by typing that completion shortcut, as shown in Figure 10-31.

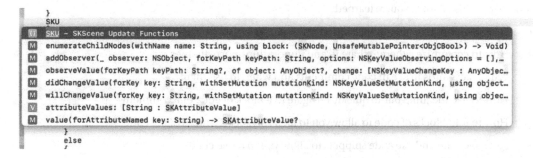

Figure 10-31. *Quickly adding the snippet to the implementation file*

It's this feature that exemplifies how Xcode has many of the same features you find in other IDEs, but Apple has taken the concept and refined it to make the developer's life so much easier. All that remains now is to run the application and watch the alien dev being bombarded by bugs, as shown in Figure 10-32.

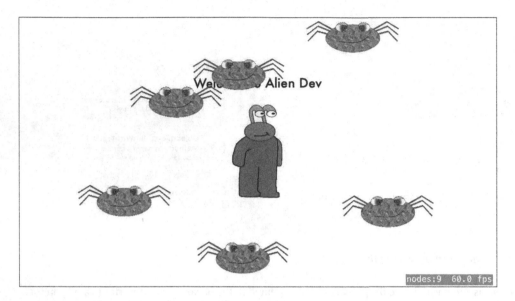

Figure 10-32. *The completedAlienDev application*

Summary

This chapter used a SpriteKit application as a backdrop to show the numerous ways Xcode can help reduce the overhead of writing code by streamlining how you code and by fine-tuning the development environment to suit your personal preferences.

Specifically in this chapter, you've learned:

- How to select a theme for the code editor
- How to customize a theme, share it, and import third-party themes
- Which keywords to use in code comments and when to use them
- How to use the jump bar to quickly navigate to a block of code or a comment
- How to fold blocks of code to allow you to focus on specific areas of the code
- How to create and use code snippets to allow you to reuse code

The next chapter will take a detailed look at how to debug issues in applications and how Xcode can give insight into what's going on behind the scenes.

CHAPTER 11

■■■

Debugging and Analysis

Chapter 10 looked at some of the ways Xcode can empower you to be a more effective and efficient developer, from tweaking the theme used to display code in the code editor, to using the jump bar and code snippets to speed up development. You learned all that by creating a SpriteKit-based animation application where the hero, the alien dev, had bugs raining down on him from above.

This leads nicely into this chapter, where you learn about debugging and analysis and, hopefully, answer the question, "How can Xcode help when the bugs start raining down?" Xcode has a whole suite of tools dedicated to making your life easier when it comes to determining why your code throws an exception or why in some cases nothing happens at all. This chapter takes a detailed look at all of these reasons. Additionally, I discuss some of the lesser-known debugging tools that aren't integrated into Xcode but are essential as you explore the breadth of the features of iOS application development with Xcode.

At the end of the chapter, I introduce you to one of the key tools exclusive for Swift programming: the Swift playground. This a code sandbox lets you focus on trying different pieces of logic and sampling the outcome.

This chapter initially focuses on three common debugging scenarios and how Xcode can be used to address them:

- *Logic errors*: Sometimes the hardest to debug, logic errors occur when your application doesn't do what you expect it to do, but they don't cause your application to trigger an exception or warning at either compile time or runtime. An example would be a button that doesn't do anything or a map view not displaying the specified area.

- *Runtime errors*: A runtime error is one that is detected after the application has compiled and it's either launching or running. Unhandled runtime errors are usually fatal to the application and cause it to crash.

- *Compile-time errors*: When you tell Xcode to run or build your application, it uses the compiler to take all of your code, linked files, and libraries and compile them into a binary. A compile-time error stops your application from compiling into a binary, so it must be resolved before you can run the application.

This chapter explains how to create an application that lists some of the European Union (abbreviated to EU throughout this chapter) member states in a table view calls EUStates. The table view uses an array as its data source, which is traditionally a great way of demonstrating runtime and logic errors because of their precise nature (they have a set number of items known as the *bounds* of the array, and going outside of those bounds can trigger a runtime or logic error).

© Matthew Knott 2016
M. Knott, *Beginning Xcode*, DOI 10.1007/978-1-4302-5005-0_11

Building the Application

EUStates is a very simple application to build. The focus here is on how to use Xcode to debug an application, so the code is minimal. To create the EUStates application, let's start with a Single View Application template and add a Table view controller. Many of these steps will be familiar to you from when you created the Twitter client in Chapters 7 and 8:

1. Open Xcode and create a new project by going to File ➤ New ➤ New Project (⌘+Shift+N) or, alternatively, choosing Create A New Xcode Project on the Welcome screen (⌘+Shift+1).

2. Select the Single View Application Template and click Next.

3. Name the product EUStates, substitute your personal information for mine, ensure that Device is set to Universal, and leave the other options set to their defaults, as shown in Figure 11-1. Click Next.

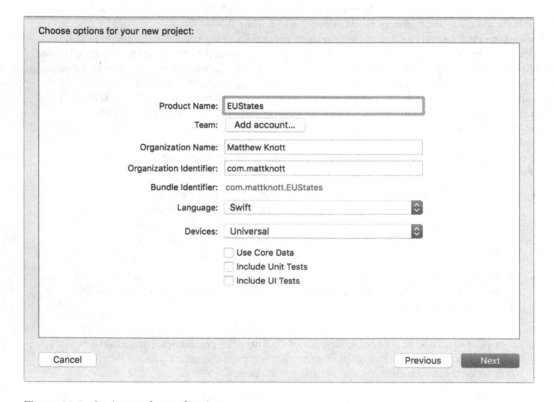

Figure 11-1. *Setting up the application*

4. The default save location is okay, so create the application by clicking Create.

5. Open Main.storyboard from the Project Navigator. It presents a single view on the storyboard; select the view and remove it so that you're left with an empty storyboard, as shown in Figure 11-2.

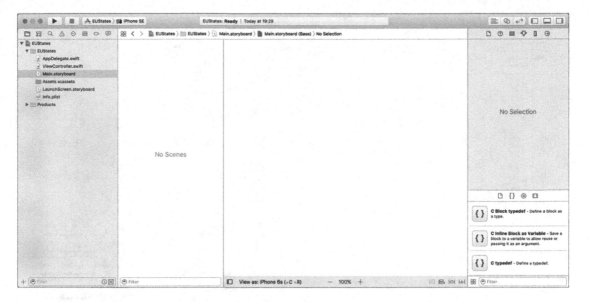

Figure 11-2. *Starting with a blank storyboard*

6. To complete the initial setup of the application, select `ViewController.swift` in the Project Navigator. Remove it either by pressing the Backspace key or by right-clicking the file and selecting Delete and then Move to Trash when prompted.

7. The application you're creating is based on a single Table view controller. That means you need to subclass `UITableViewController` to create a custom view controller and then tie that into a Table view controller on the storyboard. Choose File ➤ New ➤ File (⌘+N), choose Cocoa Touch Class from the list of templates, and click Next.

8. Set the Subclass Of value to `UITableViewController` and the Class value to `StatesViewController`. Leave Also Create XIB File unselected and click Next. Accept the default location to save the new class files and click Create.

9. Let's add the Table view controller to the storyboard. Open `Main.storyboard` from the Project Navigator. Open the Object Library and locate the Table View Controller object near the top of the list.

10. Drag a Table view controller onto the storyboard's design area, as shown in Figure 11-3.

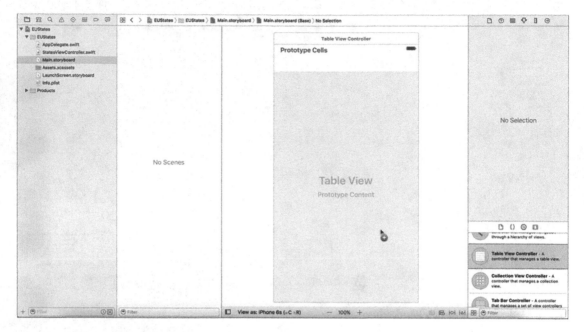

Figure 11-3. *Dragging a Table view controller onto the storyboard*

11. You need to specify the class for the new Table view controller. If the Table view controller isn't selected, select it and then open the Identity Inspector. Change the Class value to StatesViewController, as shown in Figure 11-4.

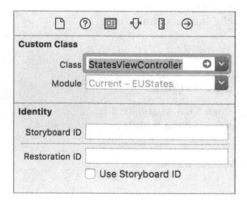

Figure 11-4. *Setting the Class value for the Table view controller to StatesViewController*

12. Click the Attributes Inspector. If it isn't selected, check Is Initial View Controller, as shown in Figure 11-5.

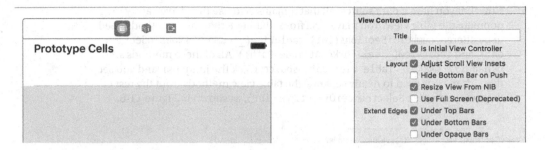

Figure 11-5. *Specifying the initial view for the storyboard*

13. With the structure of the application complete, it's time to create the array to hold the 15 EU member states. This is done by creating a String array as an instance variable and then populating it in a custom method. Open StatesViewController.swift from the Project Navigator. To declare the instance variable, add the highlighted code to the file as shown next:

```
class StatesViewController: UITableViewController {

    var states = [String]()
```

14. You need to create a method to initialize the array and populate it with 15 EU member states. After the viewDidLoad method, to create a new function called initStates, drop down a few lines and add the following stub:

```
func initStates() {

}
```

15. To populate the array, you add string values for the first 15 member states of the EU to the array. Add the highlighted code to the initStates function:

```
func initStates() {
    states.append("Austria")
    states.append("Belgium")
    states.append("Bulgaria")
    states.append("Croatia")
    states.append("Cyprus")
    states.append("Czech Republic")
    states.append("Denmark")
    states.append("Estonia")
    states.append("Finland")
    states.append("France")
    states.append("Germany")
    states.append("Greece")
    states.append("Hungary")
    states.append("Ireland")
    states.append("Italy")
}
```

16. Now that you have a data source, all that remains is to use the states array to populate the table view. You may recall from Chapter 8 that three methods need to be altered: numberOfSections(in:), tableView(_:numberOfRowsInSecti on:), and tableView(_:cellForRowAt indexPath:). All of these methods sit beneath // MARK: - Table view data source. Click the jump bar, and you see that this mark is used to neatly separate the table view methods from the rest of the view controller. Select numberOfSections(in:), as shown in Figure 11-6.

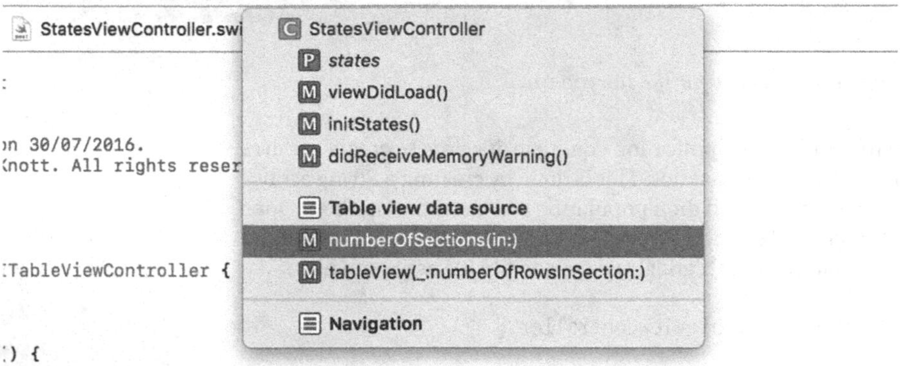

Figure 11-6. *Selecting the numberOfSections(in:) method from the jump bar*

17. Change the return value from 0 to 1, as shown next, and feel free to remove any comments:

```
override func numberOfSections(in tableView: UITableView) -> Int {
    return 1
}
```

18. Move down to the tableView(_:numberOfRowsInSection:) method, which dictates how many rows to render in the table view's section. Because you want this to be the number of elements in your array, you simply return states.count. The finished method should now resemble the following code:

```
override func tableView(_ tableView: UITableView, numberOfRowsInSection section: Int) -> Int
{
    return states.count
}
```

19. The final part of this implementation is to set the text of the table cell to the value of the corresponding index in the array. You use a string formatted to append the index number onto the table cell so that each cell appears like this: *2: Bulgaria*. Go to the tableView(_:cellForRowAt indexPath:) method, which is currently commented out, and remove the /* from the start and */ from the end of the method.

20. Add the highlighted code to display the desired text inside the cell:

```
override func tableView(_ tableView: UITableView,
    cellForRowAt indexPath: IndexPath) -> UITableViewCell {
    let cell = tableView.dequeueReusableCell(withIdentifier: "StateCell", for: indexPath)
```

```
    let cellText = "\(indexPath.row):  \(states[indexPath.row])"
    cell.textLabel!.text = cellText

    return cell
}
```

That's the last of the code you need to write for this application. Now you can run the application in the Simulator. Unfortunately, when you do, not a lot happens, as shown in Figure 11-7. All the methods are set correctly, so where's the problem? To get to the bottom of this conundrum, you need to see what's happening behind the scenes; and to do that, you need to use breakpoints.

Figure 11-7. *The application running in the Simulator, but not doing very much*

Using Breakpoints to Resolve Logical Errors

You've come across the first issue with the application. You need to use Xcode's debugging tools to analyze the problem and understand what has gone wrong and what you should do to fix it. The first tool in a developer's arsenal is the humble breakpoint.

Breakpoints allow you to specify a point in the application at which to pause the execution of the code and see what's happening behind the scenes. This way, you can associate a specific event with the line of code at fault. When a breakpoint is reached and the application pauses, you get to see the state of all of your objects and what values they contain. The application checks the numberOfSections(in:) and tableView

(_:numberOfRowsInSection:) methods to set the parameters for the table view, so these are good places to start the analysis. Because the numberOfSections(in:) method returns a fixed value, let's concentrate on the tableView(_:numberOfRowsInSection:) method first.

Setting a Breakpoint

If you've used other development environments in the past, you may find that adding a breakpoint in Xcode is very familiar; even if you haven't, you'll find that the process is intuitive. Scroll down to the tableView(_ :numberOfRowsInSection:) method and click in the gray bar to the left of the method declaration to place a breakpoint, as shown in Figure 11-8; if you have line numbers turned on, click the line number. When you add a breakpoint, a dark blue arrow appears on top of the line number.

```
override func numberOfSections(in tableView: UITableView) -> Int {
    return 1
}

override func tableView(_ tableView: UITableView, numberOfRowsInSection section: Int) -> Int {
    return states.count
}
```

Figure 11-8. *The breakpoint added for a line of code*

During runtime, when this line of code is reached, the application will pause and, hopefully, provide insight into why there isn't any information in the table view. Try running the application now. It launches in the Simulator, and then you're dropped back to Xcode with the Debug Navigator (see Figure 11-9) showing the state of the application and the debug area (see Figure 11-10) showing a selection of objects that are relevant to where the application has paused.

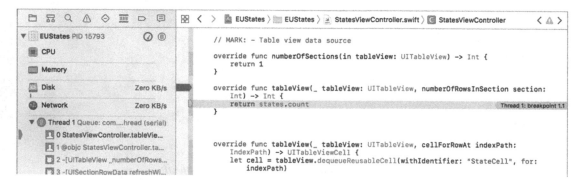

Figure 11-9. *The Debug Navigator, showing key information about the application at this point in time*

Figure 11-10. *The debug area and, on the left, a selection of objects relevant in the context of the breakpoint*

Before you look at why the application isn't working, let's examine both of these key areas in some detail to see what information they provide.

The Debug Navigator

While the application is paused, the Debug Navigator, as shown in Figure 11-11, can be used to provide a live snapshot of the activities taking place in the application. It displays the application's performance in terms of resource usage and the call stack of each thread in the thread list.

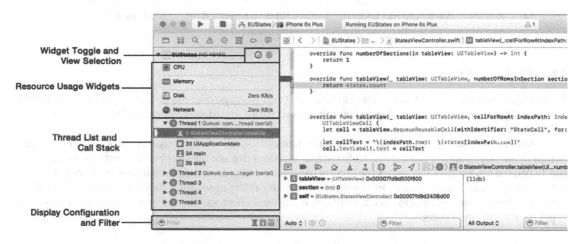

Figure 11-11. *The three key areas of the Debug Navigator, shown while debugging an application*

The resource usage is the only portion of the Debug Navigator that appears while the application is running as well as when it's paused. When you're developing for iOS, memory management is essential, but the task of ensuring that objects are correctly disposed of has been automated to a large extent with the introduction of automatic reference counting (ARC) in iOS 5. Before Xcode 5, ARC could be turned on or off depending on your preference, but with Xcode 5 it ceased to be presented as an option and was enabled by default for all iOS application templates. ARC basically automates the disposal of objects when they're no longer needed, handling almost all memory management and therefore giving you a lot of insurance against memory leaks.

The thread list and the call stack in each thread show which methods are currently being executed by each thread. You can see from the expanded call stack for the main thread (thread 1) in Figure 11-12 that the currently executed method is tableView(_:numberOfRowsInSection:), which was called by [UISectionRowData refreshWithSection:tableView:tableViewRowData:]. This can make understanding the flow of your application much easier.

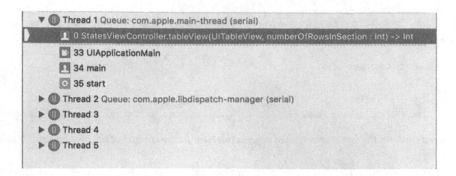

▼ ⦿ Thread 1 Queue: com.apple.main-thread (serial)
  👤 0 StatesViewController.tableView(UITableView, numberOfRowsInSection : Int) -> Int
  🗔 33 UIApplicationMain
  👤 34 main
  ⚙ 35 start
▶ ⦿ Thread 2 Queue: com.apple.libdispatch-manager (serial)
▶ ⦿ Thread 3
▶ ⦿ Thread 4
▶ ⦿ Thread 5

Figure 11-12. *A detailed look at the call stack of the main thread*

An icon adjacent to each thread reflects the thread's status:

- *No icon / blue icon*: The thread is running normally.

- *Yellow icon*: The thread is being blocked and is waiting for another thread to be unlocked or a certain condition to be met.

- *Red icon*: The thread has been suspended. While suspended, the thread doesn't execute any code when you proceed from the breakpoint.

The Debug Area

The debug area was covered in some detail in Chapter 3, so I won't go over old ground. But unlike in Chapter 3, the debug area has now come to life so you can interact with some of the controls and features you learned about earlier in the book.

Referring back to Figure 11-10 and your own instances of Xcode use for a moment, notice that the main output of the debug area at this time is the list of four variables that are relevant in the context of the method you're paused on. Figure 11-13 shows the control bar for the debug area. I explained what each icon means in Chapter 3, but at that time you didn't necessarily have the ability to see what they do. As you go through the rest of this chapter, feel free to click the buttons to see their effect and then stop and rerun the application to get back to the breakpoint.

Figure 11-13. *The control bar for the debug area*

The buttons that appear in the debug area, listed left to right, are as follows:

- *Hide*: Show or hide the debug area.

- *Breakpoint toggle*: Currently dark blue; toggles all breakpoints between enabled and disabled.

- *Continue*: Resumes execution of the application and then becomes a pause button.

- *Step Over*: Allows you to move out of the function being executed onto the next instruction.

- *Step Into*: Allows you to see in intricate detail each step of the application's execution. Think of the application as a film that's been paused: each time you click Step Into, you move a single frame ahead.

- *Step Out*: Shows the next piece of code to be executed. Use this if you've stepped too deep into your application's inner workings.

- *Debug View Hierarchy*: Visual debugging mechanism that helps you understand where elements of your view may be sitting, either offscreen or on. Sometimes a constraint may seem sensible enough when you add it but can have unexpected consequences when your application runs; this tool is invaluable in understanding what has happened.

- *Debug Memory Graph*: This exceptional new feature for Xcode 8 provides an execution map of the application allowing you to understand where memory is being consumed in your application.

- *Simulate Location*: Explained later in the chapter.

In addition to these controls, the debug area has its own jump bar. This jump bar shows the threads in the application and, in turn, each thread's call stack, as shown in Figure 11-14.

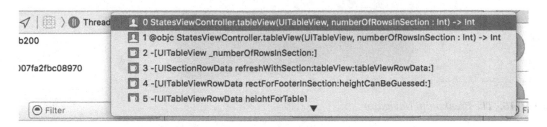

Figure 11-14. *The debug area's jump bar*

While trying to solve the current predicament of a table view with no content, you essentially have two initial lines of investigation: the data source (is there anything for the table to display?) and the application logic (did you correctly pass the information to the table view?). Looking at the objects in the debug area as shown back in Figure 11-10, you have an item called self. Click the disclosure indicator triangle next to it, and beneath self you see an array called states. Looking at the information about states, it should be obvious where the fault lies: the states array, instead of saying "15 values," says "0 values," meaning it hasn't been populated. Before you investigate why the array hasn't been populated, there are a few more things to cover in relation to breakpoints: most important, the Breakpoint Navigator.

The Breakpoint Navigator

At this point you've only created a single breakpoint, which is fine for working through the current problem, but in day-to-day development you'll come across various issues that call for a range of different breakpoints. You'll often set breakpoints on key pieces of logic and turn them on or off as required when flowing through an application. To manage these numerous breakpoints, you need to take advantage of the Breakpoint Navigator (⌘+7), which is the seventh icon in the list of navigators and resembles the shape of a breakpoint indicator.

Figure 11-15 shows the Breakpoint Navigator as it stands for this application. It gives you access to all the breakpoints in the project from a single location, and you can also use it to create an array of special breakpoints from the + symbol at the bottom of the navigator.

Figure 11-15. *The Breakpoint Navigator*

In addition to a standard breakpoint, Xcode lets you add the following breakpoints, which are used in specific scenarios:

- *Swift Error breakpoint*: Triggers when any Swift error occurs, or when a specific type of error occurs.

- *Exception breakpoint*: Triggers when any Objective-C or C++ exception is thrown or when a specific C++ exception is thrown.

- *Symbolic breakpoint*: Triggers when a specific method is triggered, which can be refined to a specific method in a specific class or even a specific function.

- *OpenGL ES error breakpoint*: Used when creating OpenGL ES-based applications (mainly games). As with standard breakpoints, these can be configured to be conditional, as I explain shortly.

- *Test failure breakpoint*: Triggers when a unit-test assertion fails, giving you an even greater level of granular analysis during testing.

Xcode also gives you a large degree of control over the behavior of your breakpoints. Right-click the breakpoint, as shown in Figure 11-16.

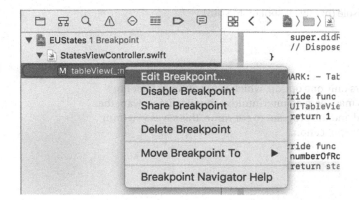

Figure 11-16. *The contextual menu displayed when you right-click a breakpoint in the Breakpoint Navigator*

You can use this menu to *edit* the attributes of the breakpoint; you can also *disable* or *delete* the breakpoint. Sharing a breakpoint makes it available to other users of the same project. This menu also continues Xcode's great support for contextual help, providing numerous useful and relevant pages on the Breakpoint Navigator and its features. Here, you focus on the edit ability.

Click Edit Breakpoint, and you're presented with a popup dialog, as shown in Figure 11-17. This dialog first shows the file and line number where the breakpoint has been added, and then provides several properties that can be set for the breakpoint:

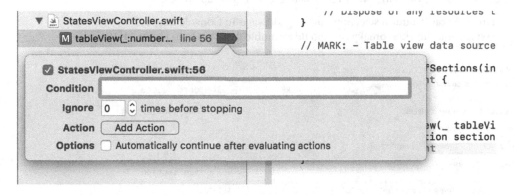

Figure 11-17. *Editing a breakpoint*

- *Condition*: A specific programming condition that must exist for the breakpoint to trigger, such as the incremental number in a for loop being equal to 10.

- *Ignore*: The number of times the condition needs to be met before it triggers a pause.

- *Action*: The action menu exemplifies Xcode's flexibility as an IDE. When the condition of the breakpoint is met, Xcode can perform any number of combinations of the following actions:

  - Execute a piece of AppleScript

  - Capture a GPU frame

  - Issue a debugger command

- Log a message to the console (or have it spoken to you!)

- Run a shell command

- Play a sound

- *Options*: Although plural, offers only one option, which is to continue after the breakpoint has triggered. This may seem counterintuitive, but if you just want the actions you add to be executed and the program to continue, this saves you from having to manually resume the application.

Conditional Breakpoints

Conditional breakpoints only trigger when certain conditions are met. In this case, it would be great if even after you fix the current issue, the debugger would notify you any time you get to a breakpoint and the states array is in a null state. Let's make the breakpoint conditional and add some humor to it at the same time (who knew that breakpoints could be fun?):

1. Right-click the breakpoint in the Breakpoint Navigator and choose Edit Breakpoint.

2. In the Condition box, type states.count == 0.

3. Click Add Action and choose Log Message from the list.

4. Set the Message value to I've fallen and I can't get up at %B.

5. Change the radio button selection from Log Message To Console to Speak Message. Your finished breakpoint should resemble that shown in Figure 11-18.

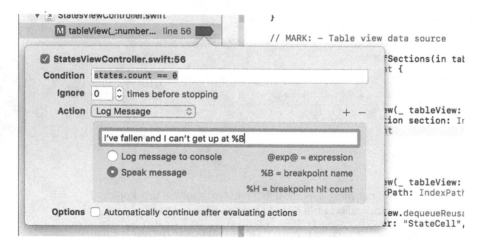

Figure 11-18. The customized breakpoint with a little added humor

Rerun the application. You're greeted by a synthesized voice saying, "I've fallen and I can't get up at table view_:numberOfRowsInSection." Although this is amusing, the issue with the application—that the array is empty—still has not been resolved. The fact that the array is empty means that the initStates method isn't being called before it tries to build the table. The real issue is that the method isn't called *at all*.

Switch back to the Project Navigator and open StatesViewController.swift. Go to the viewDidLoad method and add the highlighted code to the method:

```
override func viewDidLoad() {
    super.viewDidLoad()

    initStates()
}
```

Now rerun the application. It runs, and you're dropped back to Xcode. This isn't because of the breakpoint—as you should have noticed, there was no voice expressing its need for assistance—but rather because of a runtime error.

Runtime Errors

Although logic errors are frustrating, runtime errors are far more destructive to your application and your reputation. Outside of your IDE, a runtime error will cause your application to crash, which will annoy your users to no end and harm your reputation as a developer of bulletproof software. Because of the risk associated with software glitches, it's essential to thoroughly test your software for robustness.

The question here is how do you address a runtime error? It's often one of the hardest errors to debug, but there is a wealth of information available through breakpoints to help you get to the bottom of the issue. When the application crashed, it dumped the exception details and the call stack into the console in the debug area, as shown in Figure 11-19.

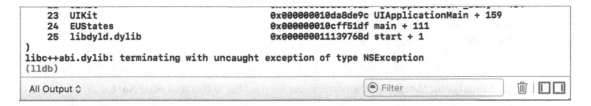

```
    23  UIKit                    0x000000010da8de9c UIApplicationMain + 159
    24  EUStates                 0x000000010cff51df main + 111
    25  libdyld.dylib            0x000000011139768d start + 1
)
libc++abi.dylib: terminating with uncaught exception of type NSException
(lldb)
```

All Output ◇		⊙ Filter	🗑	▢▢

Figure 11-19. *The console in the debug area after a runtime error has occurred*

When you first look at this mass of detail, it can be daunting, but it's actually incredibly useful. Starting at the end of the message, you can see that the application threw a standard NSException. This isn't particularly helpful at this point. Then you have the call stack in reverse order, meaning you need to scroll up through the console to get to the point of failure. As you scroll up, look at item number 4, as shown next:

4 UIKit 0x00000001032b4ef5 -[UITableView dequeueReusableCellWithIdentifier:forIndexPath:] + 266

The call stack is like the black-box flight recorder on an aircraft: just like a real black box, it gives a detailed log of what happened leading up to a crash. Item 4 is significant because this is the last event that happened before Xcode started reporting the calls to the exception handlers in items 3 to 0, which can largely be discarded.

Item 4 is significant because it shows a call to the TableView class's dequeueReusableCellWithIdentifier:forIndexPath: method. If you open StatesViewController.swift from the Project Navigator and scroll down to the tableView(_:cellForRowAt indexPath:) method, you see that this is called in the first line of the method.

Using Exception Breakpoints

To confirm your suspicions about this line, you can create an exception breakpoint to confirm the true source of the exception. Open the Breakpoint Navigator, click the + symbol at the bottom of the navigator, and then select Exception Breakpoint, as shown in Figure 11-20.

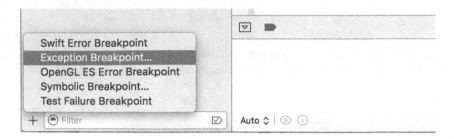

Figure 11-20. Adding an exception breakpoint

A new breakpoint to capture all exceptions is added to the list of breakpoints, as shown in Figure 11-21. All that remains is to run the application and see what Xcode can tell you about this particular issue.

Figure 11-21. A breakpoint to capture all exceptions has been added to theBreakpoint Navigator

Run the application again. Immediately the new breakpoint intercepts the exception and confirms your suspicions about the exception's source, which is indeed the call to the dequeueReusableCellWithIdentifie r:forIndexPath: method, as shown in Figure 11-22.

Figure 11-22. The exception breakpoint pinpointing the source of the exception

So, now that you know the source of the exception, how do you resolve it? It isn't always obvious, but in this case, Xcode gives you all the answers needed to get the application up, running, and error-free. What's more, the solution has been there since the initial exception.

Click the Breakpoints toggle button in the debug area to disable all the breakpoints, and then rerun the application. It crashes back to Xcode and again provides a mass of detail about the crash. This time, scroll up through the details in the console until you reach the top and see the following line:

```
2016-07-30 12:40:41.610 EUStates[48292:4152660] *** Terminating app due to uncaught
exception 'NSInternalInconsistencyException', reason: 'unable to dequeue a cell with
identifier State§Cell - must register a nib or a class for the identifier or connect a
prototype cell in a storyboard'
```

Roughly translated, this line says that you told the dequeueReusableCellWithIdentifier method to dequeue a cell called StateCell, which indeed you did in the first line of the tableView(_:cellForRowAt indexPath:) method:

```
let cell = tableView.dequeueReusableCell(withIdentifier: "StateCell", for: indexPath)
```

It's saying that you haven't set up a prototype cell in the storyboard with the identifier of StateCell, so it doesn't know what you're asking it to do. As you may recall from looking at table views in Chapter 8, you need to specify a reuse identifier for each cell you want to reference, so now you can see what happens if you don't.

To resolve this exception and move one step closer toward a working application, open main. storyboard from the Project Navigator. Select the prototype cell from the table view and then open the Attributes Inspector as shown in Figure 11-23.

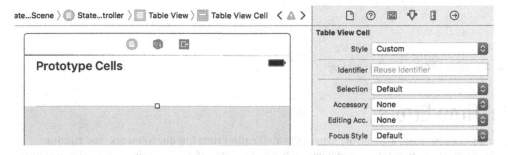

Figure 11-23. *Selecting the prototype cell from the table view in the storyboard*

In the Identifier attribute, match the cell identifier to the code to set the value as StateCell, as shown in Figure 11-24.

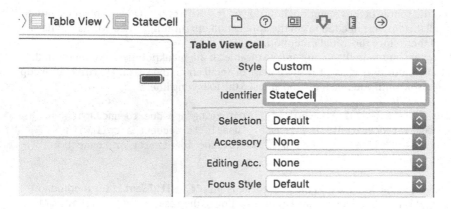

Figure 11-24. *Setting the cellIdentifier attribute*

It's taken a while to reach this point, but it's finally time to rerun the application and see it in action. Click the Run button, and your application should run successfully, as shown in Figure 11-25.

Figure 11-25. *The application, finally running!*

Compile-Time Errors

So far, this chapter has discussed logic errors, where the application runs but doesn't work, and runtime errors, where the application runs but then crashes. In both situations, when Xcode is instructed to run the application, the compiler is happy that all the code's syntax is correct, and it compiles the application.

A compile-time error occurs when the compiler is processing the code and encounters an issue with either the syntax of the code or one of the linked files. The good news is that often, compile-time errors are easily overcome, and many times Xcode even helps you overcome them by suggesting solutions.

Let's start to introduce some syntax errors into the application so you can see this in action. Open StatesViewController.swift from the project and scroll down to the viewDidLoad method. After the super.viewDidLoad() line of code, let's specify a background color for the table. Add the highlighted code exactly as shown—the case and spelling of words is extremely important:

```
override func viewDidLoad() {
    super.viewDidLoad()

    self.tableview.backgroundColor = UIColour.redColor?

    initStates()
}
```

Instantly, Xcode shows you that you have made a mistake by indicating the error with a red circle next to the line, as shown in Figure 11-26.

```
override func viewDidLoad() {
    super.viewDidLoad()

    self.tableview.backgroundColor = UIColour.redColor?

    initStates()
}
```

Figure 11-26. *Xcode indicating an error with the syntax*

Just to prove that you've created a compile-time error, try to run the application; it will fail and report the failure to build in the Activity Bar, as shown in Figure 11-27. Notice that the number of compile-time errors is reflected in the Activity Bar as a red circle with a white exclamation mark in it, next to the number of issues. To get an overview of the issues, click the red circle, which takes you to the Issue Navigator.

EUStates | Build EUStates: **Failed** | Today at 16:15   ❶ 1

Figure 11-27. *The Activity Bar reflecting the compile-time error*

TheIssue Navigator

This small issue serves two purposes: it shows you how Xcode spots syntax issues, and it serves as a great example that although Swift is a very comprehensive and advanced language, it has plenty of room for growth. You've actually created two errors in this single line of code; in Swift, Xcode identifies that there is a syntax error and shows you the line the error occurs on. If you were deliberately creating this error in Objective-C, Xcode would spot that there were two errors and offer to fix both for you. No doubt Apple will continue to develop the language throughout future versions of Xcode and through each successive release, but for now, you have to work things out for yourself.

To get an overview of any warnings or errors in the project, use the Issue Navigator (⌘+4), as shown in Figure 11-28.

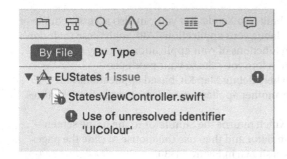

Figure 11-28. *The issue listed in the Issue Navigator*

As you can see, Xcode has seen the misspelled class name and is effectively saying it doesn't know what you're referring to. Go into the code editor and correct this by removing the *u* from the class name so that it says UIColor.

Although the class name is fixed, Xcode now picks up on the next issue. It doesn't like the `tableview` element, this is because it doesn't exist. In this instance, the object has the wrong case for the object name, change it to have a capital V so that the object is written `tableView`. That's fixed, but wait, there is another error!

Issues that are highlighted with a white dot in the red circle in the Issue Navigator can be fixed automatically by Xcode. Select the Swift Compiler Error from the list, and you're directed to the specific point in the code that Xcode feels is in error, as shown in Figure 11-29.

Figure 11-29. *The issue detail popup explaining the issue and offering to fix it*

As you can see, Xcode adds a popup explaining what the issue is, and it also gives a suggested fix. Click the Fix-it option and Xcode corrects the syntax issue.

There is now only one final issue remaining to resolve. Between Swift version 2 and version 3 Apple have made a number of simplifications to the syntax that were legacies of Objective-C. in Swift 2, `redColour` was a perfectly valid statement that allowed you to return a red UIColor object without specifying the RGB values. In Swift 3 Apple has simplified the syntax by removing Color from the statement. If you again click the red dot with white circle, you will see that Xcode is sympathetic to the fact that you have Swift v2 code, and shows you how to correct it for Swift 3; let Xcode fix this issue.

Immediately the Activity Bar loses the error indicator and the Issues Navigator says No Issues. That is how easy Xcode makes it to manage compile-time errors! Sometimes you will find it slightly more challenging than this, but powerful code completion coupled with a highly responsive editor and debug system largely prevent errors or allow you to resolve them the second they crop up.

Tools to Help with Debugging

So far, this chapter has looked at the debug tools that are built into Xcode, but you can also access a couple of extremely useful tools through the Simulator to help you debug your applications. Although these tools don't specifically debug anything, they allow you to test certain functions of your application in a way that can trigger an exception and therefore let you debug the error before you release your product.

In the next section, I explain the tools you can use to help debug Map Kit–based applications and applications that have a print function. Rather than write another application to demonstrate these features, let's use the default iOS Maps application.

To access Maps, first make sure you stop EUStates, which returns the Simulator to the home screen—but not the first page. To get to the first page, open the Simulator and then use the mouse to slide the pages across until you reach the page with the Maps icon on it, as shown in Figure 11-30.

Figure 11-30. *The main icons all appear on the first page in the Simulator*

Run the Maps application from the Simulator. Depending on previous use both the Simulator and Xcode, you should see a view resembling that in Figure 11-31: a map with no user location and no movement.

Figure 11-31. *The default starting point in the Maps application*

Debugging a Location

The challenge when developing a Map Kit–based application is your location. Unless you're commuting, using a physical device won't really help you develop your application because you want to try the application in different locations—perhaps even at different speeds, such as when driving or cycling—and using a MacBook while cycling isn't advisable!

Because of this conundrum, Apple introduced location simulation in Xcode and the Simulator, which lets you use preset locations and scenarios or create your own. As shown in Figure 11-32, you can debug the location by choosing Debug ➤ Location and then selecting Apple. Almost immediately, a blue circle appears over California. Clicking the arrow in the top-right corner of the Maps application zooms you to Apple headquarters in Cupertino.

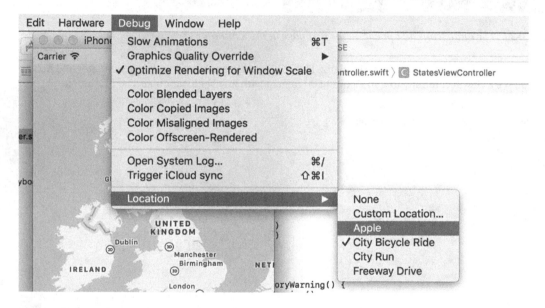

Figure 11-32. Accessing the options for debugging location from the Simulator

Next, return to the Debug ➤ Location menu and select Freeway Drive. The simulated position starts speeding around the Junipero Serra freeway, which is a great way to test an application that measures speed or distance.

■ **Note** If nothing happens, click the location arrow in the top-right corner of the Maps application. It will request access to your location and then begin tracking.

To simulate a specific location, return to the menu and choose Custom Location. From here you can specify a longitude and latitude as the user's location. Specify a latitude of 51.62228 and a longitude of -3.943491 to put the user in the middle of the Welsh city of Swansea. Simulating location is great for applications that use routing or that perhaps make recommendations based on a location.

Print Debugging with the Printer Simulator

Adding print functionality to your application is a great way to enrich its capabilities. Although the ability to print from in an application isn't overly complicated, you need to be able to test the actual print functionality. If you don't have a printer that supports Air Print, the technology for printing from an iOS device, fear not, because the Printer Simulator can solve all your worries.

Unfortunately, the Printer Simulator is no longer bundled with Xcode and must be downloaded from theApple web site. In Xcode, choose Xcode ➤ Open Developer Tool ➤ More Developer Tools, which prompts you to sign in with your Apple developer credentials.

Once you have done this, look for the newest release of Additional Tools for Xcode; the releases are in reverse chronological order, so the newest version is near the top. Click the item, and, on the right, you'll see a .dmg file for download, as shown in Figure 11-33.

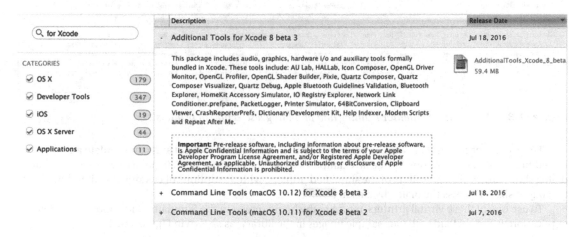

Figure 11-33. *Downloading the Additional Tools for Xcode*

Download and then open the .dmg file. Once mounted, go into the .dmg file, and inside the Hardware folder, you can open the Printer Simulator. It launches as a simple console and reports that it has set up several types of printers, as shown in Figure 11-34.

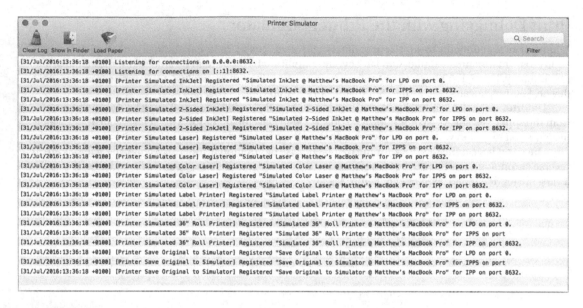

Figure 11-34. *The Printer Simulator running and providing a selection of printers*

The Simulator may not be what you expected, but it's extremely powerful and can simulate an incredible number of scenarios. To see an example of its power, click the Load Paper icon from the toolbar. A dialog slides down, showing all six of the simulated printers, with the options of customizing their functions and paper sizes. Dismiss the dialog by clicking OK.

To use one of these virtual printers, return to the home screen in the Simulator and choose the Photos application. It should load with four sample images in the library, as shown in Figure 11-35.

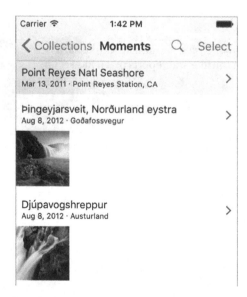

Figure 11-35. *The Photos app with default photos*

Open a photo and click the Share icon next to one of the images. The sharing action sheet appears, as shown in Figure 11-36.

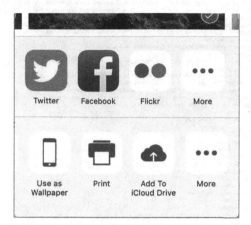

Figure 11-36. *The iOS sharing menu*

From this action sheet, swipe until you can select the Print option on the bottom row of icons. You're presented with the standard iOS print dialog, as shown in Figure 11-37.

Figure 11-37. *The iOS printer options*

Choose the first option and select a printer. You're then presented with a list of simulated printers; choose Simulated Inkjet and click the Print button. After a brief pause, the Printer Simulator springs to life. Details about the print job appear in the console; then the Preview application appears, displaying the results of your print job, as shown in Figure 11-38.

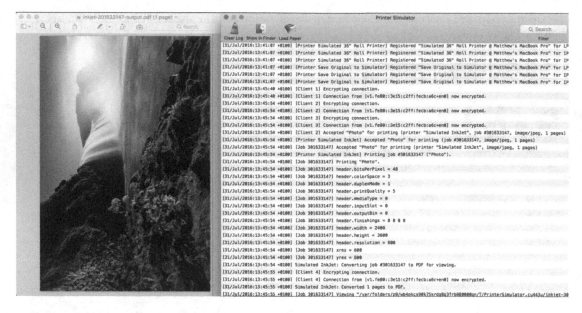

Figure 11-38. *The output of the simulated print job*

Setting up printing for your application is often done blind, with no visual indication of the output until you print, so being able to quickly test this functionality and debug any issues (such as missing pages) is invaluable. The depth offered by the Printer Simulator means that you can test print functionality on a range of device types at different resolutions and have a high degree of confidence in your finished product—and you also aren't contributing to the erosion of the rainforests with reams of test prints.

Playground

Accompanying the original announcement of the Swift programming language was the Playground feature in Xcode 6. A *playground* is effectively a code sandbox or scratchpad where you can drop in, write some Swift code, and experiment with it outside the confines of your application.

This can be great for learning the language, or even for more seasoned developers who want to perfect a regular expression, for example, or see a visual representation of the curve they're calculating. Playgrounds can be saved and shared among friends and colleagues, meaning you no longer have to rely on code snippets or large projects as ways of sharing code—you can also share playgrounds. And because Xcode is free, playgrounds surely lend themselves to computer science in schools as a great way of writing a piece of logic without having to build an interface or make full use of an IDE.

There are literally hundreds of uses for playgrounds. Although they don't strictly have to be used for debugging purposes, they can certainly help when you hit a sticky patch in your application's logic.

Let's take a moment to demonstrate the power of playgrounds. Start a new playground in Xcode by choosing File ➤ New ➤ Playground. Then enter a name for your playground; I chose BeginningXcode, as shown in Figure 11-39. Click Next and specify a location to save the playground.

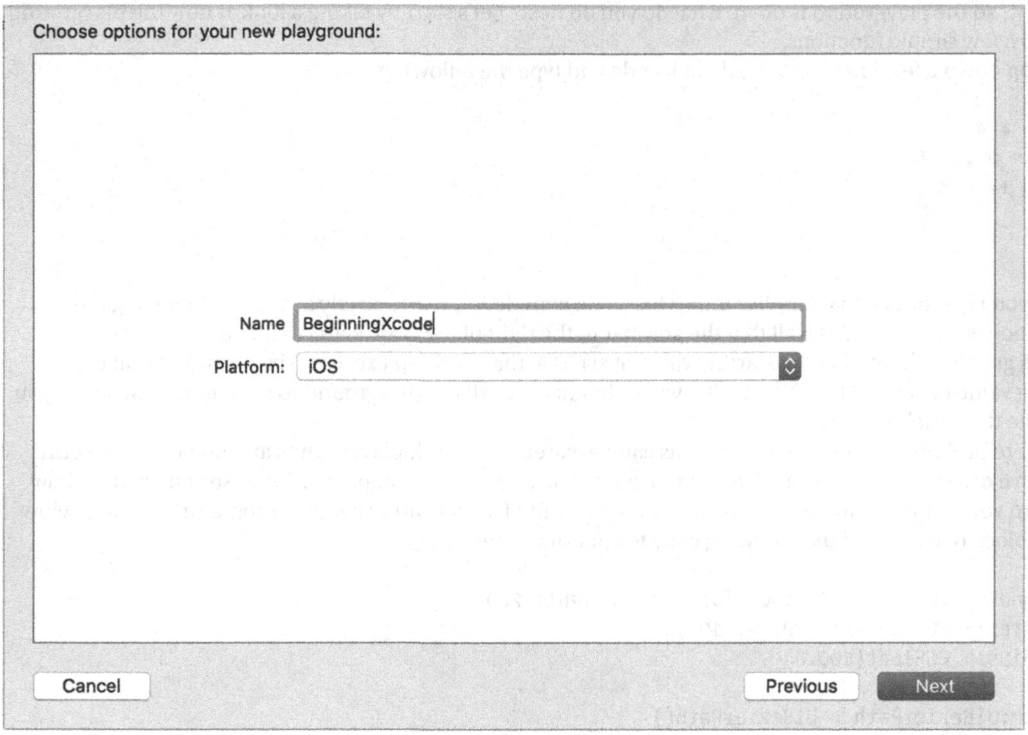

Choose options for your new playground:

Name BeginningXcode

Platform: iOS

Cancel

Previous

Next

Figure 11-39. *Setting the options for the playground*

After saving your playground, you arrive at a screen with a couple of lines of code, as shown in Figure 11-40. This is the playground: on the left is a code editor, and on the right is a light gray pane that shows relevant details of the code, such as the stored value or the number of times a loop has run.

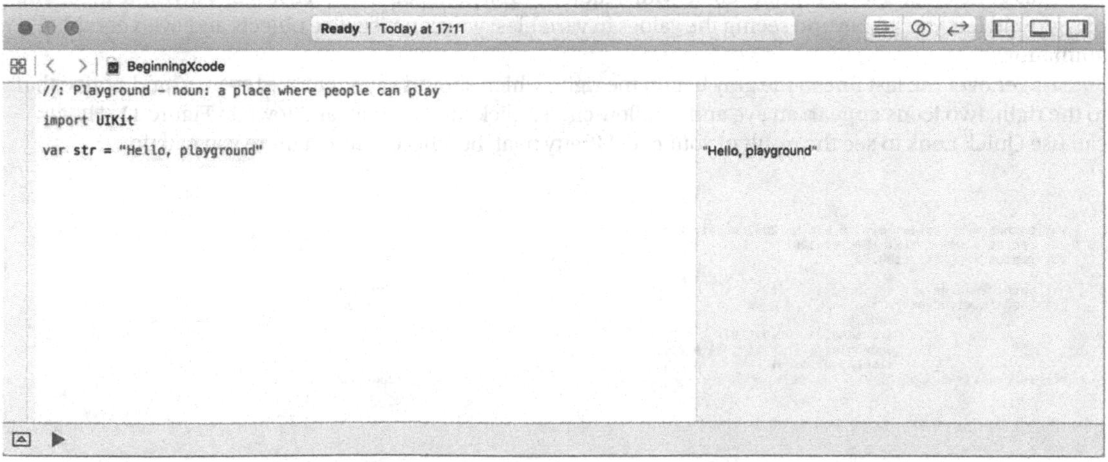

Ready | Today at 17:11

BeginningXcode

```
//: Playground - noun: a place where people can play

import UIKit

var str = "Hello, playground"
```

"Hello, playground"

Figure 11-40. *The default contents of the playground*

Okay, so the playground is open; what do you do next? Let's start by taking a look at how the playground reacts to a few simple functions.

Drop down a few lines from the default code and type the following:

```
var sum = 4
for i in 0 ..< 6 {
    sum += sum * i
}
sum
```

As you type, notice that familiar things like code completion work exactly as they do in the regular Xcode code editor. Notice as well that the gray bar to the right of the code starts to fill up.

The gray bar shows that the starting value of sum is 4, that the loop executes six times, and that the finishing value of sum is 2,880. Notice that you didn't have to tell the playground to print to the console—you just wrote the variable name.

You're probably starting to see how this can be extremely useful; playgrounds are incredibly powerful. Let's move on and add some far more complicated code and see what happens. Suppose you want to draw a circle in your application for some reason, or a segment of a circle and change it programmatically. Below the last block of code, add the following code to your playground:

```
var bounds = CGRect(x: 0,y: 0,width: 200,height: 200)
var center = CGPoint(x: 100, y: 100)
var radius = CGFloat(100.0)

var path:UIBezierPath = UIBezierPath()
path.addArc(withCenter: center,
    radius: radius,
    startAngle: CGFloat(0),
    endAngle: (CGFloat(M_PI) * 2),
    clockwise: true)
path.stroke()
```

This code creates a very simple circle with a radius of 100 in the center of a 200 × 200 invisible area. The playground lets you go beyond seeing the values in variables: you can visualize objects and even complex animations.

Hover over the last line in the gray bar on the right, which should say 5 path elements, and notice that to the right, two icons appear: an eye and a hollow circle. Click the eye icon; as shown in Figure 11-41, you can use Quick Look to see the result of your code! Pretty neat, but there is much more you can do.

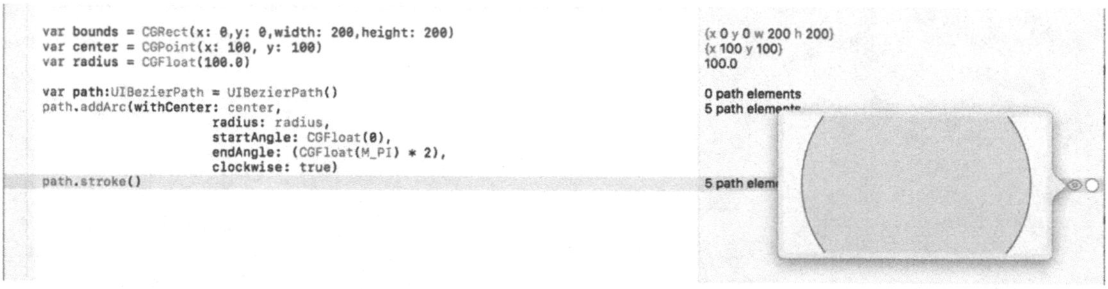

Figure 11-41. *Using Quick Look to preview the circle*

Let's say you want to modify values, add color information, or animate the circle drawing. Clicking the Quick Look icon each time would quickly become a pain. Move the mouse back to 5 path elements, and this time mouse over the empty circle, which changes to a plus symbol. Click it.

The circle that was previewed is now added to the playground editor, as shown in Figure 11-42.

Try removing the * 2 from the line endAngle: (CGFloat(M_PI) * 2), and see that immediately the circle changes to a half circle.

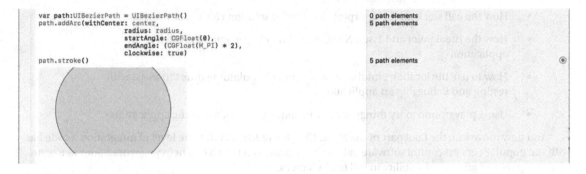

Figure 11-42. *The circle shown in the Assistant Editor*

Finally, go back up through the right column and hover over the line in the for loop that appears as (6 times) and again click the plus symbol. Notice that the playground renders a nice graph showing the rate of change during each loop, as shown in Figure 11-43. This is incredibly useful when you're trying to animate something and you want a sense of acceleration rather than movement at a constant speed.

Figure 11-43. *Viewing the values created in the for loop as well as the circle*

That's it for playgrounds in *Beginning Xcode*. If you're moving on to a Swift programming language book or learning from the free Swift programming book that Apple released, go straight to the playground and start tapping out the examples: tweak them, break them, and see what happens.

Summary

Until IDEs develop artificial intelligence and can accurately predict what programmers intend to do in our code and automatically resolve any errors, there will be a need to debug code. It's rare to write something that works fine the first time, so knowing how to debug an application in Xcode is an essential skill.

This chapter presented a detailed look at how Xcode can be used to resolve various issues with applications. You also learned how to use Simulators to put the functionality of the application to the test when physically moving or when owning additional hardware would otherwise be required.

Specifically, in this chapter, you learned the following:

- About the types of errors that can occur

- How to use breakpoints effectively to investigate logic and runtime issues

- How the call stack can be interpreted to lead to solutions for runtime errors

- How the Breakpoint and Issue Navigators can help you efficiently debug an application

- How to use the location simulation and Printer Simulator features to assist with testing and debugging an application

- Using playground to try things with Swift code outside of a specific application

You now move into the final part of the book. Chapter 12 looks at the fine level of integration Xcode has with the popular version control software called Git. You find out how it can help you work better in a team of developers and give you the ability to roll back changes.

PART III

Final Preparations and Releasing

CHAPTER 12

■ ■ ■

Version Control with Git

Chapter 11 focused on errors and exceptions and how you can use the tools in Xcode to root them out. You looked at the three most common types of errors and exceptions: logic, runtime, and compile-time errors. You also looked at how to make sense of the call stack when your application crashes.

The focus of this chapter is version control, and specifically how Xcode integrates with the Git source code management system. Xcode stands out from other IDEs in this department. Its integration is so fine and complete that it's a joy to use and so intuitive you'll wonder why you haven't used it before.

As you work through the intricacies of version control, you'll create a voice-recorder application called HearMeNow. This application has Record and Play buttons initially, but later you'll enhance the project and modify it to play back the voice at half speed—perfect when trying to listen to people like me who talk too quickly. It's important to note that although the application will run without error in the Simulator, I will show you how to deploy the application to a physical device so that you can take this neat little application out and about with you.

Why Use Version Control?

Actually, the question when it comes to version control is, why not? Have you ever developed a solution, taken a vacation, and, when you returned, discovered that while you were away, a member of your team made a small change and suddenly there were a dozen bugs as a consequence? If so, version control would have saved the day.

Version-control software, also known as *source control* or *revision control*, allows you to track and manage changes made to code over time. If something suddenly stops working, you can compare it to an older version to see what's changed and hopefully get to the bottom of what's gone wrong. Version control makes it easy to see what's changed between releases. Changes to a file are highlighted and logged against a specific user, and can even hold comments.

A wide variety of version-control systems are on the market, and unlike many software markets, some of the best systems are open source. Most software-development houses use one of several tools for version control, depending on the language they write in or their preference. The most popular systems are Git, Subversion (SVN), and Microsoft's Team Foundation Server (TFS) or Visual Studio Online. Xcode uses the extremely popular Git system to provide version control.

What Is Git?

If you're British, a *git* is that colleague who steals your lunch, even though it had your name written on it in capital letters with black marker. The Git source control management system actually has a little to do with this vernacular in its origins. It's the brainchild of the principal developer of the Linux kernel, Linus Torvalds. When none of the version-control packages available at the time supported his vision of robust distributed

© Matthew Knott 2016
M. Knott, *Beginning Xcode*, DOI 10.1007/978-1-4302-5005-0_12

development of the Linux kernel, Torvalds wrote his own system: Git. He names all of his software after himself and has quipped that this one was no different, so read into that what you will. The software is quite amazing: Torvalds designed Git to be fast, efficient, and robust, and it excels at all three.

Git is notable as a system because it can be used either locally for version control or with a server to allow global collaboration on a piece of software. Online systems such as GitHub and Bitbucket provide free Git repositories so you can back up your project online and invite people to take a copy by cloning, branching, or forking the project. Another notable feature that separates Git from other, similar systems is that when you make a change, Git snapshots the project, giving you a true point-in-time view; other systems simply track changes on individual files.

When talking about Git, many terms may sound strange or complicated. Let's look at these terms to prove there's nothing to be afraid of:

- *Repository*: Also known as a *repo*, a repository encapsulates your project, storing the different versions of the files and folders and tracking the changes.

- *Commit*: When you've made changes to a file and want to put them into the repository, you commit those changes.

- *Branch*: Branching a project allows you to work on a duplicate of that project in the repository without altering the original. Typically this is done when you want to add a new feature: you branch off from the original project, make the changes, and then merge the branch back into the master branch or trunk.

- *Fork*: If you want to work on a project but have read-only access, or you want to send a project in a brave new direction, forking is a good idea. This allows you to duplicate the repository, but it's reserved for online services such as GitHub or Bitbucket.

Creating the Project

Because it's suitable for the vast majority of iOS projects, you yet again use the Single View Application template for this chapter's project. The project focuses on using the built-in microphone of an iOS device to record a voice or sound and play it back. Here are the steps:

1. Open Xcode and create a new project by choosing File ➤ New ➤ New Project (⌘+Shift+N) or choosing Create A New Xcode Project on the Welcome screen (⌘+Shift+1).

2. Select the Single View Application Template and click Next.

3. Name the project HearMeNow, substitute your personal information, ensure that Devices is set to Universal, and leave the other options set to their defaults, as shown in Figure 12-1. Click Next.

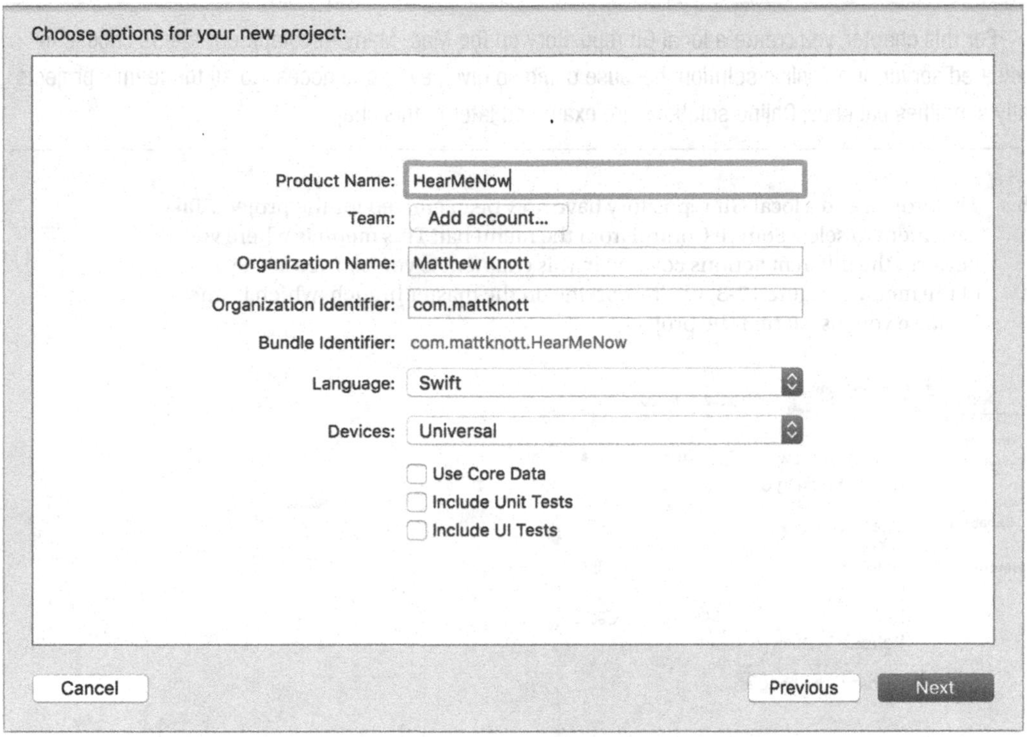

Choose options for your new project:

Product Name:	HearMeNow
Team:	Add account...
Organization Name:	Matthew Knott
Organization Identifier:	com.mattknott
Bundle Identifier:	com.mattknott.HearMeNow
Language:	Swift
Devices:	Universal

☐ Use Core Data
☐ Include Unit Tests
☐ Include UI Tests

Cancel   Previous   Next

Figure 12-1. *Setting up the initial options for the project*

4. Click the Source Control check box at the bottom of the Save dialog. This specifies that the project should use source control. Specify that you want to create a Git repository locally by choosing My Mac from the drop-down list, unless you have a server set up to house Git repositories. Be sure your settings match those shown in Figure 12-2 and click Create. (Don't worry if you don't see the Add To option—it comes and goes depending on whether you have other workspaces open.)

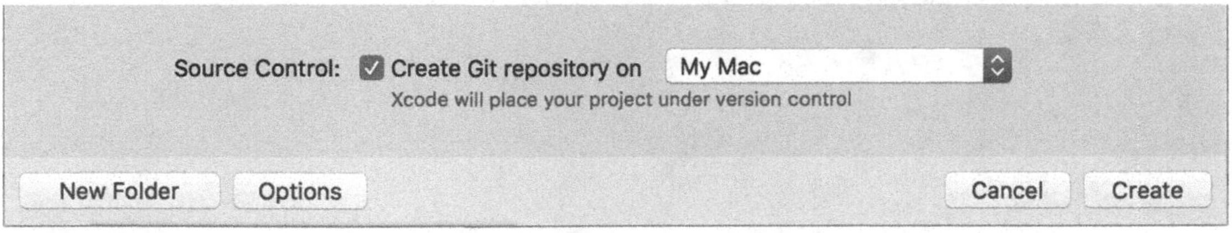

Source Control: ☑ Create Git repository on   My Mac
Xcode will place your project under version control

New Folder   Options   Cancel   Create

Figure 12-2. *Choosing to create a Git repository locally on the Mac*

■ **Note**　For this chapter, you create a local Git repository on the Mac. Many development teams choose to use a dedicated server or an online solution, because doing so gives everyone access to all the team's projects and greatly simplifies backups. Online solutions are examined later in this chapter.

---

5. The project and a local Git repository have now been created for the project. Take a moment to select Source Control from the menu bar. This menu is where you perform the different actions covered in this chapter. As you can see at the top of the menu in Figure 12-3, you're working on the master branch, which is fine because you just started the project.

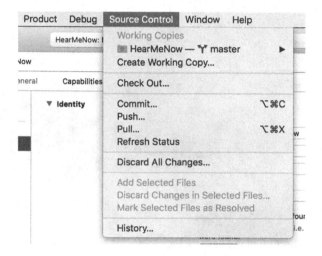

Figure 12-3. *The Source Control menu*

6. Select History from the Source Control menu. Figure 12-4 shows the history of the project in a source control context. When you created the project, a snapshot of that start point was automatically created: it's called the `initial commit`. Click Done to close the dialog.

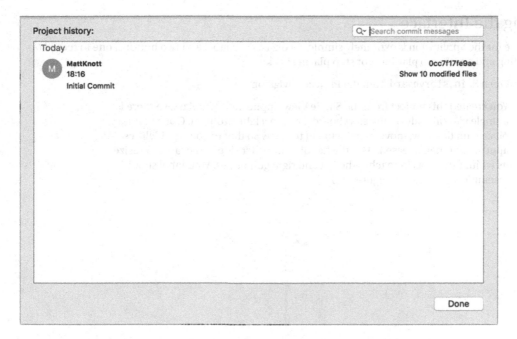

Figure 12-4. The dialog showing the history of the project under Source Control

---

■ **Note**   When you open the History dialog, you may be prompted to allow access to contacts. This is so that Xcode can try to identify who made changes to the project and the repository.

The project has been created and is under source control. You're ready to begin building the interface for the project and writing the code, which uses of a framework called AVFoundation.

The AVFoundation Framework

Before you begin an interface for the project, let's quickly take a look at what the AVFoundation framework is and what it lets you do. Although there are dedicated audio and video frameworks, AVFoundation, as its name might suggest, provides a powerful set of classes that underpin these other frameworks.

AVFoundation can be used in slightly varying forms in both iOS and macOS development. Its main purpose is to support the use of time-based audio and video functions, such as recording and playback of various media types.

In this application, you set up the view controller as an AVAudioPlayerDelegate and also AVAudioRecorderDelegate so that you can take advantage of the AVAudioPlayer and AVAudioRecorder classes, which are named to clearly indicate their purpose.

AVFoundation can be added to the project simply by using the import statement in the view controller. You don't need to physically add it to the project. Let's start building the interface.

Creating the Interface

The interface for the application is extremely simple. It consists of a label and two buttons, one to record or stop recording and another to play back or stop playing back:

1. Open Main.storyboard from the Project Navigator.

2. You created this project from the Single View Application template, so there is a single view already on the storyboard. Drag in a label from the Object Library, place it on the view, move it to the top of the view so that the blue guidelines appear, and then release it. Use the handles on either side of the label to resize its width until it again reaches the left and right guidelines. Your label should resemble that shown in Figure 12-5.

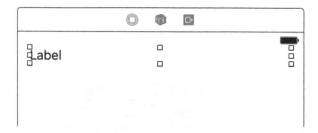

Figure 12-5. *Positioning the label in the view*

3. You need to set the label's attributes. Open the Attributes Inspector and change the Text attribute from Label to Hear me now... and Alignment to the center position, as shown in Figure 12-6.

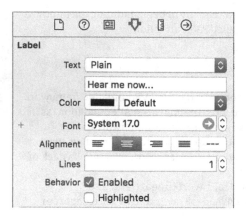

Figure 12-6. *Setting the attributes of the label*

Now that the label is configured, you can turn your attention to the two buttons. Drag in two buttons from the Object Library, positioning them one beneath the other, as shown in Figure 12-7.

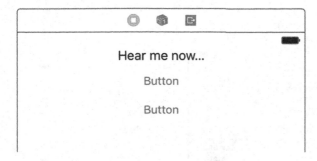

Figure 12-7. *Adding two buttons to the view*

4. Resize both buttons the same way you did the label, dragging the left and right sides until the guidelines display. Change the attributes for the buttons in the Attributes Inspector, naming the top button Record and the bottom button Play.

5. Realign both buttons so they're once again dead center. Your finished interface should resemble that shown in Figure 12-8.

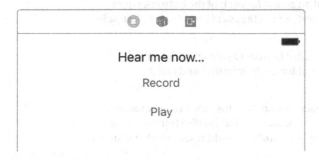

Figure 12-8. *The completed interface for the application*

6. Let's fix the elements in place using the Resolve Auto Layout Issues button. Click the button, and then click Add Missing Constraints under All Views in the view controller heading, as shown in Figure 12-9.

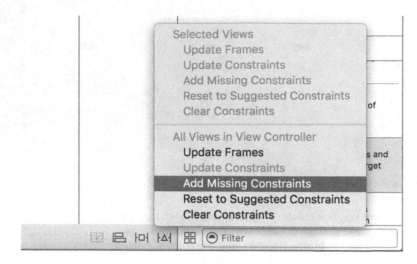

Figure 12-9. Adding constraints for the controls in the view

7. The next task is to create an outlet and an action for each of the buttons. Open the Assistant Editor and ensure that ViewController.swift is selected alongside your storyboard.

8. Control+drag a connection from the Record button. Create an outlet called recordButton; then create another outlet for the Play button and call it playButton.

9. Repeat the Control+drag process for each button, but this time create an action for the Record button called recordPressed and one for the Play button called playPressed. The beginning of your view controller should resemble that shown in Figure 12-10.

```
class ViewController: UIViewController {
    @IBOutlet weak var recordButton: UIButton!
    @IBOutlet weak var playButton: UIButton!
    @IBAction func recordPressed(_ sender: AnyObject) {
    }
    @IBAction func playPressed(_ sender: AnyObject) {
    }
```

Figure 12-10. The outlets and actions created in the header file

10. With the outlets and actions created, it's time to add the final touches. Switch back to the Standard Editor and open ViewController.swift from the Project Navigator. Earlier, when I mentioned the AVFoundation framework, I mentioned two protocols you need to add to the view controller: AVAudioPlayerDelegate and AVAudioRecorderDelegate. Add the highlighted code to the header to import the AVFoundation framework and apply the two protocols:

```
import UIKit
import AVFoundation

class ViewController: UIViewController, AVAudioPlayerDelegate, AVAudioRecorderDelegate {

    @IBOutlet weak var recordButton: UIButton!
    @IBOutlet weak var playButton: UIButton!
    @IBAction func recordPressed(sender: AnyObject) {
    }
    @IBAction func playPressed(sender: AnyObject) {
    }
```

11. In addition to adding code to the viewDidLoad method and the two actions,
     you also need two delegate methods and a number of instance variables. Let's
     add the instance variables, because they're essential for all the methods in the
     application. At the top of the file, add the variables highlighted next, and then
     add the five instance variables:

```
class ViewController: UIViewController, AVAudioPlayerDelegate, AVAudioRecorderDelegate {

    var hasRecording = false
    var soundPlayer : AVAudioPlayer?
    var soundRecorder : AVAudioRecorder?
    var session : AVAudioSession!
    var soundPath : String?

    @IBOutlet weak var recordButton: UIButton!
    @IBOutlet weak var playButton: UIButton!
```

Let's look at what these instance variables do:

- Bool - hasRecording: Determines whether a recording has been made

- AVAudioPlayer - soundPlayer: Handles all audio playback

- AVAudioRecorder - soundRecorder: Handles recording from the microphone

- AVAudioSession - session: Activates and deactivates the audio session

- String - soundPath: Holds the path for the recorded file

12. Scroll down to the viewDidLoad method. In this method, you initialize the
     session, soundPath, and soundRecorder objects. As in previous chapters, I
     won't always go into detail about the code, because that isn't the focus of this
     book. Add the following highlighted code to your viewDidLoad method:

```
override func viewDidLoad() {
    super.viewDidLoad()
    // Do any additional setup after loading the view, typically from a nib.

    session = AVAudioSession.sharedInstance()

    do {
```

347

```
        soundPath = "\(NSTemporaryDirectory())hearmenow.m4a"

        let url = URL(fileURLWithPath: soundPath!)

        try session.setCategory(AVAudioSessionCategoryPlayAndRecord)
        try session.setActive(true);

        let settings = [
            AVFormatIDKey: Int(kAudioFormatMPEG4AAC),
            AVSampleRateKey: 12000.0,
            AVNumberOfChannelsKey: 1 as NSNumber,
            AVEncoderAudioQualityKey: AVAudioQuality.high.rawValue
        ]
        try soundRecorder = AVAudioRecorder(url: url, settings: settings)

        soundRecorder?.delegate = self
        soundRecorder?.prepareToRecord()
    } catch {
        print(error)
    }
}
```

13. With the soundRecorder object initialized, it's time to write the code for the
    recordPressed action. This is called when the Record button is tapped. If the
    application is currently recording, it stops the recording process and sets the
    button title back to Record; otherwise, it uses the session object to check recording
    permissions and then either start recording, if granted, or use print to display that
    the request was denied. Add the following highlighted code to the action:

```
@IBAction func recordPressed(sender: AnyObject) {
    if(soundRecorder?.isRecording == true)
    {
        soundRecorder?.stop()
        recordButton.setTitle("Record", for: UIControlState.normal)
        hasRecording = true
    }
    else
    {
        session.requestRecordPermission(){
            granted in
            if(granted == true)
            {
                self.soundRecorder?.record()
                self.recordButton.setTitle("Stop", for: UIControlState.normal)
            }
            else
            {
                print("Unable to record")
            }
        }
    }
}
```

14. You've written the action for the Record button. Now you need to write one for the Play button, which calls the `playPressed` action. In this method, the action is determined from three possible states: if the `soundPlayer` object is currently playing back the audio file, it pauses; if the `hasRecording` object is set to `Yes` or `true`, the application plays the recorded file; and if neither of the other two states is met, the method checks to see if the player is initialized, which means it's being asked to resume from a paused state. Add the following highlighted code to the `playPressed` method:

```
@IBAction func playPressed(sender: AnyObject) {
    if(soundPlayer?.isPlaying == true)
    {
        soundPlayer?.pause()
        playButton.setTitle("Play", for: UIControlState.normal)
    }
    else if (hasRecording == true)
    {
        let url = URL(fileURLWithPath: soundPath!)
        do {
            try soundPlayer = AVAudioPlayer(contentsOf: url)
            soundPlayer?.delegate = self
            soundPlayer?.play()

        } catch {
            print("Error initializing player \(error)")
        }

        playButton.setTitle("Pause", for: UIControlState.normal)
        hasRecording = false
    }
    else if (soundPlayer != nil)
    {
        soundPlayer?.play()
        playButton.setTitle("Pause", for: UIControlState.normal)
    }
}
```

15. The final task in the implementation of this application is to write two delegate methods that are called when the recording or playing is finished, to change the text of the relevant button and, in the case of playing the audio back, to set the `hasRecording` object to no or `false`. Add the following two methods just after the `playPressed` method:

```
func audioRecorderDidFinishRecording(_ recorder: AVAudioRecorder, successfully flag: Bool) {
    recordButton.setTitle("Record", for: UIControlState.normal)
}

func audioPlayerDidFinishPlaying(_ player: AVAudioPlayer, successfully flag: Bool) {
    playButton.setTitle("Play", for: UIControlState.normal)
}
```

With those last two methods in place, the application is ready to be run. As I mentioned at the beginning of this chapter, this is a great application to run on a physical iOS device and show your friends how far your skills have come, although it still works just fine in the Simulator as long as you have a microphone and speakers. To select a physical device versus the currently selected Simulator, click the simulated device name next to the scheme, as shown in Figure 12-11, and select your physical device if you have one. Physical devices are separated from the various Simulators and are represented by the device's icon. In order for your device to appear in the list, it must be connected to your Mac via the USB cable and must be prepared for development, which is covered in Chapter 14.

Figure 12-11. *Selecting a physical device from the list of available devices*

Run the application. You should find that you have a plain but effective sound recorder. Tap the Record button and speak. When you click Stop, the sound is saved onto the device and is available for playback. Record as many times as you like, but the application uses a single filename and therefore overwrites the file every time you click Record. Figure 12-12 shows the application running on a physical device.

Figure 12-12. *The application running on a physical device*

Once you've played with this great little application you've just created, stop it and return to Xcode. Take a look at the Project Navigator: two files have been modified since the project was created (the storyboard and the view controller) and now have an M symbol next to them, as shown in Figure 12-13. This icon indicates that the project item has been modified since the last time the project changes were committed to the Git repository.

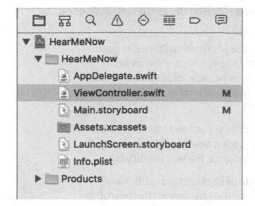

Figure 12-13. *The Project Navigator places an M next to each project item modified since the last commit*

Committing Changes

When making changes to a project under source control, just as with any other project you've created in this book, the changes take effect locally as you save the files or run the application. So why is Xcode pointing out that some of the files and settings in the project have been modified? The reason is that although the changes are being applied, they aren't saved into the Git repository until you perform an action called a *commit*. A commit action creates an updated snapshot of the project in the Git repository: you're creating a point-in-time reference for your project that you can go back to at any time.

Because you've created the first goal for the project, this is a good time to commit the project and update the Git repository. Select Source Control ➤ Commit (⌘+⌥+C). You're presented with a wealth of information about the files that have changed, as shown in Figure 12-14.

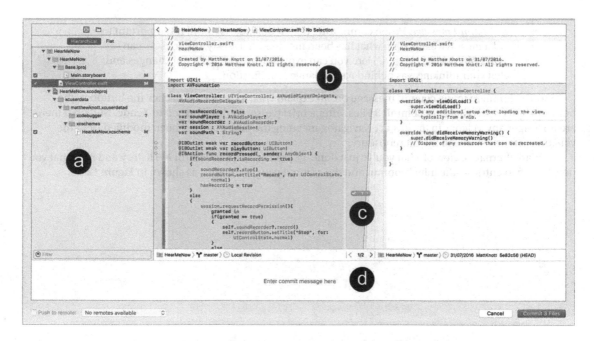

Figure 12-14. *The Commit screen, detailing all changes made in the project since the last commit*

In this instance, I selected ViewController.swift, because it received the greatest modification. As indicated in Figure 12-14, there are four key points of interest.

- *(a) List of modified items*: This area lists all items in the project that have changed. You have two options for viewing this list: Repository View, which is the default; Project View, which shows modified files in the context of their folder structure in Finder. It's important to note that each item has a check box next to it that can be deselected if you wish to exclude it from the commit.

- *(b) Highlighted changes*: When selecting an item, you're shown the changes that have occurred in that item since the initial commit, unless it's a new item. Each change is highlighted, and you can see the point at which the original file was modified.

- *(c) Change numbering*: In each modified item, Xcode dynamically identifies and groups changes to make it easier for you to ignore specific changes at the time of the commit or to discarding them entirely. Clicking the numbered item in this area presents these options, as shown in Figure 12-15. At the bottom of the list is a number that represents the number of changes that can be affected in isolation along with stepper controls that allow you to jump between the changes in sequence.

Figure 12-15. *When you click one of the numbered changes, you can choose to ignore or discard that change*

- *(d) Commit message*: When committing the modifications to Git, it's important to add a message explaining what has been modified. That way, other users can see what's physically changed. Here you can explain why you made the changes and what your thinking was behind each change modification.

Add a comment to the commit message box to explain what's changed and click the button in the bottom-right corner that says Commit 3 Files. After a brief pause, you're returned to Xcode. Note that there are no longer any M icons in the Project Navigator, meaning the project hasn't been modified from the version currently stored in the Git repository.

For an alternative view of what you've just done, go back to Source Control ➤ History and note that you now have two entries—the initial commit and the commit you just made—as shown in Figure 12-16.

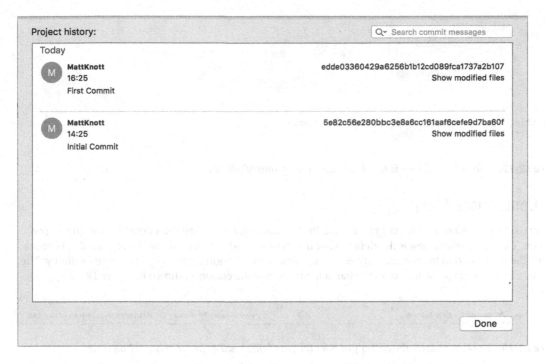

Figure 12-16. *The project history, showing the initial commit and the one just performed*

The details of the last commit appear at the top, with previous changes appearing below in reverse chronological order. Hopefully you can see the value of adding comments: they help provide a rich picture of how and why the application has changed, which is important especially if you're working as part of a team, where understanding who did what is critical. Although this view gives you a good deal of information about the changes made with each commit, Xcode has a number of ways you can compare multiple version of a file and the changes in that file.

Examining Changes with the Version Editor

One of the most valuable aspects of version control is that it gives you a safety net in which you can have multiple people working on a single project. When something stops working between commits, it's important to be able to look back at what's changed and even determine who, and most importantly what, is to blame for breaking the code. In addition to the Standard and Assistant Editors, Xcode provides a Version Editor. As you may remember from Chapter 3, the Version Editor is the third icon in the group of editors. You may also have noted the small downward-pointing arrow, which indicates that the editor has multiple views: Comparison (the default), Blame, and Log, as shown in Figure 12-17.

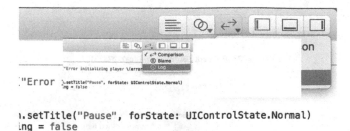

Figure 12-17. The Version Editor is the third icon in the group of editors

The Comparison View

To begin, select ViewController.swift from the Project Navigator, and then select the Version Editor icon in Xcode. The comparison view is the default view that is presented. It will be immediately familiar, because it forms the major part of the commit process, except that in the Version Editor it has far more flexibility. The difference in the view can be found on the bar at the bottom of the editor, as shown in Figure 12-18.

Figure 12-18. The bar beneath the editor provides the core functionality in the comparison view

You can configure either the left or right pane to show any available version of the file you've selected in the Project Navigator. Because the left and right sections have identical functionality, I'll focus on the left side for a moment. There are three segments: in this case, they're HearMeNow, which represents the projects in the workspace; Master, which represents the selected branch; and Local Revision, which represents the selected version of the file to be displayed. On the right, almost the exact same information is displayed, except that it's the version from the last time the file was committed.

From the pane on the right, select the Master branch item in the bar. You see the available versions of the file that can be compared, as shown in Figure 12-19. To review again what has changed since the initial commit, select the bottom item, which is the oldest one available.

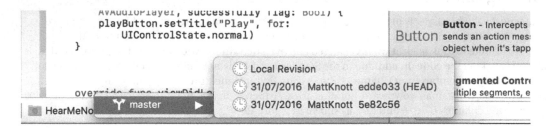

Figure 12-19. The list of available revisions in the selected branch

When you select the older version, the code comparisons appear, highlighting what has changed between the two selected versions, as shown in Figure 12-20. I've already discussed the functionality available when selecting a numbered change in the previous discussion of the commit process, so I won't go into that again. However, it's worth noting that unlike when you commit, you don't have the option to exclude code from the commit, because it's already committed (which makes sense).

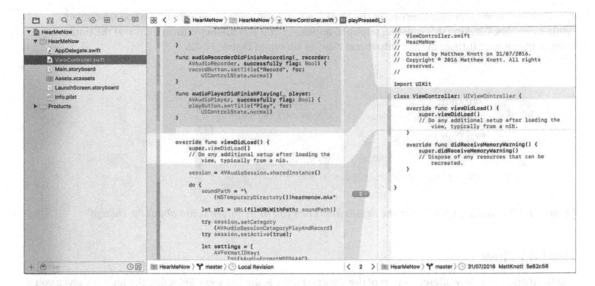

Figure 12-20. *Comparing the current local revision with the oldest version available*

The Blame View

All the Xcode integration with Git is done so that you don't have to worry about what happens behind the scenes. As with many of Apple's products, it just works; but in the background, Xcode is firing off command-line messages to the Git system to perform the action you've just asked Xcode to perform. There is a host of commands, including git blame, which is what the blame view bases its display on.

Blame is an unfair term, because often you aren't looking to actually blame anyone for anything—you just want to know who changed what in a project so you can ask them a bit more about it. It's also unfair because it adds a negative term to one of the coolest views when using Xcode's source control.

To turn on the blame view, click the Version Editor button again, and a menu will appear. Select Blame; refer back to Figure 12-17 to see the icon appropriate for your operating system.

Once you've opened the blame view, you can see why it's so powerful in a team environment. Figure 12-21 shows the detailed analysis of every change in the selected file, when it was made, and by whom. If a colleague wrote a method that you're not quite sure about, you know who to talk to about it.

Figure 12-21. *The blame view in action*

If you move your cursor over one of the blocks in the detail area to the right of the code, a circled *i* symbol appears. Clicking this causes a popup to appear, giving you further information and the option to analyze the change further in the comparison view, as shown in Figure 12-22.

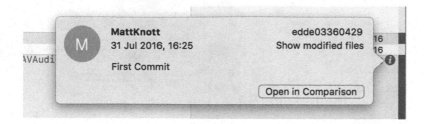

Figure 12-22. Clicking the i icon in the details area gives you more information about the change

The Log View

The third and final view offered as part of the Version Editor is the log view. Selecting the log view gives you a Standard Editor along with an additional bar, as shown in Figure 12-23, which details the change history for the current file along with any comments. The log view is the simplest of the views in the Version Editor, and as such you'll probably use either the comparison or blame view more often.

```
//
//  ViewController.swift
//  HearMeNow
//
//  Created by Matthew Knott on 31/07/2016.
//  Copyright © 2016 Matthew Knott. All rights reserved.
//

import UIKit
import AVFoundation

class ViewController: UIViewController, AVAudioPlayerDelegate, AVAudioRecorderDelegate {
```

Today

MattKnott   edde033
16:25   Show modified files
First Commit

MattKnott   5e82c56
14:25   Show modified files
Initial Commit

Figure 12-23. The log view in the Version Editor

Branching in a Repository

When you're developing a project that is under version control with Git, the master branch or trunk should always be used to hold the version of your project that is ready for release. When you want to add new features, you could just continue working on the master branch—but then if you need to modify the code to fix a bug, you have no good version to update, and the development process starts falling apart. In this situation, you can create a branch from the master. This allows you to work in total isolation from the master branch. Once you're happy that your branch is complete, and you're ready to add the changes into the release version, you can merge your branch back into the master.

To add some new functionality to the HearMeNow application, let's create a new branch called SlowDown, as shown by Figure 12-24. The master branch will remain untouched, and all of your work will be done on the new branch. In this new branch, you're going to modify the playback routine to slow down playback to half the normal speed, which is a useful feature when you're typing up dictation or trying to understand someone who talks quickly or in a language you're trying to learn.

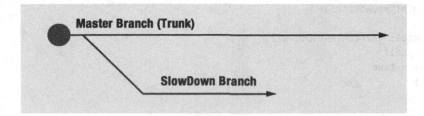

Figure 12-24. *A branch allows you to work in isolation from the master branch*

1. To create a new branch, choose Source Control ➤ HearMeNow ➤ Master ➤ New Branch.

2. You're presented with a dialog asking you to name the branch, as shown in Figure 12-25. Name it SlowDown or choose your own name. Click Create.

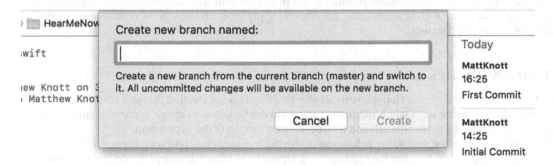

Figure 12-25. *The new branch dialog, asking you to name the branch*

3. Xcode creates the new branch and automatically switches you to it. Open ViewController.swift from the Project Navigator and ensure that you're still in the log view. Notice that as Figure 12-26 shows, you're now working on the SlowDown branch instead of the master.

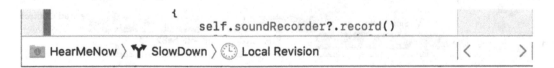

Figure 12-26. *The branch has changed from the master to the new SlowDown branch*

Now that there is a separate branch, you're free to alter the code without fear of breaking the original and working project, which safely remains in the master branch. You can add the code needed to reduce the playback speed, which can be achieved with only two lines.

If it isn't already open, select the Standard Editor and open ViewController.swift from the Project Navigator. Scroll down to the playPressed action; you need to change the rate property used by the soundPlayer object. Add the highlighted code to the second if statement just after you set the player delegate:

```
let url = URL(fileURLWithPath: soundPath!)
do {
    try soundPlayer = AVAudioPlayer(contentsOf: url)
    soundPlayer?.delegate = self
    soundPlayer?.enableRate = true
    soundPlayer?.rate = 0.5
    soundPlayer?.play()

} catch {
    print("Error initializing player \(error)")
}
```

Before you commit the changes to the current branch, run the application to test the new functionality. When the application runs, record yourself saying something and play it back. If all goes well, you should come across as sounding slightly tired or a little drunk, but most important the sound is half the normal speed.

When you're satisfied with the change, commit the changes the same way as you did earlier in the chapter, and remember to add a suitable comment. You're well on your way to mastering Git—but now that you've changed this branch of the application, how do you apply those changes to the master branch? With unbelievable ease, as it happens.

Merging Branches

You've been able to develop your changes without affecting the working solution that you created in the master branch. But having successfully made the changes to the SlowDown branch, it's time to merge this arbitrary branch with the master branch and release another version of the application.

Merging is incredibly simple to do. Before you merge the two branches, take a moment to compare the ViewController.swift file between the two branches. Open the Version Editor and the default compare view, and then select ViewController.swift from the Project Navigator.

By default, Xcode present you with the local revision on the left and the last committed version on the right. This tells you nothing, because they're effectively the same at this point. At the bottom of the pane on the right, click SlowDown, and a menu appears. Hover over Master, and then select the most recent version, as shown in Figure 12-27. Doing so loads the version of ViewController.swift that you committed the last time.

Figure 12-27. Selecting the version of ViewController.swift from the master branch for comparison

When the other version of the file appears, scroll down to where you modified the playPressed method. As Figure 12-28 shows, Xcode has singled out the change you made, so you can clearly see that the code you just wrote doesn't exist in the master branch.

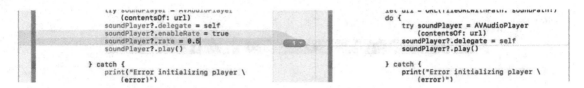

Figure 12-28. *Xcode showing the difference between the* ViewController.swift *file in both branches*

Now that you're certain there is a difference between the files, you should be able to merge the branches and see the code added into the master branch. Open the Source Code menu again, and hover over the HearMeNow – SlowDown item. As you can see in Figure 12-29, Xcode gives you two options for merging branches: Merge From Branch and Merge Into Branch. Which branch you're currently working on will influence your choice here:

- Use Merge From Branch if you're currently working on the target branch—the one you want to add the changes to. You can then select a source branch that has the changes you want to merge from.

- Use Merge Into Branch if you're currently working on the source branch—the one that holds the changes—as you currently should be. You can then select the branch you want to use as the target to merge into.

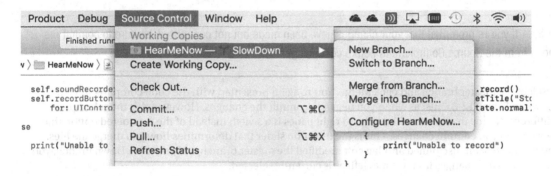

Figure 12-29. *Examining the options for merging branches*

Based on these two cases, the latter is needed in this scenario. Choose Merge Into Branch, and, as shown in Figure 12-30, you're presented with a screen to select a target for merging into.

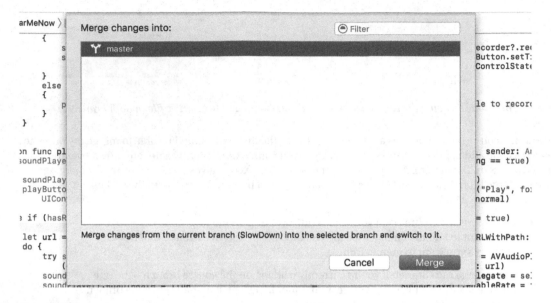

Figure 12-30. Selecting a target branch

■ **Note**   If you're prompted that your changes have been made but not committed, be sure to commit the changes from the Source Control menu before continuing.

Select the master branch and click Merge. You're again presented with the code comparison view, as shown in Figure 12-31, just as when you began to commit the changes. However, this time the options are different. Notice that between the left and right panes is a switch instead of the numbered option that appears when you commit changes. This is the direction slider that determines how you merge the files. Because you've been disciplined and haven't modified the master branch, only the SlowDown branch, you need to merge the changes from right to left, as is currently selected.

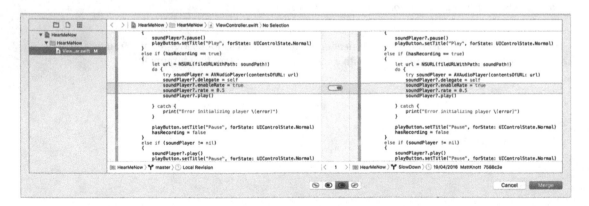

Figure 12-31. The code comparison view, shown before merging

You could very realistically have a scenario where both you and a colleague have separate branches where you're adding new features independently of each other. In this scenario, you may want to merge the two branches before merging them into the master branch. Alternatively, you may want to merge one of the branches with the master, create a new master branch, and have your colleague merge their branch with the new branch for testing purposes before ultimately merging that branch into the master.

When you're happy that the dark part of the switch is pointing to the newer SlowDown branch as the source, click Merge.

Once you've made your choice, the merge operation is complete, and you return to Xcode and the ViewController.swift file in the master branch. Run the application. The application being built from the master branch has the half-speed playback you added in the SlowDown branch. Neat!

Removing a Branch

Now that you've successfully merged your branches, it's considered good housekeeping to remove the SlowDown branch because it's no longer needed. Go to Source Control ➤ HearMeNow ➤ Master ➤ Configure HearMeNow and select the Branches tab, as shown in Figure 12-32.

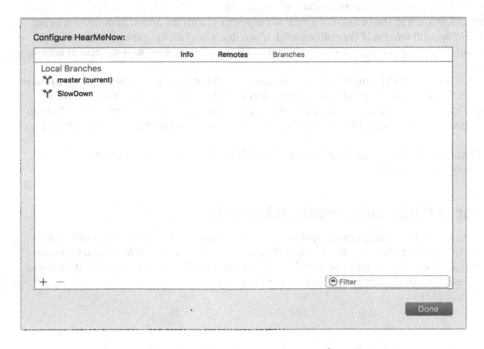

Figure 12-32. *The Branches tab in the project repository configuration view*

Select the SlowDown branch from the list, and then click the – icon in the bottom-left corner. You're prompted to confirm the removal, as shown in Figure 12-33. Click Delete Branch. The branch is permanently removed, leaving you with a neat and tidy repository.

Figure 12-33. Xcode prompting you to delete the branch

Using a Remote Repository

Up until this point, this chapter has concentrated on using a local Git repository; but as I've mentioned, it isn't the only option. A number of online solutions are available to you for hosting or backing up your Git repository online, such as the massively popular GitHub, Bitbucket, and a number of others. Strangely enough, one of the best Git solutions for teams is Microsoft's Visual Studio Online, because of the tools built in for teams working using the Scrum Agile methodology.

With these services, you get all the benefits of a local Git repository, with the added benefits of it being available for collaboration with the rest of the online world. If you don't have all the expertise you need to finish your application or game, you can push your repository online and enlist your friends' help in adding those killer features.

In this era of open source software, more and more people are turning to online Git repositories to share their source code with the world. Making your software publically available can be incredibly rewarding when you see people making interesting new applications based on your code. Being online doesn't have to mean being open to everyone, however. You can create a private repository and restrict access to it based on your preferences.

To finish this chapter, I take you through signing up for a GitHub account and sharing your repository online. Doing so is unbelievably simple.

Registering for GitHub and Creating a Repository

Registering for a GitHub account is made extremely simple because of the clever way the web site has been designed. Head to http://github.com. As you can see in Figure 12-34, the registration form is right on the front page. Fill in the username, e-mail, and password boxes, and click the Sign Up for GitHub button. If you already have an account, click the Sign In button in the top-right corner.

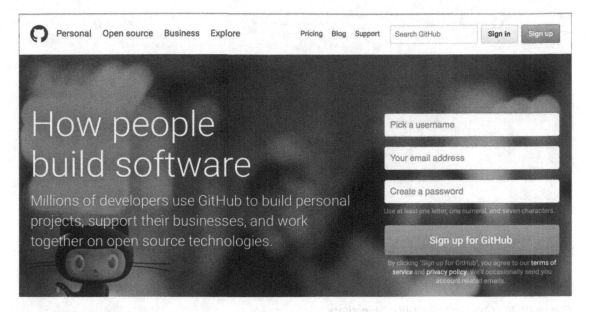

Figure 12-34. *The GitHub home page*

Once you've signed in to GitHub, you're presented with the launch page shown in Figure 12-35. The first thing you need to do is create a repository to add to Xcode by clicking the New Repository button.

Figure 12-35. *Adding a new repository from the GitHub sidebar*

Creating a new repository in GitHub is super easy. Just give the repository a name, as shown in Figure 12-36, and choose whether you want the repository to be public or private. I named my repository HearMeNowSwift after the project name, but you can name it anything within reason. Although it's optional, if you're creating a public repository a description is very helpful. After you've added a name, click the Create Repository button.

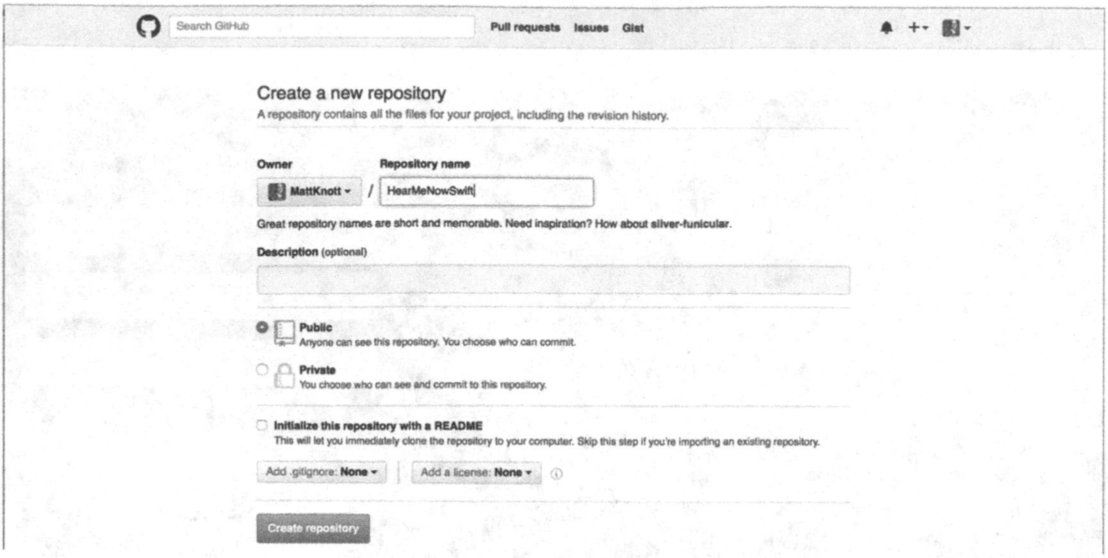

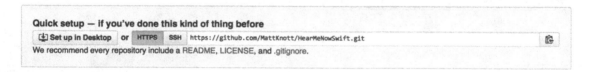

Figure 12-36. *Creating a new GitHub repository*

Once you've created the repository, you're taken to the repository page, which is effectively empty at this point. But there are some key details you need to make note of. Figure 12-37 shows the Quick Setup box, which holds the HTTP address for the repository. At the end of the address is a Copy To Clipboard button. Click it to copy the repository address so it's ready to add to Xcode.

Figure 12-37. *The Quick Setup box on the GitHub repository page*

Adding a GitHub Repository to Xcode

Whether you've worked with Git before or you're trying it for the first time, hopefully one thing that's apparent is how easy Apple has made its interface into this fantastic technology. Linking with the remote repository you just created is no exception, and Apple gives you two ways to do it: in the repository configuration or with Xcode preferences.

Adding a Remote Repository in Repository Configuration

You can quickly add a link to a remote repository by choosing Source Control ➤ HearMeNow - Master ➤ Configure HearMeNow and selecting the Remotes tab. Click the + symbol in the bottom-left corner, and click Add Remote, as shown in Figure 12-38.

Figure 12-38. *Adding a remote repository in the repository configuration's Remotes tab*

Give the remote repository a reference name and then paste in the address you copied from the Quick Setup box in GitHub. Your completed configuration should resemble that shown in Figure 12-39. Click Add Remote to add the reference to Xcode.

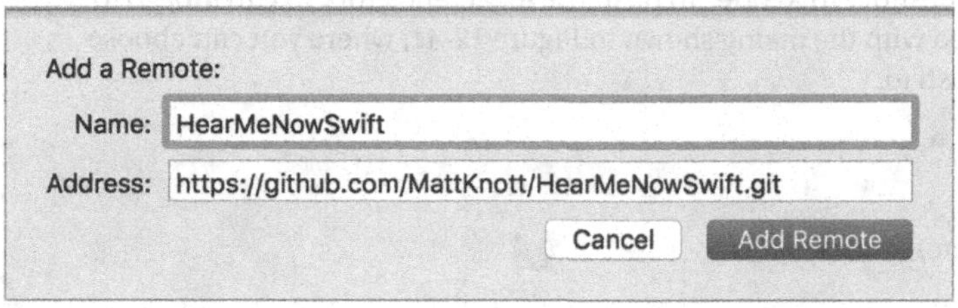

Add a Remote:

Name: HearMeNowSwift

Address: https://github.com/MattKnott/HearMeNowSwift.git

Cancel   Add Remote

Figure 12-39. *Configuring a reference to a remote repository*

One of the limitations with this method is that it doesn't let you add the GitHub username and password that are required to write to the repository, which brings me nicely to the second way of adding a remote repository.

Adding a Remote Repository with Xcode Preferences

The second method for adding a remote repository is my preferred way and often the quickest way to get your repository ready for action. For this method, you need to access Xcode's preferences: the area of Xcode you went to when you customized the Xcode interface in Chapter 10. To access the preferences, go to Xcode ➤ Preferences (⌘+,). When the preferences appear, select the Accounts tab, as shown in Figure 12-40. In the left column, select the reference to the GitHub repository you just added.

Figure 12-40. *The incomplete reference for the GitHub repository*

Change the Authentication type to User Name and Password and those corresponding fields will appear: these refer to your GitHub credentials. Take this opportunity to enter them now. When you enter the username and click into the password box, Xcode tries to validate the details online. Once you've entered the details, click the red dot in the top-left corner to close the preferences.

You have successfully added a remote repository to Xcode. Next I show you how to push your entire repository to the cloud in your GitHub repository.

Pushing to a Remote Repository

You've set up a remote repository and linked it into Xcode; all that remains is to somehow duplicate your repository onto GitHub. Because Git was developed with this type of working in mind, it has two features designed specifically for working with remote repositories: Push and Pull.

Issuing a Push command copies the entire repository over to your GitHub repository, and it's incredibly easy to do now that you've added the repository to Xcode. To push the local repository to GitHub, go to Source Control ➤ Push. You're presented with the dialog shown in Figure 12-41, where you can choose which remote repository you want to push to.

Push local changes:
⅄ HearMeNowSwift/master (Create)
Cancel   Push

Figure 12-41. *Selecting the remote repository*

You only have a single repository available, so the choice here is simple: click the Push button. Xcode takes a few moments (depending on your connection speed) as it sends the entire repository to GitHub. When the process is complete, the dialog automatically closes.

Now for the exciting part! Head back to your web browser and the GitHub web site and refresh the page on your repository. The contents of your project appear, as shown in Figure 12-42.

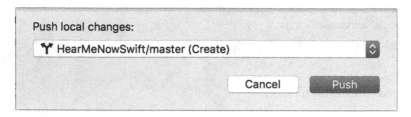

Figure 12-42. *The files from the project are now also hosted on GitHub*

In just a few quick steps, you've taken a piece of work that was stuck in the confines of your Mac and shared it with the world. Anyone can look at your code if you let them. They can copy it to their own Git repository or offer to update yours, and you'll come to learn the collaborative joy that is Git version control.

Updating the Remote Repository

Now that you've pushed your code to a remote repository, you need to think about maintaining it as your project continues to develop locally. Xcode makes linking your local and remote updates a piece of cake.

To demonstrate this, you need to make a small modification to one of the files in the project. Open ViewController.swift from the Project Navigator and ensure that you're using the Standard Editor.

There is no need to make a drastic change; the only goal is to differentiate the file somehow from the last committed version. To do this, I added a line to the comments at the top of the file to say that this is the view controller. Modify your file in a way similar to this highlighted code:

```
// ViewController.swift
// HearMeNow
//
// Created by Matthew Knott on 31/07/2016.
// Copyright © 2016 Matthew Knott. All rights reserved.
// This is the View Controller
```

After you do that, commit the change to the repository by going to Source Control ➤ Commit. Before you click the button to commit the files, look in the bottom-left corner of the commit view and note the Push To Remote check box. Check it, as shown in Figure 12-43, and your GitHub repository automatically appears.

Figure 12-43. *Electing to also push to the remote repository*

You may notice that the Commit button changes to read Commit 1 File And Push. Add a commit message, as the button suggests, and then click it to see what happens. After a brief pause, the view closes and the operation is complete.

To verify what happened in the remote repository, go back to your web browser and the page for the GitHub repository you created. When you refresh the page, note that, as shown in Figure 12-44, the number of commits is now listed as 4.

Figure 12-44. *The number of commits on the repository now shows 4*

To see the level of replication between the local and remote repositories, click the number of commits. You're taken to a page showing the commit history, as shown in Figure 12-45. As you see, it has all the previous commits and their comments exactly as the local repository does.

Figure 12-45. *The GitHub commit history matches the local repository*

Summary

In this chapter, you learned the ins and outs of software version control in Xcode using Git while writing a basic voice recorder application. Specifically, you did the following:

- Created a local repository

- Learned about committing changes to the repository

- Looked at the Version Editor and seen how it allows you to compare files and roll back changes

- Made and merged branches

- Added and used a remote repository

Whatever your hopes for Git, you now have an excellent grounding in all the skills needed to make the most out of it. In the next chapter, you learn about localization with Xcode and how to make your application support multiple languages in a single version.

CHAPTER 13

■■■

Localization

Chapter 12 looked at how Xcode uses Git to create some of the finest version control ever seen in an IDE. You created a simple voice recorder under Git source control, branched the repository to add extra functionality without altering the original, and then merged the two branches together.

This chapter looks at the localization of an application. *Localization* is the term given to the ability of a single application to appear in multiple languages. Making your application available in various languages is a key step to maximizing your success on the App Store, because you can offer your app in the native language of every country in which you choose to advertise.

> *If you talk to a man in a language he understands, that goes to his head. If you talk to him in his language, that goes to his heart.*
>
> —Nelson Mandela

Localization works best when the user doesn't even have to make a language selection—the application simply detects the language that the user has set for their operating system and loads the correct language files. In the past, with other programming languages and IDEs, this could create massive development overheads; but developing applications for iOS and macOS with Xcode makes this process simple and requires minimal development. Once you've created your application in one language, you'll be amazed how easy it is to add more.

In this chapter, you create an interesting application called SayMyName. This application uses the Contacts UI framework to let you select a contact from your Contacts list and then uses the text-to-speech API in the AVFoundation framework to say the person's name though the device's speakers.

You localize the application and make it available in Spanish. Specifically, you learn about three types of localization: storyboards, images, and strings in code. Figure 13-1 shows the finished application running in English and Spanish.

© Matthew Knott 2016
M. Knott, *Beginning Xcode*, DOI 10.1007/978-1-4302-5005-0_13

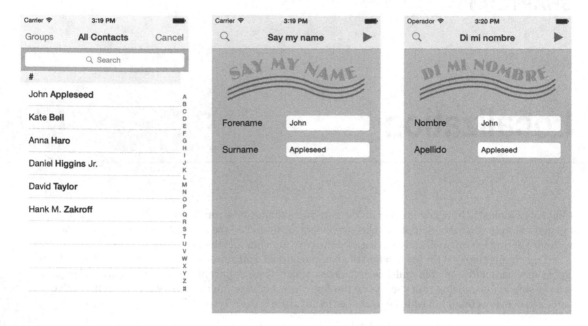

Figure 13-1. *The finished application, picking from the Contacts list and running in English and Spanish*

Another point about the SayMyName application is that it's the last application you create in this book. The final two chapters use this application to explore functionality before you see how to submit it to the App Store, so be sure to keep it handy when you finish this chapter.

Creating the SayMyName Application

One thing that I've always found to be true about localization is that you should do it at the end of the development process. This doesn't necessarily mean you shouldn't write your application with localization in mind, such as by using the NSLocalizedString macro for all user-facing strings, but it's not essential. When you're starting out with Xcode, focus on getting your code right and your application working the way you want it. This is the approach you take with the SayMyName application. You write the code in a familiar way and then, when the application is finished and working, you start to localize the strings in your code, images, and storyboard:

1. Open Xcode and create a new project by choosing File ➤ New ➤ New Project (⌘+Shift+N) or, alternatively, choosing Create a New Xcode Project on the Welcome screen (⌘+Shift+1).

2. The SayMyName application operates on a single view, so select the Single View Application template and then click Next.

3. Name the product SayMyName and ensure that the Devices option is set to iPhone. Substitute your personal information, leaving the other settings as shown in Figure 13-2. Click Next.

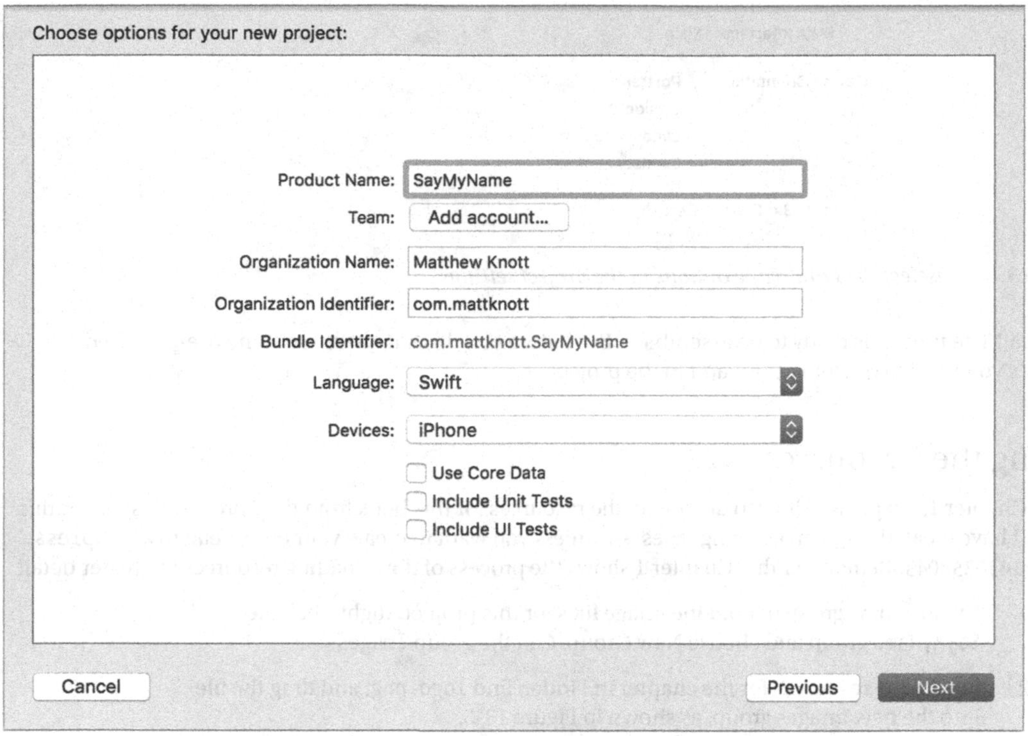

Figure 13-2. *Specifying the settings for the new project*

4. On the next screen, ensure that the Source Control option is selected, as shown in Figure 13-3, and click Create. Using source control, you can commit the changes once you have a working application and before embarking on the localization of the application, during which it can be easy to break the application or lose some values.

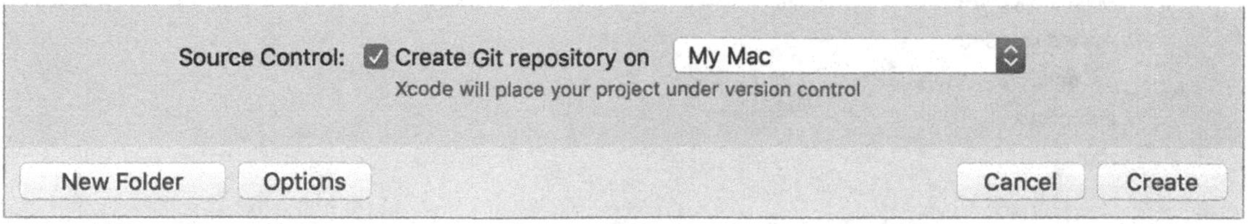

Figure 13-3. *Choosing to create a Git repository*

5. You're taken to your new project and its settings. Look for the Deployment Info section. Because this application only needs to operate in portrait mode, uncheck the Landscape Left and Landscape Right options, as shown in Figure 13-4.

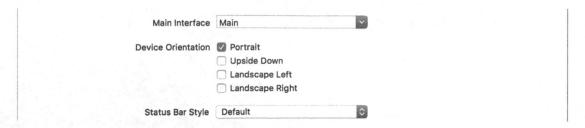

Figure 13-4. *Unselect the Landscape options in the project settings*

Great! The project is ready to be assembled. But before you do that, there are some pre-prepared resources you need to download and add to the project.

Adding the Resources

Back in Chapter 1, I explained how to download the resources for this book from the Apress web site. For this chapter, I have created a logo in two languages; so, unless you want to create your own, head to www.apress.com/9781430250043. Remember that Chapter 1 shows the process of downloading resources in greater detail:

1. Create a new group to hold the image files for this project. Right-click the SayMyName group and choose New Group. Call the group Images.

2. Locate the resources for the chapter in Finder, find logo.png, and drag the file into the new Images group, as shown in Figure 13-5.

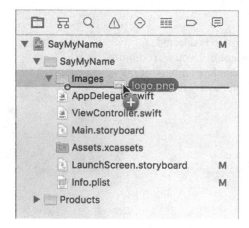

Figure 13-5. *Adding the* logo.png *file to the Images group*

3. When you release the image into the Images group, be sure to choose Copy Items If Needed, as shown in Figure 13-6.

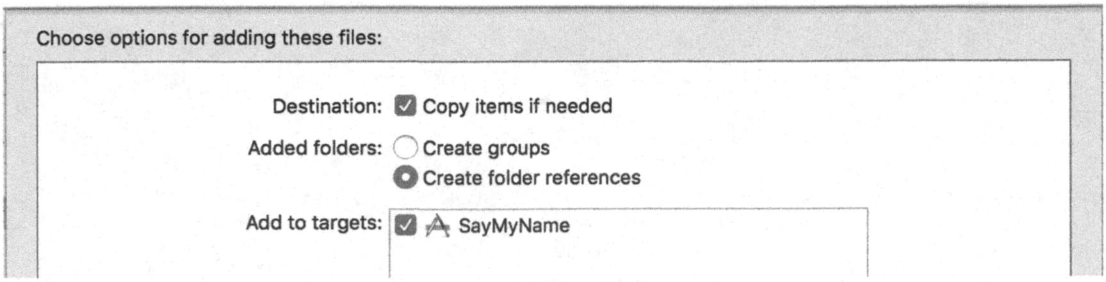

Choose options for adding these files:

Destination: ☑ Copy items if needed

Added folders: ○ Create groups
○ Create folder references

Add to targets: ☑ A SayMyName

Figure 13-6. *Importing the English language logo*

That's it: the logo has been added to the project and you're ready to begin building the user interface.

Creating the Application Interface

Now that your project is configured and has all the required resources, all that remains is for you to create the interface and write the code for this application. One of the most important attributes of this application isn't just the experience of making an app that works seamlessly in different languages, but also the way you use the Contacts API to display your Contacts list and retrieve information from it. Notably, you don't have to create any view controllers or other interface elements—it's all done with a few lines of code. A great thing about developing for the iOS ecosystem is that Apple provides different hubs of data that are easy to interface with, such as the Contacts list, Photo Library, and Calendars.

Laying Out the Views

In Figure 13-1, I gave you a preview of the application's user interface. It consists of a navigation bar, two bar buttons, an image view for the logo, two labels, and two text fields. Select Main.storyboard from the Project Navigator to start building the interface:

1. Zoom out your view and drag a navigation controller onto the design area, as shown in Figure 13-7. Positioning isn't too important at this stage.

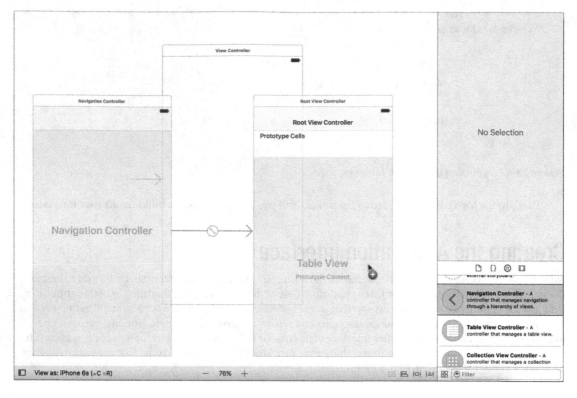

Figure 13-7. *Dragging a navigation controller onto the design area*

2. Select the root view controller that came with the navigation controller and delete it using the Backspace key.

3. Position the navigation controller to the left of the initial view controller in the design area, as shown in Figure 13-8.

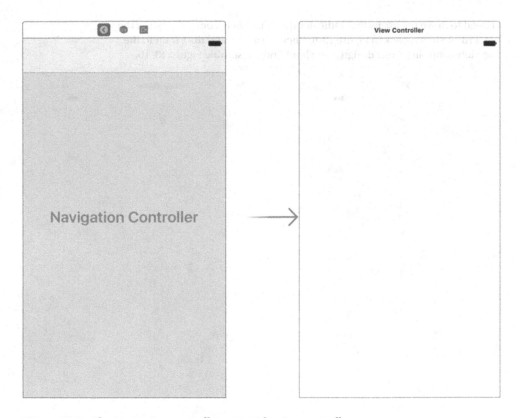

Figure 13-8. *The navigation controller next to the view controller*

4. Control+drag a connection from the navigation controller to the view controller to link them. When you release the mouse, select Root View Controller under Relationship Segue (see Figure 13-9).

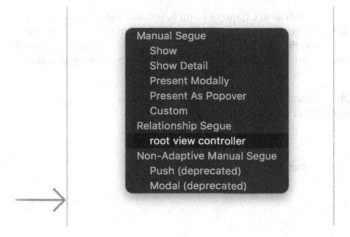

Figure 13-9. *Creating a root view controller relationship with the navigation controller*

5. You need to move the arrow that indicates the initial view controller when the project runs, shown back in Figure 13-8. Click the arrow and drag it on to the navigation controller. Your design area should now resemble Figure 13-10.

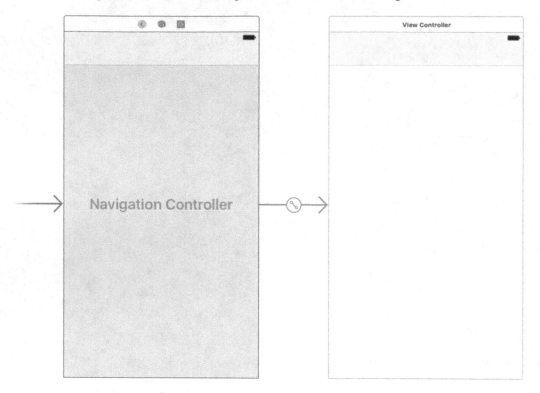

Figure 13-10. *The views laid out, ready for the interface to be built*

Building the Interface

The interface for this application is straightforward. Just as in Chapters 7 and 8, you use bar button items to control the application. Xcode provides a number of great icons for use in bar buttons; in this case, you use the search icon to trigger the Contacts list picker and the play button to make the application say the name of the chosen contact. You also add two text fields to show the selected contact's first and last names, and two labels for each of the text fields:

1. Locate Bar Button Item in the Object Library and drag one to each side of the navigation controller. Your view controller should resemble Figure 13-11.

Figure 13-11. *The navigation bar with two bar buttons added*

376

2. Select the left button; this one will trigger the display of the Contacts list. Open the Attributes Inspector and change the System Item attribute to Search.

3. Select the bar button on the right; this one will cause the selected name to be spoken by the iOS device. In the Attributes Inspector, change the System Item attribute to Play. Your interface is developing nicely and should resemble Figure 13-12.

Figure 13-12. *The bar button items changed to their respective icons*

4. Drag in an Image View item from the Object Library to hold the application logo. Place it just below the navigation bar.

5. Resize the image view so it takes up the full width of the view up to the guidelines but isn't too tall, as shown in Figure 13-13.

Figure 13-13. *Adding the image view to the view*

6. In the Attributes Inspector, change the image to `logo.png`.

7. Change Mode to Aspect Fit. Because the logo has text, you want the image to remain fully visible, whatever shape the view takes on, but it should also maintain its shape. This is what Aspect Fit does. Your evolving view should now resemble Figure 13-14.

Figure 13-14. *The image view positioned and set to Aspect Fit mode*

8.   You need to add the two labels and two text fields. Refer back to Figure 13-1, and you see that they're positioned side by side. Drag a label onto the view, position it on the left so it fills about one third the width of the view, drag a text field beside it, and expand it to occupy the other two thirds, as shown in Figure 13-15.

Figure 13-15. *Positioning the first label and text field*

9.   Once both elements are positioned, change the label's text to read First Name.

10. Repeat the previous two steps, creating the same two elements underneath the first name row, but this time changing the label text to Last Name. Your completed views should resemble Figure 13-16.

Figure 13-16. *The completed view*

11. At this point, take a moment to set the constraints for this layout. Click a blank area of the view, and then click the Resolve Auto Layout Issues button. Click Add Missing Constraints under the All Views In View Controller heading. Your interface elements have been created; take a moment to run the application and preview the layout so far.

You have completed the interface. It's time to create the outlets and actions for this application before moving on to the code:

1. Switch to the Assistant Editor and ensure that ViewController.swift is being displayed in the code editor.

2. Control+drag a connection from the first text field to just below the line that says class ViewController: UIViewController. Create an outlet called firstnameField.

3. Create an outlet for the second text field just below the previous outlet and call it lastnameField.

4. Control+drag a connection from the magnifying-glass icon in the navigation bar to just below the last outlet. This time, create an action called getContact.

5. Create another action, this time for the play button. Position it just below the getContact action and call it sayContact.

Congratulations—you've created all the actions and outlets for this application. Before switching back to the Standard Editor, ensure that the start of your view controller's code resembles the following:

```
import UIKit

class ViewController: UIViewController {

    @IBOutlet weak var firstnameField: UITextField!
    @IBOutlet weak var lastnameField: UITextField!
    @IBAction func getContact(_ sender: AnyObject) {
    }
    @IBAction func sayContact(_ sender: AnyObject) {
    }
```

Writing the Code for the SayMyName Application

For this chapter's application, I've already mentioned that you're using the Contacts UI framework. The Contacts UI framework gives you access to standardized views and classes for browsing, editing, and retrieving Contacts entries.

Just as in Chapter 5's project, using a standardized view to perform a task as basic a selecting a contact from a Contacts list gives you the benefit of having a view that is common to other applications. This makes it more familiar to the users while also removing the development overhead of updating the view for different devices and, in many cases, across multiple versions of iOS.

In iOS 9, Apple deprecated the Address Book framework, which has been in use since developers were first able to write their own iOS applications. The Contacts framework that has replaced it actually simplifies the task of interacting with the Contacts list, and this application since iOS 9 is less than a quarter of the code than the previous version.

In this chapter's application, you once again use the AVFoundation framework, which you first used in the previous chapter. AVFoundation contains the AVSpeechSynthesizer class, which provides the text-to-speech function. Because it's good practice, you write the code in a separate custom class that you can reuse in any applications where you want to handle spoken text.

Now that you have a brief outline of how to approach the code, let's get started by implementing the Contacts list lookup in the getContact action.

Retrieving a Contact

In iOS, whenever you see the Contacts list picker that lets you browse your contacts, you're looking at an instance of the ContactsUIPickerViewController class. Presenting this view is far simpler than using Contacts predecessor, the Address Book. First, as with many of the core functions within iOS, you need user authorization. Second, you write a dedicated function to encapsulate your access to the Contacts list, this is to make future re-use easier. And finally, you implement two delegate functions: one for handling the user's selection, and a second for when the view is cancelled. Here are the steps:

1. Be sure you have the Standard Editor enabled and then open ViewController. swift from the Project Navigator.

2. The first thing you need to do is to make all the Contacts classes available by importing the ContactsUI framework. Add the highlighted code to your view controller:

```
import UIKit
import ContactsUI
```

3. I've already mentioned that you're using two delegate functions relating to the CNContactPickerViewController class, so the next logical step is to add the CNContactPickerDelegate protocol to the ViewController class. Do this by adding the highlighted code shown next:

```
class ViewController: UIViewController, CNContactPickerDelegate {
```

4. As mentioned at the start of this section, you're writing a function to display the Contacts picker. The function is called showPeoplePicker. Very simply, it creates a new instance of the CNContactPickerViewController, specifies its delegate, and then presents it to the user. Effectively, you're presenting a complete view controller with just three lines of code! After the last action, write the highlighted function as shown next:

```
@IBAction func getContact(_ sender: AnyObject) {
}
@IBAction func sayContact(_ sender: AnyObject) {
}

func showPeoplePicker() {

    let picker : CNContactPickerViewController = CNContactPickerViewController()
    picker.delegate = self

    self.present(picker, animated: true, completion: nil)
}
```

5. Now you're ready to write the getContact action that calls your new function. Add the highlighted code in the getContact action:

```
@IBAction func getContact(sender: AnyObject) {
    let cn = CNContactStore()
    cn.requestAccess(for: CNEntityType.contacts) {
        (success: Bool, error: Error?) -> Void in
        DispatchQueue.main.async() {
            if (success == true) {
                self.showPeoplePicker()
            }
        }
    }
}
```

──

■ **Note**   Rather than returning a result, the requestAccess(for:) method call uses a *Swift closure* to handle the outcome of the request. This is signified with the open brace and the in keyword. In Objective-C, this is known as a *block*. If you're referring to the Apple Swift Programming Guide mentioned in Chapter 1, there is a section titled "Closures" that can provide more information.

──

6. Because this application is going to request access to the iOS Contact data, you need to modify your info.plist with an appropriate usage description or the application will crash. Open info.plist from the Project Navigator.

7. Click the plus symbol next to Information Property List and then, from the newly added row, choose Privacy - Contacts Usage Description.

8. Next, set a value of Demonstrating Contact Selection. Your view should now resemble Figure 13-17.

⊞ ‹ › 🖼 SayMyName › 🗀 SayMyName › 📄 Info.plist › No Selection		
Key	Type	Value
▼ Information Property List	Dictionary	(14 items)
Privacy - Contacts Usage Descript... ⬍	String	Demonstrating Contact Selection
Localization native development re... ⬍	String	en
Executable file ⬍	String	$(EXECUTABLE_NAME)

Figure 13-17. *Setting a privacy message to be displayed when requesting Contact access*

Take this opportunity to run the application. When it launches in the Simulator, click the search icon; immediately you should be prompted to allow access to the device's contacts, as shown in Figure 13-18. When you grant permission, the Contacts picker appears, showing a list of fictional contacts. You can select any of the contacts and cancel the view controller, which at the moment is the only way you can return to your application. Next you need to make it possible to select one of the contacts and return to the application with that information; this is done using a delegate function.

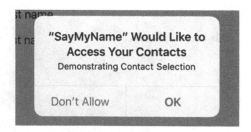

Figure 13-18. *Allowing access to the device's contacts*

Whenever you tap a contact in the picker, a call is made to see whether you have implemented the con tactPicker:didSelectContact: function. When you implement this function, the Contacts list no longer shows you the user's details, but rather returns to your application with the contacts information.

Let's implement that function now:

1. Drop down a couple of lines and type contact, as shown in Figure 13-19. Code completion appears with a number of options. Highlight the first method and press the Tab key twice to create the function stub.

One of the parameters passed to the function you just created is a CNContact object; this contains all the information about the contact the user selected.

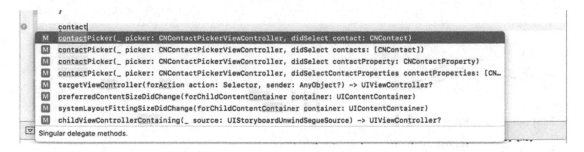

Figure 13-19. *Using code completion to start the function*

2. Add the following highlighted code to retrieve the first and last names from the supplied contact object and then assign those values to their respective text fields:

```
func contactPicker(_ picker: CNContactPickerViewController, didSelect contact: CNContact) {
    firstnameField.text? = contact.givenName
    lastnameField.text? = contact.familyName
}
```

3. Now you will write the second ContactsUI delegate function. This one has only a very limited implementation in this application, but it's important that you remember it for your own applications. This function is called when the user cancels the contacts picker; in this application, that doesn't really matter—the text fields simply remains empty, but in other applications, this could break an entire process, and that possibility needs to be handled. Beneath the previous delegate function, add the following:

```
func contactPickerDidCancel(_ picker: CNContactPickerViewController) {
    print("Cancelled")
}
```

4. Run your application. Click the search button and select a name from the Simulator's Contacts list. When you do, the view dismisses itself, and the selected contact's details appear in the text fields, as shown in Figure 13-20.

Figure 13-20. *The selected name is added to the First Name and Last Name fields in the application*

Converting Text to Speech

You've already done something amazing by interacting with data held in another iOS application. Now you take it further and add the wow factor by making the device say the name of the person the user chose. This is possible thanks to the AVSpeechSynthesizer class in the AVFoundation framework. To make the code you write more reusable, you create a separate class called TextToSpeech to encapsulate the type method you write in it. As mentioned in Chapter 5, a type method in Swift is a function that exists in a specific class and that can be called without instantiating the parent class. Here are the steps:

1. Create a new file for the project (⌘+N).

2. Select Source under iOS at left, and then choose Cocoa Touch Class. Click Next.

3. The class name is TextToSpeech, and you're subclassing the generic NSObject. Ensure that your values match those shown in Figure 13-21 and click Next.

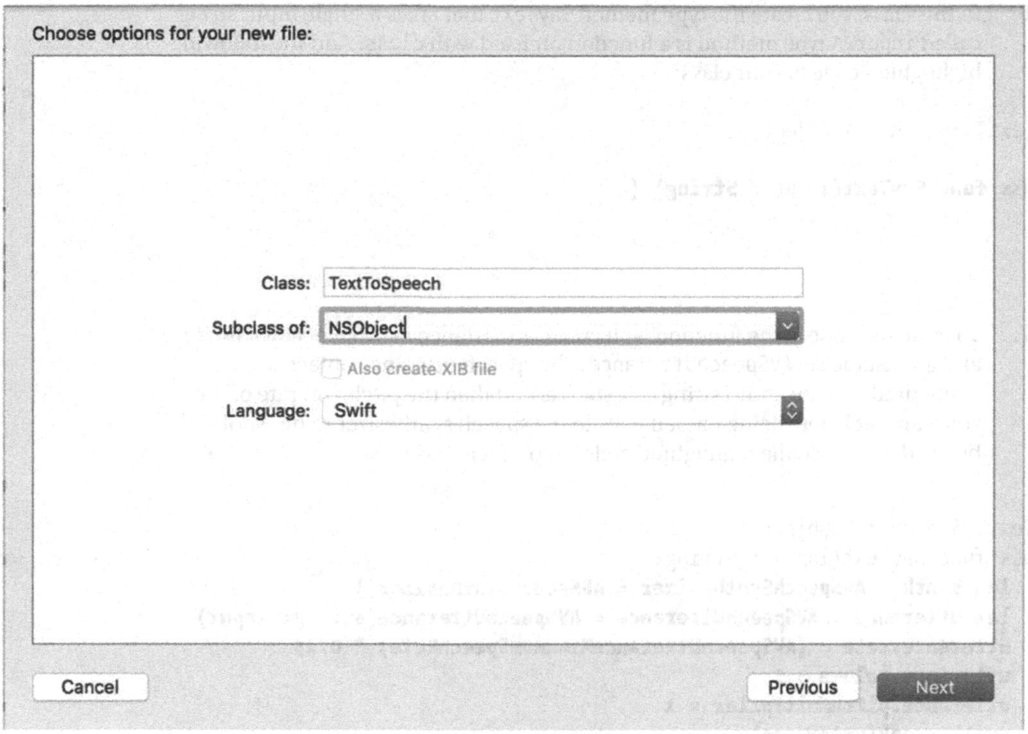

Figure 13-21. *Creating the new class, TextToSpeech*

4. Let Xcode create the new class in the project structure and click Finish. You're presented with a nice, fresh class.

5. The first step as always is to import any frameworks; and as you know, you need the AVFoundation framework to access the required classes. Import the framework as shown in the highlighted code:

```
import UIKit
import AVFoundation

class TextToSpeech: NSObject {

}
```

6. In this class, you create the type method SayText that takes a single input string called input. A type method is a function prefixed with class. Add the following highlighted code to your class:

```
class TextToSpeech : NSObject {

    class func SayText(input : String) {

    }
}
```

7. To write the code in the function, you create an instance of AVSpeechSynthesizer and an instance of AVSpeechUtterance. The speech utterance object is configured with the input string as a source, and then the pitch and rate of the voice are set before being passed back to the speech synthesizer to be "spoken" by the device. Add the highlighted code to complete this class:

```
class TextToSpeech : NSObject {
    class func SayText(input : String) {
        let synth : AVSpeechSynthesizer = AVSpeechSynthesizer()
        let utterance : AVSpeechUtterance = AVSpeechUtterance(string: input)
        utterance.rate = (AVSpeechUtteranceMinimumSpeechRate) * 0.25
        utterance.volume = 1
        utterance.pitchMultiplier = 1
        synth.speak(utterance)

    }
}
```

That's it—you've completed the TextToSpeech class, and it's ready for implementation. It's not much at the moment, but you can add your own functions and type methods to this class over time to create a useful, reusable library of text-to-speech functions; or you can overload the SayText method with other parameters. For now, you call this new method from the sayPerson action back in the view controller:

1. Reopen ViewController.swift from the Project Organizer.

2. Locate the sayContact action. You need to build a string with the person's first and last names in it based on the values of the two text fields; you can then pass the string to the SayText method you just wrote. Add the highlighted code to do this:

```
@IBAction func sayContact(sender: AnyObject) {
    var personName : String = "You have chosen "
    if let forename = firstnameField.text {
        personName += forename
    }

    personName += " "

    if let lastname = lastnameField.text {
        personName += lastname
    }
}
```

3. You want to pass the `personName` variable to the `SayText` type method in the `TextToSpeech` class. Do this with the following line of highlighted code:

```
@IBAction func sayContact(sender: AnyObject) {
    let personName = "You have chosen \(firstnameField.text!) \(lastnameField.text!)"
    TextToSpeech.SayText(input: personName)
}
```

■ **Note**   Unlike in other programming languages (including Objective-C), you don't have to import or include the `TextToSpeech` class in order to use it. Swift works hard in the background to simplify and streamline the development process.

At this point, you've completed the base application for this project. Run the application in the Simulator and enjoy the neat little application you've written using only a small amount of code. Next, it's time to get down to the primary purpose of this chapter: localization.

Localizing the Application

So, you may be wondering what's involved in taking your single-language application and turning it into one that supports multiple languages. It's easy to have a sense of foreboding at this point, but the process is surprisingly simple. With Xcode 7 and iOS 9, Apple has further refined the steps you need to go through to localize an application, making life much easier for you, the developer. But before you dive in, take a moment to think about all the elements in this application that are user facing and need to be translated for each language you localize to:

- Logo image
- Label text
- String passed to the `SayText` method

Fortunately this application is small, so it won't take a huge amount of effort to localize, but don't think you're missing out on anything. I purposely selected this variety of elements because each one needs to be handled in a completely different way.

Before going any further, I hope you kept Source Control enabled as requested when you created the application. Commit the changes into the repository by choosing Source Code ➤ Commit (⌘+⌥+C). Add an appropriate comment and click the Commit Files button.

Enabling Localization

Just as in a number of other development platforms, when you're developing apps for iOS 10 in Xcode 8, localization is already enabled for the default language, which in this case is English. Localization isn't something you strictly enable in Xcode, your application is ready and waiting to be localized; all you need to do is specify which languages you want to make it available in and then add the relevant content.

To understand this a bit better, as shown in Figure 13-22, select the SayMyName project from the Project Navigator in Xcode, and ensuring that the projects and targets list is enabled, select the SayMyName project from that menu instead of the SayMyName target heading.

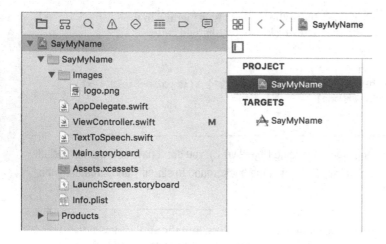

Figure 13-22. *Accessing the project settings*

In the project settings, and specifically the default Info tab, you find all the details about the different languages that have been added to the project in the Localizations section, as shown in Figure 13-23.

▼ Localizations

Language	Resources
English — Development Language	2 Files Localized

\+ —

☑ Use Base Internationalization

Figure 13-23. *The default localization settings*

There are two things to note here. First, there is already a single language: English. Second, Base Internationalization is enabled. The Base Internationalization feature isn't unique to Xcode, but it's a great concept. Basically, a base language is your primary language and a fallback for the application; in a situation where a value hasn't been translated to one of the other localizations, the application falls back on the base language to determine the value to display. This obviously isn't ideal but is better than an exception.

When developing an application that will be localized, you must ensure that every string and value has been set at a base level, which is why I encourage you to write the application first before starting translations. Once you're happy with your base localizations, that's when you move on to adding other languages to the project.

For the sake of building progressively toward the end goal of a localized application with more than one language, in this example you create the strings for the base language at the same time as the Spanish translation in some sections. Ordinarily you would get your base translation right before adding any additional languages.

Adding Another Language

Now that you understand what the base language is, it's time to add another language to the project. As I've already stated, the second language is Spanish:

1. To add a new language, click the + symbol at the bottom of the Localizations section shown in Figure 13-23. When you do this, a list of available languages appears, as shown in Figure 13-24.

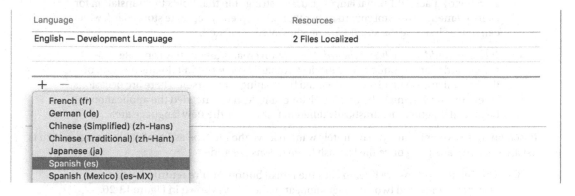

Language	Resources
English — Development Language	2 Files Localized

+ −

French (fr)
German (de)
Chinese (Simplified) (zh-Hans)
Chinese (Traditional) (zh-Hant)
Japanese (ja)
Spanish (es)
Spanish (Mexico) (es-MX)

Figure 13-24. Selecting the Spanish language to add to the project

2. Select Spanish from this list. A popup appears, as shown in Figure 13-25, listing all the files that will be localized, their reference language, and, if applicable, the destination file type.

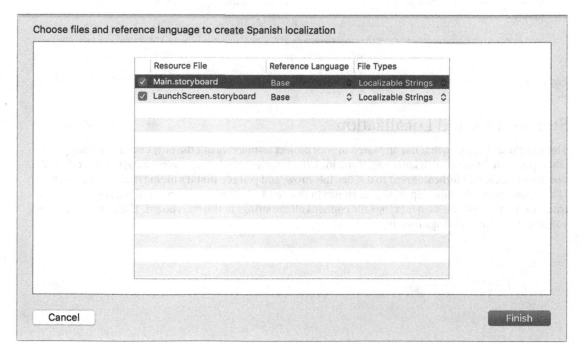

Choose files and reference language to create Spanish localization

Resource File	Reference Language	File Types
✓ Main.storyboard	Base	Localizable Strings
✓ LaunchScreen.storyboard	Base	Localizable Strings

Cancel   Finish

Figure 13-25. Choosing the files to localize to Spanish

This is the most important part when adding a new language. You must ensure that it's using the correct reference language for each resource file. In this case, the files are sourced from the only languages they're available in; but if you're adding multiple languages, you have a degree of variability, so be sure the settings are correct.

Each row has a destination File Types option that can be changed from the default Localizable Strings option to Interface Builder Storyboard. The following descriptions will help you understand the differences:

- *Localizable Strings:* Selecting this option means you only have a single base storyboard. Each additional language uses a strings file that holds the translation for every element in the storyboard rather than a completely separate storyboard, which can make changing the storyboard needlessly complicated.

- *Interface Builder Touch Storyboard:* This option creates an entirely separate storyboard that is unique to this locale. Ordinarily you wouldn't do this because of the administrative headache you would be creating for yourself. There are occasions where this option might be beneficial: for example, if you needed the application to be pieced together in a drastically different fashion for the new language area.

Based on these explanations, you definitely want to leave the file type as Localizable Strings, which is the first area you're translating once the Spanish localizations are added.

3. The default options are fine, so click the Finish button. You're returned to the project settings, and two languages appear in the list, as shown in Figure 13-26.

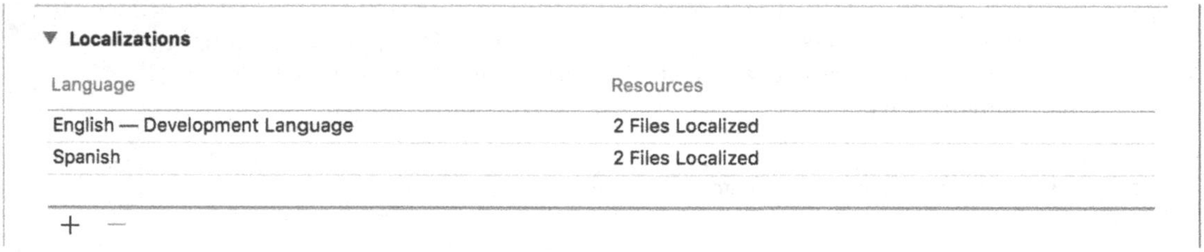

Figure 13-26. *The list of localizations now features the Spanish language*

Storyboards and Localization

The additional language that has appeared in your project settings wasn't the only change that happened when you added the Spanish language. If you look at the Project Navigator, notice that Main.storyboard now has a disclosure indicator next to it. Click the arrow, and you see that it's hiding Main.storyboard (Base) and Main.strings (Spanish), as shown in Figure 13-31. The base storyboard is a reference to the true storyboard, and the Main.strings file contains all the strings in the storyboard. The more languages you add, the more .strings files appear here.

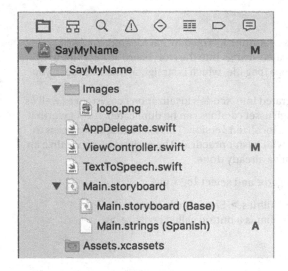

Figure 13-27. *Expanding the disclosure indicator next to* Main.storyboard *exposes the localization strings*

Click Main.strings to examine its contents. Your file should contain several lines similar to the following:

```
/* Class = "UILabel"; text = "First name"; ObjectID = "GOv-Ba-CQc"; */
"GOv-Ba-CQc.text" = "First name";

/* Class = "UILabel"; text = "Last name"; ObjectID = "txr-iB-qbM"; */
"txr-iB-qbM.text" = "Last name";
```

The first line is a comment, and the second is a key/value pair that links the translation to the label's text. The first part of the key GOv-Ba-CQc points to the label's unique object ID, which is automatically assigned when the label is added to the storyboard. The second part, text, indicates that the string is the text attribute for the label.

■ **Note**   Your label object IDs will be different from mine because the value is randomly generated when the object is added to the storyboard.

The value of First name is taken directly from the base translation and is the first part you need to change. Change First Name to Nombre and Last Name to Apellidos, as in the following code:

```
/* Class = "UILabel"; text = "First name"; ObjectID = "GOv-Ba-CQc"; */
"GOv-Ba-CQc.text" = "Nombre";

/* Class = "UILabel"; text = "Last name"; ObjectID = "txr-iB-qbM"; */
"txr-iB-qbM.text" = "Apellidos";
```

You have translated two values in the user interface, but you won't preview these changes until all the other elements in the application have been translated. Next you localize the application's logo image.

Localizing Images

Hopefully you're starting to sense that localization isn't as daunting as you may have feared. You've successfully added a new language and a couple of translated strings into the storyboard strings files to change the text on your button. It's time to localize the logo.png file, which is straightforward because you *didn't* use an asset catalog to store the image.

Asset catalogs are great, but they haven't been integrated into Xcode's localization ecosystem as well as other more well established elements have been. Although asset catalogs can be duplicated, it isn't worth it when you have a single image in your catalog that needs a localized version. This is because the process to localize the catalog involves duplicating it in its entirety, which isn't practical. The easiest way to localize an image in Xcode 8 is to add it to the project as a file, as you've already done.

1. Expand the Images group in the Project Navigator and select logo.png.

2. Open the File Inspector by choosing View ➤ Utilities ➤ Show File Inspector (⌘+⌥+1). Contained in the File Inspector sidebar is a button called Localize, as shown in Figure 13-28.

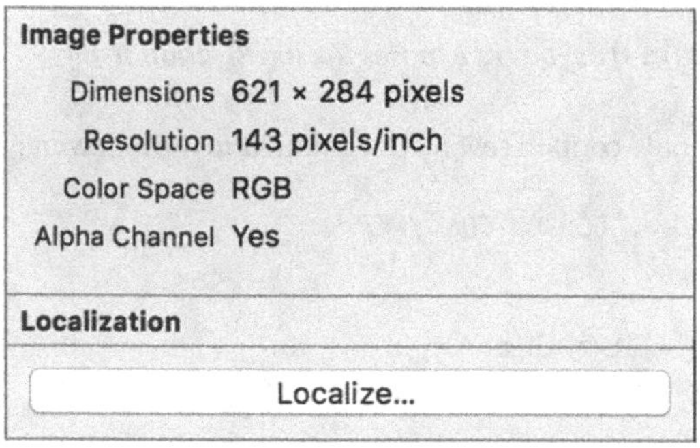

Image Properties

Dimensions 621 × 284 pixels

Resolution 143 pixels/inch

Color Space RGB

Alpha Channel Yes

Localization

Localize...

Figure 13-28. The Localize button in the File Inspector

3. Click the Localize button. You will be prompted for which language you want to localize to, as shown in Figure 13-29. Leave the selection as the default base language and click Localize.

Figure 13-29. Selecting the Base language as the target for localization

4. When the dialog has closed, the area that contained the Localize button in the File Inspector changes to reflect the languages available for localization. Select Spanish, as shown in Figure 13-30. There is no need to select the English box, because English is also the base language, so you would be doubling up needlessly.

Image Properties

Dimensions --

Resolution --

Color Space --

Alpha Channel --

Localization

☑ 🖻 Base

☐ 🖻 English

☑ 🖻 Spanish

Figure 13-30. logo.png can be localized to any available language

5. If you look at logo.png in the Project Navigator, just as with the storyboard, there is now a disclosure indicator alongside the image. Expand it. As shown in Figure 13-31, you now have two versions of the image: the base version and a Spanish one.

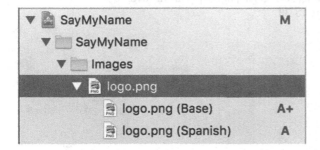

Figure 13-31. The logo.png file now has two language versions

A Peek Behind the Scenes

As with many things, Xcode does a great job of creating the appearance of simplicity on top of what is going on behind the scenes in your project, presenting you with a nice, easy-to-use interface. To see what Xcode is really doing, right-click the project name in the Project Navigator in Xcode and select Show In Finder.

As you can see in Figure 13-32, if you select the SayMyName folder, there is an es.lproj folder in addition to the base.lproj and en.lproj folders that you normally find in an iOS 9 project folder. In this folder are all the files that are localized to Spanish, including logo.png. It's here that you need to replace the overlay image, currently written in the English language, overwriting it with a Spanish version:

Figure 13-32. *Behind the scenes, the SayMyName project folder has a folder for each localization*

1. Open an additional Finder window. To do this, in Finder, go to File ➤ New Finder Window (⌘+N).

2. In the new Finder window, navigate to the resources for this chapter and open the Spanish folder, which contains a single file: logo.png. Drag this file over to the es.lproj folder, as shown in Figure 13-33.

Figure 13-33. *Dragging the Spanish logo.png over to the es.lproj folder*

3. When you release the file, you're told that the file already exists and asked how you want to handle the duplicate files. Choose Replace.

You have now learned how to localize a storyboard and a project resource, in this case an image file. All that remains is to look at localizing the string that is passed to the SayText method; then you'll be ready to explore previewing and texting localization.

Localizing Code with Localizable.strings

The last area of application localization that I cover in this chapter is code localization. When localizing code, you don't have to translate all of it—just the strings used in the code. Here I have highlighted the string you construct in the sayContact action:

```
@IBAction func sayContact(sender: AnyObject) {
    var personName : String = "You have chosen "
    if let forename = firstnameField.text {
        personName += forename
    }

    personName += " "

    if let lastname = lastnameField.text {
        personName += lastname
    }

    TextToSpeech.SayText(input: personName)
}
```

As you can see, three strings need to be translated. There are a number of ways to localize these strings, but all of them use the same method of retrieving the localized string: NSLocalizedString. In this instance, you're using NSLocalizedString to retrieve a localized string value from a file you haven't created yet: Localizable.strings.

Creating Localizable.strings

The Localizable.strings file, like the Main.strings file for the storyboard, holds localized strings in a key/value format. Unlike Main.strings, Xcode hasn't created this file for you automatically. Creating a strings file is a quick and easy task, so let's take a moment to create the file:

1. Select the SayMyName group in the Project Navigator and then choose File ➤ New ➤ File (⌘+N).

2. When the New File pop-over appears, select the Resource category under iOS on the left, and then choose the Strings File template on the right, as shown in Figure 13-34. Click Next to continue. (You may have to scroll down to see the Strings File template.)

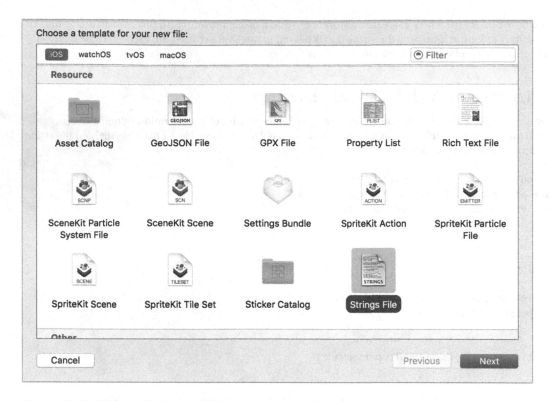

Figure 13-34. *Selecting the Strings File template from the Resources category*

3. You need to name the file correctly in the Save As box. Be sure you name it
    Localizable, as shown in Figure 13-35. Click Create to add the new strings file to
    the project.

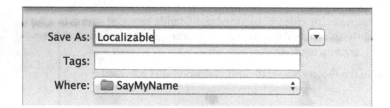

Figure 13-35. *Naming the new strings file*

4. In your Project Navigator, you should now see a Localizable.strings file. Select
    the file, and it appears in the code editor. Currently the file is empty, apart from
    the opening comments. Beneath the comments, add the following code:

```
"SELECTED" = "You have chosen ";
```

The first item in quotes, SELECTED, is the *key*. This is the value you reference in your code to retrieve the *value*, which is the item on the right of the equals symbol. Although there isn't a specific convention for naming keys, it's good to think semantically and name the key as either a whole word or a part of the sentence.

■ **Note** It's important to remember that .strings files aren't Swift code, and as such they require you to end each line with a semicolon. Without a semicolon, the application won't compile.

You've successfully created a string for the base translation. Now you need to localize this file and translate it.

Localizing Localizable.strings

When you created Localizable.strings, it wasn't associated with any language. In order to have a language-specific version of the file, you need to localize the file just as you did with the overlay image:

1. Select the Localizable.strings file in the Project Navigator, and then open the File Inspector by going to View ➤ Utilities ➤ Show File Inspector (⌘+⌥+1).

2. Look for the Localize button in the File Inspector (refer to Figure 13-28 if you can't find it) and click it. As before, leave the language as Base, and click Localize.

3. Again, the Localize button is replaced with a list of available languages with check boxes. Select the Spanish check box, as was shown in Figure 13-30. This creates a base version and a Spanish version of the file.

4. Expand the disclosure indicator next to Localizable.strings in the Project Navigator, as shown in Figure 13-36, and select the Spanish version.

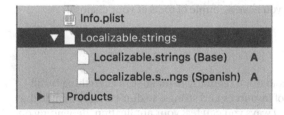

Figure 13-36. Displaying the base and Spanish versions of Localizable.strings

5. In the code editor, you should find that the contents are exactly the same as the base version of the file. Change the values highlighted in the following code to their Spanish counterparts:

```
"SELECTED" = "Has elegido ";
```

Great! You now have base and Spanish versions of your Localizable.strings file, fully translated and ready to go. Next you need to work the contents into your application's code.

Retrieving Localized Strings with NSLocalizedString

With the localized strings in place for both languages, all that remains is to retrieve the values from the Localizable.strings file using the NSLocalizedString macro. To do this, you replace the static strings that you've already written with the NSLocalizedString macro. NSLocalizedString does the hard work in retrieving the correct strings for the selected language, meaning all you as the developer need to do is supply the correct key.

NSLocalizedString takes a number of arguments, but it requires you to supply it with a minimum of two specific arguments: the key that corresponds to the string you want to display, and a comment that allows you to add context but is completely optional. I provide a string, but you can just as easily specify nil.

Open ViewController.swift from the Project Navigator, and scroll down to the sayContact action. Replace the highlighted code as shown here:

```
@IBAction func sayContact(sender: AnyObject) {
    var personName : String = NSLocalizedString("SELECTED", comment: "Selected Person")
    if let forename = firstnameField.text {
        personName += forename
    }

    personName += " "

    if let lastname = lastnameField.text {
        personName += lastname
    }

    TextToSpeech.SayText(input: personName)
}
```

That was easy. You've replaced the string that was there with a call to the NSLocalizedString macro, so whenever your application runs, the value from the Localizable.strings file will be displayed.

Now you're ready to test the application. To do that, you have a couple of tools at your disposal.

Testing Localizations

Once you begin to localize an application, it's a good idea to test it regularly to make sure everything is still as it should be. You may be dealing with a large number of resources and strings, so don't underestimate the potential for making a mistake. Xcode provides a couple of ways you can test your application, depending on the type of localization you want to test.

Testing Localization with Xcode 8

Xcode allows you to test your interface localizations in real time as you build your interface by using the preview option in the Assistant Editor. This is a quick way to ensure that your interface stands up to changing string lengths without constantly recompiling the application:

1. Select `Main.storyboard` from the Project Navigator.

2. Select the Assistant Editor.

3. Click Automatic on the jump bar and move down to Preview. Select `Main.storyboard`, as shown in Figure 13-37.

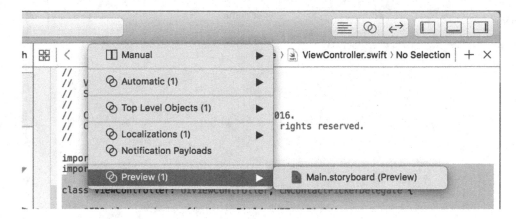

Figure 13-37. *Selecting the preview for the storyboard*

4. Select the view controller in the design area. The preview shows your interface neatly duplicated, as shown in Figure 13-38.

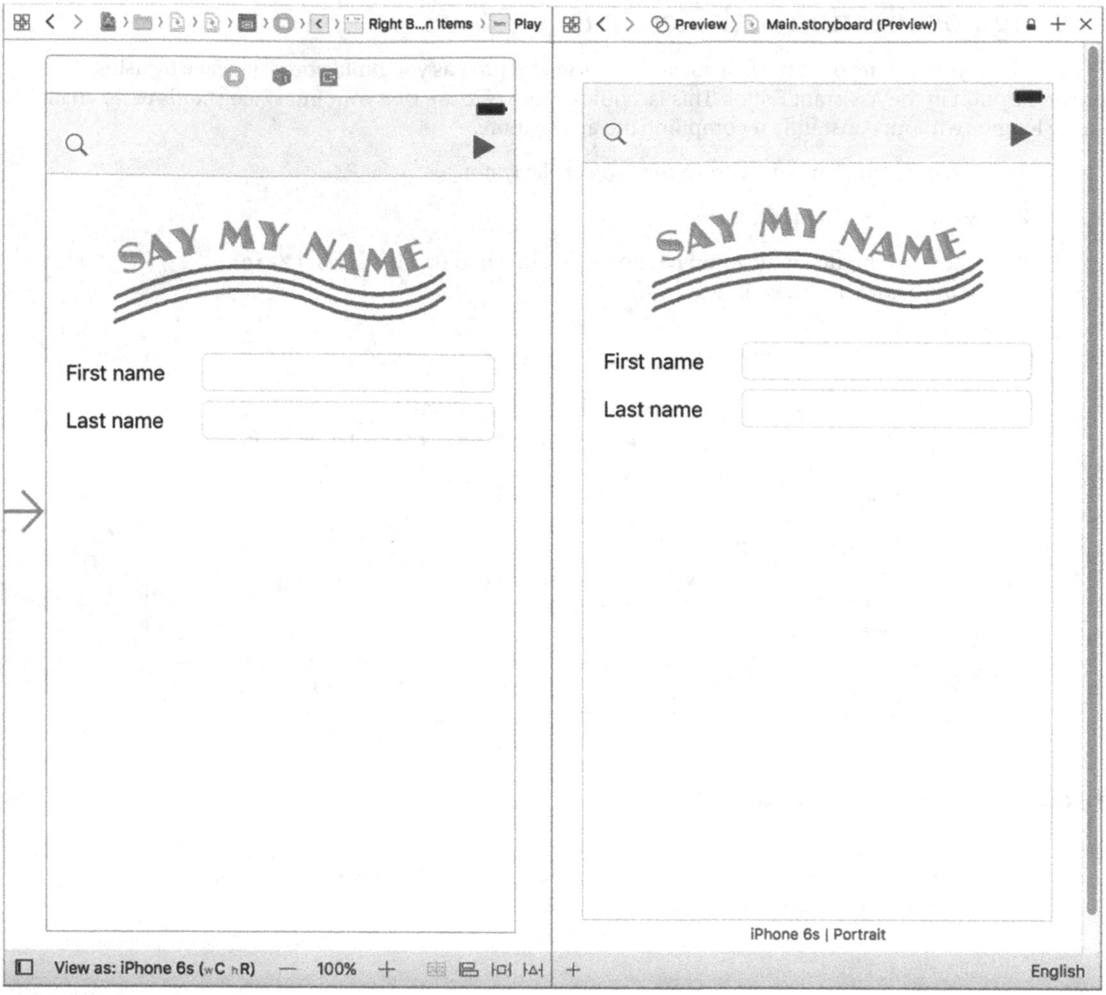

Figure 13-38. *Previewing the SayMyName application*

5. In the lower-right corner of the preview area is a language selection, currently set to English. Click it, and a menu appears, as shown in Figure 13-39.

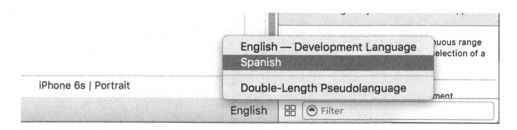

Figure 13-39. *Selecting a different language for the preview*

6. Choose Spanish from the language selection and as Figure 13-40 shows, the strings are translated in the preview area.

Figure 13-40. *Translated strings in the preview area*

You're lucky that the translations you're using fit nicely into the labels you created. To test how they might behave with longer strings, the language menu has another option, Double-Length Pseudolanguage, that doubles the length of the base language string for testing purposes.

7. Bring up the language selection as you did in Figure 13-39 and select the Double-Length Pseudolanguage option. As you can see in Figure 13-41, the label's text is truncated.

Figure 13-41. *The strings truncate when switched to the Double-Length Pseudolanguage option*

8. There are a couple of ways to fix this, but the quickest is to enable autoshrink for the field. Click the First Name label in the design area and open the Attributes Inspector.

9. Locate the Autoshrink attribute and change it from Fixed Font Size to Minimum Font Size, as shown in Figure 13-42.

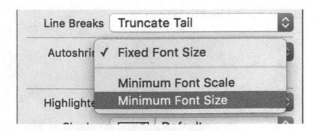

Figure 13-42. *Setting a minimum font size*

10. Click back into the preview. Now the label text fits perfectly. Repeat this step for the Last Name field.

When autoshrink is enabled, iOS shrinks the font size no smaller than the specified minimum until it can fit into the label. If the string is still too long, it's truncated. At times like that, you might want to set up a two-line label as you did when preparing the prototype cells for SocialApp back in Chapter 8.

In Preview, you can't see localized images, and you can't experience the localized string passed to the SayText method. For this, you need the Simulator.

Setting the Application Language in the Scheme

You probably know that iOS allows you to choose from a range of languages within the actual operating system; however, this is a time consuming and very fiddly technique for testing your localizations. Xcode allows you to change the application's language by editing the active scheme. Here's how:

1. Click the SayMyName scheme and then click Edit Scheme, as shown in Figure 13-43.

Figure 13-43. *Editing the application's scheme*

2. Select Run from the column on the left and then click the Options tab.

3. In this tab, you see an option called Application Language. When you click the drop-down list for this option, you can specify a language to run with, which overrides the settings of the operating system (see Figure 13-44).

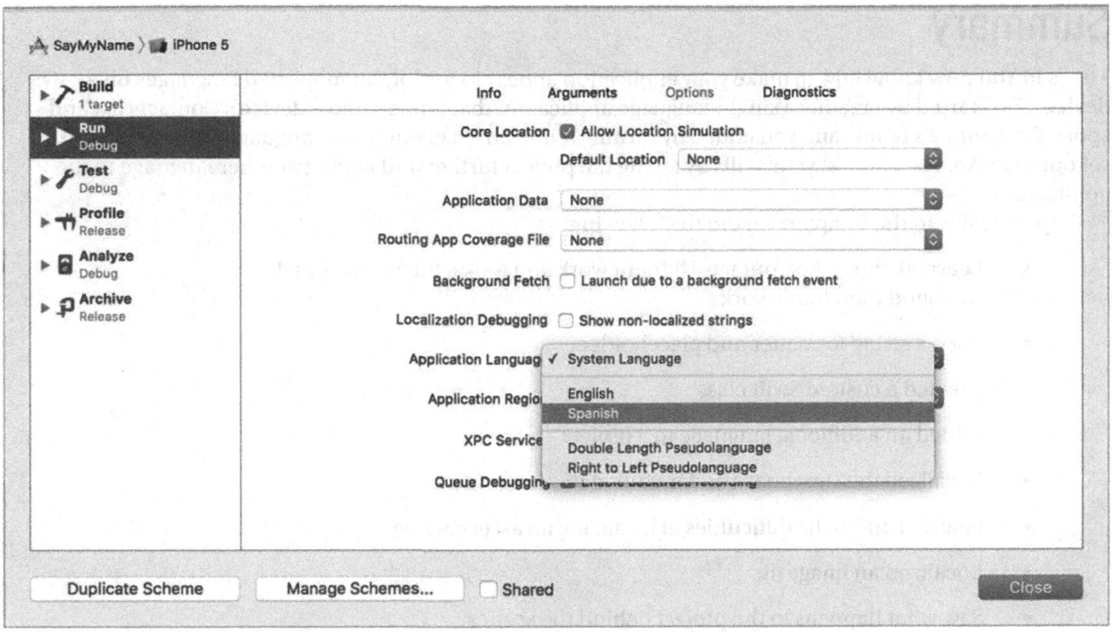

Figure 13-44. *Changing Application Language in the Scheme options*

By changing the language this way, you never have to face the necessity of remembering how to change the language of the operating system back into your native language, when you don't understand the language that you changed it to!

Run through the application, select a contact, and click the play button. Not only is your spoken string the Spanish one you created using placeholders, but iOS speaks it in a Spanish accent! This shows the fantastic level of localization that can be achieved with an application in iOS—and writing with Swift makes it even easier. The finished, localized application is shown in Figure 13-45.

Figure 13-45. *The finished application*

Summary

That's it! You now know how to make your application appear in any of the supported languages on an iOS device. You started by creating a single-language application that tapped into a device's Contacts list and spoke the contact's name, and you ended by turning it into an excellent multi-language application you set out to make. You can test your skills by taking the project further and adding another language to the application.

Specifically, in this chapter you did the following:

- Learned about the Contacts UI framework and took a further look at the AVFoundation framework

- Used a string formatter and placeholders

- Created a custom Swift class

- Added an additional language to a project

- Localized the storyboard and modified its strings file

- Learned about the difficulties of localizing an asset catalog

- Localized an image file

- Saw what happens to the project behind the scenes

- Created a `Localizable.strings` file and populated it with string for both languages

- Implemented `NSLocalizedString` to pull in the string values

You've achieved a lot in this chapter and learned some important skills that can cement your application's success in the App Store. Before you move on, here's a hint: keep the `SayMyName` application handy, because you use it in the next two chapters as you learn about the Organizer and then publish an application in the App Store!

CHAPTER 14

■ ■ ■

Devices and the Organizer

Chapter 13 taught you about localization and how you can enable your application to appear in multiple languages with minimal effort. To learn about localization, you built the SayMyName application, where you used the ContactsUI framework to pick a contact and the AVFoundation framework to say it.

The SayMyName application, which is really cool, is used in both this chapter and the next as you step away from coding and focus on Xcode's functionality. This chapter explains the Organizer, originally a single part of Xcode that is being downsized and cut up with each successive release of Xcode. In Xcode 8, the Projects Organizer has been removed altogether.

Chapter 1 showed you how to register for an Apple Developer Account. This chapter explains how to upgrade this to a fully paid Developer Account, allowing you to deploy applications to a physical device; then, in Chapter 15, you publish to the App Store. This chapter delves into the real nitty-gritty of Xcode's Organizer and Devices areas and explains many advanced activities such as obtaining crash logs, capturing screenshots to your computer from a device, and learning about derived data and snapshots.

■ **Note** To make the most of this chapter, you need a physical iOS device such as an iPhone, iPad, or iPod Touch running iOS 10. If you don't have one of these devices, then it will be hard for you to follow some of what is shown in this chapter.

The Role of the Organizer in Xcode 8

The Organizer is one of the areas of Xcode has been streamlined yet again in the latest release of Apple, a trend that has been ongoing since Xcode 5.

The Organizer groups two useful functions into a single location:

- *Archives Organizer*: Manage archived applications; one of the ways you can publish an application to the App Store

- *Crashes Organizer*: Access crash reports from your published applications, including device information and specific details about the nature of the crash

You access the Organizer from the menu bar by choosing Window ➤ Organizer, which loads the Archives Organizer by default, as shown in Figure 14-1. Because so much of this chapter requires an active developer account before you can take full advantage of the Organizer or Devices windows, it makes sense to go through the Developer Program enrollment process now.

© Matthew Knott 2016
M. Knott, *Beginning Xcode*, DOI 10.1007/978-1-4302-5005-0_14

Figure 14-1. *The Organizer: specifically, the Archives Organizer*

Preparing Xcode for Deploying to a Device

Deploying an application to a physical device allows you to take your innovative applications with you and test them in the real world. Prior to the all-in-one Apple Developer Program, Apple required you to be an active subscriber to test on your device. Thankfully this is no longer the case unless you want to publish the application to the App Store or share within your organization. In preparation for the next chapter, the first thing you will do in this chapter is to enroll in the Apple Developer Program and become a fully fledged Apple Developer.

Enrolling in the Apple Developer Program

If you want to publish to the App Store, then you must be enrolled in the Apple Developer Program. Although everything that has been covered in the book to this point could be done with the free account, the next chapter requires enrollment in the Developer Program, which costs $99 per year (at the time of this writing). If you're not ready to enroll in the Developer Program, or you're already a paid-up Apple developer, skip ahead to the section "Adding Your Developer Account to Xcode."

There's nothing wrong with holding back on enrollment into the program. When I started developing for iOS, I signed up immediately and then didn't make full use of my account until my second year. It might make financial sense for you to hold back until you've got an application that you're ready to release to the App Store.

Note that there's much more to the Developer Program than just being able to publish apps and test on a device. You get access to beta versions of system software, Xcode, and Apple TV firmware, which gives you a head start on adapting any existing apps for the new versions of iOS. You can also show off all the new features Apple brings to its devices months before Joe Public gets a look.

To begin the process, follow these steps:

1. Go to the Apple Developer Center in your web browser at `https://developer.apple.com`. Click the Account link in the upper-right corner and enter your Apple ID account details.

2. After you've entered your details and accessed the developer account page, you will notice at the bottom of the page a banner inviting you to join the Developer Program, as shown in Figure 14-2. Click this link to proceed.

Join the Apple Developer Program

Membership in the Apple Developer Program includes everything you need to develop, distribute, and manage your apps on the App Store. you'll also gain access to beta software, advanced app capabilities, beta testing tools, and app analytics.

Figure 14-2. An advertisement for the iOS Developer Program

3. The landing page for the Apple Developer Program is shown in Figure 14-3. This page holds lots of information about what the program enables you to do, and this is where you start the enrollment process. Click the Enroll button when you're ready.

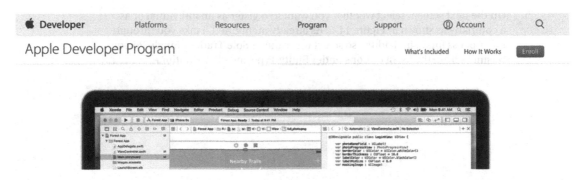

Figure 14-3. The landing page for the Apple Developer Program

4. You're provided with information about how the enrollment process works, as shown in Figure 14-4. I'll take you through registration as an individual; if you're registering as a business in the United States, you need to supply your D-U-N-S number; or if you're in another part of the world, you're asked for alternative information for validation. Once you have read this information, click the Continue button near the bottom of the page.

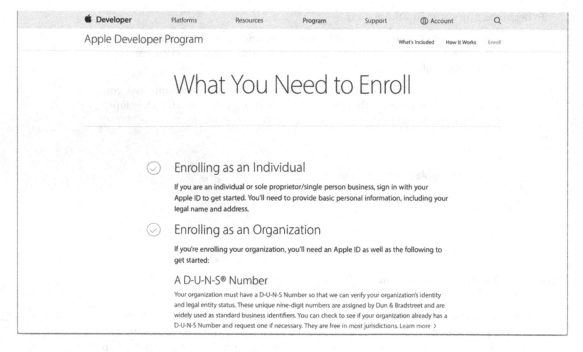

Figure 14-4. *The enrollment process, explained*

5. On the next screen, select whether you want to register as an individual or as a company as shown in Figure 14-5. As already mentioned, I take you through the process for an individual, so select Individual / Sole Trader / Single Person Business from the list of options under Entity Type and click Continue.

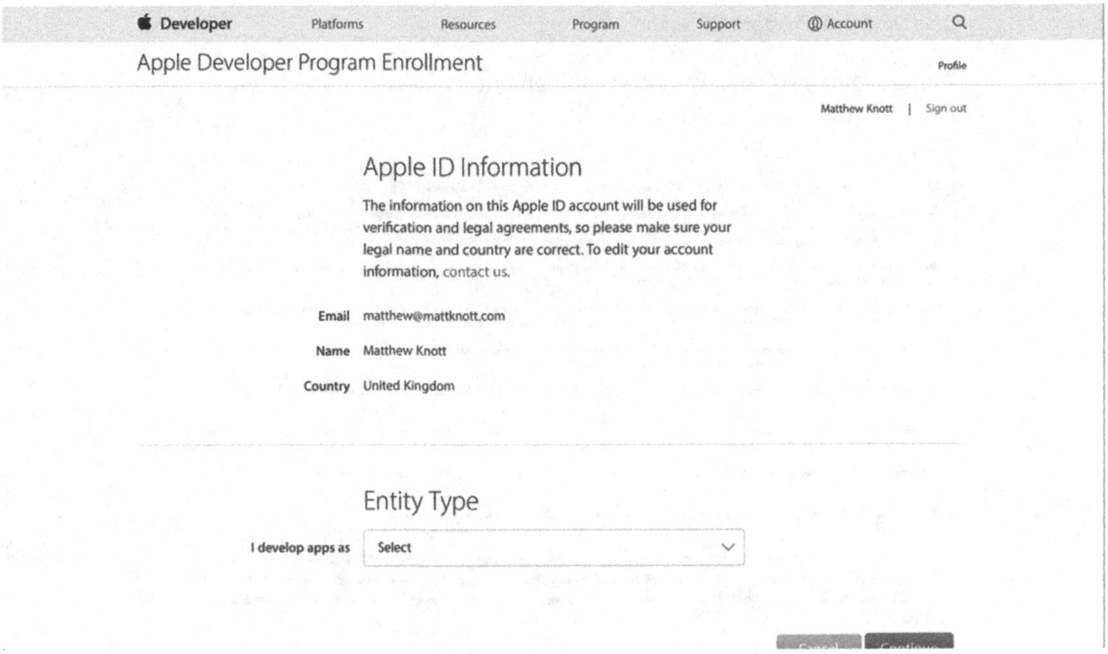

Figure 14-5. *Choosing the enrollment entity type*

6. Next enter your contact information including telephone number and address, click Continue, and then click Continue again after confirming Romanized contact details.

7. You will be asked to accept the license terms, as shown in Figure 14-6. Apple presents you with the license agreement, which is legally binding. If you're planning to take iOS app development seriously, then, contrary to how you may usually approach such things, I recommend that you read it and save a copy by using the link to the PDF version of the agreement. This document protects you as much as it protects Apple, so keep a copy for your records. When you're ready, check the disclaimer box below the license agreement and click the I Agree button.

Figure 14-6. *The license agreement for the Apple Developer Program*

8. With your options for enrollment set, you see a summary of the proposed purchase, as shown in Figure 14-7. At this point the price of enrollment adjusts to your local currency. You are also presented with the option to auto renew your membership. When you're ready to do so, click Continue.

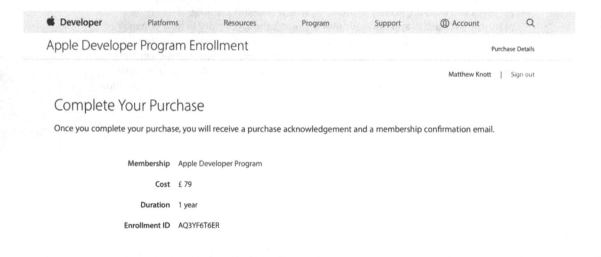

Figure 14-7. *Reviewing the details of your enrollment*

9. Next, you will be taken to the Apple Store and prompted to sign in. Confirm your payment details and complete the purchase. Once you've completed the purchase and your enrollment is approved, you receive an e-mail confirming that you're a part of the Developer Program!

■ **Note** If you live in a country that has no online Apple Store, the process for paying is very different from that shown in this chapter. You can still sign up; it just takes a little longer.

Adding Your Developer Account to Xcode

Being enrolled in the Apple Developer Program is one thing, but if Xcode doesn't know you have a Developer Account, you can't take advantage of any of the extra functionality it gives you. You may have already added your developer account details through your own experiences with Xcode; but if not, this section guides you through adding the account details. Then it's on to the devices. Follow these steps:

1. Open Xcode. From the menus, choose Xcode ➤ Preferences (⌘+,). Once you're in Preferences, select the Accounts tab, as shown in Figure 14-8. If you set up an online repository in Chapter 12, you will see those account details here.

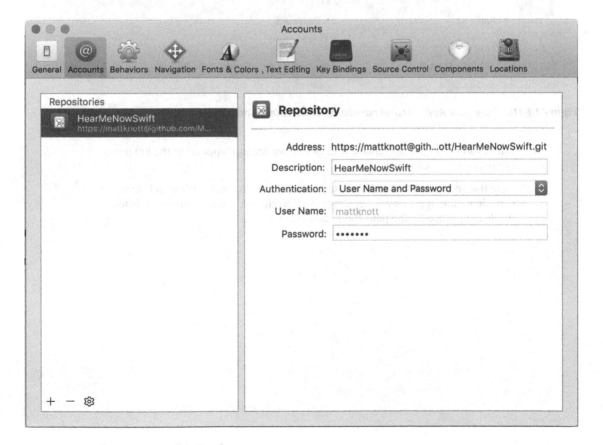

Figure 14-8. The Accounts tab in Xcode

2. Click the + symbol at the bottom of the left page and select Add Apple ID, as shown in Figure 14-9.

Figure 14-9. *Selecting the option to add an Apple ID to Xcode*

3. A popup appears, asking for your Apple ID and password, as shown in Figure 14-10. Enter your credentials and click the Sign In button.

Figure 14-10. *Enter your Apple ID and password to integrate the account with Xcode*

4. When you return to Preferences, your developer account appears in the left pane of the account preferences.

5. Note that in Figure 14-11 to Role is set to Free. This is because although I have completed the Apple Developer Program subscription, it takes a short while for Apple to approve the the paid-for membership status.

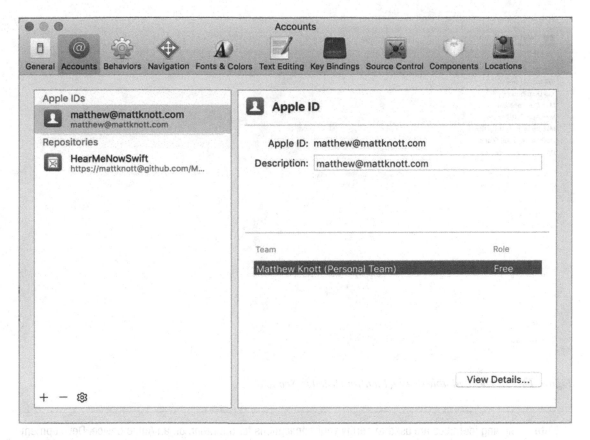

Figure 14-11. *The Apple ID added to Xcode*

6. Click the View Details button. Figure 14-12 shows that the free account status allows you to create signing identities for iOS and Mac development.

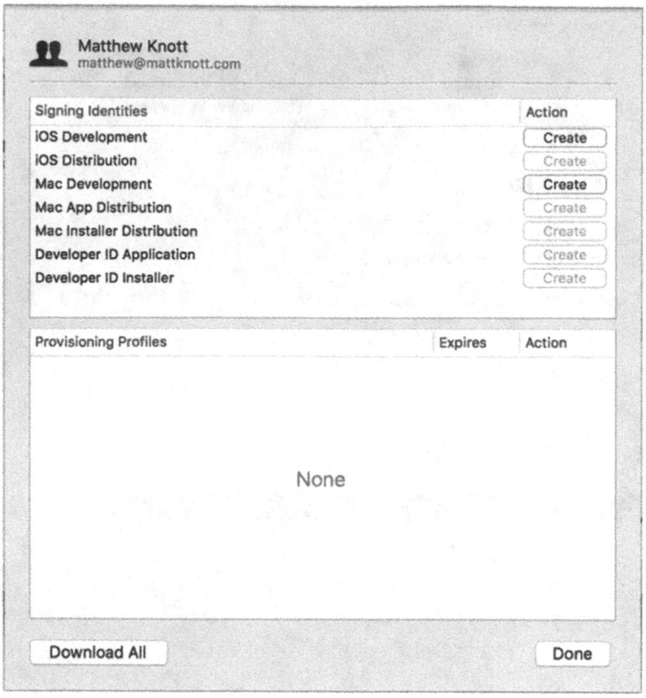

Figure 14-12. *The available signing identities listed in Xcode*

■ **Note**   Signing identities are used to certify your applications for operation on an Apple device. Development identities allow you to run your application on a device, but do not allow you to distribute the application either within your organization or on the App Store.

---

   7.   Click Create next to iOS Development to be able to deploy applications to your
         own hardware and then click Done.

The account has been added to Xcode, but there are a few more steps you need to go through before you can deploy your application onto a device. This is a great opportunity to get familiar with the Devices area, which allows you to finish preparing your device for deployment.

Preparing a Device for Deployment

Deploying any of your applications to a physical device is a process that is becoming increasingly simple, especially in this latest release. In order to deploy applications onto a device, you must register the device with Apple on your developer profile.

Prior to Xcode 5, if you wanted to use a physical device for development, you had to obtain the device's unique identifier through the Devices Organizer and then add it manually to the Certificates, Identifiers, and Profiles area of the Apple Dev Center. This was a long-winded and tedious process.

Apple has continued to simplify this process so that in Xcode 8 it is incredibly simple and intuitive. To demonstrate this functionality, follow these steps:

1. Ensure that you have the SayMyName project open.

2. Connect your physical device running iOS 10 to your Mac via USB cable. Other applications, such as Photos, may open at this time; if so, dismiss them. Click the list of devices, as shown in Figure 14-13, and select your device. In this instance I've selected my unregistered iPhone, called Matthew's iPhone.

Figure 14-13. *Select your physical device from the list of available devices*

3. One thing that you must do now that has been omitted from every project until this point is select a development team. Start by selecting the SayMyName project from the Project Navigator, and then the SayMyName target if it has not appeared automatically.

4. Next, click the drop-down list and select the correct development team, as shown in Figure 14-14.

Figure 14-14. *Specifying the development team when it was not done during project creation*

5. If the product name is valid, Xcode will remove the warning status and show a provisioning profile and signing certificate, as shown in Figure 14-15.

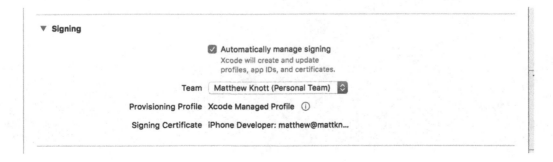

Figure 14-15. *Xcode after specifying a development team*

415

6. Ensure that your device is unlocked and on the home screen. If prompted by the device, trust the computer you're connected to.

7. Run the application from Xcode, and it will appear within a few seconds on the attached device.

At this point, Xcode does a number of things in the background: it creates a developer certificate on your Mac, it registers your new device on the developer portal, it creates a code-signing identity that is used to secure and encrypt the binary during the build phase, and it creates a provisioning profile on the device itself. All this before it deploys the app to your device!

■ **Note** Make sure that if you have a PIN lock on your device, the device is unlocked and on the home screen. Otherwise, Xcode will give you an error message.

You can now play around by selecting names from your actual contacts list and making the device speak their names. Deploying an application to physical Apple hardware for the first time is an incredible feeling.

Apple has made some huge strides in creating a process that, by and large, sorts itself out. Next, let's take a look at how you can use the Devices area of Xcode to manage and control your devices, as well as gather useful information about your application.

Managing Devices in Xcode

Now that the preparatory work has been done, you're all set to get your device ready to be used for development. If you haven't already, close Xcode's Preferences and open Devices by going to Window ➤ Devices (⌘+Shift+2).

The Devices area not only allows you to manage your physical hardware in great detail, but also, in Xcode 8, gives you access to information about the different iOS simulators. With each physical device, you can access crash logs, take screenshots, add provisioning profiles, and view the device's console data.

Assuming that your device is still connected to the Mac via the USB cable, it appears in the sidebar. Select it, and you're presented with an overview of all the information that is relevant to you as a developer, as shown in Figure 14-16.

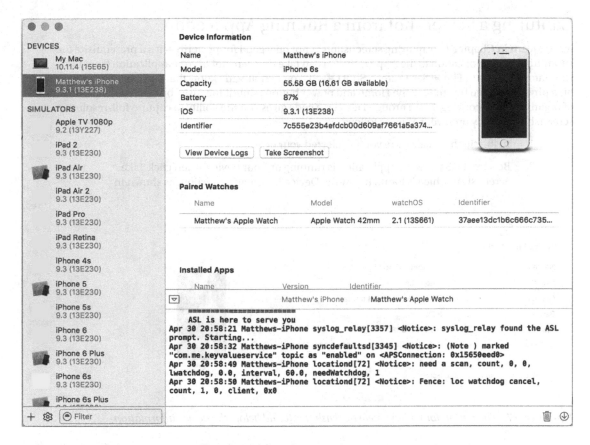

Figure 14-16. *The Devices area, with a device selected*

- *Sidebar*: In the sidebar you're able to select your Mac, any connected physical devices, and any of the simulators as shown in Figure 14-16. To find specific devices, you can use the filter box at the bottom of the sidebar to display only devices with "iPad" in the title, for example. The + symbol allows you to create new simulators; the cog lets you rename a device, remove a simulator, see provisioning profiles, or remove the device from the Run Destinations list.

- *Device Information*: In this area you can view important information that is unique to your device, such as the serial number and the unique identifier. You also can view the log files created by applications on the device and capture a screenshot to the desktop.

- *Paired Watches*: Purely for information purposes, this section lists the core details of any paired Apple Watch.

- *Installed Apps*: Any applications that you deploy to the device can be found here. You can interact with the applications by viewing their containers or by downloading and replacing them. You can also remove the application or add one from an .ipa file.

- *Device Console*: Here you can see in real time the activity being captured to your device's console, including any connected Apple Watch. You will see everything from Wi-Fi and iOS errors to individual applications adding comments to the console. This a great tool to use when debugging applications and OS behaviors.

Capturing a Screenshot from a Running Application

As you learn in Chapter 15, capturing screenshots is not only good for posterity—it's a prerequisite for submitting your application to the App Store. You can take a screenshot of your application from the simulator by going to File ➤ Save Screen Shot (⌘+S). You may already know that you can take a screenshot on a physical device by pressing the Home and power buttons simultaneously, but then you have the hassle of organizing and copying files. Through Devices, Xcode gives you the ability to capture full-resolution screenshots directly onto your Mac, as follows:

1. In the sidebar, make sure you've selected your device.

2. Be sure the SayMyName application is running on your device. Then click Take Screenshot, which is found below the Device Information section, as shown in Figure 14-17.

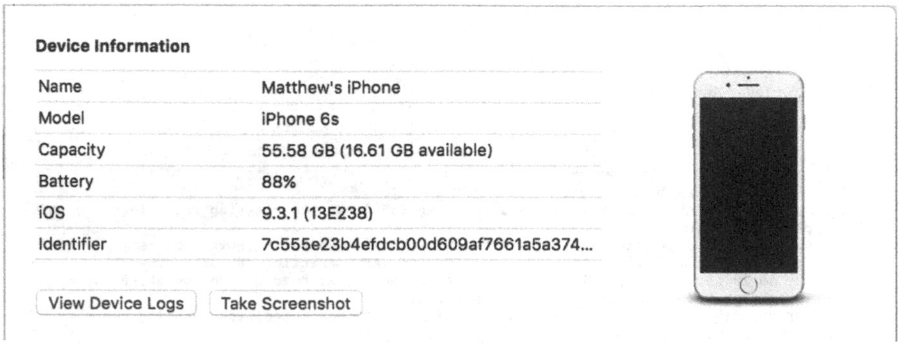

Figure 14-17. *The button for taking a new screenshot is found below the device information*

It may appear as though nothing has happened, but in fact a screenshot has been captured and saved to your desktop in the .png format.

Taking a screenshot may not seem like an important function. But as I mentioned previously, it's essential for when you submit your application to the App Store, because Apple requests that you supply screenshots of the application in action.

The Archives Organizer

The Archives Organizer represents one of a couple of ways that you can submit applications to the App Store. Because App Store submission is the topic of Chapter 15, I focus here on how you can create an archive of your application and then use the Archives Organizer to analyze it.

Start by opening the Organizer (choose Window ➤ Organizer). Right now, your Archives Organizer probably looks empty, like the example in Figure 14-18, because it contains no archives. In order to make more sense of the Archives Organizer and its capabilities, the first thing you need to do is archive the SayMyName application.

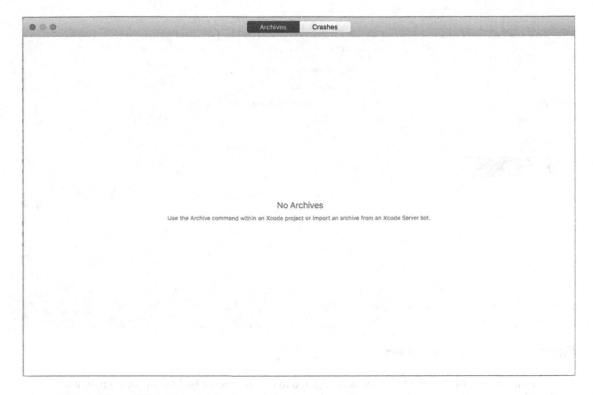

Figure 14-18. *The Archives Organizer, minus any archives*

Archiving Your Application

When you archive your application, it is compiled, readied for release, and then compressed into an Xcode archive file (.xcarchive) on your computer. The actual archiving process takes two clicks of the mouse, so rather than starting with that, I'll take you behind the scenes so you have a better understanding of what happens when you ask Xcode to archive an application.

When you choose to archive your application, you're performing an action that is customizable as part of the currently active scheme. To see how the action is configured, close the Organizer and go back to Xcode. Next, choose Product ➤ Scheme ➤ Edit Scheme (⌘+<) and select the Archive action from left column, as shown in Figure 14-19.

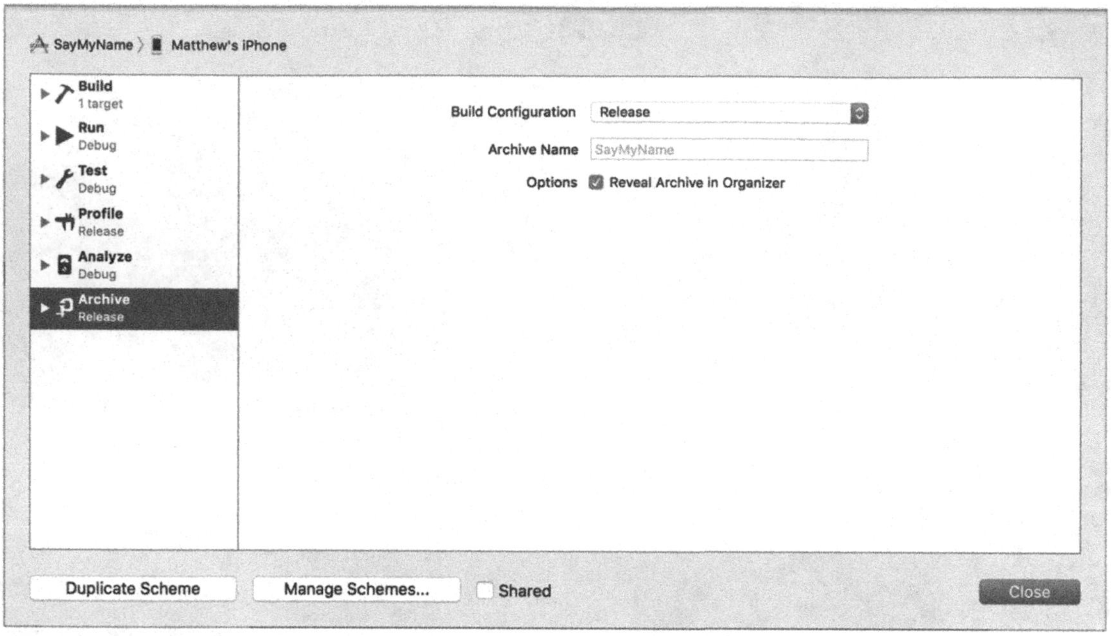

Figure 14-19. *The Edit Scheme dialog*

You can see that by default, the action is configured to use the release build configuration, that it uses the default name SayMyName, and that upon completion, it will launch the Archives Organizer. You can customize any of these options according to how they would best suit you. Click Close to dismiss this dialog; it's time to try archiving the SayMyName application.

To create an archive of your application, choose Product ➤ Archive from the menu bar. Xcode goes through a build process before reopening the Archives Organizer, which now contains an archive, as shown in Figure 14-20.

Figure 14-20. *The Archives Organizer, looking much more useful with some content*

■ **Note** If the archive is unavailable, ensure you have an iOS device selected as your target, not a simulator. You can use Generic iOS Device if you do not want to connect your own.

The main information pane on the right shows the application version and bundle identifier, which is useful for differentiating among multiple archives. The Validate, Upload to App Store, and Export buttons are covered in Chapter 15, which leaves several small pieces of functionality to discuss here.

If you right-click the archive, as shown in Figure 14-21, you can perform actions and access contextually relevant help files. Choosing Show in Finder launches a Finder window in the folder containing the selected archive. This archive can then be distributed to other users on your development team.

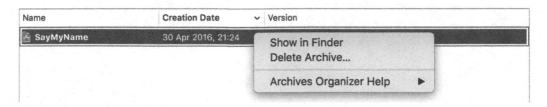

Figure 14-21. *Right-clicking the archive reveals several options*

Finally, choosing Delete Archive removes the archive from the file system. Before removal, you're prompted whether you want to delete the archive; in this instance, you would simply confirm the action by clicking the Delete button.

That's as far as I can take you through the Archives Organizer without encroaching on the next chapter. There you learn how to validate your application and submit it to the App Store from this very window.

Summary

As you approach the end of the book, you are learning some of the least commonly used, but no less important, parts of Xcode. You looked in detail at the key areas of Devices and the Archives Organizer and saw how they can be used to manipulate and manage your applications and hardware.

Specifically, in this chapter, you did the following:

- Learned how to sign up as a paid member of the iOS Development Program

- Registered a physical device, prepared it for development, and deployed your application to it

- Captured an application screenshot

- Archived your application so it's ready for distribution on the App Store

In the next and final chapter, you complete your knowledge by publishing an application to the App Store!

■ ■ ■

CHAPTER 15

Building, Sharing, and Distributing Applications

Chapter 14 looked at Devices, Projects, and the Organizer. Together these elements of Xcode let you perform a vast array of actions, from managing iOS devices and project snapshots to preparing archives for submission to the App Store. This chapter continues that theme as you learn how to take your finished application and submit it for hosting on Apple's App Store, the single storefront for both free and paid applications for iOS.

You make the final touches to the SayMyName application that you first created in Chapter 13, by adding an icon to the project. You then move online, where I introduce you to the iTunes Connect portal, a one-stop shop for publishing to the App Store and reporting on download numbers and revenue. You use the iTunes Connect portal to prepare for publishing by creating a profile for your application with all the text and images required for submission.

Finally, this chapter looks at two ways of uploading your application to iTunes Connect, before submitting the application and all the required files to Apple for approval. I'll give you some hints and tips along the way to improve the likelihood of first-time acceptance. You also learn how you can distribute your application. And that's it! Once you've completed this chapter, you'll be ready to dive into writing and sharing your own apps and games!

It's worth noting that being enrolled in the paid iOS Developer Program is essential before you start on this chapter. I covered enrollment in Chapter 14, so if you need to register, now is a good time.

Final Checks Before Publishing Your Application

Before I take you through the process of submitting the SayMyName application to the App Store, you need to add a final touch of polish to complete the application. One of the focal points of this chapter is ensuring that your application has everything it needs to get through the Apple review process and be published to the App Store the first time. One key element that is currently missing from the SayMyName application and that is an absolute prerequisite is an icon.

If you haven't already downloaded the collective resources for the book, then refer back to Chapter 1, where I cover how to access this book's page on the www.apress.com web site and download the resources file. In the Chapter 15 folder, you'll find all the icons needed for both the application and the iTunes Connect portal. The icon provided for the SayMyName application is shown in Figure 15-1.

© Matthew Knott 2016
M. Knott, *Beginning Xcode*, DOI 10.1007/978-1-4302-5005-0_15

Figure 15-1. *The icon you use for the SayMyName application*

I covered the process of setting an application icon in Xcode; but that was back in Chapter 2, so I take you through it again because here you need to set three icons, not just one. Each icon file is named according to its resolution: the main application icon, for example, is named icon_120.png because it is 120 pixels × 120 pixels. Here are the steps:

1. Open the SayMyName project in Xcode.

2. Open Assets.xcassets from the Project Navigator.

3. Select the AppIcon image set, as shown in Figure 15-2. Notice that there are six image wells, all of which will hold icons used in different locations in iOS 10.

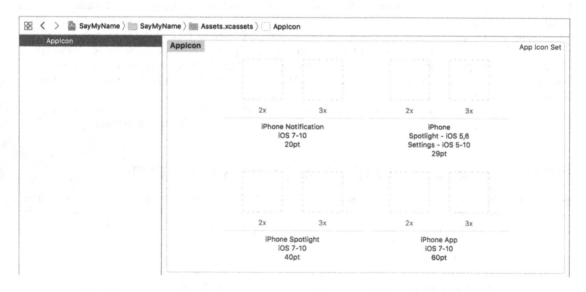

Figure 15-2. *Select the AppIcon image set from the Images asset catalog to see the six image wells in the set*

■ **Note**   Only one of these sets is a requirement, but you'll set them all for the sake of completeness. Another thing to note is that because this is an iOS 10–only application, and only for iPhone or iPod Touch, all of the image wells are subtitled with 2x or 3x, indicating that they're all retina images. The 3x images are specifically for the new iPhone 6. This is because all the devices in the iPhone form factor that run iOS 8 have retina screens. If you were creating an application that was backward compatible with iOS 6.1, or a universal application, then there would be far more icons to set.

4.   Open a Finder window and navigate to the resources for this book. In the Chapter 15 folder, all the icons are listed. Above iPhone Notification iOS 7-10, drag the file named icon_40.png into the 2x image well and icon_60.png into the 3x image well. Next, for iPhone Spotlight iOS 5,6 Settings – iOS 5-10, drag the file named icon_58.png into the 2x image well and icon_87.png into the 3x image well.

5.   Now repeat the last step by dragging icon_80.png and icon_120.png into the 2x and 3x wells in the iPhone Spotlight iOS 7-10 set and icon_120.png and icon_180.png into the iPhone App iOS 7-10 set, as shown in Figure 15-3.

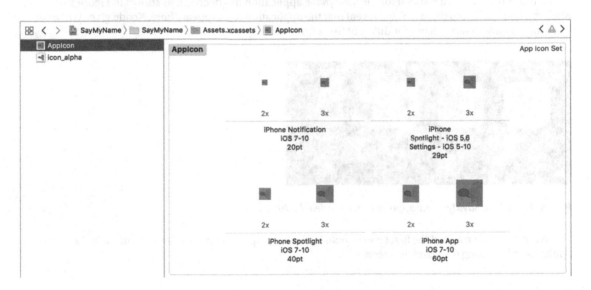

Figure 15-3. *A complete set of icons in the AppIcon image set*

With your four icons in place, run the application either on a device or in the Simulator to ensure that there are no warnings regarding the icons. If you add an icon with the wrong resolution to an image well, when you build and run the application, you receive a warning similar to that shown in Figure 15-4. If you receive this warning, be sure you added the correct image to the correct well.

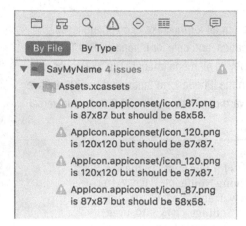

Figure 15-4. *Xcode warns you if your icons are the wrong resolution*

If you're running your application in the Simulator, choose Hardware ➤ Home (⌘+Shift+H); or, if you're using a physical device, press the Home button to return to the home screen with all the application icons. You should see that the icon for the SayMyName application has been set, as shown in Figure 15-5. Also, searching in Spotlight in iOS will reveal that the application icon appears here. Xcode gives you great flexibility to have different icons for different functions.

Figure 15-5. *The SayMyName application, completed with an icon*

Now that you've added the first layer of polish by setting up the icons, it's time to complete the application by setting up a launch screen.

Building a Launch Screen

Prior to Xcode 6, the preferred, default approach to display an image while your app was loading was to use a launch image. This harkens back to when iOS devices were far slower and a screenshot of the app was used to give the impression that the app had loaded before it actually became responsive. In Xcode 6, Apple changed tactics for the first time since iOS was introduced to use a .xib file however in Xcode 7, the new preferred approach became to use a storyboard.

Many app developers use the launch screen to display product branding or partner information. For this app, you create a launch screen that displays the application's logo in the center:

1. If you're not still looking at the Assets.xcassets asset catalog, select it from the Project Navigator.

2. Open a Finder window and navigate back to the resources for this chapter. Drag the icon_alpha.png icon into the asset catalog sidebar, as shown in Figure 15-6, to create a new image set.

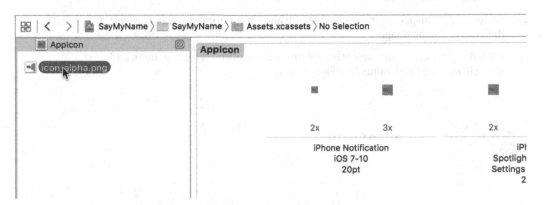

Figure 15-6. *Adding* icon_alpha.png *to the asset catalog*

3. Open *LaunchScreen.storyboard* from the Project Navigator. The default launch screen is completely blank, as shown in Figure 15-7.

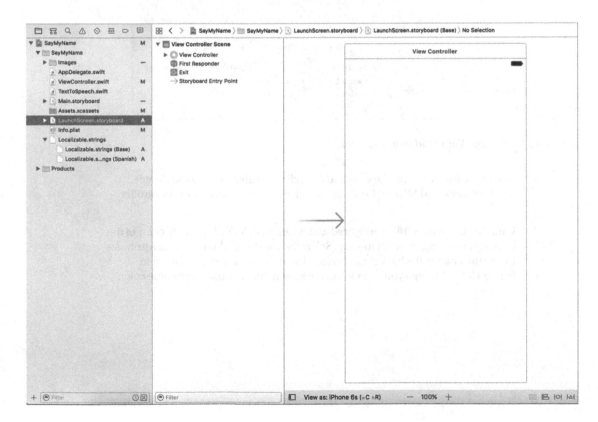

Figure 15-7. *The default* LaunchScreen.storyboard *created by Xcode*

4. Drag an image view onto the canvas.

5. Go to the Attributes Inspector with the image view selected and set the Image attribute to `icon_alpha`.

6. Go to the Size Inspector and set both Width and Height for the image view to 120 then re-center the image.

7. Click the pin icon, fix the Height and Width constraints by selecting them, and then click Add 2 Constraints (see Figure 15-8).

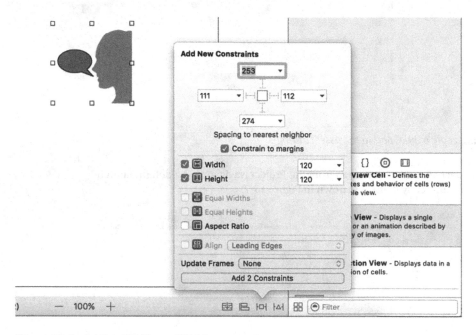

Figure 15-8. *Adding Width and Height constraints*

8. Center the image within the view and then click Resolve Auto Layout Issues, and then click Add Missing Constraints under the All Views in View Controller heading.

9. With the image view fully configured and positioned, let's change the color of the view to something more interesting. Select the canvas, and then, in the Attributes Inspector, change the background color to anything you want, as shown in Figure 15-9. Although you can't tell in the screenshot, I chose a light blue color.

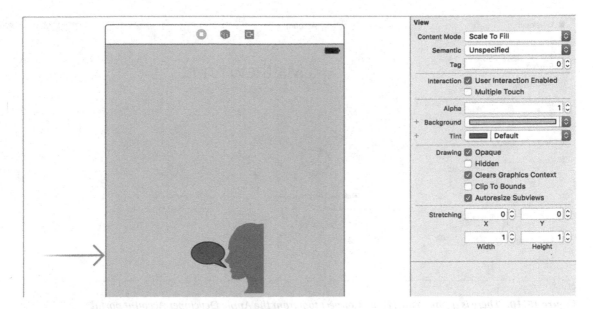

Figure 15-9. *The completed launch screen that will greet users every time the app runs*

Congratulations: you've just built and configured your first launch screen. If you want to see it in action, run the application. It's time to get down to the nitty-gritty of this chapter and load your application into the App Store.

Discovering iTunes Connect

You now leave Xcode behind for a moment and focus on the functionality available through the iTunes Connect portal. Here you create a profile for your application and set some initial details about the application and its audience.

■ **Note** A large portion of this chapter relies on you having an Internet connection and a web browser. I use the default Safari browser, but you should be able to use almost any modern web browser and achieve the same results.

To access iTunes Connect, go directly to https://itunesconnect.apple.com or, alternatively, reach it from the Developer Account area you were introduced to in Chapter 14, as shown in Figure 15-10.

Figure 15-10. *There is a link to the iTunes Connect tool from the Apple Developer Account portal*

When you arrive at the iTunes Connect portal, you're asked to sign in. Because of the highly sensitive nature of the content in iTunes Connect, your connection will time out if left unattended for a short while, so you'll be seeing a lot of the screen shown in Figure 15-11. Enter your Apple Developer ID details and click the button on the right side of the password box.

Figure 15-11. *Accessing the iTunes Connect portal for the first time*

If this is your first time accessing the iTunes Connect portal, you're asked to review and agree to a separate set of terms and conditions. As with other terms and conditions presented to you, it's a good idea to review them before accepting them.

Once you have agreed to the terms and conditions, you arrive at the iTunes Connect dashboard, shown in Figure 15-12.

Figure 15-12. *The dashboard of the iTunes Connect portal*

As you can see, numerous sections are available from this dashboard:

- *My Apps:* As far as this chapter is concerned, this is where it all happens. Here you create and manage your application profiles and control how they appear on the App Store.

- *App Analytics:* A recent addition to the iTunes Connect portal that provides developers with detailed information about the behaviors of the users of their applications.

- *Sales and Trends:* Get reports on the number of downloads for a particular timeframe.

- *Payments and Financial Reports:* Get a detailed breakdown of payments, and also view trends in your app-generated earnings.

- *iAd:* Soon to be discontinued, iAd was Apple's ad network.

- *Users and Roles:* You can give others access to the iTunes Connect portal. You can control permissions—restricting users from seeing the financial aspects, for example.

- *Agreements, Tax, and Banking:* Here you can view your tax details and request contracts in relation to the developer program. You can also view any transfer agreements you may have in place.

- *Resources and Help:* You can access various support mechanisms for issues when submitting your apps, including FAQs, a contact form, and a link to the developer forums, where you can crowdsource a solution from iOS developers the world over.

Clearly there is a lot you can do with iTunes Connect. For now, click My Apps so you can begin creating an application profile for the SayMyName application:

1. You're taken to an empty list (assuming you haven't created any applications already). At the top of the page is a + icon. Click it, as shown in Figure 15-13, and you're presented with three options: New App, New Mac App, and New App Bundle.

Figure 15-13. *The Add dialog on the My Apps page in iTunes Connect*

2. Click the New App link. A dialog appears in which you need to specify some basic information about your application, as shown in Figure 15-14:

    a. Set the platform to iOS.

    b. The Name field should contain the name of the application as you want it to appear on the App Store; I chose "Say My Name!".

    c. Set Language to English.

    d. The SKU field is for you to specify an identifier that is unique for you that will help you differentiate this app from others you may publish; I chose SayMyName.

New App

Platforms ?
☑ iOS   ☐ tvOS

Name ?
Say My Name!

Primary Language ?
English

Bundle ID ?
Choose
Register a new bundle ID on the Developer Portal.

SKU ?
SayMyName

Cancel   Create

Figure 15-14. *Setting the basic app information*

3. The Bundle ID select list shows a wildcard app ID when you select it. Depending on what you want your application to do now and in the future, it's worthwhile thinking about this step very carefully. For now, below the select list is the text Register a New Bundle ID on the Developer Portal; click Developer Portal. A new window or tab opens, showing the New App ID page.

Creating an App ID

An App ID links your application into Apple services such as iCloud, Game Center, and Pass Book; it also allows you to enable push notifications. There are two types of App ID, and the services you want your application to access both now and in the future will influence the type you use:

1. Click the plus icon at the top of the new page.

2. Give the App ID the name SayMyName, as shown in Figure 15-15.

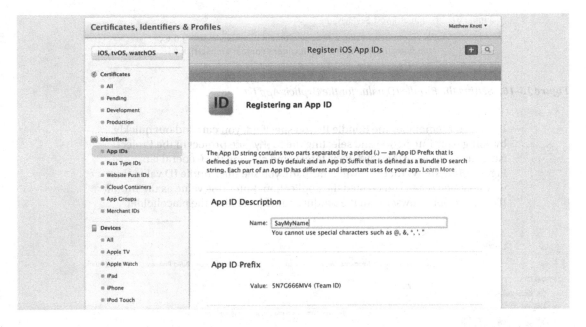

Figure 15-15. *Registering a new App ID*

3. You need to specify the type of App ID you want to register. I briefly explain each type next:

    •   ***Wildcard App ID:*** Can be shared between multiple applications. You can enable Data Protection, iCloud, Inter-App Audio, and Passbook services with a Wildcard App ID. This type of App ID is useful if you have a series of really basic applications that don't need access to the full range of Apple services.

    •   ***Explicit App ID:*** Gives you access to all Apple services that are available to the Wildcard App ID, with the addition of Game Center, In-App Purchase, and Push Notifications. If you aren't sure what you want to do with your application in the future, choose an Explicit App ID to reduce future hassles.

In this instance, choose Explicit App ID. Enter the Bundle ID that was set for the SayMyName application when you created it in Xcode in Chapter 13 (see Figure 13-2), which in my case was com.mattknott.SayMyName, as shown in Figure 15-16.

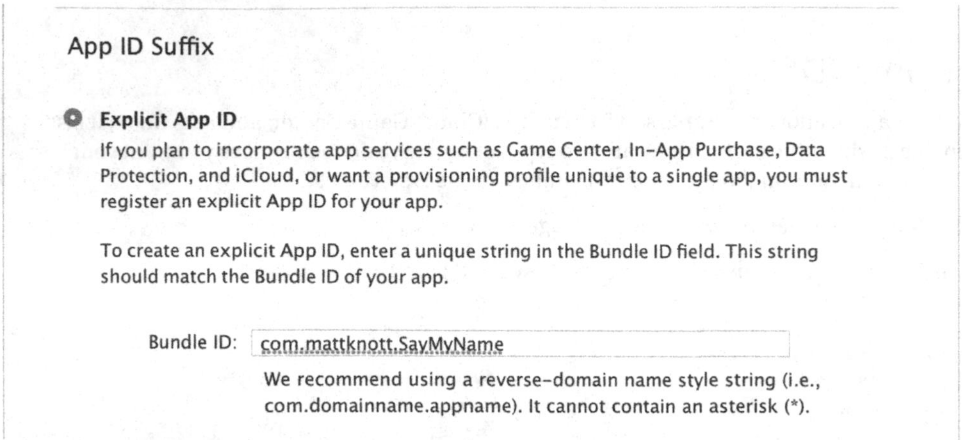

App ID Suffix

○ **Explicit App ID**

If you plan to incorporate app services such as Game Center, In-App Purchase, Data Protection, and iCloud, or want a provisioning profile unique to a single app, you must register an explicit App ID for your app.

To create an explicit App ID, enter a unique string in the Bundle ID field. This string should match the Bundle ID of your app.

Bundle ID: com.mattknott.SayMyName

We recommend using a reverse-domain name style string (i.e., com.domainname.appname). It cannot contain an asterisk (*).

Figure 15-16. Setting the Bundle ID value for the Explicit App ID

If you can't remember the Bundle ID you specified, you can find out quickly by going back into Xcode and selecting the SayMyName project in the Project Navigator, choosing the SayMyName target, and clicking the General tab. Figure 15-17 shows that following this path, you see the Bundle ID value that was specified when you created the application. Enter this value as the Bundle ID in your web browser with the product name instead of the placeholder.

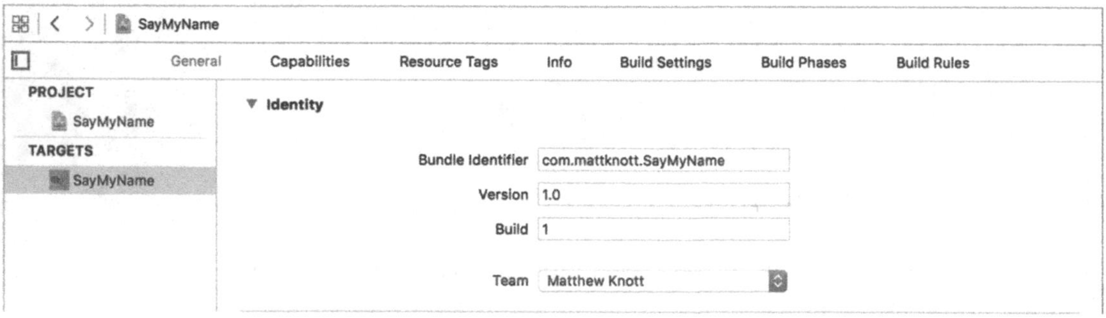

	General	Capabilities	Resource Tags	Info	Build Settings	Build Phases	Build Rules

SayMyName

PROJECT
SayMyName

▼ **Identity**

TARGETS
SayMyName

Bundle Identifier com.mattknott.SayMyName

Version 1.0

Build 1

Team Matthew Knott

Figure 15-17. Checking the Bundle ID is quick and painless

4. There is no need to enable any additional services, so scroll to the bottom of the page and click the Continue button.

5. On the next screen, you're shown a summary of the App ID details, including which services are enabled (see Figure 15-18). Don't worry that Game Center and In-App Purchase are enabled; this is the case for every Explicit App ID, and you don't have to use them. When you're happy with everything, click the Register button at the bottom of the page.

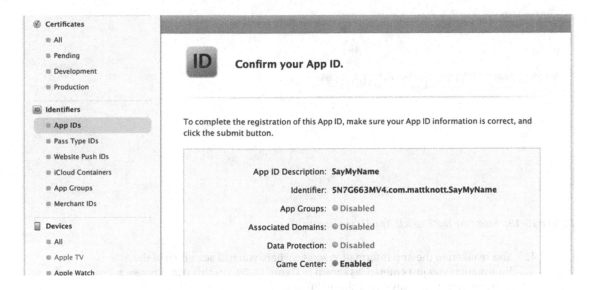

Figure 15-18. The App ID summary page

6. You're taken to a repeat summary page. The App ID has been created. Click Done to return to the list of App IDs, which now contains your Explicit App ID.

That's it: you have everything you need to create an application profile.

Creating an Application Profile

It's frustrating when you have to rip something up and start again as you just did when you abandoned the Application Profile, but in this case, at least you only typed a couple of words:

1. Go back to the iTunes Connect window or tab you were using in your browser, click the Back button, and then once again click the Add New App button that was shown in Figure 15-14.

2. Again, specify English as the default language, enter the app name (mine is "Say My Name!"), and enter the SKU value SayMyName.

3. This time, when you click the Bundle ID select list, your new App ID is in the list. Select it, as shown in Figure 15-19, and click Create.

Figure 15-19. *Selecting the Explicit App ID you created*

4. You're taken to the App Information screen where you will see much of the information you just entered, as shown in Figure 15-20. On this page choose a primary category; in my case I chose Utilities.

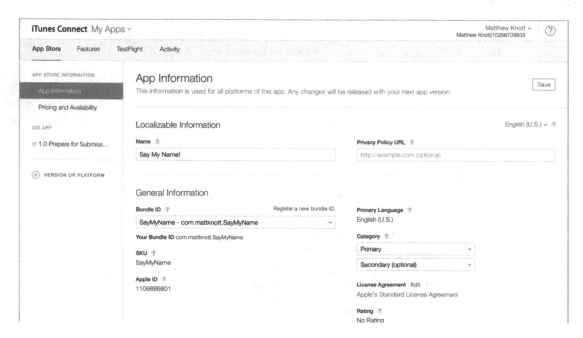

Figure 15-20. *The Say My Name! application management page*

5. Click Save and then choose the Pricing and Availability link on the left of the page.

6. Beneath Price Schedule is a drop-down list with the different pricing tiers. This will display in your local currency; however, the actual price paid differs from region to region. Choose the Free tier, as shown in Figure 15-21.

Figure 15-21. *Setting the pricing information*

■ **Note** If you choose to release a paid application, you're asked to supply your bank account details and also to accept the iOS Paid Applications Agreement, which explains your rights and entitlements. The temptation is to skip through these agreements, but you should always save anything you agree to, because it's legally binding.

---

7. Click Save and then click the 1.0 Prepare for Submission link on the left of the page.

Adding Screenshots and Video Previews

As you scroll down the page, the first section to be configured is for App Video Preview and Screenshots. There are five different formats for screenshots: 4.7-inch (iPhone 6s), 5.5-inch (iPhone 6s Plus), 4-inch (such as iPhone SE), 3.5-inch (such as iPhone 4s), iPad and iPad pro. This is not an iPad app, so you only need to set the first four screens. To save time, the resources for this chapter contain four different sizes of screenshots, ready for upload, in the screenshots folder.

Start by making sure the 4.7-Inch tab is selected, and then drag in the screen47.png file from the Finder, as shown in Figure 15-22. Repeat this step for the remaining tabs until one screenshot is uploaded for each applicable screen size. Click Save once all the screenshots have been added.

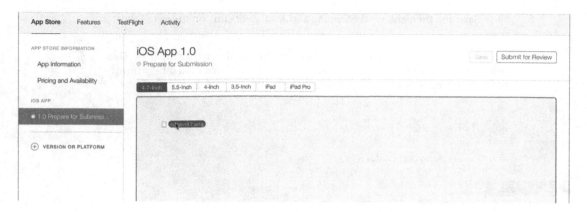

Figure 15-22. Dragging in a screenshot for upload

Adding Application Metadata

Scroll to the next section, traditionally referred to as the metadata area, as shown in Figure 15-23. In this segment you can specify six pieces of information, two of which are optional:

- *Description:* This will appear on the App Store page for your application and should focus on the app's purpose and key features.

- *Keywords:* Words that help your application appear when users search the App Store. You can have 100 characters' worth of keywords, which you separate with commas.

- *Support URL:* The primary support URL for your application. You must have a web site set up to support users with your application. The site doesn't have to be specifically about your application; it can be your personal or business web site.

- *Marketing URL:* This is optional, but a marketing URL is displayed to users in the App Store so they can discover more about your app before they purchase or download it.

Enter the values you feel are relevant. You must provide a description, at least one keyword, and a support URL.

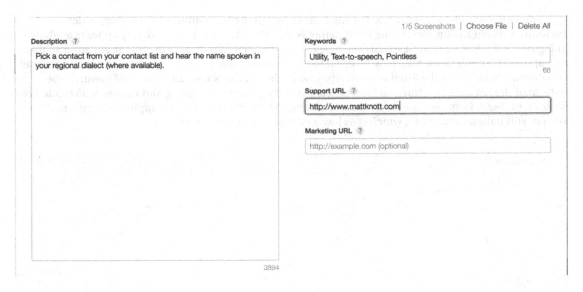

Figure 15-23. *The metadata area contains searchable information and key URLs for the SayMyName application*

Adding General Application Information

It's good to click Save periodically, so go ahead and do this now. Then scroll down to the next section: General App Information. The section is split into two columns. The right column is automatically populated with your personal address information, so let's start with the left column.

First, you need to set the icon for the application that will appear in the App Store. This is straightforward: click the icon, and a file browse dialog appears, as shown in Figure 15-24. Navigate to the resources for this application and select the file named `icon_1024.png`.

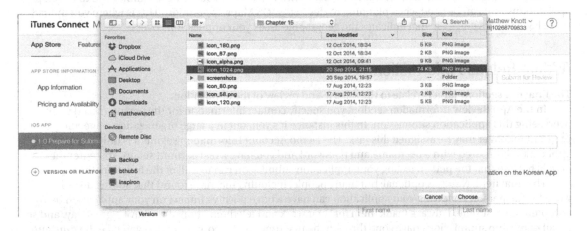

Figure 15-24. *Selecting the large format icon for the App Store*

The Version is already set at 1.0. The next item to set in the left column is the rating, which currently says No Rating. Next to the word Rating is an edit link; click it, and a dialog appears as shown in Figure 15-25. Here you must specify the types of content that may appear in your application so that an appropriate content warning may be given to users downloading the application. The Say My Name! app doesn't have any of the listed content types, so I selected the None value for all of them. At the bottom of the list are new values for Unrestricted Web Access and Gambling and Contests; I selected No for both of these. Complete this form and click Done. When you return to the application information screen, you have a rating of 4+, which is as low a rating as can be achieved.

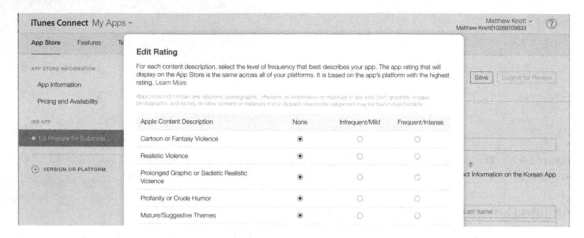

Figure 15-25. *Obtaining the application's rating by specifying its content*

In the right column, for the Copyright field, you usually enter the year and your name or company. I entered 2016 Matthew Knott.

The Address field should be filled in, but if it isn't, specify the required values.

The final segment, Routing File, was introduced with iOS 7 and Xcode 5, which allows you to develop applications that can be used when planning routes in the iOS Maps application. This is where you upload the associated coverage file that indicates the geographic areas your application covers.

Adding Release Information

The final few sections largely relate to the release and review of the application.

In the App Review Information section, you specify contact information for the person tasked with overseeing this application submission. In this instance it's you, but in a large organization a specific program manager may be assigned this task. The Demo Account Information segment is only used if your application is secured with a username and password and you have a test account set up. You enter the details here so that the person testing your application submission can test all of the functionality.

The final field, Notes, is optional; but many people, including me, have found that adding a kind word for the person reviewing your application can have a huge positive impact on your application being accepted the first time. I always thank them for their work and tell them I hope they have a great day, and so far all of my app submissions have gone through the first time. So, I recommend that you take the time and write your own positive message, as shown in Figure 15-26.

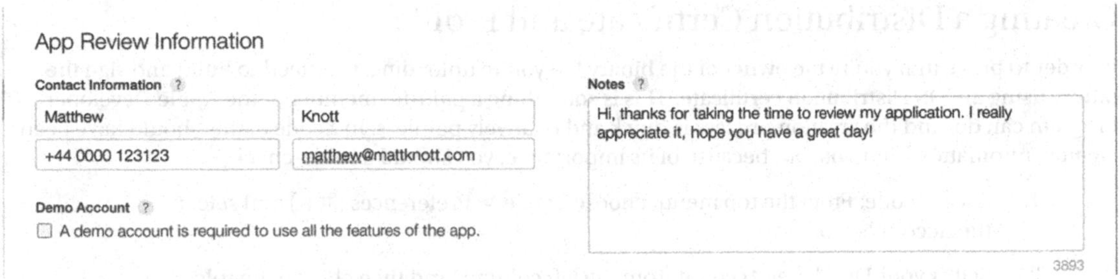

App Review Information

Contact Information ?

| Matthew | Knott |

| +44 0000 123123 | matthew@mattknott.com |

Notes ?

Hi, thanks for taking the time to review my application. I really appreciate it, hope you have a great day!

3893

Demo Account ?

☐ A demo account is required to use all the features of the app.

Figure 15-26. *Setting the app review information*

The last configurable section on this page is the Version Release section. Here you simply specify whether you want the application to be released the minute it's approved, or whether you have a more specific date in mind or you want to manually release. In this instance, select Automatically Release This Version, as shown in Figure 15-28.

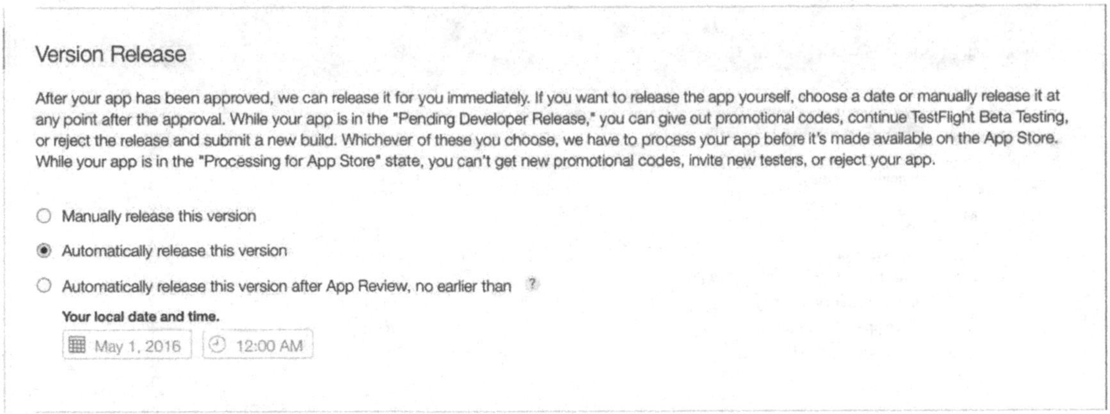

Version Release

After your app has been approved, we can release it for you immediately. If you want to release the app yourself, choose a date or manually release it at any point after the approval. While your app is in the "Pending Developer Release," you can give out promotional codes, continue TestFlight Beta Testing, or reject the release and submit a new build. Whichever of these you choose, we have to process your app before it's made available on the App Store. While your app is in the "Processing for App Store" state, you can't get new promotional codes, invite new testers, or reject your app.

○ Manually release this version

◉ Automatically release this version

○ Automatically release this version after App Review, no earlier than ?

Your local date and time.

🗓 May 1, 2016   🕐 12:00 AM

Figure 15-27. *Setting the version release information*

Finish by clicking the Save button at the top of the page, and then address any validation errors.

Congratulations: you've just completed your first application profile in iTunes Connect! You're ready to move on to uploading your application.

Uploading an Application to iTunes Connect

You've completed your application's profile, but there are still some key steps to go through in order to submit your application to the App Store. In a sense, all the information you just entered is metadata; it's there to support the real thing you want to share, which is the binary file for your application.

Creating a Distribution Certificate and Profile

In order to prove that you're the owner of the binary file you're uploading, you need to build and sign the binary using an iOS Distribution certificate. This is something a paid-up member of the Apple Developer Program can do, and the creation process is quick and relatively painless. In Xcode 8, this should have been created automatically for you; but because of its importance, you should double-check:

1. Go to Xcode. From the top menu, choose Xcode ➤ Preferences (⌘+,) and select the Accounts tab.

2. Select your Developer Account from the left column, and then choose the role denoted as Agent and click the View Details button. A popup containing details about your Developer Account and any linked signing identities and provisioning profiles will appear. If there is a Create button next to iOS Distribution, as shown in Figure 15-31, the identity has not been created. You can either do so here by clicking Create or allow Xcode to create it automatically later.

Figure 15-28. *With your Developer Account selected, click the View Details button to see the available identities and profiles*

3. If you click Create, Xcode communicates with Apple while it generates the relevant certificates on Apple's servers and then removes the Create button. Click Done to dismiss the popup and close the Preferences.

Validating Your Application

You may remember that in Chapter 14 I discussed the Archives Organizer, but I didn't cover the validation or distribution features available for an archived application because they form an essential part of the uploading process. By validating your application in Xcode before submission, you can identify any major issues with the app and rectify them, creating a smoother submission process for yourself. Validating your application doesn't take long at all:

1. In the Archives Organizer, select the newest archive for SayMyName, as shown in Figure 15-29, and click the Validate button.

Figure 15-29. *The Archives Organizer has a validation feature built in*

2. You're prompted to select a development team. There should only be one entry for you to choose from; select it and click Choose.

3. Xcode presents an overview of the libraries and components that make up the SayMyName application, as shown in Figure 15-30. Click Validate.

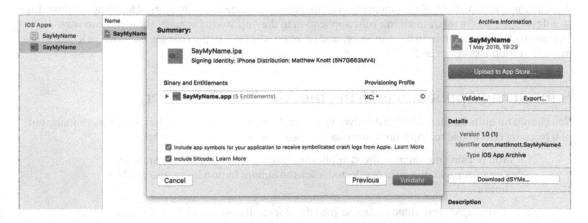

Figure 15-30. *Xcode gives you an overview of the elements to be validated*

4. After about 30 seconds, your application should either succeed or fail. If it succeeds, as it should, you're presented with the confirmation shown in Figure 15-31. Click Done to dismiss the validation.

Figure 15-31. *The SayMyName application has been successfully validated*

Now that you know your application has a clean bill of health, it's time to submit it to the App Store! If there are any issues with your submission and you aren't clear on the reason for rejection, head to the Resources and Help section of iTunes Connect that was shown earlier in the chapter, where you can find all the information you need to set about correcting the issue.

Submitting Your Application to the App Store

After all the buildup, it's finally the moment of truth, the culmination of 15 chapters of learning and growing as a developer. You're ready to submit your application to the App Store. I actually show you two ways of submitting your application to the App Store, and I explain why later in the chapter. For now, let's take a look at the first submission method.

Submitting Applications Using the Archives Organizer

You should be quite familiar with the Archives Organizer by now. Let's wring the last bit of functionality out of it by using the Upload to App Store feature to complete your submission to the App Store:

1. You're using the same archived application you just validated. In the Archives Organizer, with the archive selected, click the Submit button below the Validate button.

2. You're again prompted to choose your development team. As in the validation step, you probably have just one account to choose from: select it and click Choose.

3. You see a summary of the application as you did back in Figure 15-30. Click Upload. The archive is re-validated and then uploaded to Apple.

Your application will take a while to upload. Then Xcode will present you with the message shown in Figure 15-32 that confirms your submission has been made. The moment your application has been uploaded, the Apple review process begins automatically. This is no longer the case, which is helpful, because next you learn the second way Xcode can submit your application to the App Store.

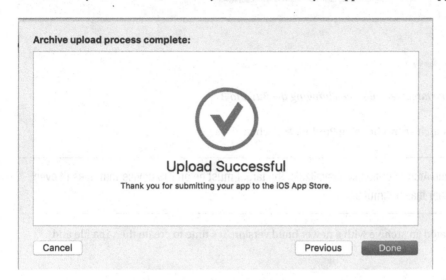

Figure 15-32. *Your application has been successfully uploaded to iTunes Connect and the App Store*

Submitting Applications Using the Application Loader

Next, I'll show you the Application Loader. You may wonder why you need to use it after what should have been a fairly painless upload process using the Archives Organizer. Some organizations have a specific person who is responsible for App Store submissions. The fact that you can use the Application Loader as a stand-alone application makes that process far simpler, because this person only needs to contend with one simple application rather than working through different Xcode screens and project files.

The Application Loader is distinctively different visually from other parts of Xcode. Although it can be downloaded separately from the Developer Portal, it is currently bundled in the Xcode package. Rather than uploading the binary file from an archive, the Application Loader works by uploading a pre-signed .ipa file to the App Store.

Changing Build Numbers

Before you can use the Application Loader, you need to change the build number and create a signed copy of the application in the .ipa file format. You do so using the Archives Organizer with the Export feature.

Let's start by creating a new build number. It's important to know that a build number is not the same as a version number. The SayMyName application is currently on version 1.0 and build 1. If you try to use the Application Loader to upload the binary with the same version and build numbers, you'll receive an error because even if the code has changed, Apple will view these as one and the same and therefore prevent your upload. Changing build numbers is a piece of cake:

1. Open the settings for the SayMyName target.

2. Change the Build value to 2, as shown in Figure 15-33.

Figure 15-33. *Opening the target settings and changing the Build to 2*

3. Create a new archive by choosing Product ➤ Archive.

■ **Note**   Remember, if the Archive option is unavailable, the target must be an iOS device that doesn't even need to be connected, rather than a Simulator.

Now that you've created an archive with a newer build version, it's time to create the .ipa file and upload it to the App Store.

Creating an .ipa File

If you've not come across the extension before, an .ipa file is an application archive: that is, your entire application contained in a single, signed file that can be distributed in a number of ways, including among members of your organization or to the App Store. You can create an .ipa file by using the Export function in the Archives Organizer:

1. Open the Archives Organizer and select the latest SayMyName archive.

2. Click the Export button. You're presented with four options, as shown in Figure 15-34; choose the first option, Save for iOS App Store Deployment and click Next.

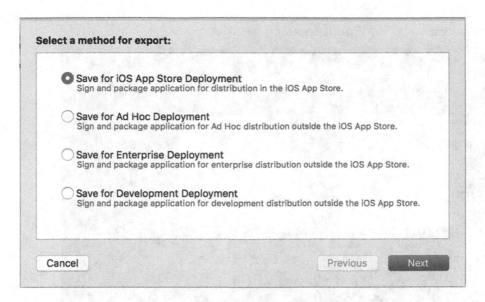

Figure 15-34. *Exporting the SayMyName application to an* `.ipa` *file*

3. As you have done several times, select the development team and click Export.
    Once again you see a summary of the application's contents; click Export.

4. You're prompted to save your file somewhere; remember which location
    you select and click Save. You have now created the `.ipa` file, ready for the
    Application Loader.

5. To launch the Application Loader, go to the menu bar and choose Xcode ➤ Open
    Developer Tool ➤ Application Loader.

6. When the Application Loader first loads, you're presented with a terms and
    conditions page and then asked to log in. Enter your credentials and click Next.

7. Once your information has been verified, click Done. You see the screen shown
    in Figure 15-35; this is the Application Loader.

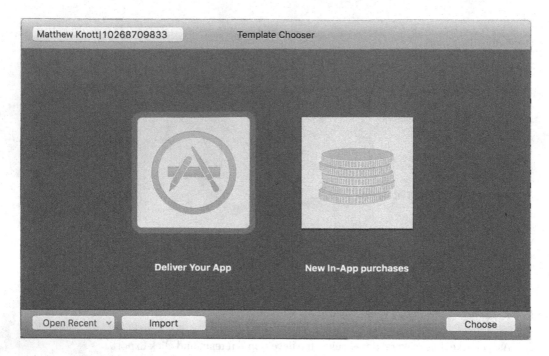

Figure 15-35. *The Application Loader main screen*

8. Click the Deliver Your App button and then click Choose. Locate and select your .ipa file, as shown in Figure 15-36.

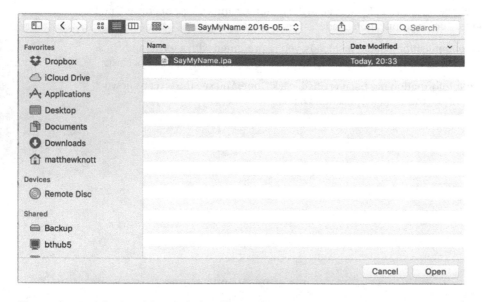

Figure 15-36. *Selecting the signed .ipa file to submit it to the App Store*

9. After a moment, you're presented with a summary of the Say My Name! application, as shown in Figure 15-37. Click Next.

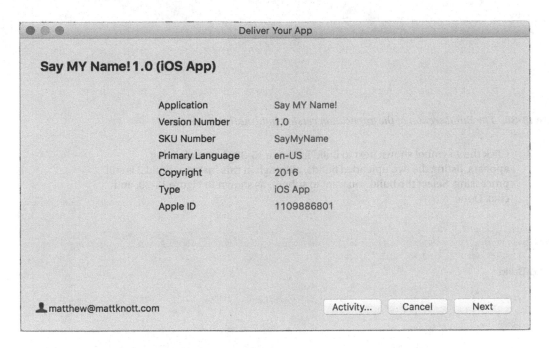

Say MY Name! 1.0 (iOS App)		
	Application	Say MY Name!
	Version Number	1.0
	SKU Number	SayMyName
	Primary Language	en-US
	Copyright	2016
	Type	iOS App
	Apple ID	1109886801
▲ matthew@mattknott.com		Activity... Cancel Next

Figure 15-37. *Summary of the Say My Name! app*

10. You're shown a screen titled Adding Application. The .ipa file is being uploaded to Apple.

11. When it has finished uploading, you're presented with a thank you screen; click Done.

You've submitted two builds of your application to Apple; all that remains is to complete the submission process. In the past this would have started the moment you uploaded the binary file, but Apple has changed this process to make it more flexible to users' needs, as described next.

Submitting an Application for Approval

You've written the application and uploaded your build, and it is time to complete the process and submit your application to Apple for approval and addition to the App Store. For this stage, you need to return to iTunes Connect, so open your browser and navigate back to the iTunes Connect web site:

1. On the iTunes Connect web site, click My Apps, and then click the Say My Name! application.

2. Scroll down until you see the Build section, as shown in Figure 15-38.

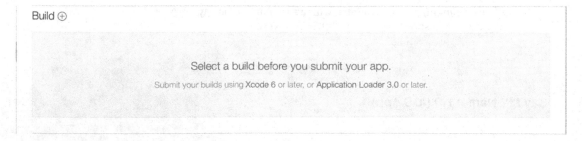

Figure 15-38. *The Build section of the application version information screen*

3. Click the + symbol shown next to Build in Figure 15-38. A modal dialog appears, listing the two uploaded builds, although in this instance build 2 is still processing. Select the build you want to submit, as shown in Figure 15-39, and click Done.

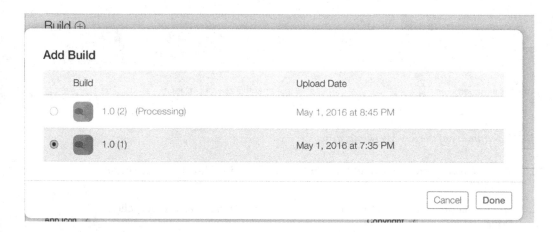

Figure 15-39. *Selecting the latest build that has been uploaded to iTunes Connect*

4. You're ready to submit your application for review. At the top of the page, click the Save button; this enables the Submit for Review button, as shown in Figure 15-40.

Figure 15-40. *The Submit for Review button becomes active after you click Save*

5. Click the Submit for Review button. You're presented with several checks to confirm; select No for each of these, as shown in Figure 15-41, and then click Submit.

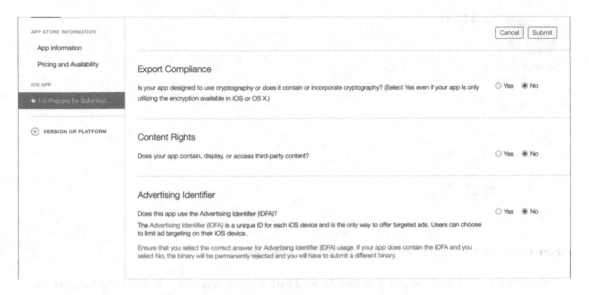

Figure 15-41. *Final checks before submitting for review*

You return to the application version information screen, as shown in Figure 15-42, but the status has changed to Waiting for Review. Congratulations: you have a wait of roughly two weeks ahead, during which your application will be reviewed by Apple engineers. The first time you submit an application, the wait is horrendous—you will probably check daily for updates even though Apple e-mails you with each status change.

Figure 15-42. *The application is now waiting for review*

Using the iTunes Connect App

As a footnote to this chapter and indeed the entire book, I want to take a moment to tell you about the iTunes Connect app available for iPhone. Although it has nothing to do with Xcode, as an iOS developer you'll want to check on the profitability and popularity of your apps wherever you are, and the iTunes Connect app is a great way to do this. On your iPhone, open the App Store and search for iTunes Connect, as shown in Figure 15-43.

Figure 15-43. *Searching for iTunes Connect in the iOS App Store*

Once you've downloaded and installed the application, open it and sign in. Click the Projects tab, and you see your applications listed. Select Say My Name!, and you see that its status is displayed as well as the ability to reject the binary if you realize there is a problem with the build you submitted (see Figure 15-44).

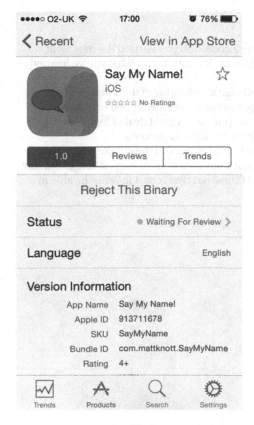

Figure 15-44. *Examining the Say My Name application using the iTunes Connect application*

The iTunes Connect application has a number of the web site's features, including sales reporting, and is certainly something you should be aware of.

Summary

In this chapter, you added the last feather to your cap, and you can now use Xcode to a high standard. Where you go from here is up to you, but you have all the skills necessary to become a professional iOS developer. Specifically, in this chapter you did the following:

- Finished the SayMyName application by adding icons
- Configured a loading screen using the LaunchScreen.storyboard file
- Set up an application profile in iTunes Connect
- Created a provisioning profile in the Dev Center
- Learned how to verify your application separately from the upload process
- Uploaded your application two different ways
- Learned how to submit your application for review
- Discovered the iTunes Connect iOS app

Next Steps

You're now armed with an excellent understanding of how to use Xcode, and you've used the new Swift programming language to create a number of really neat applications. It's time to take what you've learned and put it into practice by building your own apps and games.

If you're wondering where to go from here, Apress has published a wide array of titles that can help you get to the next level, whether that's iOS, macOS, or game development. As I mentioned at the start of the book, iTunes U is also a great source of material to help and inspire you. A great deal of help is available online; start small and build up to grander projects, and you'll be more likely to succeed.

My sincerest hope is that you've found this book useful and that it's given you the confidence to try something yourself. If it has, I'd love to hear from you; or, if you have any questions or suggestions about how I might improve a future edition, please send me an e-mail at matthewknott@me.com. I may not be able to reply right away, but I will certainly do my best.

Good luck!

Index

© Matthew Knott 2016
M. Knott, *Beginning Xcode: Swift 3 Edition*, DOI 10.1007/978-1-4302-5005-0

Get the eBook for only $5!

Why limit yourself?

Now you can take the weightless companion with you wherever you go and access your content on your PC, phone, tablet, or reader.

Since you've purchased this print book, we're happy to offer you the eBook in all 3 formats for just $5.

Convenient and fully searchable, the PDF version enables you to easily find and copy code—or perform examples by quickly toggling between instructions and applications. The MOBI format is ideal for your Kindle, while the ePUB can be utilized on a variety of mobile devices.

To learn more, go to www.apress.com/companion or contact support@apress.com.

Printed in the United States
By Bookmasters